NELSON'S FAVOURITE

Horatio, Viscount Nelson, by John Hoppner. (In the possession of Her Majesty The Queen)

Nelson's Favourite

HMS Agamemnon at War 1781–1809

ANTHONY DEANE

CHATHAM PUBLISHING

LONDON

In memory of my father
Captain Gerald Newnham Deane, RE (1886–1962)
who sailed with me in spirit throughout these pages

© Anthony N Deane 1996

First published in Great Britain in 1996 by
Chatham Publishing,
1 & 2 Faulkner's Alley,
Cowcross Street,
London EC1M 6DD

Chatham Publishing is an imprint of
Gerald Duckworth & Co Ltd

British Library Cataloguing in Publication Data
A catalogue record for this book is available from the British
Library

ISBN 1 86176 001 9

Typeset by Dorwyn Ltd, Rowlands Castle, Hants

Printed and bound in Great Britain by
Bookcraft (Bath) Limited

Contents

Foreword

A few years ago while on a brief visit to Punta del Este, Uruguay, as Chairman of the Race Committee of the Whitbread Round the World Race, I had the good fortune to meet Anthony Deane who told me that he was writing the history of HMS *Agamemnon*, one of Nelson's early commands. We chatted about the remarkable Admiral, and I remember mentioning my admiration for him in one particular episode in his career when he remained at sea for two whole years. I have spent six months at sea in a modern warship with all its creature comforts, yet I found that extremely testing.

Anthony Deane has drawn together details about life aboard *Agamemnon* during the Great War against Napoleon. His keen eye and vivid powers of description conjure up the hardships of naval life, rules and practices that shock our sensibilities today: marooning a culprit on a desolate shore, flogging him with the cat o'nine tails, or hanging him from the yardarm. Such brutality was the only known way for the majority of officers to maintain authority over men who were often garnered from the ranks of the misbegotten and displaced, if not actually criminals recruited from the jails. I could not help thinking, in reading Deane's account, of certain similarities experienced by modern yachtsmen. Today we have, of course, developed more humane modes of discipline but men living in cramped conditions of a modern ocean racing yacht and exposed at close quarters to the relentless elements for long periods build up tensions which can be difficult for skippers to handle. The breaching of human limits remains in any age.

As the Commander-in-Chief Naval Home Command in Portsmouth, it was my privilege to have Nelson's *Victory* as my flagship. I therefore had the opportunity to dine in his Great Cabin and to imbibe the atmosphere of the distinguished Admiral and hero. As can be imagined, I was the more interested on arrival in Uruguay to discover not only that the famous HMS *Agamemnon* had foundered in 1809 close offshore, but that her remains had been found by a team of divers, ushering in Deane's account with an uncanny heraldry.

Admiral Sir Jeremy Black
GBE, KCB, DSO.
March 1996

Crabtree Farmhouse
Durley, Southampton.

Preface and Acknowledgements

AGAMEMNON
. . . that ship immortal in naval memory. . .

Billy Budd
HERMAN MELVILLE

On the eve of my finishing this book, divers discovered the remains of HMS *Agamemnon* at the bottom of Maldonado Bay in Uruguay. After years of sifting through log books and archives, I felt almost as if I had been personally acknowledged by this sounding from the deep; as though my own fingers had touched her keel. The barriers which had separated us — history, distance, the leaden sea — dropped away for an instant in the joy of an explorer's find.

For six years, under the auspices of the Museo Nacional de Antropología, a group of marine archaeologists had searched for the sunken ship, basing their calculations on the captain's bearings when she ran aground.[1] As so often happens with history's random illuminations, it was only when two of the divers strayed from the marked area that they encountered her remains, stout ribs sticking above the sea bed barely 300 metres east of where she was believed to have foundered on 16 June 1809.

Strewn around the site were hundreds of copper bottom plates embossed with the Broad Arrow mark as well as a 24-pounder cannon, parts of her pumping apparatus and large quantities of shot, bolts, and copper nails.

Upon sifting through small objects and sherds, the divers made a remarkable discovery. What first looked like a pebble was revealed to be a silver pocket seal, complete with fob chain. On its face of translucent stone, it bore a star-shaped emblem with the name 'NELSON' in mirror image incised in a curve above. Although there was no doubt of the identity of the wreck, finding the seal with Nelson's name on it gave me the curious feeling he had willed it.

Since my youth I have associated Nelson's name with the *Agamemnon*. When he took command of her in 1793 he considered her 'without exception the finest 64 in the service'. Bound together through their many exploits — perhaps especially because of sailing into the Bay of Naples and a first meeting with Lady Hamilton — the *Agamemnon* was always Nelson's favourite ship. Beyond his tenure, she fought in the weather line at Trafalgar under Sir Edward Berry. What became of her after that is rarely mentioned. I supposed that she had been broken up at the end of her useful life, and that her ghost had simply wafted away into the sea-quiet dusk, as ships' ghosts do.

However, an account of two intrepid British yachtsmen who in 1880 crossed the Atlantic in a 30-ton yacht and arrived at the entrance to the Río de la Plata supplied me with the first clue to her actual fate.

> We rounded Pt. Este, and sailing inside Lobos Island, famous for its many seals, entered Maldonado Bay. This little harbour seemed but little protected, should the wind choose to blow hard from seaward. It is but a shallow bay surrounded by sand-banks, with one little island called Goriti [*sic*], overgrown with wild asparagus, and inhabited by rabbits alone, in the centre of it. It was here that HMS *Agamemnon*, Nelson's old vessel, was lost.[2]

Other allusions to the sinking then followed. The *Manual de la Navegación del Rio de la Plata* of 1868 mentions 'a bank on the northern extremity of Gorriti Island that owes its origin to the British ship *Agamemnon* having sunk there, over whose remains sand and shingle have collected forming a very hard bottom.'[3] A modern author, listing the shipwrecks in the vicinity, places the *Agamemnon* in an area northeast of Gorriti Island, called *el placer de los chinos* on early charts, *placer* being an old Spanish term for quiet, shallow water.[4] Although these descriptions seemed to be good clues to locating the wreck, they proved inconclusive in the end.

Hunting for accurate information on the ship has brought its share of blind alleys. One instance involved a comment made in Herman Melville's short story *Billy Budd, Foretopman*. Before the innocent Billy is convicted and hanged at the yardarm on a trumped-up charge of mutiny and killing a petty officer, he befriends a veteran sailor, an old Dane:

> He was an *Agamemnon* man, some two years prior to the time of this story having served under Nelson when still captain in that ship immortal in naval memory, which dismantled and in part broken up to her bare ribs is seen a grand skeleton in Haden's etching.

Clearly this seemed to refer to the ship I was interested in. My maritime researcher in London set out to look for the engraving, and established that the etching was in the British Museum. There she visited the Department of Prints and Drawings only to have her hopes dashed when she discovered that the vessel in the print mentioned by Melville as 'dismantled and in part broken up to her bare ribs' had in fact been laid down in 1849, 72 years later than the *Agamemnon* we sought. Furthermore, the Haden etching has buildings in the background which placed the 'grand skeleton' in the Thames near Greenwich, a setting which in no way resembled the primitive scenery of Maldonado Bay! If Melville was confused in his day, how must we feel today? The many wild tangents of our research tell the tale.

One of my objectives was to find accurate detailed drawings of the *Agamemnon*. The Ships Department of the National Maritime Museum at Greenwich supplied me with copies of the plans drawn by the naval architect Sir

Thomas Slade in 1766. The plans were actually for HMS *Ardent*, the prototype of a series of seven, of which *Agamemnon* was the third. Unfortunately, only parts of the ship were clearly visible. Taking these to the drawing board, and with the help of notes and sketches I had made during my research at Greenwich, the body-plan, inboard profile, and line drawing with masts and sails slowly emerged. Copies hang today in the Buckler's Hard Maritime Museum at Beaulieu where the ship was built, and in both the National Historical and the National Maritime Museum in Montevideo.

Throughout the *Agamemnon*'s period of history, Britain was engaged in the struggle against the French, and for a time, the uprising of her own colonies in America. The delicate balance of late eighteenth century politics had become upset, and there were moments when the British fleet alone protected the country from disaster. That Napoleon never achieved his aim of destroying Great Britain was due largely to the high standards set by the Royal Navy. Nelson illustrates this point well in a letter to Lady Hamilton's young cousin:

> As you from this day start in the world as a man, I trust that your future conduct in life will prove you both an Officer and a Gentleman. Recollect that you must be a Seaman to be an Officer, and also that you cannot be a good Officer without being a Gentleman.

His words were the criteria of the time and they went hand in hand with the ideals of honour, courage and loyalty to king and country. This code of conduct, coupled with unrelenting discipline, rigid training, and superior seamanship, gave the British navy the edge over its adversaries during the 22 years that the conflict lasted, and indeed for many more afterwards. Among the vessels of that fighting force, *Agamemnon* figured most prominently.

The story starts with the *Agamemnon*'s launch at Buckler's Hard on the Beaulieu River. Her construction by Henry Adams at this famous yard and her armament and fitting as a 64-gun ship of the line is followed by an introduction to the harsh life of the Royal Navy. Some of the themes explored include discipline and punishment; women on board; homosexuality; the ever-present danger of scurvy.

An account of the many naval actions in which *Agamemnon* took part forms the core of the book, illustrated by diagrams, lists of the fighting ships involved, names of their commanders and details of casualties. The *Agamemnon*'s engagements were numerous, extending from Ushant in 1781 through to Trafalgar in 1805, and beyond to the Blockade of Lisbon in 1807.

As with most stories, the more outrageous and unusual people of the time provide the excitement: Nelson and the Hamiltons; the grotesque Ferdinand and Maria Carolina of Naples; Sir Edward Berry, commander at Trafalgar; Carlota Joaquina, plotting wife of the Portuguese regent in Brazil; Santiago Liniers, victor over the British invasions of the Viceroyalty of the Rio de la Plata; the flamboyant Admiral Sir William Sidney Smith; and finally, the last commander of HMS *Agamemnon*, Captain Jonas Rose.

These characters provide a human background to the story of the *Agamemnon* herself, from launching to foundering. Her commanders numbered among the most famous ever to walk a quarterdeck, and her crew bore the honour of their station throughout the British fleet. In the military parlance of her day, the *Agamemnon* never shirked a confrontation nor showed her stern and ran, but stood her ground in battle, meting out more punishment than she received. Buoyed by the knowledge that her remains have now been found, I hope her history finds a new immediacy and a new audience through this account.

Anthony N Deane
Punta del Este, Uruguay.
August 1993

Acknowledgements

In writing *Nelson's Favourite*, help came to me from many quarters. I am particularly grateful to Jennifer Feeley of San Francisco, California, whose sage advice and clarity of style made it look as if writing difficult passages were the easiest thing in the world. To Soledad Hernandez de Robaina of Montevideo, for her faith and unfailing assistance throughout, crowned by undertaking the translation of the manuscript into Spanish. To Americo P Guzzetti of Buenos Aires, draughtsman supreme, whose masterful drawings, maps, and charts illuminate this book. To Dennis Skillicorn, yachting correspondent of BBC Radio Solent, my arms away from home, for his help and kindness stretching beyond the normal limits of friendship. To Andrea Cordani of London for her professional expertise encompassing both scholarly research and an acute editorial eye. To Admiral Sir Jeremy Black, GBE, KCB, DSO, for accepting with the best of grace my request to write the Foreword to this book. His wit and taste for conversation made every one of our encounters a pleasure. I also give my warm thanks to Luisa Angel Cash of Uruguay for allowing me to research the rare books in her collection. To my brother Brian who without a murmur of complaint searched the manuscript for missing words and accents. To Geraldo Tollens Linck of Porto Alegre, Brazil, author and expert sailor, who shared with me his experiences of sailing the Brazilian coast. To Lord Montagu of Beaulieu for his interest in the *Agamemnon* project and for his hospitality.

I wish to express my gratitude as well to Claudia Paredes of the Museo Histórico Nacional, Buenos Aires. To Captain Sergio Henrique Lyra Barbosa, Vice-Director Serviço Documentacâo Geral Da Marina, Rio de Janeiro, for much valuable information. To Elsa Minetti de Vidal Perry Director of the Museo Histórico Nacional, Montevideo. To Margaret Rule, marine archaeologist in charge of salvaging the *Mary Rose* at Portsmouth, for her sage advice on what *not* to do if the wreck of the *Agamemnon* were found, and finally to Emily Boyles, Director of the History Department of the Public Library of

San Francisco, California, who collected the information I needed by fax from other libraries around the United States when the reference books I was working on were buried beneath the rubble of the Loma Prieta earthquake of 1989. Without the kind help of all of these people, as well as many others I haven't mentioned, this book might have remained nothing more than a phantom in my mind.

NOTES

1. Hector Bado and Sergio Pronczuk, members of a Uruguayan diving team, made the lucky find.
2. E F Knight, *The Cruise of the Falcon: A Voyage to South America in a 30-ton Yacht* (London: 1887).
3. Lobo & Riudavets (compilers), *Manual de la Navegación del Río de la Plata* (Madrid 1868).
4. Carlos Seijo, *Maldonado y su Region* (Montevideo 1965).

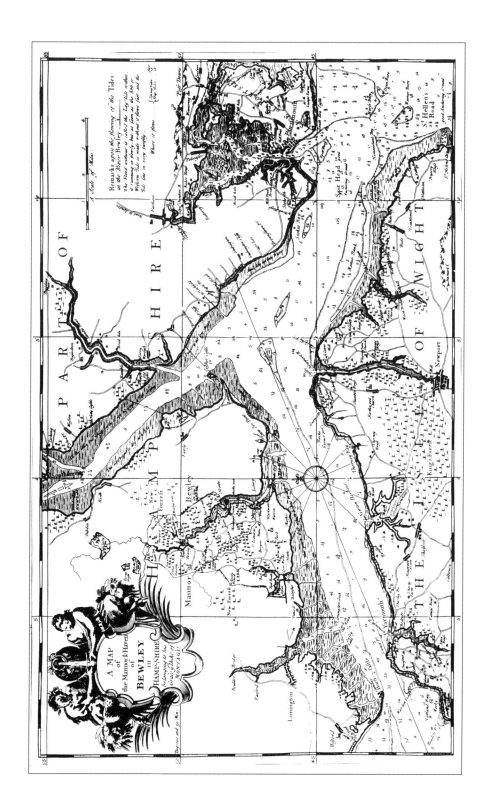

A MAP
of
the Manner & Haven
of
BEWLEY
in
HAMP-SHIRE
belonging to his
Grace ye Duke of
MONTAGU

CHAPTER 1

The Ship is Born

> That art untouched by softness, all that line
>   Drawn ringing hard to stand the test of brine;
>   That nobleness and grandeur, all that beauty
>   Born of a manly life and bitter duty . . .
>   They mark our passage as a race of men,
>   Earth will not see such ships as those agen.
>
> *Ships*
> JOHN MASEFIELD

Buckler's Hard, with its cluster of red brick buildings, was the home of the shipbuilding yard where HMS *Agamemnon* was built. The yard had been established in 1698 on the banks of the beautiful Beaulieu River where Hampshire touches the Solent. It was well chosen, for the bend in the river is wide at that place and sheltered from the prevailing westerly wind by Clobb Copse. It is also the highest navigable point at the river's tidal head, where a hard gravel bed, barely beneath the topsoil of the bank, stretches to the low water mark, providing a firm ground for landing and for building berths. Buckler's Hard derives its name from this particular feature. The term 'hard', common in the south of England, has denoted for centuries a natural landing place. The origin of the name Buckler is obscure today but may relate to the Buckle family registered in the Beaulieu parish as of 1668.[1]

The origins of Buckler's Hard date back to 1204, when the Cistercian monks were granted by King John in a royal charter an area which was then part of the New Forest: a tract of country 'afforested' by William the Conqueror to preserve its animals for the royal chase. In a departure from custom, the charter included important rights to the Beaulieu River. It specified ownership of the river bed, as well as rights to wrecks, fishing, flotsam, jetsam and lagan, this last referring to objects that lie on the river bed itself.

The Cistercians preserved their autonomy over the river for 300 years until 1538, when Beaulieu Abbey was dissolved by Henry VIII. Thomas Wriothesley, later Earl of Southampton, acquired the property. His youngest daughter married Ralph Montagu, and for the next 300 years the Montagu descendants have owned Beaulieu manor with its contingent rights to the river.[2]

(left) A contemporary map of the manor and haven of 'Bewley' (Beaulieu)

The master shipbuilder Henry Adams in later life. (Buckler's Hard Museum)

Master Shipbuilder

Henry Adams, builder of the *Agamemnon*, was to become the most famous of all the Buckler's Hard shipbuilders. He arrived in 1740 to oversee the construction of naval vessels for the Admiralty. After 8 years, he personally took over the lease of the yard, replacing the previous contractor who had run into financial difficulties. By the time of his death in 1805, Adams had transformed Buckler's Hard into the most successful private yard in Hampshire, having built twenty-seven naval vessels there, some of which achieved great renown in the fleet. As credit to his craftsmanship, three of the thirty-three British ships that took part in the Battle of Trafalgar were built by him at Buckler's Hard. *Agamemnon*, commanded by Sir Edward Berry, was one of them, the other two being *Euryalus* and *Swiftsure*.

Henry Adams had not gained his reputation as a master shipbuilder by chance. Understanding basic mathematics and geometry, he was able to work directly from the designer's plans while many other builders worked only from models. He was meticulous and honest, and he had an instinct for knowing if a ship was balanced. This knowledge was critical in avoiding costly alterations after launching.

Honesty in the shipyards was not to be taken for granted, particularly during the time the *Agamemnon* was built, when Britain was at war with its

Sir Anthony Deane (1638–1721), naval architect to Charles II and ancestor of the author. (National Maritime Museum, London)

rebellious American colonies and the royal dockyards were under pressure. Despite the vigilance of the Navy Board surveyors, dubious navy contracts and shoddy materials often undermined the construction of a vessel, the resulting problems only to be discovered at a later date when the ship was at sea.

Although shipbuilding had been an art for many centuries, it evolved only slowly into a science as ships were designed specifically for war. At the time of the *Agamemnon*'s building, science and seaworthiness had yet to be joined by precision. In many ways, the larger men-of-war with their heavy tiers of guns were often less seaworthy than their smaller predecessors, since the mistakes in design of the smaller were repeated by geometric progression in the design of the larger vessels.

Apart from changes in size, the last major technological breakthrough had occurred over a century before, when the author's ancestor Sir Anthony Deane, Charles II's scientific naval architect, worked out a system for calculating the displacement of a ship and hence its draught before launching.[3] Shipwrights of Henry Adams' time, however, although skilful with their adzes and saws, often depended more upon an experienced eye than on mathematics and geometry. Although a detailed specification accompanied every Navy Board contract, the success of a ship's construction rested considerably on the builder's personal experience, and only builders who met its exacting standards were consistently patronised by the Navy.

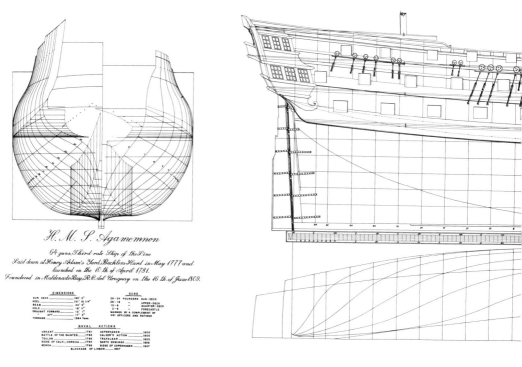

H. M. S. Agamemnon

64 guns, Third-rate Ship of the Line
Laid down at Henry Adam's Yard, Bucklers Hard in May 1777 and
launched on the 10th of April 1781.
Foundered in Maldonado Bay, R.C. del Uruguay on the 16th of June 1809.

Sheer and body plan of HMS *Agamemnon*.

The lack of science on the drawing board was all too often illustrated by the loss of ships at sea. For instance, in September 1782, only 17 months after the *Agamemnon* was launched at Buckler's Hard, Admiral Thomas Graves, in command of nine ships of the line and a frigate, was escorting eighty-eight merchantmen from Jamaica when they encountered a violent storm off Cape Sable. Not well designed or built to withstand continual wrenching and pounding, every vessel suffered severe damage. Thirteen merchantmen sank; three ships of the line were lost with all hands; and the flagship *Ramillies* sank after the admiral, officers, and crew transferred to another vessel. Only one of the warships arrived in England, while five others turned back, and altogether 3,500 lives were lost.[4]

The designer

The *Agamemnon* was one of seven ships built to the same design, drawn by the famous naval architect Sir Thomas Slade, senior surveyor of the Royal Navy and author of the plans of the *Victory*. Not that Slade had necessarily penned the drawings himself. Then, as now, junior draughtsmen usually carried out the actual detailed work under the authority and supervision of the official surveyor. Slade was probably one of the greatest naval architects of wooden ships of war that Britain has ever had and, as in the case of *Agamemnon*, ships

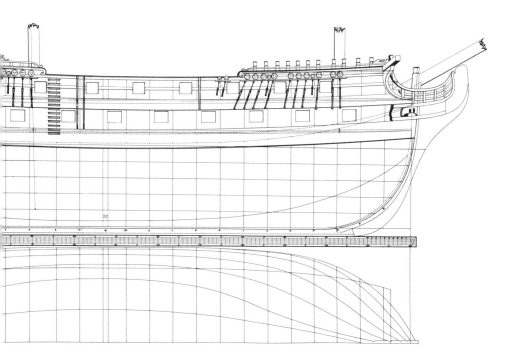

were still being built to his drawings after his death in 1771. He gave to his
series of brilliant designs the magic touch of proportion and balance that made
vessels outstanding for their speed and manoeuvrability.[5]

The surviving plans attributed to Slade and used for the construction of the
Agamemnon are kept at the National Maritime Museum, Greenwich. These
plans were actually drawn for *Ardent*, the first ship of the series to be built.[6]
The *Ardent* was built by Hugh Benjamin Blades at Hull in 1762; the second of
the series was the *Raisonnable*, laid down in 1763 at the Royal Dockyard at
Chatham. Being built alongside her was the *Victory*, still two years from
completion. The third of the series was *Agamemnon*, and right on her heels but
at different yards, the *Belliqueux* was laid down in 1778 at Perry's yard in
Blackwall and the *Stately* in 1779 at Raymond's yard at Northam. In 1781,
just one month after the *Agamemnon* was launched, Henry Adams started
construction at Buckler's Hard of the *Indefatigable*. The last of the series was
the *Nassau*, laid down at Hilhouse's private yard in Bristol in 1783.

No two ships were ever entirely identical when built to the same design,
not even sister-ships constructed in the same dockyard. Each had a character
of its own and was more or less stable, faster, or slower than its counterparts.
Of course, how each one handled depended on the captain's own experience
and skill in getting the most from his ship, since he was allowed to make

changes to the rig and ballast as long as he recorded what he had done in order to pass it on to his successor in command. Essentially, these vessels were floating platforms for guns and could hardly be expected to have more than moderate speed or sailing abilities. They were cumbersome, and their immense mass had to be propelled through the water by means of the most complicated assortment of spars, ropes, tackle, and sails ever devised by man to harness the wind. It took as much knowledge and dexterity on the part of the captain and his officers to sail and do battle on such floating fortresses as it needed a courageous, disciplined and well-trained crew to man them.

On the stocks at Buckler's Hard

The *Agamemnon* must have been a marvellous sight on the stocks at Buckler's Hard on the day of her launch. Her massive elmwood keel, resting on blocks, stretched nearly 132 feet. Her majestic hull, made of the finest English oak, boasted outer and inner skins almost two feet thick. The newly painted surface gleamed bright yellow in the sun, with the area below the gundeck and the top rails painted black.

In the centre of the bows, proudly flaring from the beakhead of the stem, soared the carved figurehead of Agamemnon, King of Mycenae, his torso covered by a breastplate and his body draped in folds of white. He brandished a sword in his hand and his dark tresses flowed backward from beneath his golden helmet. Depicted with a fierce and determined countenance, black beard parted in the middle and eyes creased as if straining through some imaginary fog at the battlements of Troy, his image was to become more a talisman than mere decoration on the bows. (For the origin of the name see Appendix 1.)

His name figured in boldly-painted letters on the stern below the windows of the maindeck, with a carved scroll on each side. A masterpiece of intricate design and beauty, the stern featured a gallery projecting from the quarterdeck, surrounded by a yellow railing of pilasters. Connected to the captain's stateroom by a pair of glass-paned doors, the gallery was a private balcony for the captain's personal enjoyment. The elegance of the stern was a concession to the comfort of captain and officers, yet for this very reason it was the weakest part of the ship. While it was widely acknowledged that shot from an enemy astern would sweep devastatingly through it and possibly bring about disaster, the benefits of luxury were considered worth the risk of such vulnerability in battle.

Nearly four years before, in May 1777, the *Agamemnon* had begun to take shape from 2,000 loads of timber, the approximate equivalent of 40 acres of century-old oaks of the *quercus robur* variety from the Beaulieu estate. A civilian shipbuilder such as Henry Adams would ride about the countryside to select and purchase growing trees appropriate for 'compass timber'. Compass timber had to have a natural curve suitable for frames and ribs. It was also necessary for the

A model of a ship on the stocks at Buckler's Hard. (Buckler's Hard Museum)

tree to yield 'thick stuff' for stout planking, and 'knees' for crooked timber used to support beams.[7] He usually sought a trunk circumference of at least ten feet. The structural ribs of the ship or 'futtocks' he built in sections and bolted together on the ground before hoisting into place. The knees, which fastened deck-head to hull, were made from the junction of the small branches with the trunk, so that the grain ran true in both directions. Other woods than oak, such as elm and beech, made up some 14 per cent of the total.

Building the *Agamemnon* had also absorbed many thousands of wooden pegs, known as treenails, varying from one to three feet long. These pegs were used as fasteners and, in order to avoid rot, were made from the same variety as the wood being fastened. In addition, some 35 tons of copper nails and bolts and over 100 tons of wrought-iron fittings were used in the ship's construction.

A Third Rate ship of the line like HMS *Agamemnon* was an expensive vessel to build, even in the hands of accomplished carpenters who knew how to use the wood to full advantage with minimum wastage. The construction of the ship's hull with yards and masts fitted would cost the Admiralty £20,579 (in today's terms, approximately £12 million), a figure that did not include the cost of sails, cordage, copper plating, hardware, and armament.[8]

The launch of HMS *Agamemnon*, 10 April 1781, from a painting by
Harold Wyllie. (National Motor Museum, Beaulieu)

The launch of HMS Agamemnon

The *Agamemnon* was commissioned into service on 28 March 1781. That same
day, the young Thomas Masterman Hardy, destined to become Nelson's
famous flag-captain, joined the ship as an officer under Captain Benjamin
Caldwell, who had been appointed only three weeks earlier.

Tuesday 10 April 1781 broke a blustery day and the rain came down in
torrents, unfortunate for the launch. Although the crowds were less than expected, those that came gathered on the banks of the Beaulieu River surrounding the shipyard. A tent had been rigged for the visiting Lords Commissioners of
the Admiralty and the Navy Board surveyors. A proud display of flags flew from
spars rigged to *Agamemnon*'s mastless decks. Launching tallow had been used
generously to grease the slipway that led into the water. In early afternoon, with
the ceremonial speech and christening over, the band struck up, and the chocks
were hammered out beneath her cradle. The great hull inched sternwards down
the incline and gathered momentum until she met the water. Slowly moving to
mid stream, she freed herself from her cradle's grip and floated unassisted for the
first time, accompanied by cheers and a great waving of hats and scarves by
those on shore and in the surrounding boats.

Although she had iron ballast of 100 tons, which would be reduced to 70 tons once completed, she rode high in the water, looking somewhat incongruous without her masts and rigging and as vulnerable as a beached whale. Two large open boats with oarsmen had met at her bows and made fast the ropes passed to them from the ship. Pulling them taut, the men towed the *Agamemnon* slowly down river to Fiddler's Reach, where she remained throughout the night. The crew awaited high tide to move her onward next morning, then, with relays of rowers in the open boats, they towed the *Agamemnon* down the river to its outflow in the Solent and beyond to Portsmouth. She arrived there on Monday 16 April at 5pm, six days after leaving Buckler's Hard.[9]

Finishing touches

She was moored alongside the sheer hulk, an old vessel fitted with 'sheer-legs', a type of derrick to lift heavy weights and step lower masts.[10] As soon as the *Agamemnon* was made fast beside her, carpenters and riggers were sent on board to complete their tasks. On Friday 20 April the lower masts and bowsprit were hoisted in and stepped, and many coils of cordage of different strands and thicknesses, which were to be employed in the rigging, were brought aboard.

'HMS *Agamemnon*, 64 guns getting in lower masts alongside the sheer hulk at Portsmouth 1781' by Harold Wyllie. (National Motor Museum, Beaulieu)

The three masts, fore, main, and mizzen, were made of oak, as was the bowsprit, but the extensions to these, the royals, topgallants, and topmasts, as well as all the yards, the jib, flying-jib, and main booms, were of pine. Although firmly stepped in the ship's keel, the masts required additional support against the strain of the sails. This was provided by the stays and backstays, ropes of great girth that ran fore and aft from the upper masts, and the shrouds that ran down either side of the ship. These last had ropes spliced across them, 'ratlines', which formed a ladder up aloft and were attached by deadeyes and lanyards to the 'chains' secured to the ship's hull. There was a platform on each of these masts known as the 'fighting tops', useful for watching the horizon and as an action station in battle for men armed with muskets and grenades.[11]

The yards positioned across the *Agamemnon*'s masts determined the shape of the sails. The higher up the yard on the mast, the shorter it was in length, so

Sail plan of HMS *Agamemnon* (the sails are shown drying in a calm)

1. Flying jib; 2. Jib; 3. Fore topmast staysail; 4. Fore staysail; 5. Fore course; 6. Fore topsail; 7. Fore topgallant; 8. Main staysail; 9. Main topmast staysail; 10. Middle staysail; 11. Main topgallant staysail; 12. Main course; 13. Main topsail; 14. Main topgallant sail; 15. Mizzen staysail; 16. Mizzen topmast staysail; 17. Mizzen topgallant staysail; 18. Mizzen sail; 19. Spanker; 20. Mizzen topsail; 21. Mizzen topgallant. (Drawn by Américo P Guzzetti)

the sails became shorter, tapering upwards the higher they were set. Each sail took its name from the mast on which it was set; therefore there were fore sails, main sails, and mizzen sails. The largest of these were the lower courses and, moving upwards, they became topsails, then topgallants, and finally royals. On her mizzen mast she carried a spanker held at the foot by a swinging boom. In fine weather when the wind was light, she would also carry studding sails or stunsails, which were attached to extensions of the yards. Apart from all these 'square' sails, which were actually rectangular in shape, she carried an assortment of fore-and-aft sails, mostly triangular. These were the jibs, which ran to the bowsprit, and the staysails, which were fitted to the stays that supported the masts. All set, the *Agamemnon*'s sails would cover an area of nearly three-quarters of an acre.

The blocks of the running rigging were made of wood, with internal sheaves and axles of iron. Introduced in 1750 by Walter Taylor, an English blockmaker, metal sheaves enabled the blocks to be one-third smaller than the previous all wooden ones made from the hard and oily *lignum vitae*, from which the deadeyes were still made.

The two wooden capstans had barrels that ran from the upper deck to the lower gundeck, so they could be turned individually at either level or together if the load were especially heavy. The capstans were worked by men pushing on the bars that were inserted into the drum heads. They were invaluable for heavy jobs such as weighing anchor, lifting guns or hoisting yards.

Many of the items on board, certainly the most valuable ones, were embossed or engraved with the Broad Arrow mark, which denoted that the item was government property. Each strip of copper bottom plating, for instance, had the mark in one of its corners. The Broad Arrow, still in use today, dates back to 1330 when the king's *pincerna* or cupbearer sealed a document with it for the purchase of wine.

Below the waterline

On 23 April the ship was hauled into dry dock to have her underwater section coppered. Introduced 20 years before in 1761, coppering a ship's bottom was the first effective means of preventing the accumulation of marine growth in cool climates and the destruction of wooden hulls by the wood boring shipworm *teredo navalis* in the tropics. Coppering helped to keep the vessel's speed constant and cut down the time a ship was out of service in the dockyard.[12]

During Sir Anthony Deane's time, lead sheathing of a ship's hull had been tried but due to electrolytic action between the lead, the seawater and the iron fastenings, the metals had rapidly decayed. Putting a layer of felt paper between copper plating and the hull solved the problem but only in the short term. The final answer came 40 years later when the iron bolts of the hull were replaced by ones made of a copper and zinc alloy.[13]

While work was going on below and above decks at a feverish pace, workers were busy on the hull below the waterline. Over a thick coating of felt paper stuck on with pitch, they were nailing to the hull some 3,000 pieces of copper plating.

Provisioning and final touches

On 3 May the *Agamemnon* was provisioned. An entry in the master's log mentions: '. . . received on board 120lb of Bread, one firkin of Butter, one half Hhd of Cheese, one Barrel of Oatmeal, and one Hhd of Pease . . .'[14] The ship was slowly taking on a life of her own.

A J Holland, in his book on Buckler's Hard, notes the following schedule of events on board the *Agamemnon*:

> On Thursday 17 May the officers' stores were put on board; on 4 June 277 tons of shingle ballast was placed in the hold. The rest of June saw both the dockyard workmen and a skeleton crew busy; the former finishing the fitments, the latter engaged in splicing ropes, washing and scraping decks, and setting up the rigging. On 4 July two hundred seamen from HMS *Nonsuch* were seconded temporarily to help in readying the ship for sea. Two days later the guns were taken on board and on the following Monday, 9 July, the *Agamemnon* sailed out of Portsmouth Harbour to begin her long and illustrious career.[15]

According to the master's log, she was loaded with provisions for six months at sea. These included 154 tons of water, 24 tons of beer, 48 tons of coal, and 39 tons of wood.

The maiden voyage

Let us go back in time and visualise the scene of the *Agamemnon* leaving harbour for the first time. It is 7am on 9 July 1781. The ship is moored up to the Portsmouth dockside. Though missing many hands to make up her full complement of 491 officers and men, she has her full detachment of 141 marines on board dressed in their colourful red cloth coats with white waistcoats and breeches.[16]

There is a bustle of activity. Horse-drawn carts unload the last boxes and barrels on the dockside, which in turn are hoisted on board several at a time in nets, to be lowered into the hold. A group of sailors stripped to the waist handle the last water casks under the watchful eye of a petty officer, 'starter' rope in hand. Perhaps a bedraggled bunch of wretched men are being herded on board minus their belts, the latest harvest of the press gang from the brothels and taverns of Portsmouth.

Captain Caldwell steps through the hatchway from his cabin onto the clean white of the quarter deck, cocked hat on head and left hand on his sword hilt. The officers are already there, in their blue and gold, together with the midshipman of the watch, the quartermaster behind the wheel and the ship's surgeon. The stamp and crash of the marines presenting arms is heard. On the deck below men heave on hawsers, driven on by the cane of the boatswain; others climb the ratlings to reach the spars high above, in readiness to unfurl the sails. There are sounds of scurrying feet, of shouted orders, of sheaves running in the blocks, and the groaning of the wooden hull. From the dockside comes a fluttering of handkerchiefs and loud goodbyes from a group of womenfolk who have stayed until the bitter end, knowing in all likelihood they might never see their men again.

At 9am Caldwell gives the orders for a gun to be fired and to hoist the signal for leaving port. A white puff of smoke amidships hangs suspended in the morning air, followed almost immediately afterwards by the noise of the cannon as it reverberates off the surrounding buildings. A shout from the boatswain up forward signals that the bridles have been slipped, and the bows slowly swing away from the dock as the men in the boat below heave on their oars. Such are the complications of the manoeuvre that it takes two hours for the ship finally to leave the dockside.[17]

Caldwell glances up at the long, narrow pendant at the top of the main mast as the ship suddenly heels, catching the first gust of wind in her sails. Water breaks beneath her bows. She springs to life, responding dutifully to the helm, better even than Caldwell's expectations. The ship moves smartly under her billow of new, white canvas, making a good 6 knots as she clears Dockyard Point. Moments later, she passes Round Tower leaving Fort Blockhouse to starboard and moves into the Sound. The ship rises to the waves under her bows in the freshening wind as she heads towards the open sea. Caldwell nearly loses his footing as she gives a sudden heave when a rogue wave rolls under her bows from stem to stern. Helm to leeward, she picks up speed, making a good 6 knots as she sails into the Solent. Caldwell is pleased with her performance but keeps in mind a few adjustments to the angle of the masts that he thinks will make a difference when sailing to windward.

Later in the afternoon the *Agamemnon* arrived at Spithead and anchored with her best bower in 12 fathoms of water.[18] She remained there for 5 weeks to receive her full complement of men. Some were put to work scraping and touching up the paintwork of the hull, while others helped the officers to adjust the shrouds according to Caldwell's orders.

On 11 August, the crew received their pay, £3 for able seamen and £2 for landmen. On 16 August, the ship sailed to St Helen's Roads and three days later, in company with HMS *Prothée*, she headed south of the Isle of Wight towards Land's End. There she cruised for 5 days to tune up her rigging and conduct her sea trials before returning eastwards to Torbay to join the Channel fleet of twenty-one ships of the line under Admirals Darby and Sir John Ross. On 13 September the fleet sailed to Berry Head and then cruised up and down the English Channel for more than three weeks. Returning to Spithead, dockyard workers were brought out to the anchorage to help with yet more

'HMS *Agamemnon* leaving Portsmouth Harbour 9 July 1781' by Harold
Wyllie. (National Motor Museum, Beaulieu)

adjustments to masts and rigging and to recaulk a considerable amount of
planking, mainly on the second deck where the hull had leaked.[19]

Nothing on record tells us the results of the *Agamemnon*'s first trials. Nevertheless, there are detailed explanations of those conducted later in 1796 (see
Appendix 2). An even later report of 1802 provides the clearest summary of
her performance:

> Very good Roader [i.e., rides at her anchor well]; 10½ knots before the wind
> and rolls deep; Steers easy, more dependent in Staying than in Wearing; In a
> gale, easily brought to her bearings and sails 7 knots; Best sailing draft of water
> when victualled, afore 20 ft and abaft 22 ft.[20]

Hidden amongst the measurements and commentaries in the reports of her
trials were other notable facts. The *Agamemnon* was an outstandingly fast ship
for her size. What she lacked perhaps in firepower, she made up for in
manoeuvrability.[21] Nelson, who commanded the *Agamemnon* from 7 February 1793 until 10 June 1796, wrote in glowing terms about her to his wife
Fanny. She was, he said, 'without exception one of the finest 64s in the
service, with the character of sailing most remarkably well'.[22] In another

instance, after twelve days under storm stay-sails in the Mediterranean, he wrote of 'gales and lumping seas . . . but in the *Agamemnon*, we mind them not; she is the finest ship I ever sailed in, and were she a 74, nothing should induce me to leave her while the War lasts'. And again, '*Agamemnon* sails admirably, we think better than any ship in the fleet'.[23] He later wrote of leaving behind the 74-gun *Robust*, with which the *Agamemnon* was frequently in company. Even the enemy commander Admiral Alemand expressed the view that she was one of the fastest ships in the British Navy. Swift and manoeuvrable, she handled like a frigate, inspiring fear in her adversaries and respect among the fleet.

NOTES

1. A J Holland, *Buckler's Hard, A Rural Shipbuilding Centre* (Emsworth, Hampshire: Kenneth Mason, 1985) pp 14, 31.

2. Holland, pp 19, 29. John, second Duke of Montagu, planned to build a major port on the site in 1722, 24 years after its establishment as a shipyard. He abandoned the idea after launching an ill-fated colonising expedition to the West Indies, in which he lost £10,000. The present owner of the estate, Lord Edward Montagu, has shown outstanding ingenuity in creating the Beaulieu Museum complex. By making a business out of his inheritance he has secured its preservation for the enjoyment of its many visitors.

3. Sir Anthony Deane began life as a supporter of the Commonwealth, served in the navy, and was present at some of the engagements with the Dutch under his famous cousin Richard Deane, General and Admiral at Sea. After the Restoration he had a post in the Woolwich Dockyard. He became a friend of Samuel Pepys and is frequently mentioned by him in his *Diary*. Deane was promoted to Master Shipwright of the Harwich Dockyard, and represented Harwich in Parliament in 1673. He was knighted and was appointed Master Shipwright at Portsmouth a short time after. Pepys states that Deane invented the method for calculating the displacement of a vessel and hence its draught of water before launching. It is also most likely that he was the inventor of the slide-rule. His *Doctrine of Naval Architecture* was written in 1670, 'at the instance of Samuel Pepys Esq.' and is one of the most important texts in the history of naval architecture. He designed some twenty-two ships for the Royal Navy, as well as several royal yachts, possibly contributing more to the development of the sailing warship than anyone else in his time. He and Pepys, who were almost the only pair of honest men in the public service of the time, were attacked by enemies in the pay of the Duke of York for misappropriating stores. The accusers backed down when the principal witness retracted his bribed accusations. Pepys and Deane resigned as commissioners at the dethronement of James II but between them they had restored the Royal Navy from a state of decay and discredit to one of efficiency. Sir Anthony outlived his friend Pepys, whose pall he bore at his funeral, and died himself at the age of ninety, in 1713. *The Diary of Samuel Pepys*, 5 May 1663 and 19 May 1666.

   Mary Deane, *The Book of Dene, Deane, Adeane, A Genealogical History* (London: Elliot Stock Pub., 1899), pp 59–61.

4. *Encyclopaedia Britannica*, Vol. 3, p 221.

5. Antony Preston, *History of the Royal Navy*, (Greenwich: Bison Books, 1980), p 40.

6. Pencilled notes on the profile drawing (Drawing No. 1091, National Maritime Museum, Greenwich) mention: '. . . fitted to accommodate 24 Officers and 600 soldiers. The length of the Roundhouse admits of the Commanding Officer of the Troops dividing the accommodation with the Captain of the Ship and, presuming that this class of ship might sometimes be required to embark a whole Regiment, great accommodation should be provided'. It is evident that these drawings detail her proposed modification for use as a troopship, although there is no evidence to suggest that she was in fact modified in this way.

7. For information about timber used for shipbuilding, see Holland, pp 46, 111, 113. By the time *Agamemnon* was built, England had all but used up the most accessible of her considerable resources of timber. The depletion of forests was to be a major reason for her stubborn resistance to surrendering her American colonies, which were a great natural source of pine for masts and spars.

8. Admiralty: Ships built, repaired, etc., 1771–1783 (ADM 95): ADM 95/84.

9. Admiralty: Masters' Logs (ADM 52): ADM 52/2113, HMS *Agamemnon*.

10. Gershom Bradford, *The Mariner's Dictionary* (Massachussetts: Barre Publications, 1972); Graham Blackburn, *The Overlook Dictionary of Nautical Terms* (Woodstock, N.Y: Overlook Press, 1981).

11. HMS *Victory: Official Guide* (Waterlow Ltd., 26th Impression, 1984).

12. Graham Blackburn, *The Overlook Dictionary of Nautical Terms* (Woodstock, N.Y: Overlook Press, 1981).

13. Brian Lavery, *The Ship of the Line* (London: Conway Maritime Press, 1983), Vol 1, p 116.

14. Admiralty: Masters' Logs (ADM 52): ADM 52/2113, HMS *Agamemnon*. Hhd is the abbreviation for hogshead, a large cask or barrel equivalent to 63 US gallons.

15. Holland, p 130.

16. W A Falconer, *A New Universal Dictionary of the Marine* (London, 1815; reprinted 1970). The detachment of marines on a 64 was made up of one captain, two second lieutenants, three sergeants, three corporals, two drummers, and 130 privates. The standing orders regarding uniforms were specific and meticulous in detail, including how marines had to wear their hair in 1784: 'battalion officers allowed a curl on each side', but light infantry officers strictly 'no curl'. Then, almost as an afterthought: 'the men to be provided with trousers'.

17. Admiralty: Masters' Logs (ADM 52): ADM 52/2113, HMS *Agamemnon*.

18. Admiralty: Masters' Logs (ADM 52): ADM 52/2113, HMS *Agamemnon*.

19. Holland, p 130.

20. Holland, p 131, with reference to National Maritime Museum, *Observations of the Qualities of HMS Agamemnon*, 29 April 1802.

21. Tom Pocock, *Nelson and His World* (London: Thames & Hudson, 1974), p 38.

22. Carola Oman, *Nelson* (London: Hodder & Stoughton, 1947), p 97.

23. Ibid, p 136.

CHAPTER 2

The Wooden World

. . . have you ever considered what the traditions
of the Royal Navy are? I will tell you in three
words: rum, sodomy, and the lash!

Winston S Churchill[1]

The *Agamemnon* was a 64, Third Rate ship of the line. The name derived from
the fact that she was armed with sixty-four guns and was expected to give
battle in line, meaning in single file, as per an Admiralty order of 1653. Once a
British commander sighted the enemy, his instructions were to form a line of
battle and pair off his ships with opponents of approximately the same speed
and armament. To define their fighting power, warships were divided into
rates according to the amount of guns they carried. Although the rating varied
over the years, in the *Agamemnon*'s time a First Rate ship bore over ninety
guns, a Second over eighty, a Third over sixty, a Fourth over forty-four, a
Fifth over twenty-eight, and, finally, a Sixth over twenty guns. Only the first
three rates were considered powerful enough to fight in the line; consequently, these became known as ships of the line.[2]

Armament

Guns were designated by the weight of the ball they fired. On the *Agamemnon*, twenty-six 24-pounders were mounted on the gun deck, thirteen to a
side. The upper deck also carried twenty-six guns, but they were 18-
pounders. Above, on the quarter deck there were five 9-pounders on each
side, two of which graced the captain's stateroom with their ominous black
bulk. There were also two of these on the forecastle. In addition to its sixty-
four cannon, *Agamemnon* carried twelve 24-pounder carronades, distributed
around the forecastle and roundhouse. Much lighter and shorter in the barrel
than an ordinary cannon, the carronades had a powder chamber similar to a
mortar and fired a large ball at short range. Invented by General Robert
Melville, they derived their name from the Carron ironworks in Scotland
where they were initially produced, and after subsequent improvements,
they became standard in the Royal Navy in 1779. Simple to use, they were
manned by a crew of three or four men, and at a short distance they could
wreak terrible damage if properly aimed.[3] A painting of the *Agamemnon* by
Nicholas Pocock at the National Maritime Museum, Greenwich, shows her
with two chase ports in her stern. These were for 9-pounders, which must
have been particularly useful on a manoeuvrable ship like the *Agamemnon*.

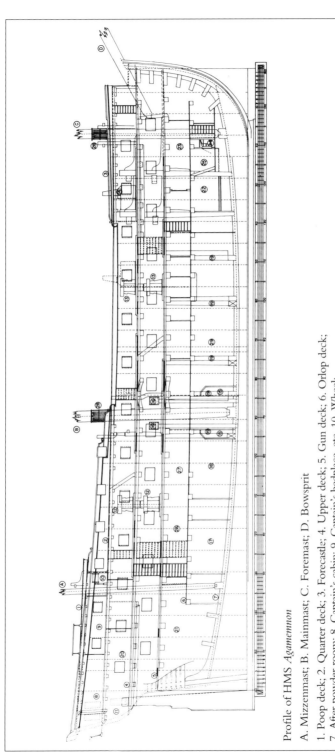

Profile of HMS *Agamemnon*

A. Mizzenmast; B. Mainmast; C. Foremast; D. Bowsprit

1. Poop deck; 2. Quarter deck; 3. Forecastle; 4. Upper deck; 5. Gun deck; 6. Orlop deck;
7. After powder room; 8. Captain's cabin; 9. Captain's bedplace, etc. 10. Wheel;
11. Wardroom (officers' mess and cabins); 12. Main capstan; 13. Fore jeer capstan;
14. Galley fire hearth (with chimney to forecastle deck); 15. Shot lockers; 16: Cistern at
head of chain pumps; 17: Wine & spirits storage; 18. After hold; 19. Deck-beam supports;
20. Master's cabin (port), 1st Lieutenant's cabin (starboard); 21. Bread room; 22. Magazine;
23. Gunner's, carpenter's & boatswain's store rooms; 24. Light room (illuminates filling
room); 25. Filling room (cartridge store); 26. Surgeon's cabin & dispensary; 27. After
cockpit (dressing station & sickbay when in action); 28. Boarding Pikes; 29. Main hold

The cannons were of cast iron with trunnions that projected from either side of the barrel. These were fitted into grooves cut into the top of the wooden truck carriage, then secured by two cap squares. The lumbering wooden carriage rested on wooden wheels so that it could be run out to the hinged gunport by pulling on a harness of heavy hempen breechings and side tackles. These ropes were secured to the ship's sides and tarred black to match the funereal hue of the guns, and the rammers and linstocks lodged in loops overhead. If the gunner wished to aim the shot higher or lower, he would do so by moving in or out a wooden wedge, called a quoin, under the breech.

In order to load a gun through the muzzle, it was necessary to run the gun inboard. First a cartridge of powder was pushed to the rear of the barrel and on top of this a wad of felt, then came the cast-iron cannonball and another wad rammed on top to avoid the shot from moving as the gun was run out.

Once a gun was loaded and ready to fire, the powder cartridge in the barrel was pierced with a spike through the touch hole and a little powder to act as a fuse was poured down the vent and into the fire channel and pan by one of the gun crews, from a powder horn hanging from his belt. The gun was then run out and aimed as well as experience dictated. Then a slow match was taken from a tub on the deck and applied to the pan to ignite the gunpowder. But this procedure, that involved keeping lighted matches on a deck inevitably scattered with particles of powder, had obvious dangers. In the late 1750s, hollow tin tubes were inserted in the touch holes for priming and flintlocks started to replace the lighted matches. Later, the tin tubes were replaced by goose quills of which a ship like *Agamemnon* might carry up to 3,000. The flintlock system, which greatly increased the rate of fire, became standard in

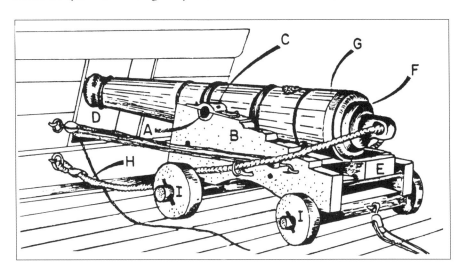

A 24-pounder gun and tackle.

A. Trunnion; B. Truck carriage; C. Cap squares; D. Gun port; E. Quoin;
F. Breech; G. Touch hole; H. Breeching tackle; I. Trucks

the Royal Navy towards the late 1770s and, while one can be reasonably sure that they were fitted to the *Agamemnon* at some date, it is difficult to say exactly when.

The gun captain fired the gun by pulling on a lanyard attached to the lock, while standing to the side, so as to keep out of the way of the gun's recoil. The gun recoiled with colossal force, and was checked from catapulting across the deck by the breeching ropes secured to the frames of the ship, which passed through a ring cast into the breech of the gun. A hit was possible from about a mile but it was considered a lucky one and warranted much cheering from the crew. Accuracy, born of long practice, was expected only at a quarter of that distance, which is why close range action was so popular in the *Agamemnon*'s day.

On the orlop deck in the bow and stern were the powder magazines, their walls and floor quilted in leather to prevent any sparks igniting the explosives. The powder boys, known as 'powder monkeys', wore special leather slippers when carrying the powder cartridges to the guns.[4] Powder monkeys were usually boys as young as ten. With the agility of their youth, they could bound and weave like veritable monkeys over and around every obstacle on deck to carry the powder charges from either magazine to the hatchways that led to the guns above. No precaution could be too much in the area of the magazines, as an accident could cause an explosion that would blow the ship apart. Even illuminating this room by means of a lamp could cause disaster, so a special lamp room was provided next to it with a small double glass window through which a feeble beam was cast. The powder magazine was certainly the most perilous space in the ship, and it was guarded by marines day and night. In 1808 the Regulations and Instructions Relating to His Majesty's Service at Sea stated:

> [The gunner] is never to go into the Magazine without being ordered to go there. He is never to allow the doors of the Magazine to be opened but by himself; he is not to open them until the proper Officer is in the Light-room; and he is to be very careful in observing that the men who go into the Magazine have not about them any thing which can strike fire, and he must take care that no Person enters the Magazine without wearing the leather slippers supplied by the Ordnance.[5]

The gun crews

Two hundred and fifty-six men lived on the *Agamemnon*'s gun deck, nearly half of the whole ship's company. Most of them made up the gun crews, who were divided into groups of twelve men to each 24-pounder plus a powder boy. The gun crew would be reduced to six if required to operate the port and starboard guns at the same time. The complement of crews was also dependent on how many were sick or wounded. Rarely was any provision made for standby crews, and people had to make do as best they could. As the navy

A view of the gun deck of HMS *Bellerophon* by H Hodgson, showing the guns run out. (National Maritime Museum, London)

procedures were not to be fully standardised until 1830, there was much improvisation in any given action.

The leader of each group was the captain of the gun who had beneath him in rank a second captain, a loader, a sponger, four side-tackle men, two hand-spike men, a primer, and a train-tackle man.[6] All slept among the guns they served and were allowed a space for their hammock equivalent to the width of their shoulders, (more or less 18 inches, or 45 centimetres.) Anyone caught stretching his allotted space was flogged, but as spaces were allocated alternately to port and starboard watches, one of which was usually on duty, it was not quite so cramped as it might seem.

A table was rigged between each pair of guns, hooked up by ropes to the beams above. The seamen had their meals at these tables and whiled the time away sitting on wooden benches. Each had a knife that he wore about him, as well as a spoon, an earthenware bowl, and a platter. No smoking was allowed except in the galley, but as most of them chewed tobacco, this was not a problem. Ventilation and light came mainly from the gunports, which had to be closed in bad weather. Then lanterns and candles provided the only light. After a few days with all the ports and hatches closed, the stench of sweat and filth was overwhelming.

When the hammocks were not in use, they were rolled up and lashed and then stowed between the double line of nettings strung around the ship's top sides and in front of the poop deck. The padding they formed was protection

A boarding action, from a anonymous graphite drawing of around 1820, showing the range of weapons used in these vicious hand-to-hand struggles. The seaman in the left foreground is wielding a boarding pike against an opponent with a cutlass, whilst the rest of the boarding-party is largely armed with hatchets ('tomahawks'), as much to cut rigging and cables as to be used in actual combat. (National Maritime Museum, London)

of a sort against musket balls and flying splinters. Together with the boarding nets set up across the upper deck, the hammocks became an obstacle for enemy boarding parties trying to hack their way on board. To the shouted order of 'Stand by to repel boarders,' every man on deck and those from the decks beneath would grab for the closest weapon — cutlasses or pikes were preferred — and charge into the fray to fight for their lives.[7] Conversely, when the ship was placed alongside a crippled opponent during a battle, the crew had to be prepared for the order, 'Boarding parties away.' Shouted by the officers, this cry would unleash a fierce assault over the enemy bulwarks, resulting in vigorous and bloodthirsty hand-to-hand fighting that was usually decided one way or another in a relatively short time.[8]

The harsh life

The galley stove was the only means of cooking food for the whole ship's company of nearly 500 officers and men. Made of iron, its funnel passed through the deck above to reappear on the forecastle. On its front, it had a copper device, a crude form of water condenser that could distil a small amount of pure water each day for the surgeon's use. The galley floor was of brick and either coal or charcoal the normal fuel, but the risk of fire being an ever-present worry, the fire was extinguished after each meal.[9] The ship's cook used huge copper pots for boiling the salt 'junk' and making gruel. The regulation victuals, which were strictly limited in quantity, varied in quality from bad to atrocious. These included biscuit, pork, beef, oatmeal, peas, sugar, butter, and cheese. Meat out of the salt vats was gristly and fibrous. Left in the sun for a short period it became hard enough for the sailors to make boxes from it that would take on a fine polish like mahogany.[10] But the more ancient the 'salt junk', as the meat was called, the better it kept in the tropics. Steeped in saltpetre, tough and malodorous, it kept well even after travelling a couple of times around the globe. On the other hand, meat salted too re-cently, and especially meat with a fairly high fat content, tended to spoil and had to be thrown overboard. In the same manner, if in a short-sighted love of luxury a captain in a foreign port were induced to supply his vessel with barrels of sea biscuit made from high-quality flour, it would most likely be attacked by mildew and swarm with weevils and maggots before the end of the voyage. A more common quality of biscuit was said not to spoil quite so readily. Insects thrived best, and multiplied amazingly, on biscuits made from first-class flour.

Food was stored and kept under lock and key in designated storerooms beneath the waterline for coolness, either on the orlop deck or in the hold. The captain as well as the officers had their own storerooms on the orlop deck where they kept provisions they had personally paid for, as well as a generous supply of wines and liquor. Usually these provisions included such things as hams and bacons; sausages preserved in lard; salted, dried, or pickled herrings; preserved fruits; dried Smyrna figs, and cheeses from Cheshire, Suffolk, or Holland. Coffee, which had been introduced to England in the 1660s, was relatively inexpensive in the *Agamemnon*'s day, as was tea, which had arrived in England through Holland in 1540. The invention of the cork in 1660 permitted long-term storage in bottles, but being fragile, casks were still preferred on board.[11] Mustard, pepper, and certain spices were necessary to disguise the taste of food that lacked refrigeration to prolong its freshness. The captain's larder usually also contained a bag or two of stone-milled flour to make bread.[12]

To preserve his authority, although not perhaps his mental health, the captain led a lonely life on board. When not on deck, he kept to the confines of his cabins and usually had his meals on his own. The officers led a more sociable life in the officers' ward-room, which was aft on the deck below. With its dining table twenty feet by four, this cabin looked over the water through the great stern windows that partially encased its three sides. Leading off it was a pantry where cutlery, plates, dishes, and glass were kept and where food brought from the galley was prepared prior to serving.

Although the captain's and officers' quarters were crampled, they lived in relative luxury compared to the rest of the ship's company, who lived in subhuman conditions partly because the ships of the Royal Navy were victualled by naval contractors on orders from the Admiralty, whose total lack of dietetic imagination had not varied for over 200 years.

No one has stated the plight of the ordinary seaman in those days better than Leo Heaps in *Log of the Centurion*, his account of Lord Anson's circumnavigation of the globe.[13] Although the voyage he relates took place 40 years before the *Agamemnon*'s time, very little had varied, except perhaps that grog had become part of the sailor's daily fare and there was a new awareness of the causes of scurvy.[14]

> . . . the confined quarters in which the men lived, the lack of simple hygiene, filthy clothes, and vermin were a fertile ground for the breeding of disease.
>
> Toilets [heads] were built into the bows, over the water. Their exposed position, and the effects of illness, weakness, and dysentery meant that quarters below decks tended to stink of sewage at sea on long voyages. Food was eaten by the sailors normally in the limited space between the big guns. If the weather was fine, meals were consumed on deck.
>
> The diet was one of unrelieved monotony. Salted meat came out of the great vats and was served five days a week, and on the banian days, which were Friday and Tuesday, salted fish and cheese were hacked up by the cook and passed to the men from out of the store boxes. Beans, rice, oatmeal, and split peas were issued as long as they lasted. Vegetables, consisting of onions and potatoes, soon rotted on long voyages so that the staple diet reverted to either salt pork or salt beef. Meat was pickled in strong brine and, even after steeping, increased the thirst. On protracted voyages the water ration was reduced to less than a pint a day per man. Wines, spirits and beer were the usual drinks and large quantities of alcohol were consumed. A sailor was allowed a gallon of beer a day or a pint of wine and a half pint of rum. Biscuit was made of flour and water and had the consistency and appearance of clay and was broken by either smashing it on deck or splitting it with a hammer. More frequently than not the weevils had already bored through this delicacy before it was issued so that weevil and biscuit were eaten together. Officers kept their own hen coops as well as live geese, goats and cows which were tended below deck, near the mens' quarters. The larders of the officers were stocked with private provisions and copious supplies of fine wines. In the year 1739 His Majesty's Navy had altered little in its ways since Elizabethan times. The system was cruel, vicious, unrelenting.[15]

Of 'foul stinkes', 'pestilential funkes', roaches and rats

Keeping a ship clean, especially on long voyages, was a constant preoccupation for the officers. The space below decks close to the keelson was filled with stone, sand or shingle over 'pigs' of iron ballast, placed there to keep the ship counterbalanced. Wooden ships were prone to take in a certain amount of seawater which collected in the lowest part of the hull, the bilges. To this leakage was added, more often than not, vomit, urine and remnants of food contributed by lazy sailors regardless of rules prohibiting such behaviour. If confronted they would shrug and say that the pumps would take care of it, which these did, but only up to a point. The ship's carpenter would check the level of this fluid daily by sounding the well, an opening in the ship's hold close to the pumps. If there was a leak, the water would rise to a dangerous level. Then the only hope was that the pumps could gain enough for the leak to be plugged. If the leak was bad the cry 'Man the pumps' would ring throughout the ship. It was a back-breaking task that could cause the men to collapse with fatigue in extreme cases.

Regardless of punishments and threats the bilge and ballast could become so utterly disgusting discharging its 'pestilent funkes' that the vessel would have to be careened on a convenient beach. This meant heeling her over on her side, throwing the ballast overboard for the surf to wash it and scraping the muck from the inside of the bilge before washing it down with vinegar. Then the ballast would be replaced and the vessel refloated on a rising tide.

Such conditions bred several varieties of vermin. Cockroaches abounded and could only be dealt with by stepping on. Old hands were prone to say that shipboard insects remained shy until the vessel reached the tropics. Then they would venture out in force to enjoy the climate, and the crew. Rats, however, were by far the worst health hazard on any ship, either afloat or in dry dock. Even though the law of the sea prescribed keeping one or more cats aboard to keep the population in check it was impossible totally to exterminate the creatures. Thomas Swaine, ratcatcher to His Majesty's Royal Navy, gives the following unique and somewhat horrifying picture of ship conditions in the eighteenth century. His lists of rats destroyed on HM ships of war includes, from *Victory*, 171; *Achilles*, 704; *Diligente*, 665 and on two separate occasions, 140 and 141; *Prince of Wales*, 1,015; *Duke*, 415 and a spectacular 2,475.[16]

Scurvy

As a result of the ship's crew not being able to preserve fruit and vegetables at sea for any length of time, scurvy was an ever-present threat. Since it is a deficiency disease caused by the lack of Vitamin C, it would occur when fresh fruit and vegetables were unobtainable and disappear when they were administered again. For this reason, throughout history it had quite frequently broken out among soldiers on campaign, in beleaguered cities, among communities in times of scarcity and in prisons and workhouses, but in these instances it took place on land where it was at least feasible to reverse the situation. On a long voyage at sea it was an entirely different matter, for once the hardiest of vegetables, such as potatoes, onions, carrots, and turnips, had been given out or had rotted, there was little hope, other than reaching port and obtaining green provisions.

The inevitable deaths would escalate day after day after the symptoms of weakness, spongy gums, and internal haemorrhages had started to appear. Finally, fatal, hopeless depression took over as the men affected withdrew

Seamen around a ship of the line's galley stove, from a lithograph by
Schetky. (National Maritime Museum, London)

deeper and deeper into themselves with no energy and died. 'And we only
used to envy those whose good fortune it was to die first.'[17]

The fatalities in Anson's squadron due to this disease, and perhaps others,
numbered 1,051 out of the 1,955 men who had originally embarked at
Portsmouth. On board the flagship, for example, while rounding Cape Horn,
forty men died and most of the remainder were unable to perform their duties.
Almost all of the seamen were stricken, and all the marines on board were
either sick or dead.[18] Of the total ship's company of 521 on board the flagship
at the commencement of the voyage, only 201 men were alive by the time the
ship reached Canton. Of these only forty-five, out of an initial 367, were able
seamen.[19]

In terms of human life, Anson's circumnavigation was a disaster, but it
prompted the noted physician Dr James Lind, a Scot and graduate of Edin-
burgh University, to carry out the first dietetic experiment on record.[20] Later,
in 1753, he published his *Treatise of the Scurvy*, in which he revealed that he
had found the answer in the juice of lemons, oranges, and Sicilian limes.
Twenty-two years later, Lind's discovery was put to the test and confirmed by
Captain James Cook after his second voyage to the Pacific.

Cook's voyage took place between July 1772 and July 1775. During those
three years he covered more than 20,000 leagues, nearly three times the

equatorial circumference of the earth. On one occasion he was at sea for 122 days consecutively and on another for 117 days, during which time he covered more than 10,000 miles before sighting land. He provisioned his expedition with a wide variety of foods, hoping that Lind's conclusions were correct. These foods included sauerkraut, dehydrated soup, and the boiled, sweetened juice of oranges and lemons. Although there were outbreaks of the disease, only one man out of 118 was lost through sickness, after remaining at sea for longer than anyone else in history.

James Lind's discovery was a tremendous scientific breakthrough that could have wiped out the scourge from the day it became known. Even so, it took the Admiralty until 1795, 42 years, when Horatio Nelson was in command of the *Agamemnon*, to make the administration of lime juice compulsory in the British Navy. Thereafter, sailors of the Royal Navy became known as 'Limeys'. The intake of citrus virtually extinguished scurvy in the service forever. In 1781, however, its devastating effect was something Captain Caldwell and the ship's surgeon had to keep much in mind.[21]

James Kirk, the surgeon of *Agamemnon*, had his cabin and dispensary on the orlop deck, which was not wholly planked over to the stern. It was dark and gloomy beneath the waterline and poorly lit by lanterns and candles in tin sconces. Being below the waterline, however, it was a safer deck than the rest above it. The section aft of the mainmast was used as a dressing station and hospital for the wounded when the ship was in action. Known as the cockpit, its deck was painted blood red, in order to disguise the real blood that flowed when casualties were sustained and amputations done with only the help of rum as a numbing agent. These tasks were performed by the surgeon and the assistant surgeon, with the help of the surgeon's mates. Contrary to popular belief, some surgeons in the navy were surprisingly competent, considering the primitive tools and limited medicines at their disposal. In particular, they were notably advanced for their time in the treatment of burns.[22]

Naval recruiting

Given the hardships at sea and the low scale of wages, recruitment of seamen was an ongoing concern that grew particularly intense in times of war when the navy required up to 40,000 extra men a year. Recruitment stations along the coasts encouraged volunteers, and ship commanders often distributed posters and handbills advertising the name of the ship and the captain and enhancing the possibilities of a particular expedition. Sometimes it was necessary for the government to take compulsory measures by means of the Quota Acts, which obliged counties or cities to supply their proportionate share of men.

The navy had an insatiable demand for men and could ill afford to be selective. Muscle alone worked its great warships with their innumerable sails and batteries of cannon. Inevitably, a ship became a haven for many of those that voluntarily enlisted. Men running from the long arm of the law sought

'The Liberty of the Subject' by James Gillray, a cartoon from 1779
showing a press gang in action. Although 'impressment' is almost
synonymous with naval recruitment in the Nelsonic era, recent studies
have claimed that less than 2 per cent of seamen were recruited by force.
(Witt Library)

refuge at sea just as transgressors of the Middle Ages found sanctuary in the
shadow of the altar. So too, drafts from the nearest prisons made good a lack of
hands on board in an emergency. A strong element of the outcast and the
desperate were steady fare for the crew of a man-of-war.

The most infamous method of recruitment involved the press gangs. These
were detachments of men, usually under the command of a lieutenant, sent by
the captain of a naval vessel to 'impress' people into service. Always an
unsavoury affair, unwitting folk were taken by force from taverns, brothels,
and even seaport homes. Legally, the press was confined to professional
seamen, but at the height of the war almost anyone would do — be they
farmers or merchants, pickpockets or bridegrooms, all were considered fair
game, and previous experience as seamen was not a requirement, although
experienced seamen were still preferred if possible. The hapless subjects were
usually herded on board without their belts to make any attempt to escape
hazardous. Equally unlucky were those serving as merchant seamen when
their return to home port coincided with a call for hands on a man-of-war. In
that case, a returning sailor would not be likely to see his long-awaited wife
and children for months or years to come.

Although the dramatic brutality of the press gangs gained them public
notoriety, in actual fact the numbers of men pressed into service were said to

be small compared to more traditional methods. One analysis of ships' muster books of the time estimates their inclusion at about 2 per cent.[23]

Contrary to popular belief, naval officers did not always originate from well-to-do families. Commissions in the navy could not be bought in the same way as they could in the army. Since a career in the army was generally the preferred choice of the first and most financially able son, many naval officers came from among the less affluent, younger sons in a family. A man's career in the eighteenth century hinged considerably on his influence. However great his personal merit, these qualities might go unrecognised for the duration of his career. A powerful patron, however, could ensure a man's position and completely change his fortune. While war could draw attention to an individual's actions and speed promotion, in peacetime influence became essential.

Apart from heroic loyalty to king and country and the hope of glory, the lure of service was mainly prize money awarded by the Admiralty for a captured ship. This made war a far more lucrative time than peace for men on active service. If the Admiralty could be persuaded that a captured prize was valuable enough to save the navy the cost of building a new ship, so much greater was the reward, proportionately divided among the successful captain, officers, and crew.

Perhaps a fate worse than death

In the first Articles of War, laid down in 1652 and not reformed for 180 years, almost all offences were considered major and merited the death penalty. But for what might be considered lesser offences, punishment took on a variety of barbaric forms. 'Mastheading,' which meant a spell on the top mast crosstrees without food or water, was perhaps the most lenient. 'Gagging' with a marlinespike between the teeth could be the penalty for using bad language or arguing with an officer. 'Marooning' an offender on a deserted coast or island was not usual but did happen, as with the case of the Scots seaman Alexander Selkirk in 1719. He was found on the island of Juan Fernandez off the coast of Chile after living there for 4 years and 4 months entirely alone. He was later immortalised by Daniel Defoe in *Robinson Crusoe*. Later, in 1807, Robert Jeffrey, accused of theft, was marooned on the small deserted island of Sombrero in the Caribbean.

The most terrible of all punishments was 'keelhauling', which consisted of dragging the unfortunate man under water for the whole length of the hull, which was usually covered in barnacles. This punishment was not inflicted after about 1750. 'Running the Gauntlet' was a grisly punishment where the offender was either carried on a grating or prodded around at swordpoint in front of the ship's company. The assembled men stood in line around the main deck, each armed with a knotted rope with which to flay the prisoner's back.

By far the most common, horrible and enduring method of punishment in the Royal Navy was flogging. The offender was usually confined in irons a day or two before with his ankles shackled to an iron bar secured to the gundeck. He was brought up to the light of day at the appointed hour and lashed sometimes to a cannon but more often to a grating taken from one of the hatches. Sentence was carried out by one of the boatswain's mates with the cat-o'-nine-tails before the captain, lieutenants, and a full muster of the hands. The 'cat' had a wooden handle with nine knotted cords about 2 feet long. Theoretically, a court martial was necessary for a sentence of more than twelve lashes. This technicality, however, could be sidestepped by awarding the twelve for each regulation breached within the one offence. For instance, being drunk, starting a fight, and swearing all at the same time could bring upon the offender thirty-six lashes. Moreover, the penalty often did not fit the crime. A man could be lashed for whistling in the presence of an officer, for example, which was considered not only bad luck but also disrespectful. There

'The Point of Honour', a famous cartoon by Cruickshank in which a sailor is saved from an unjust flogging by the real culprit confessing at the last moment. It shows the condemned man tied to a grating, the bosun's mate with the cat-o'-nine-tails and the ship's company assembled to witness punishment. Note also the carronades on their sliding carriages. (National Maritime Museum, London)

was, however, no limit to the amount of lashes that could be awarded by a court martial. For example, for having 'written anonymous letters, endeavouring to make mutinous assemblies and uttered seditious and mutinous words', King, a seaman of HMS *Active*, was condemned in April 1801 to receive 500 lashes (a sentence undoubtedly worse than death), and two of his shipmates, Beetham and Forrest, were condemned to 300 each. On 6 January 1802, fourteen alleged mutineers of the *Téméraire* were sentenced. Thirteen were condemned to death and one to receive 200 lashes.[24] The cruel irony was that the maximum penalty (being hanged from the yard-arm) was, in the long run, considerably more humane than a sentence of over twenty lashes, prescribed for a lesser offence.

An even worse alternative to flogging at the gratings was flogging round the fleet. In this case, the prisoner was rowed alongside every ship at the anchorage, and to the dramatic drum beat of the Rogue's March, he was flogged by a boatswain's mate at every stop.

With their characteristic grim humour, seamen referred to a flogging over a cannon as 'kissing the gunner's daughter', and to flogging in general as 'putting on the red-checked shirt'. But, making light of this barbaric custom did little to hide the fact that apart from usually causing unconsciousness and permanent disfigurement, it could also cause death. With resentment deep in his heart, such abuse could at the very least break a man's pride, his spirit, or his mind. He would rarely strive to do his best again.[25]

Mirth and festivity

Most sensible captains encouraged music and dancing as good for community spirit and sustaining morale on board. In 1793 Cuthbert Collingwood, Nelson's close friend, wrote from the Channel Fleet, 'We have lately been making musical instruments and have now a good band. Every moonlit night, the sailors dance, and there seems as much mirth and festivity as if we were in Wapping itself.'[26]

Dancing on deck to the tune of a fiddler was a traditional pastime. Jigs and hornpipes were the most popular and had been adopted by sailors because they could be danced by men alone. On festive occasions and during their leisure hours at anchor, the seamen would show their abilities. With upright bodies and rapid, nimble movements of their feet they would trace rhythmic patterns on the deck, touching the floor with great speed and dexterity. Captain and officers would often watch from the side and clap their hands in rhythm to the beat.

Seamen believed from early times that a ship had an invisible rope attached to her bows with its other end held by their loved ones back home. When the ship raced through the sea with a fair wind abaft the beam, sailors imagined their women were pulling hard on the rope. But when the wind turned foul and the ship made little headway, they would growl there was a knot on the rope that stopped it sliding through the block, a sure sign the women had forgotten their sailor lovers and were out consorting with soldier lads. Every time the women heaved in the throes of passion, they would jerk the rope, causing the ship to toss on rough seas and making life miserable on board. The richness of shipboard folklore evolved partly from the rigours of confinement, where barren loneliness gave way to fertile imagination.[27]

Women and sex in a floating world

The attitude of the Royal Navy towards women and sex has been rather unsympathetic, not to say hypocritical, throughout its history. From time immemorial, women on board were an accepted custom when a ship was in port, as sometimes they also were on short trips between home ports. But at sea, when a ship was on active service, it became an entirely different matter and their presence became strictly contrary to regulations.[28] The fact was that women on the lower decks could be a serious menace to morals and discipline, one of their chief offences being the quantities of illegal liquor that they brought aboard.[29]

For the most part captains were tolerant of women coming on board when a ship was at her moorings. In fact, some went so far as making arrangements ashore for women to be provided for the crew upon arrival. One frigate captain, on reaching the West Indies, had 300 black women sent on board his ship from a neighbouring plantation, so that each man might have a mistress while in port.[30] Only occasionally did a strict and narrow minded captain, such as James Gambier in 1793, insist that any females coming on board show their marriage lines. This raises the question of what was exactly meant by marriage. It seems to have been largely a matter of expediency and the fact is that many 'wives' were not married at all. 'One can find a rag of a wife anywhere', said a Scottish sailor of that time.[31] There is no precise evidence of the proportion of men in the navy who actually were married but it would seem that they were in the minority.

> The evidence suggests that the proportion of the officers and men of the Navy who were permanently married was no more than a fifth or a quarter, disproportionately concentrated among the officers, petty officers and older seamen. The majority of ships' companies were young men without ties, and it's hardly surprising that when given leave with money in their pockets, they tended to spend it unwisely. Captain Wheeler (a colourful officer whose outspokenness got him into trouble on occasion), reproached his men in these terms: 'I have observed too, whenever ye get any money paid, ye do not act with it like rational creatures and lay it out on clothes and necessaries, but ye throw it on dirty whores and in stinking gin.'[32]

Cases of venereal disease ran, on average, at over 8 per cent of complement a year, and in some ships, over 20 per cent.[33]

It was not altogether unusual, however, for some wives to live on board, contrary though it was to regulations. Captain Thomas Fremantle, for instance, who had married Betsey Wynne at the Palazzo Sessa, Sir William and Emma Hamilton's home in Naples, took his bride to sea. She was on board his ship, the *Seahorse*, at Santa Cruz when Nelson's right arm was shattered. Nelson was rowed to the *Seahorse*, which was the nearest ship, but although nearly unconscious and in great pain, he refused to go on board because he did not wish to alarm Betsey, anxiously awaiting her own husband's return from the beaches. 'I will die', said Nelson, 'rather than alarm Mrs Fremantle by seeing me in this state when I can give her no tidings of her husband.'[34] We are also told of Captain Arbuthnot who earned a mild reprimand for giving the wives of his boatswain and master passages to Virginia. While there were, indeed, some useful tasks that women such as these could do aboard ship, it was more or less understood that only those that were either plain or elderly would be accepted on board. That a young, attractive woman would have been a disruptive danger, was clear in a sensible captain's mind.[35]

Some officers arranged to bring their wives to foreign stations and set them up comfortably on land, but in the Admiralty's view these husbands were often tempted to linger with their wives when they should be at sea. Captain Richard Watkins damaged his career by staying ashore at Barbados with his new bride after being ordered to sea.[36]

'Dinner on board a ship at Gravesend' by Captain Wright, painted c.1810. The presence of women on board ship whilst in port was a long-established custom. Note the hammocks above, and the use of the sailors' sea-chests as chairs. (National Maritime Museum, London)

As for bachelor officers away from home, the Navy offered possibly more scope for amorous adventures as visitors than were available to settled members of the community.[37] That many kept mistresses was true and of course they also fathered bastards in many foreign ports.

The morality of the lower deck was as equally strained as it was in the officers' quarters; more so, as privacy hardly existed there. Fifty-three per cent of all able seamen in the Navy were aged twenty-five or under, and therefore at the height of their sexual libido. It is not surprising that women were smuggled aboard and hidden.[38] Sometimes, in an emergency, they would come out of hiding and help to man ship, or even fight a gun. John Nicol records of the Battle of the Nile in 1798, being stationed at the powder magazine in the *Goliath*:

> Any information we got was from the boys and women who carried the powder . . . I was much indebted to the Gunner's wife who gave her husband and me a drink of wine every now and then . . . Some of the women were wounded . . . One woman bore a son in the heat of action.[39]

Surprising as it seems, it was possible for a woman to keep her secret on a crowded ship with little privacy. Jane Townshend fought aboard the *Defiance* at Trafalgar, as did Ann Hopping and Mary Ann Riley. Forty years later they individually proved their legitimate claims to the General Service Medal, but the Admiralty turned down their requests saying it would create too dangerous a precedent.[40] Mary Ann Talbot, known as the 'British Amazon', who had served as a drummer boy in Flanders, later took to the sea as a cabin boy and was wounded at the battle of The Glorious First of June in 1794.[41]

Many allusions are to be found in the logs and journals of the time to the presence of women aboard warships. For instance, after the 44-gun *Resistance* had blown up in the Strait of Banca on 24 July 1798, Thomas Scott, who was one of only four survivors, gave evidence at the court martial that among those that perished in her were three English women, and one Malay woman of Amboyna. In the rules and orders written by the ringleaders, to be observed by the mutinous crews of the ships at the Nore in 1797, occurs the amusing but significant paragraph: 'No woman shall be permitted to go on shore from any ship, but as many may come in as please.'[42]

The incidence of homosexual behaviour

That three-quarters of ships' companies were not married, coupled with the sexual frustration of their being confined for some times months at sea, brings up the matter of the incidence of homosexual behaviour. In fact, a ship at sea with so little privacy, and with over a thousand eyes scanning the decks, must have been a very difficult place to commit an act of sodomy, especially with the fear of being caught and brought to trial. Sodomy was a capital offence in England until 1861, and from that date until 1967 was punishable by life imprisonment.

From the seventeenth century onwards, buggery was specifically mentioned in the Articles of War. Article 29 of the 1749 Articles stated:

> If any person in the fleet shall commit the unnatural and detestable sin of buggery or sodomy with man or beast, he shall be punished with death by the sentence of a Court Martial.

No doubt many officers simply looked the other way when evidence of sodomy was presented to them. As for the crew, knowing that conviction would most likely mean death for the offenders, they seldom reported known cases. Some captains preferred to put a man ashore at a convenient port of call, when faced with 'suspicious behaviour' by a member of his crew.[43] Occasionally, however, there were cases that came to trial, and others that never did. For instance, Captain Churchill of the *Canterbury*, confronted with a complaint against him from one of his men, denied it and shot himself. The purser of the *Newcastle* 'detected in some things not so decent to name', deserted before he could be arrested. Then there was the case of Captain Henry Angel of the *Stag*, who was arrested by his own officers. Angel at once resigned his commission, begging his commander-in-chief to 'represent him as favourably as possible' at the court martial, which reads like a man with a guilty conscience.[44]

Gilbert has noted that in courts of law, sodomy presented problems very similar to those presented by rape: at what point was the act deemed 'committed'. For example, murder can easily be distinguished from attempted murder because the victim is either alive or dead, and robbery can be separated from attempted robbery by determining whether or not the attempt was successful. Rape and sodomy present more serious difficulties. In the latter case, conflict arose over whether sodomitic acts were deemed complete if an emission took place, or if penetration occurred, or both. In 1631, for example, the Earl of Castlehaven was convicted of buggery on proof of emission only. Generally, however, it was necessary to prove penetration, and according to a judicial decision of 1781, both penetration and emission had to be established for a sodomy conviction to be sustained.[45]

If, in a case of sodomy, the death sentence was not imposed, either because the act was not proven or because the charge was changed to 'uncleanliness', the punishment was extremely harsh in comparison to other crimes. In 1760, for example, one seaman was sentenced to 700 lashes for desertion and theft, another to 600 for desertion only. Five men were sentenced to 500 lashes apiece for crimes ranging from mutiny to striking an officer. The following year a sailor convicted of drunkenness, disrespect and mutiny charges was given 600 lashes and another received a similar sentence for desertion. In contrast, two men accused of buggery in 1762, which could only be partially proved, received 1,000 lashes each.[46]

If we take the lash average as a measure of how seriously courts martial boards rated crimes, deviant sexual behaviour topped the list throughout the Napoleonic Wars. Over twice as many lashes per sentence were awarded for

moral offences during that time, than for the perennial military crime of
desertion.[47]

Log and muster books

A considerable amount of paperwork had to be accomplished to sail a ship of the
line. An hourly diary of a ship's life was kept in the logs. A copy or sometimes the
original of these was handed into the Navy Board periodically, later to become an
invaluable historical record. The log recorded navigation details such as the wind
direction, courses steered, speed and distances made good hour by hour. Recorded also were lists of stores taken on board, duties and punishments carried
out, signals hoisted and received, and casualties sustained in action.[48]

The captain's journal and the master's log were official and obligatory in the
Royal Navy until the middle of the nineteenth century, when they were
superseded by the ships' logs. Apart from the captain and master of the vessel,
the midshipmen had to maintain a log as part of their training. They had to
submit it regularly to one of the officers for his examination and signature.
Other officers, including lieutenants, often kept logs as personal diaries and
even embellished them with pencil or watercolour drawings of the coastline
and foreign ports. All the logs were usually based in one form or another on
the master's log. The master kept his log first on a large, rough slate, which he
kept in the binnacle box. At the end of the day and in the privacy of his cabin,
he would copy the information from his slate onto paper in rough draft, and
then into his log book. One fair copy at least had to be made to send to the
Navy Board; the original he kept for himself. It was prudent to do so, since it
was a record of his own service, which he might need later.

From the master's original was then derived the captain's log, which added
any items of general information that the captain might think proper, or
which he was obliged by regulation to give. Usually, he added little beyond
shipboard routine and loss or damage to stores and supplies. The master's log
also supplied the basic information for the lieutenant's and midshipmen's logs.
In practice, there could easily be a dozen logs kept on board, all derived from
the master's original.[49]

Another important task involved the keeping of musters, that is to say, a listing
of the ship's company in the muster book or roll. It was the captain's responsibility
to record in it the name of everyone on board, mainly to determine his wages.
The purser, for the purpose of his own accounting, recorded the consumption of
victuals and articles of clothing chargeable to each officer and member of the
crew. Both the captains' and pursers' accounts had to be accurate, as errors or
omissions could be, and often were, charged against their pay. Consequently,
both officers had a strong incentive to keep the records correct.

As with logs, the captain and the purser did their work in rough, to be
written up later in the muster book. A fair copy was sent to the financial
officer of the ship's home port, the Clerk of the Cheque. He in turn

forwarded the muster to the Navy Office, where it was entered in the pay book in order to disburse the pay of the ship's company.

A ship became an administrative unit when the first officer arrived on board and hoisted the pendant. From that day the musters commenced. While in the dockyard, the ship was under the control of the Clerk of the Cheque, who paid the men and victualled them, when she was said to be 'under the cheque'. Only when the ship was ready to put to sea, did she enter on 'sea victualling', under full control of her own officers.

Once a week, a muster was carried out on deck, and each person was recorded in the muster book under such headings as 'Ship's Company', 'Marines Part of Complement', 'Supernumeraries for Wages and Victuals', or 'Supernumeraries for Victuals Only'. Those sick or absent without leave were marked in as such and included in the total. Moreover, there would often be all sorts of people on board who were not part of the ship's company but still had to be fed. These might be soldiers, passengers, prisoners of war, customs officers, shipwrecked mariners, pilots, and even admirals' retinues. It is interesting to note that those not engaged in the actual work of the ship were usually recorded for 'victuals only' but at two-thirds of the daily allowance.

The ship was a self-contained unit of intricate accountability in the hands of its officers. The clerical recording system was highly complex, but followed its own intrinsic logic.[50]

The key to success

There was no such thing as privacy on board for anyone but the officers. Men in the forecastle or on the gundeck understood privacy primarily in social, not in individual, terms. The hardships of life in confined quarters, surrounded by the alien sea, was in fact the very fabric from which seamen derived their self-understanding 'when private life was everywhere, and yet nowhere'. The very design of a wooden walled man-of-war reflected this and forged its occupants into a family, a clan, a community, whose success in beating the odds, be they enemies or elements, lay precisely in its unity.

NOTES

1. After becoming first Lord of the Admiralty in 1911, Winston Churchill converted the fleet from coal to oil and scrapped the older ships in favour of smaller and faster ships. An admiral indignantly said to Churchill, 'Sir, you are scuttling the traditions of the Royal Navy', to which Churchill answered, 'Well, Admiral, have you ever considered what the traditions of the Royal Navy are? I will tell you in three words: rum, sodomy, and the lash'. Sir Peter Gretton, *Former Naval Person: Winston Churchill and the Royal Navy* (London: Cassell & Co, 1968).
2. Lavery, Vol 1, p 126. These were the theoretical rates assigned to British battleships but as Lavery states, the nominal force of a ship, as it appeared on the Navy List, now gave only a rough guide to its real strength. In the past it had understated it, in that carronades were never counted as part of the total. After 1797 it also overstated the true position in one sense, in that few ships carried as many long guns as their nominal listing.
3. W A Falconer, *A New Universal Dictionary of the Marine* (London, 1815; reprinted 1970), p 77.
4. Grant Uden & Richard Cooper, *A Dictionary of British Ships & Seamen* (London: Allen Lane, 1980), p 390.
5. Ibid.

6. Major J Elvin, *Handbook of Smooth Bore Cannon* (1805).
7. Highly valued as weapons were the boarding pikes, 6 feet long with steel blades on their tips, which were stacked neatly on end like billiard cues around the base of the main and foremast on the quarter deck and forecastle.
8. Preston, op. cit.
9. *HMS Victory: Official Guide* (Waterlow Ltd., 1984).
10. Oliver Warner, *A Portrait of Lord Nelson* (London: Penguin Books, 1987), p 78.
11. Christopher Driver & Michelle Berriedale-Johnson, *Pepys at Table* (Berkeley: University of California Press, 1984).
12. The flour was not white as we know it today. It was not until the advent of the roller mill in the nineteenth century that it became possible to crush the wheat germ to obtain flour of a chalky white and long-lasting consistency.
13. Leo Heaps, *Log of the Centurion* (New York: Macmillan, 1973), pp 25–29.
14. In 1687, when Jamaica was annexed by Britain, rum was substituted for the brandy which had been consumed before. In 1740, Admiral Vernon, nicknamed 'Old Grogram' for the coarse material from which his cloak was made, ordered that a daily allowance of half a pint of rum, diluted in a quart of water, be ladled out to each sailor in the presence of the officer of the watch. The mixture became known immediately as 'grog'.
15. Heaps, pp 25, 28.
16. Thomas Swaine, *The Universal Directory for Taking Alive, or Destroying, Rats and Mice* (1788).
17. Heaps, p 90.
18. Ibid, p 87.
19. Ibid, pp 12, 26.
20. Ibid, p 13.
21. Identifying the disease as a deficiency of vitamin C did not become possible until the discovery of vitamins in the twentieth century.
22. Preston, p 53.
23. Uden & Cooper state that a study in 1803 indicates that out of 39,600 men recruited, 37,000 were volunteers and less than 2,000 were pressed. However, this was at the renewal of war after the short-lived Peace of Amiens; as the navy's requirements for men escalated, a higher proportion of pressed men would have been needed.
24. William Laird Clowes, *The Royal Navy, a History from Earliest Time to the Present* (London: Sampson Low, Marston, 1898), Vol 4, p 181.
25. Uden & Cooper, pp 161–162, 287, 797, & 442.
26. Warner, p 79.
27. Bruce Chatwin, *In Patagonia* (1977), p 151.
28. Uden & Cooper, p 565.
29. Ibid, pp 565–566.
30. Ernle Bradford, *Nelson: The Essential Hero* (London 1977), p 71.
31. N A M Rodger, *The Wooden World* (London: Fontana Press, 1988), p 79.
32. Ibid.
33. Ibid, p 80.
34. Uden & Cooper, p 169.
35. Ibid, pp 76–77.
36. Rodger, p 75.
37. Ibid, p 76.
38. Ibid, p 78.
39. Uden & Cooper, p 566.
40. Ibid, p 527.
41. Ibid, p 506.
42. Clowes, Vol 6, p 84.
43. Arthur N Gilbert, 'Buggery and the British Navy', in *Journal of Social History* (1976), Vol 10, No 1, p 79.
44. Rodger, pp 79–80.
45. Arthur N Gilbert, 'Buggery and the British Navy', in *Journal of Social History* (1976), Vol 10, No 1, p 73.
46. Ibid, pp 82–83.
47. Ibid, p 84.
48. Uden & Cooper, p 273.
49. I am grateful to N A M Rodger, senior archivist and authority on Admiralty Records at the Public Record Office, London, for providing information on naval logs.
50. N A M Rodger, *Naval Records for Genealogists* (London: Public Record Office, 1984).

CHAPTER 3

First Engagements 1781–1782

Kepe then the sea that is the wall of England:
And then is England kept by Goddes hande.

A libel of English policie, c.1436.

When war broke out between Britain and its rebellious American colonies in
1775, the Royal Navy was weakened not only by neglect but by a reduction
in the number of its ships. It was to be weakened even more by party politics
and by the loss of America itself as a source of manpower, ships, stores, and
timber.

Britain had come to depend on its American colonies, and principally New
Hampshire, for mast timber since 1652. The supply had ceased abruptly with
the commencement of hostilities. To make matters worse, it appeared that
some of its existing naval vessels had been hurriedly built of unseasoned wood.
No fewer than sixty-six of them were to founder during the war, one being
the *Royal George*, which sank at her moorings.

The Declaration of American Independence[1]

Britain's attempt to quell the revolution, which began in Lexington and
Concord on 19 April 1775, included a naval blockade of the coast. The
colonists countered by building privateers, using the excellent timber of New
England and manning them with their experienced deep water sailors.[2]

On 17 June, the British successfully assaulted Bunker Hill, although it cost
them more than 40 per cent of their force. A few days after the battle, George
Washington took command of the colonial troops and gradually instilled a
degree of order and discipline among them.

On 4 July 1776, influenced by the British attack on Charlestown, the
colonists proclaimed their independence in a document whose principal
author was Thomas Jefferson. Their Declaration of Independence was seen by
the British as a reckless and provocative move, and they set about further
subduing the colonies by securing some key strategic areas.[3]

In a pincer manoeuvre from Montreal, the British sent two forces to isolate
New England. Approaching from Canada by means of the St Lawrence River,
Lieutenant Colonel St Leger seized Fort Stanwix and marched east to join
forces with General John Burgoyne. Burgoyne planned to take Albany and
win control of the upper Hudson Valley, but the colonist forces under Major
General Benedict Arnold drove St Leger from Fort Stanwix and went on to

help his compatriot Major General Horatio Gates to force Burgoyne's surrender at Saratoga on 17 October 1777. This was to be the turning point in the war, which brought France, then Spain, into an alliance against England, followed shortly after by the Netherlands. With the other states of northern Europe, these three powers undertook to defend the interests of neutral states against what they saw as the arrogant enforcement by Britain of the right to search any vessel at sea.

Britain and France vie for naval supremacy

England was now confronted by the larger part of Europe and the war became to a great extent a contest between the two most powerful navies in the world, her own and that of the French, and the scene of their actions became mainly the West Indian and European seas.

From April 1778 until September 1779, the French fleet in American waters under the command of Admiral D'Estaing met with little or no success, even though it was more heavily equipped with cannon than the British fleet under Admiral Howe. D'Estaing first blockaded Howe at Sandy Hook. Then, by agreement with the American generals, he planned an attack on Newport, Rhode Island, but put to sea to fight the British before the attack took place. After a storm shattered his fleet, he put into Boston for repairs, then sailed for the West Indies to capture the islands of St Vincent and Grenada. After fighting an indecisive battle with a British fleet under Admiral John Byron, he set sail to attack British-occupied Savannah. He could not achieve his aim, however, and was repulsed with a heavy loss of life. He returned to France in 1780.

Due to its better discipline, training, and tactical skills, the British navy, after many battles, was proving to be the more formidable fighting force. The navies of Holland and Spain had already been defeated. Now it became vital for the British to defeat the French fleet in the West Indies under the command of Admiral de Grasse, in order to assert their power in the area unhindered and take command of the Atlantic seaboard.

The Comte de Grasse, who was sixty years old at the time, had fought the British successfully for two years in the American war. He was an experienced sailor who had started his career at sea at the early age of twelve and was well known for his cunning, competence, and valour. After France had joined the American cause, he had been sent across the Atlantic as commander of a squadron. In 1781 he had been promoted to the rank of Admiral and successfully defeated Admiral Samuel Hood, seizing Tobago. Later, he cooperated with Washington in the final stages of the land war by sailing his fleet into the Chesapeake and bringing 3,000 French troops to supplement the armies of Washington, Rochambeau and Lafayette. De Grasse's naval intervention in the Chesapeake was more than instrumental in the decisive siege of Yorktown, the last major land action of the American Revolution. In the drama of that historic event, which was to change the world and secure a new nation, it was French naval power, coupled with American strategy, that brought about the surrender of the patrician British Lieutenant General Lord Charles Cornwallis and his army of more than 7,000 men. After Cornwallis' surrender, de Grasse returned to the West Indies where in January 1782 he captured the island of St Kitts, properly called St Christopher.[4]

The action off Ushant

The British were aware that de Grasse had been imploring his government throughout the summer of 1781 to send him reinforcements of ships and supplies for his next campaign in the West Indies. The transports and war material could not be collected at the port of Brest, however, until December of that year.

On 2 December 1781 Rear Admiral Richard Kempenfelt, having hoisted his broad pendant in the *Victory*, left England with a fleet of twelve ships of the line, one 50-gun ship, four frigates, and a fireship. His orders were to cruise down the English Channel towards the tip of Brittany and stand off Ushant, and once there, lie in wait for the French expedition. Among the ships of the line was the *Agamemnon*, ready for her first engagement with the enemy.[5]

Captain Benjamin Caldwell, first commander of HMS *Agamemnon* , by Samuel Medley. (National Maritime Museum, London)

The French suspected correctly that the British would attempt to intercept the convoy. Rear Admiral de Guichen was ordered to accompany it from Brest clear of the Bay of Biscay with twelve line-of-battle ships and then sail on to Cadiz.[6] Five ships of the line destined for de Grasse and two going to the East Indies raised to nineteen the total fighting force with which de Guichen left Brest on 10 December 1781. The merchant vessels, loaded beyond their normal capacity and wallowing heavily, numbered over twenty.

Nineteen French ships of the line should have been amply sufficient to ward off any attack, but de Guichen, ordinarily a careful officer, had allowed his faster fleet of line-of-battle ships to sail to leeward and ahead of the convoy. Six hours later this lack of foresight proved to be a fatal and irreparable mistake.

On the afternoon of 12 December 1781 the weather, which had been thick and squally, suddenly cleared. To windward, in the pale sunshine of that winter's afternoon, silently bearing down upon them, rising and falling in the troughs and under short canvas, appeared the British fleet. In the column, with sterns and bowsprits almost touching, the *Agamemnon* had taken her place in the line. Her gun decks were cleared of everything but fighting equipment. The ports were raised and the guns run out.

As the British column approached the convoy at right angles, de Guichen realised that the outcome would be disastrous. Being too far ahead and to leeward, he could not manoeuvre his warships back in time to protect the transports. They had scattered in every direction as the British swooped down upon them. There was no escape, and the French line-of-battle ships remained helpless spectators while the victims were hauling down their flags in surrender left and right.[7]

With night coming on some prizes escaped but fifteen were captured. The captives were laden with military and naval stores of considerable monetary value and even greater military importance.[8] The booty would later bring welcome prize money to both officers and men, once their values were assessed by the High Court of Admiralty.

A few days later, a violent storm dispersed and shattered the remainder of the French fleet. Only two ships, the *Triomphant* of 84 guns and the *Brave* of 74, plus five transports, ever reached de Grasse in the West Indies. The rest struggled back to Brest.[9] There had been no losses aboard the *Agamemnon* and only minor casualties within the fleet while boarding the French vessels.[10]

Kempenfelt, before returning to England, sent off to the West Indies the fireship *Tisiphone*, under the command of James Saumarez, to advise Rear Admiral Hood of the possible arrival of the French ships that had escaped capture.

Agamemnon *joins the West Indian fleet*

On 30 December 1781, *Agamemnon* was back at anchor at Spithead, where she remained until 6 February 1782. She then sailed for the Caribbean as part of a squadron of twelve ships of the line and a convoy of merchant vessels under the command of Admiral Sir George Rodney, who had hoisted his broad pendant in the *Formidable*.[11]

Rodney was 64 and an ailing man at the time. An unusual man for a seaman, he had rather an effeminate air. His friend Sir Nathaniel William Wraxall was later to give the following description of him in his memoirs:

> His person was more elegant than seemed to become his rough profession. There was even something that approached to delicacy and effeminacy in his figure; but no man manifested a more temperate and steady courage in action.[12]

On 25 February, to windward of Antigua, Rodney's squadron met up with the British West Indian fleet under the command of Rear Admiral Sir Samuel Hood, bringing the British force in the area to thirty-six line-of-battle ships.

The Comte de Grasse was based at Martinique with thirty-three ships, which made both opposing forces practically equal in numbers. His immediate objective was to give the British the slip and capture Jamaica, no simple matter, since the problem confronting de Grasse was in reality an extremely difficult and risky one. To make the enterprise possible, he would have to convoy to Cap François the supply vessels with the troops essential for the scheme. He would also have with him merchant vessels to send on to France. This would make a total of over 150 unarmed vessels to be protected by his thirty-three fighting ships, as against the British opposing force of thirty-six line-of-battle ships.

Since a fleet can only sail at the speed of the slowest ship, large bodies of ships commonly moved less rapidly than smaller ones, so adding this disadvantage to the fact that the British owned the strategic island of St Lucia which they used as their outpost, de Grasse was tremendously handicapped from the outset. A further condition needed to ensure his success was the safe arrival of another great convoy from Brest to replace the losses that Kempenfelt's raid had inflicted off Ushant in December.

Rodney, who had taken over as Commander-in-Chief upon his arrival, took his fleet to St Lucia to refit and prepare for the coming campaign. While there, Hood, his second in command, suggested to Rodney that he halve the fleet, letting one part cruise between Dominica and Deseada while the other guarded the southern area between Martinique and St Lucia. Rodney was unwilling to agree to this plan and instead, as was his way, he adopted a half measure, which consisted in restricting the area under surveillance only as far north as Dominica, but not beyond.[13] It would seem, however, reading between the lines, that Hood tried to stretch his cruising ground northwards, convinced that it was worth the effort, but he was later recalled and reprimanded.

True to Hood's reasoning, the convoy from Brest sailed through unhampered, north of Deseada, escorted by only two French ships of the line. The convoy reached Martinique safely on 20 March 1782, raising de Grasse's fighting force to thirty-five ships of the line as against the British thirty-six.

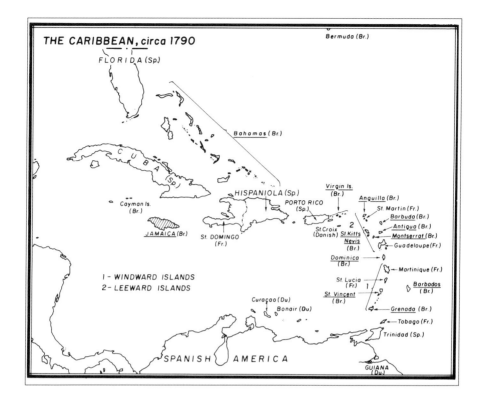

At the end of the month, Rodney returned to St Lucia and remained at anchor, though carefully keeping watch on the French fleet in Fort Royal by means of a chain of frigates.[14]

Preliminaries to the Battle of the Saintes

De Grasse's scheme for his conquest of Jamaica hinged on the chance of him slipping out of port unseen whenever he had a favourable trade wind and then skirting the inner edge of the Caribbean Sea. This would permit him the use of a close succession of friendly ports where the convoy could take refuge in case of need. Accordingly, he set sail on the 8 April 1782. This was reported promptly to Rodney, relay-style by his chain of frigates, and by noon the whole of the British fleet was clear of its anchorage and in pursuit.[15]

By six next morning, both the French fleet and the enemy convoy were visible from the deck of Hood's flagship, the *Barfleur*, then in the van. Hood could see them bearing northeast, spread out between the centre of Dominica towards Guadeloupe, at a distance from him of only 4 to 12 miles. His squadron had gained much in the night and early morning, taking every advantage of the catspaws coming through the Channel at infrequent intervals. Gradually working its way clear of the high land of Dominica that had cut it off from the wind, Hood's division was the first among the British to get the breeze, and with eight ships he stood north in order of battle.

Rodney had hoisted the signal to engage at 6:38am, but, ambivalent, hauled it down almost immediately. Wary of the consequences, Hood would not fire without orders, so when two French vessels that had been separated from their group boldly sailed down and impertinently crossed the bows of the *Alfred*, leader of Hood's column (so close, in fact, that it had to bear up to let them pass) Hood fumed but held his fire as the two French ships sailed by and rejoined their main body unharmed.

Seeing that the British were gaining on him, de Grasse knew that unless he divested himself of the convoy, he stood a good chance of losing it in the ensuing battle. He therefore directed two of his line-of-battle ships to accompany the transports into Guadeloupe, where they arrived safely that day, and he took his fleet to windward, midway between Dominica and Guadeloupe, towards a group of small islands called Les Saintes, the Saints. By this manoeuvre, De Grasse hoped to draw the British away from pursuing the convoy and also to escape action due to his superior speed.

French ships were usually better sailers. They were longer on the waterline, which, all other things being equal, made them faster than the British, a fact that even coppering had not been able to overcome entirely. When speed was a factor, as in this case, the Royal Navy was often at a disadvantage against the French.

As de Grasse made headway into mid-channel, a subtle and irresistible temptation assailed him.[16] Watching from his quarterdeck, he noticed that Hood's squadron was now exposed. Having caught the wind at last, Hood's ships had picked up speed and separated from the rest of the British column, which was still becalmed under Dominica. If de Grasse attacked with all his thirty-five ships, he knew he could crush Hood and render the remainder of the British fleet hopelessly subordinate to the French. Still, he would prefer not to expose his total force. If he risked only half his fleet, he might be able to damage Hood's column sufficiently to deter the British from further pursuit.

Like many a commander before him, de Grasse was confronted with a fateful choice, whose outcome — whether victory or defeat — only history would reveal. In our mind's eye, we can see him pacing the quarterdeck of the *Ville de Paris* in his frock coat, knee breeches, white stockings and buckled shoes, his hat slightly askew to permit raising the telescope to his eye. We can see him carefully following the movements of Hood's column, which by now was shortening sail to avoid pulling further away from the British centre and rear. He draws a handkerchief from his sleeve and mops his brow. Though only 9am, the day is proving to be unbearably hot again, and he is glad of the breeze strengthening from the northeast. He raises the telescope to his eye once more and focuses. Hood's squadron is getting closer and slowly entering the trap. He weighs the odds and swiftly makes up his mind. Squeezing the telescope shut with a click, he turns to his flag captain and gives the order to hoist the signal for only half his fleet to attack. The die is cast. The plan is to be carried out by the Marquis de Vaudreuil, his second in command.

The action of 9 April 1782

De Vaudreuil formed his squadron in line of battle and bore down from windward to attack Hood's rear ships. Then, sailing up parallel to them, he fired at long range until, having overtaken the leaders, he tacked back, repeating the manoeuvre again in an elliptical curve. Having the choice of distance, his ships fired high at sails and rigging and cautiously kept out of range of the British carronades.

The storm of shot that raked the British column until 1:45pm did not deter Hood from keeping up a good barrage of his own. One of the French ships, the *Caton*, was so crippled that she left the battle and limped into Guadeloupe. The captain of the *Alfred* was cut in two by chain shot and several seamen were killed by the same volley. The *Royal Oak* lost her main topmast as did the *Warrior* and, although considerable damage was inflicted to spars, sails, and rigging, de Grasse was far from having accomplished the purpose of crushing

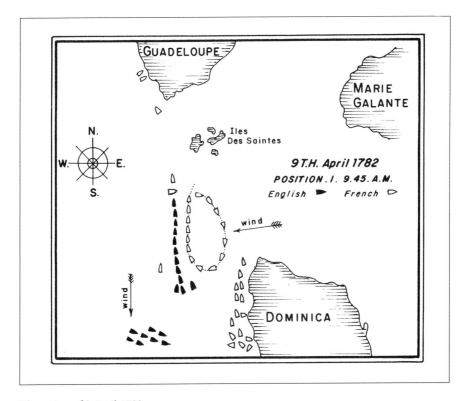

The action of 9 April 1782.

Hood's squadron. In fact, the damage he had achieved was nothing that the seamen could not readily repair to enable them to continue the chase.[17]

During the night the British lay to for repairs. Rodney contented himself with reversing the order of battle, putting Hood in the rear so he would be able to refit. The next morning they resumed the pursuit but on the whole lost ground throughout that day and the next, with the French barely in sight from the deck of the leading British vessel.

The Battle of the Saintes

The *Agamemnon*, which had seen action on the 9th, firing from a distance, now lay sixteenth in the line, ahead of and separated from Rodney's flagship, the *Formidable* only by the *Duke*, of 98 guns. At 2am on 12 April, de Grasse's flagship, the *Ville de Paris* of 110 guns, and another French ship, the *Zélé*, crossing on opposite tacks in the dark, collided with each other. The *Zélé* lost both her foremast and bowsprit. A frigate was summoned to tow her to Guadeloupe, but by daybreak the sudden loss of wind during the night brought them, becalmed, to within six miles of the *Barfleur*, Hood's flagship. Rodney signalled Hood to cut out of the line with three of the rearmost ships and capture the *Zélé*. Seeing this, the impulsive de Grasse made his second and final mistake. He bore down to try and save the crippled ship, making all sail but losing the ground he had gained during the last few days. An hour later, at 7am, he gathered his fleet in line. Shortly afterwards, the opening salvos of the great battle of the Saintes were heard.[18]

Having abandoned his previous cautious policy, de Grasse hurried his fleet into action, but some of the ships were scattered over ten miles to windward of his own. Though they crowded on sail to rejoin the flagship, there was not enough time for them to take up their stations in the line before the battle began at 8am. 'Our line of battle was formed under the fire of musketry', wrote the Marquis de Vaudreuil later, who being in the rear of the fleet had a good vantage point from where to observe the action. To make matters worse, de Grasse added to his errors by sailing his fleet towards Dominica and into the calms and intermittent puffs of wind that clung to the shoreline. The move deprived him of the power to manoeuvre and the blunder was evident at once, even to his own officers. 'What evil genius has inspired the admiral?' exclaimed du Pavillon, de Vaudreuil's flag captain, who was recognised as one of the best tacticians in France and who later fell in the battle.[19]

At five minutes past eight, Rodney made a general signal for close action and his flagship the *Formidable*, eighteenth in the line, began to fire at 18:23am. The great ships slowly sailed by each other on opposite tacks, firing their guns in murderous succession, the enemy often disappearing from sight in the billows of the smoke that each created. The *Agamemnon* had been cleared for action and her boats hoisted out and towed astern. Her decks had been sanded to avoid the crew slipping in the blood that soon would flow around their

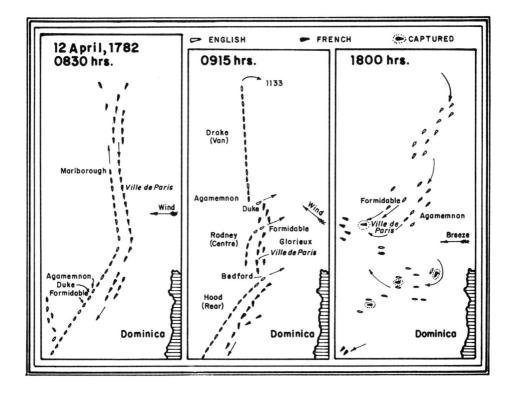

The Battle of the Saintes, 12 April 1782, showing Rodney's breaking of
the French line. It is still a matter of debate whether this manoeuvre was
deliberately planned.

feet. As protection against flying splinters, all hammocks had been stowed in
the netting strung around the upper decks, and large ones were spread over
the bulwarks from bows to stern to fend off any attempt of enemy boarders.
To lessen the ever present risk of fire and also to clear the field of vision,
seamen had been ordered to climb the rigging and clew the courses up to the
yards.

At 9:15am, Captain Caldwell saw the *Formidable*, the second ship behind
his, cut across the French line astern of the *Glorieux*, firing both broadsides as
she broke through. Then, seeing Rodney's manoeuvre, the ship immediately
astern of the *Agamemnon*, the *Duke*, imitated his action and broke through the
French line as well.

As he watched, Caldwell could see that the *Formidable*'s broadsides had
blown away the main and mizzen masts of the *Glorieux*. Minutes later her
foremast and bowsprit fell. Huddled together and effectively sandwiched
between Rodney's ship and the *Duke* were four French ships taking repeated
broadsides at close quarters from the two British vessels. As Caldwell could
see, they were severely mauled. Looking astern he could make out the

Bedford. Probably unable to see the ship ahead of her through the smoke, she had luffed and cut across the French line as well, followed by twelve ships behind her.

The *Agamemnon*, which had been firing her starboard guns since 8:30am from her position in the column, had now passed the rearmost French ship and was out of the action for now. As the last ship in the van, she continued to sail northward with the others, hastily repairing the damage to her rigging inflicted by the French broadsides.

At 11:33am Rodney signalled the van to tack. The *Agamemnon*, having been the last in line, now was closest to the enemy and closing the range fast. With a favourable wind the van descended upon the French and, passing in a column alongside the *Glorieux*, *Hector*, and *César*, they inflicted such damage that had no parallel among the British vessels. The French ships were totally dismasted and lay motionless between the enemy lines.

Towards evening, when the smoke of battle had cleared, the *Agamemnon* lay in tatters. All her sails and rigging had been cut to pieces and her foretopmast had been shot away. Still, she fired her guns until 6:29pm, when Rodney signalled to cease the battle. The master's log of Sunday 14 April states tersely:

The French flagship *Ville de Paris* (right) strikes her colours at the Battle of the Saintes, by Thomas Whitcombe. She had suffered some 300 casualties during the battle and expended all her powder and shot. (National Maritime Museum, London)

> PM Calm & clear Airs. Departed this Life Lieutenant William Brice. At 2 also departed this Life James Hawkins Mariner. Employed about the Rigging as before. Mustered the Ship's Company and found 14 Men killed 22 wounded . . .[20]

The British practice of firing at the hull, as opposed to the French preference for firing mainly on the upsurge at the rigging, probably accounted for the heavier losses in the French fleet, although nobody would ever know exactly their precise number. On the *Ville de Paris* alone losses were reckoned at 300. British losses were stated at 243 killed and 816 wounded. The French lost six captains and the British two.

Towards sunset the French flagship *Ville de Paris*, to many the finest ship afloat, had expended all her ammunition, even to the point where it was said that her last broadsides were fired with powder scooped by hand from the empty kegs in the magazine. She finally hauled down her colours, and Admiral de Grasse formally surrendered to Hood on the *Barfleur*. Shortly after this, Rodney made the signal for his fleet to anchor. They remained there for the night as the French continued to retreat under the orders of the Marquis de Vaudreuil, now commander in chief since de Grasse had surrendered. The British had captured five French ships of the line, one of which had blown up, but twenty-six ships had sailed away as best they could, making for Cap François and Curaçao.

The aftermath

Hood was furious at what appeared to be Rodney's slothful attitude in not bothering to pursue the French. He had strong words of condemnation for his commander:

> Why he [Rodney] should bring the fleet to because the *Ville de Paris* was taken, I cannot reconcile. He did not pursue under easy sail, so as never to have lost sight of the enemy in the night, which would clearly and most undoubtedly have enabled him to have taken almost every ship the next day . . . Had I had the honor of commanding his Majesty's noble fleet on the 12th, I may without much imputation of vanity say the flag of England should now have graced the sterns of upwards of twenty sail of the enemy's ships of the line.[21]

But another remark by Hood summed up Rodney's attitude conclusively: 'I lamented to Sir George on the 13th that . . . he did not pursue so as to keep sight of the enemy all night, to which he only answered, "Come, we have done very handsomely as it is." '[22]

Despite Hood's indignation and open criticism about the lack of initiative shown by his elderly superior, it was also argued that Rodney was a level headed and sensible commander who had put caution above impulse and passion.

Regardless of whether or not he should have pursued the French fleet after the battle, Rodney had regained command of West Indian waters and had struck the French a staggering blow. He had captured their commander in chief, killed and injured no less than 2,000 of the enemy in one day, including six post-captains, and had put the rest of their fleet to flight.[23] What would have been the purpose of ordering a general chase throughout the night with a fleet of ships nearly hacked to pieces during the previous day and carrying their 816 wounded on board? The risks of chasing an enemy fleet at night through the shoal waters and coral reefs of the Caribbean are obvious, especially when the draught of most of the line-of-battle ships was over 21 feet and the larger ones even more.

In answer to Hood's and others' criticisms, Rodney delivered an unconvincing argument, saying:

> The enemy, who went off in a body of twenty-six ships of the line, might, by ordering two or three of their best sailing ships or frigates to have shown lights at times, and by changing their course, have induced the British fleet to have followed them, while the main of their fleet, by hiding their lights, might have hauled their wind, and have been far to windward by daylight, and intercepted the captured ships and the most crippled ships of the English.[24]

Apart from Hood's criticism of Rodney's conduct, the battle itself had been significant in that for the first time in over a century, British ships had broken the sacred line of battle, taking on their adversaries in a sort of 'free-for-all'. Moreover, they had won a decisive and morale-boosting victory.[25] So demoralised were the French by the defeat of de Grasse that later, at the peace negotiations in Paris, they virtually abandoned their American allies to deal with the British by themselves.[26]

Two days after the battle, Captain Caldwell mustered ship for the burial of the fourteen members of the crew that had fallen in action. We can visualise the scene as he reads over them the service for the dead from his prayer book, not a break in his voice as the bodies, sewn in canvas and weighted with shot, are consigned to the deep from under the ensign. Around him is a group of men with weather beaten faces, some young ones too, streaming with tears and clutching their hats to their breasts as a roll on the drums accompanies each splash. Caldwell reads on to the end, then closing his book, turns to his first lieutenant with the request that he accompany him on a tour of the ship.

The gun deck is in order except for a plank of the hull beside the number eight gunport. The gunport had received a direct hit which had killed two of its gun crew and maimed another. The ship's carpenter and his mate are at work repairing the damage with the help of two of the crew. The decks have been swabbed of most traces of blood, and the ports are open to catch the faint traces of the breeze and ventilate the stench of gunpowder that still hangs heavy in the air.

Admiral Samuel Hood
(1724–1816), by Sir
Joshua Reynolds. He
had wanted to pursue
the escaping French
after the Battle of the
Saintes and complained
bitterly when Rodney
prevented him.
(National Maritime
Museum, London)

As Caldwell makes his round of the deck he stops briefly with each gun crew to congratulate them on the accuracy of their firing, making a joke or two about how much better their marksmanship had been than that of the French who, he said, had fired so high that the three trucks of the *Princess* had been shot away.[27] His remark causes hilarity among the men.

From the gun deck they descend beneath the ship's waterline to the gloom of the orlop deck where they are met by the moans of the wounded. Some are in a state of delirium caused by shock after amputations performed the evening before. Surgeon William Pettigrew, still with his shirt sleeves rolled up and his apron on, greets Captain Caldwell and proceeds to give him a case by case account of each of the wounded and their chance of survival. In the dim candlelight cast from the sconces attached to the bulkheads, Caldwell moves from one pain-wracked figure to the next. When recognised, he proffers some words of comfort, shallow and insufficient as they seem to him. With this most unpleasant business over for the time being, he and the first lieutenant climb the companion way to the quarterdeck and the light of day to supervise the repair work on the masts and rigging.

The fleet remained near Guadeloupe for five days after the battle, refitting and searching without result among the neighbouring islands for any stray members of the French squadron. On the fifth day, Hood was detached to seek out the French, taking with him ten sail of the line, including the

Agamemnon. Left to his own devices, Hood made for the Mona Passage between Puerto Rico and Santo Domingo carrying studding sails 'aloft and alow' in his haste. Two days later, after sighting the western tip of Puerto Rico, they came upon a small French squadron, which they chased. They captured the *Jason* and the *Caton*, both 64s, which had parted from the fleet before the battle. They also took two smaller vessels, *Aimable* and *Céres*.

Rodney, in the meantime, had sailed for Jamaica with the rest of the fleet, arriving there only three days later than had de Vaudreuil at Cap François. The French, though, had had enough and did not attempt further offensive action. They were demoralised not only by their defeat, partial though it was, but by the ignominious news that their commander de Grasse had been sent to England, a prisoner of war aboard HMS *Sandwich*.

Rodney stayed at Jamaica until 22 July 1782, when he sailed for England having been replaced by Admiral Hugh Pigot. With his departure, the war in the West Indies and North America had come to an end, as by then the British Government had abandoned all hope of subduing their rebellious American Colonies.[28] Still, taken over all, the British had reason to be grateful. Had it not been for Rodney's victory at the Saintes, it was more than likely that they would have lost Canada as well. The British actually emerged from the conflict better than they could have anticipated before the Saintes was fought.

The Comte De Grasse surrenders his sword to Admiral Rodney. At the Battle of the Saintes, the French commander and his flagship were captured, with four other ships of the line, and six post-captains were killed, among some 2,000 casualties, destroying French naval power in the West Indies. (National Maritime Museum, London)

The *Agamemnon*, as part of Hood's fleet, sailed for New York to greet Admiral Pigot, the new commander-in-chief, who had on board the heir to the throne, Prince William Henry. On the return voyage to Barbados they were joined by the frigate *Albermarle*, commanded by Captain Horatio Nelson, who had managed to get his ship placed under Hood's flag.

Towards the end of 1782, the *Agamemnon* sailed for England. The musters record the vessel at the River Thames and then at the Medway, still under the command of Benjamin Caldwell.[29] At Chatham on 16 June 1783, she was paid off. Nothing more is mentioned of her during the ten-year gap coinciding with the period of peace with France, when the ship was laid up.

The harrowing years during which the *Agamemnon* had seen her first naval actions had been of invaluable experience, especially for the younger officers of the Royal Navy who were to take on the French in the greater war ten years later. Once again it was sea power that had decided the issue even though the Navy was severely tested in the struggle and sustained heavy losses.

The consequences

At the end of the conflict with her American colonies, England's power and repute were very low. George III, in the agony of defeat, even talked of abdicating and retiring to Hanover. After the collapse of the government led by Lord North, the King had to come to terms with the Marquis of Rockingham, the leader of the opposition. Rockingham's conditions were independence for the American colonies and a diminishing of the Crown's influence in politics. The King was forced to accept, and Rockingham took over as Prime Minister. It fell to him to save what he could from the wreckage. Such was the plight to which the political obstinacy of George III had reduced the British Empire.[30]

NOTES

1. While it was true that the American War of Independence stemmed from the British Crown's obstinate inflexibility in restraining trade with America and imposing taxes on a large list of commodities, it was also true that many of the colonists were driven by a strong inherent desire for freedom and self-government, quite in keeping, after all, with the spirit of their English character. Those colonists who were able to follow everyday events had long felt they were being enveloped in circumstances over which they had not only no control but no power of decision. They despaired that the important matters concerning the colonies were seldom seriously debated by Parliament. Furthermore, it had become apparent to them that they were just a part of a large expanding empire, in which their affairs were treated with indifference and even disdain by British officials.
2. By 1781, they had 449 of these privateers preying on British merchantmen, which by the end of the war had captured 600 British vessels.
3. *Encyclopaedia Britannica* (1959), p 785.
4. Alexandre de Grasse, *Notice bibliographique sur l'Amiral Compte de Grasse d'apres les documents inedits* (1840).
5. Admiral Kempenfelt lost his life tragically a year after this engagement. He was writing a letter in the main cabin of the *Royal George* while the ship was moored at Spithead being repaired. The ship capsized and sank, drowning him and some 900 men, women, and children, mostly visitors, who went down with the ship.

His sword was in its sheath
His fingers held the pen
When Kempenfelt went down
With twice four hundred men.
The Loss of the Royal George
William Cowper

6. Clowes, Vol 4.
7. Ibid, p 509.
8. Ibid, p 509.
9. Ibid, p 510.
10. Admiralty: Masters' Logs (ADM 52): ADM 52/2113, HMS *Agamemnon*; Clowes, p 510.
11. Rodney had fought and won several naval battles during his career. He had been governor of Newfoundland for a time and was later elected to Parliament. Fame and fortune had eluded him, however, until his victory at the Battle of the Saintes. In 1761, he was appointed commander-in-chief of the Leeward Islands station and during the first three months reduced Martinique, St. Lucia, and Grenada. Three years later, he was created baronet and was appointed rear admiral in 1771. In 1780, he defeated the Spanish Admiral Don Juan de Langara off Cape St. Vincent on the southeast tip of Portugal. On 3 February 1781 he assaulted the Dutch island of St Eustatius with its port of neutral trade full of valuable booty, which of course he confiscated.
12. Uden & Cooper, p 430.
13. Clowes, p 519.
14. Ibid, p 519.
15. Ibid, p 520.
16. Ibid, p 522.
17. Ibid, p 524.
18. Known in France as the Battle of Dominica.
19. Clowes, p 530.
20. Personal copy of the log of Thomas Dixon, Master of *Agamemnon*, in the Buckler's Hard Maritime Museum, Beaulieu, Hampshire.
21. Clowes, p 535.
22. Ibid, p 537.
23. The six Post-Captains killed in the encounter were: Captain de la Clocheterie of the *Hercule*, Captain de Saint-Césaire of the *Northumberland*, Captain de La Vicomté of the *Hector*, Captain Bernard de Marigny of the *César*, Captain Comte d'Escars of the *Glorieux*, and Captain du Pavillon of the *Triomphant* (Rapport du Marquis de Vaudreuil).
24. Clowes, p 535.
25. Uden & Cooper, p 449.
26. Preston, p 70.
27. Trucks are circular pieces of wood which cap the masts.
28. The formal peace treaty with France, Spain, Holland, and America was not actually signed until 3 September 1783.
29. Admiralty: Ships' Musters (ADM 7): ADM 7/437, HMS *Agamemnon*.
30. Winston Churchill, *A History of the English Speaking Peoples* (London: Cassell, 1957) pp 174, 193.

CHAPTER 4

Nelson

He standeth in stone
Aloft and alone,
Riding the sky
With one arm and one eye.

ROBERT BRIDGES

Horatio Nelson was born on 29 September 1758. He was the sixth child and
fifth son, although two of his elder brothers had died in infancy. His father, the
Reverend Edmund Nelson, was descended from a long line of clergymen: in
fact fifteen of his forbears had been men of the cloth. He had married well, to
Catherine Suckling, a great-niece of Robert Walpole, who had been Prime
Minister of England for 21 years. Unfortunately, Catherine died when
Horatio was at the vulnerable age of nine.

Beginnings

When Horatio was twelve, the Reverend Edmund wrote to his brother-in-
law, Captain Maurice Suckling, to ask if he would take Horatio aboard his
new command, the *Raisonnable*, a 64-gun ship captured from the French,
which was lying at Chatham at that time. Suckling answered with his wry
sense of humour: 'What has poor Horatio done, who is so weak, that he above
all the rest should be sent to rough it out at sea? Let him come and the first
time we go into action a cannon ball may knock off his head and provide for
him at once.'[1] It was 1771, and with the Falkland Islands a bone of contention
between Britain, France and Spain, war seemed imminent. But the crisis
passed, and Horatio's predicted experience with a cannon ball was postponed,
though he served aboard the *Raisonnable* for five months and a day until the
ship was paid off.

Captain Suckling then arranged for his nephew to go on a voyage in a
merchant ship to the West Indies, his first experience of going abroad. The
voyage lasted about a year and brought home to Nelson the resentment
merchant seamen felt against the Royal Navy. In the seamen he saw men who
had been pressed into service and who feared the very sight of a naval uniform.
'If I did not improve my education', wrote Nelson later, 'I returned a practical
seaman, with a horror of the Royal Navy, and with a saying constant with the
seamen, "Aft the most honour, forward the better man." '[2]

His uncle took Horatio into his next command, the *Triumph*, which was
acting as a guardship at the Nore. Now fourteen, he was given command of

Captain Maurice Suckling, Nelson's maternal uncle and patron, later Comptroller of the Navy. Influential relatives were a useful advantage to an ambitious young naval officer in the late 18th century. (National Maritime Museum, London)

MAURICE SUCKLING.
CAPTAIN . R . N .
AFTER BARDWELL.1764.
DIED . 1778.

the ship's cutter and the decked long boat to ply between the ship and the Port of London. He gained valuable experience in navigating shallow tidal waters with their shoals and tricky currents. 'By degrees I became a good pilot . . . and confident of myself amongst rocks and sands, which has many times since been of great comfort to me,' he was to write before he died, possibly remembering the actions at Aboukir Bay and Copenhagen.[3]

Still fourteen, he served as captain's coxswain on HMS *Carcass* on a discovery voyage to the North Pole. Then he joined the 20-gun frigate *Seahorse*, bound for the East Indies under a stern disciplinarian captain who during the two-year voyage not only had the first lieutenant court-martialled and relieved of his duties but administered punishment by flogging over 200 times.

During the trip, Nelson was sent home sick and wasted almost to a skeleton by a tropical disease, which was probably malaria. He would slump into fits of depression and had feverish fantasies about his future. 'I could discover no means of reaching the object of my ambition', he later wrote. 'After a long and gloomy reverie, in which I almost wished myself overboard, a sudden glow of patriotism was kindled within me, and presented my King and Country as my patron. My mind exulted the idea. Well then, I exclaimed, I will be a hero, and confiding in Providence I will brave every danger.' He also talked of having seen 'the radiant orb' beckoning him on.[4]

In the meantime, his uncle Suckling had been appointed Comptroller of the Navy, a position of considerable influence. It was now a simpler matter to find a ship for his nephew, so when he had recovered from his illness, Nelson was appointed fourth lieutenant in the *Worcester*.

From Lieutenant to Post-Captain

On 8 April 1777, Nelson took his examinations and passed as a lieutenant. The very next day, no doubt as a result of patronage, he received his commission as second lieutenant of the 32-gun frigate *Lowestoffe* under the command of Captain William Locker, who was to become his lifelong friend and counsellor. He served two years under Locker in the West Indies until he was made Post-Captain and given command of the frigate *Hinchinbrook*, of 28 guns. Now qualified to command the largest ship the navy could provide, he felt that his professional future was assured. Only death or disability could stop him from eventually becoming an Admiral. He was not yet twenty-one.

When Spain and France joined in an alliance with the American colonists, the *Hinchinbrook* was sent to stage an amphibious attack against a Spanish settlement on the Mosquito Coast of Nicaragua. Nelson took an active part in the action, which consisted in embarking over 200 soldiers in a flotilla of boats and ascending the San Juan river through swamps and tropical jungle. The objective was to take by assault, first the Spanish fort of San Bartolomé on an island in the river, and then the fort of San Juan itself.

By the time the Spanish garrison surrendered, yellow fever had taken hold of the British troops, who sweltered in their thick uniforms designed for European campaigns. Nelson came down with dysentery and was evacuated to the *Hinchinbrook* waiting at the coast. This move probably saved his life, since of the ship's complement of 200 men, only ten survived the 'Yellow Jack'. It is now thought that Nelson himself may have had yellow fever, albeit in a milder form, as well as dysentery. In any event, he was so ill that he could hardly stand and had to command the ship from his cot. Upon arrival at Jamaica he could not walk and had to be carried ashore.

Invalided home, he convalesced at Bath and after three months felt well enough to go to sea again. In August 1781 he was given the *Albemarle*, a 28-gun frigate. After a harsh winter in the North Sea, he conducted a convoy to St John's, Newfoundland, and sailed on to Quebec.

A few months later, during the final year of the War of Independence, he joined Lord Hood's fleet lying in the narrows of Staten Island, New York. *Agamemnon*, still commanded by Benjamin Caldwell, was a member of Lord Hood's fleet at that time, after the Battle of the Saintes.

Prince William Henry was midshipman of the watch on Hood's flagship, the *Barfleur*, when Captain Nelson's barge pulled alongside to pay his respects to Hood. He wrote later that he had encountered 'the merest boy of a Captain I ever beheld; and his dress was worthy of attention. He had on a full lace

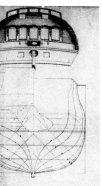

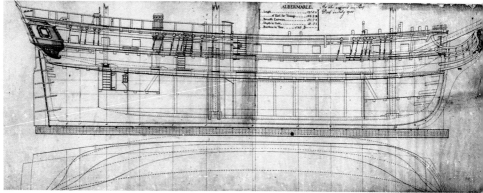

Sheer and body plan of HMS *Albemarle* (28), Nelson's ship in 1781 when he
served in North American waters. (National Maritime Museum, London)

uniform: his lank unpowdered hair was tied in a stiff Hessian tail of extraordinary length; the old-fashioned flaps of his waistcoat added to the general
quaintness of his figure . . .' The royal midshipman, who had never before
had the experience of meeting such a simultaneous combination of youth and
antiquity, saluted at the entry port the figure who climbed the side, wonder-
ing who on earth he was. The Admiral later introduced him to Captain
Nelson, whose pleasant manner and knowledge of ships and naval matters
caused Prince William to note that he was 'irresistibly pleasing in his address
and conversation, and displaying an enthusiasm, when speaking on professional subjects, which showed that he was no common being.'[5]

Nelson gained experience of fleet work under Admiral Lord Hood, but the
end of the American War of Independence brought him home. He was now
twenty-four and an officer of extensive and varied experience.

The Boreas *and marriage*

Nelson went with a brother officer to France, intending to learn the language.
There, he fell in love with an English girl who refused him. On his return to
England he was given command of the 28-gun frigate *Boreas*, bound for the
West Indies. The assignment turned out to be a difficult one for Nelson, who
stubbornly insisted on enforcing the Navigation Acts. These Acts denied the
colonial settlers in the West Indies the right to trade using American ships,
even after American independence. They required that all trade with British
colonies be carried in British ships via British ports, and with at least three-
quarters of the crew being British subjects. The rules were often ignored or
circumvented by smuggling, but when Nelson tried to enforce the Acts he ran
foul not only of the merchants and traders but of his own admiral and the
governor of the Leeward Islands. Some traders attempted to take out legal
actions against him. He became so unpopular that he was, for a time,

completely ostracised ashore, the exception being his friend Mr Herbert, the President of the Council of Nevis Island.[6]

Mr Herbert's large household was run by his widowed niece, Frances, 'Fanny', Nisbet. Fanny had married a doctor on Nevis who died shortly after they had moved to England, leaving her with an infant son, Josiah, and with no money with which to support herself. Mr Herbert came to her rescue and, with her little boy, she returned to the island to take up the position of housekeeper at 'Montpelier', her uncle's home. In March 1786, Fanny was twenty-eight, slightly older than Nelson by a few months. She had been a widow for 4 years and her son was five.

Soured by recent events, lonely, and starved of feminine company, Nelson was emotionally susceptible when in March he anchored off the island. He fell in love with Fanny, and after a year of courtship, they were married at Nevis on 11 March 1787. Prince William Henry, who was by now Nelson's close friend, had arrived at the island in command of HMS *Pegasus*. Bedecked in the finery of his full dress uniform, he acted as father of the orphan bride, and gave her away at Nelson's wedding. He later wrote to his father King George III, 'And I had, my Lord, the honour of giving her away. He is now in for it. I wish him well and happy and that he may not repent the step he has taken . . .'. Thinking of the pale, sickly bridegroom as he wrote, he was prompted to add, 'He is in more need of a nurse than a wife.'[7]

Two months after the wedding, the Nelsons sailed for England. Fanny and Josiah departed on the *Roehampton*, a comfortable West Indian merchantman, Nelson on the *Boreas*. Her tour of duty completed, the *Boreas* sailed for Portsmouth, where the ship was paid off.

'On the beach', Nelson was awarded only half pay, which for a post-captain came to barely £53 12s. 6d. paid every half year. In fact, were it not for £100 granted yearly by his uncle William Suckling, plus another £100 that Fanny received from an uncle of hers, they would have been reduced to a life of penury. For reasons of economy as much as practicality, Nelson, with Fanny and Josiah, went to live at the modest home of his widowed father, the Reverend Edmund Nelson. They settled in with him at the Parsonage House of Burnham Thorp, in the county of Norfolk. Fanny applied herself to her watercolours and her needlework, Josiah was sent to school and, except for the times when the boy came back for the holidays, there was little variation to the spartan ritual of rural life.

In a county well known for its shooting, Nelson was a bad shot. Though it was said he did once shoot a partridge, it was also known that he carried his gun at full cock and fired at the birds from the hip.[8] This dangerous habit caused most of his neighbours to give him a wide berth whenever he went out with his fowling piece. He had a passion for greyhounds and coursing, and when the trees began to bud in the spring, he would take Fanny on bird nesting expeditions in the surrounding countryside. At about this time, he began to have trouble with his eyesight. A small growth known as a *pterygium*

Frances Nelson, whom Nelson married on 11 March 1787. Although later virtually abandoned by him for Emma Hamilton, she was never divorced and remained Lady Nelson until her death in 1831. (National Maritime Museum, London)

had formed in the corner of each eye and was to restrict his vision for the rest of his life.[9]

The five years 'beached' at Burnham Thorp, with their hardships and the ever-present frustration of not being granted a ship, seemed easier for Horatio to bear than for Fanny. While Fanny would take to her bed for days with fever and depression, hating the long cold winters of Norfolk after a life in the sun, Horatio had many interests to occupy him. Occasionally he would take his ageing father and Fanny on a tour of his Norfolk relations. They would stay with his sister Kitty, married to Matcham, and then go to visit his other sister Susannah, married to Bolton, or to his brother William's family, and once a year visit relations on his mother's side, the lordly Walpoles, from whom his name Horatio derived.

Nelson was an avid reader of newspapers and the London periodicals. He whiled away his evenings with his nautical charts, and read Dampier's *Voyages*, which he thought the most interesting book he had ever encountered. He also bombarded their Lordships at the Admiralty with letters, hopeful of a command. One letter he followed up with a personal visit to London. Nelson was unable to get an interview with the First Lord, Lord Chatham, so he went to Lord Hood's house instead. Hood, who never minced words, said that he could not ask the First Lord for a ship for Captain Nelson.[10] Staggered,

Nelson asked Hood the reason. The reply was to be engraved on his brain forever: 'The King was impressed with an unfavourable opinion of me.' He left Hood's house determined never to trouble his Lordship again. Thinking his King and country did not need him and extremely hurt at being the victim of a misunderstanding, he wrote of 'a prejudice at the Admiralty, evidently against me, which I can neither guess at, nor in the least account for'. The radiant orb still shone brightly, however. 'Neither at sea nor on shore, through the caprice of a Minister, can my attachment to my King be shaken. That will never end but with my life.'[11] He returned crestfallen to Norfolk where he told his expectant and affectionate family that he had done everything that he could.

Nelson and the Agamemnon

Had he but known it, his pessimism was not justified. In January 1793, with war clouds gathering on the horizon, Nelson's luck changed. The trial and sentence of death imposed upon King Louis XVI in December made war a distinct possibility. Nelson was in London by early January. Mobilisation was the order of the day and Post-Captains with 14 years' seniority were in demand. On 7 January Nelson learned from Lord Hood that he had been chosen to command his first ship-of-the-line, the 64-gun Agamemnon. He was now aged thirty-four.

Nelson would never be more content than at the commissioning of the Agamemnon. 'Post nubila Phoebius', he quoted in ecstasy to Fanny by letter from London.

> Your son will explain the motto. After clouds come sunshine. The Admiralty so smile upon me that really I am as much surprised as when they frowned. Lord Chatham, [the First Lord of the Admiralty] yesterday made many apologies for not having given me a Ship before this time, and said, that if I chose to take a Sixty-Four to begin with, I should be appointed to one as soon as she was ready; and whenever it was in his power, I should be removed into a Seventy-Four. Everything indicates War. One of our Ships, looking into Brest, has been fired into: the shot is now at the Admiralty. You will send my Father this news, which I am sure will please him. Love to Josiah, and believe me,

> Your most affectionate Horatio Nelson.[12]

The Great Experiment in Democracy

During December 1792, Nelson had listened with horror and fascination to the news of increasing violence in Paris, brought about by the great experiment in democracy that was shaking France to its very core. King Louis XVI, who had been imprisoned with Marie Antoinette and their children in the Tuileries for 18 months, was then separated from them, formally deposed, and brought to trial as Citizen Capet.

The trial was not a formal one but rather an interrogation before the National Assembly, where he was found guilty. The range of alternative sentences available to the deputies consisted of exile, imprisonment, or death. For this last, a majority vote was needed. Put to the Assembly of 721 members present, 361 declared for death, a majority of one. On 21 January 1793, Louis XVI was taken to the Place de la Révolution, today the Place de la Concorde, and there, amid cries of '*Vive la Nation*' he was executed by the instrument of death recently invented by Dr Guillotin. As his severed head was held up by the hair for all to see, the Republic strode another bloody step forward.

Europe had been at war since the previous April when France's Girondin ministers, in an effort to uphold their toppling government, had declared war on Austria. Austria, in turn, in alliance with the Prussian and émigré armies, invaded hapless Poland, dismembered it and then prepared to invade France.

No sensible person in the outside world believed that the rabble army of the citizens' militia would ever be able to resist the combined professional might of Austria and Prussia. Little did they realise, however, that France was rapidly becoming a state under arms with its total resources and power dedicated to war. To the astonishment of the world, General Dumouriez not only repulsed the Prussians at Valmy but advanced to invade and occupy the Austrian provinces of the Netherlands. In his army there were officers whose names were to become legendary: Ney, Soult, Massena, Junot, Murat, Lannes, Marmont, Davout, Berthier, Victor and Bernadotte. These and other men were to gain for France the era of its greatest military glory.[13]

The siren song of '*liberté, égalité, et fraternité*', plus the more radical views of the French revolutionaries, took hold amongst a few minority groups in England, where only equality had been denied. The groups were mainly made up of idealistic youths, scientists, progressive political thinkers, a few misguided politicians, and some poets and writers. 'Bliss was it in that dawn to be alive', wrote Wordsworth.[14]

Some of the more radical working men's clubs corresponded with the Jacobins and even sent delegates to attend the meetings of the National Assembly in Paris. The British government took action against them; however, it was not this but their own later disillusion which made them change their minds. The indiscriminate massacre of the aristocracy, the political prisoners, and finally the execution of the King, brought them to their senses. Danton was shouting in defiance, 'Allied Kings threaten us, and we hurl at their feet as a gage of battle, the head of a King'; Marat was saying with hatred, 'We must establish the despotism of liberty to crush the despotism of Kings.' These sentiments, coupled with the hysterical purges of the terrible Committee of Public Safety, were a further shock to any aspiring revolutionaries in England.[15]

War with France

The British government under the shy and austere Prime Minister William Pitt did not wish to enter another war, but on 28 November 1792, the French fleet bombarded Antwerp and the city was taken. With the French occupation of the Flemish coast, the English Channel was no longer safe and British trade with the Continent was in danger. On 31 January 1793, the French Convention, successor to the Assembly, decreed the annexation of the Austrian Netherlands to the French Republic. The next day France declared war on Great Britain and Holland in the mistaken belief that revolution in England was imminent.

Confronted with the task of a major war effort, the situation in Britain could hardly have been worse. The lack of equipment, leaders, and men made her more vulnerable than perhaps at any time in history. The Royal Navy had only some 110 ships of the line and 20,000 men, down from the 100,000 she had had towards the end of the American War of Independence. The intention had been to reduce the Navy to 15,000 men, but the outbreak of hostilities put an end to that idea. The situation of the Army was equally bad and Pitt was barely able to send 5,000 men to help his Dutch allies defend their frontiers. These forces were beaten back by the French to the German border and eventually evacuated home.

However, while the French army worked successfully under a new cadre of officers, the French navy was in disarray. The Revolution had left it almost leaderless and consequently devoid of the discipline and tactical advantage of which it used to boast. Morale was at its lowest ebb. The younger officers lacked the experience and confidence of their counterparts in the British navy, who had been trained in adversity and encouraged by the example of Rodney and Sir Samuel Hood. Such was the shortage of naval officers in revolutionary France, due to the relentless efficiency of the guillotine, that it was not uncommon for a lieutenant to be promoted to captain and then to rear admiral in the course of 3 years, or even less.

At the outbreak of the war the British Admiralty had established two large fleets. The first, for home and Atlantic waters was put under the command of Lord Howe; the second, for the Mediterranean, under Lord Hood. There was no doubt which of the two elderly Admirals Nelson would prefer to serve under. Regardless of his previous disagreement, it was definitely Hood whom Nelson looked up to. 'Lord Hood,' he wrote to Locker, 'has been very civil indeed. I think we may be good friends again.'[16] Hood, who was to hoist his flag in the *Victory*, hinted that the *Agamemnon* might be ordered to join his fleet at Gibraltar.

At the Admiralty their Lordships agreed to Nelson's request that no bills asking for men for the *Agamemnon* be posted up in London until the name of her captain was announced. Nelson had already posted his own bills throughout his home county of Norfolk and had sent a lieutenant and four midshipmen there to recruit as many men as they could persuade to enlist. Norfolk volunteers, Nelson contended, were worth two of any other men. He had also written to his friends in the north to send him recruits from Whitby and Newcastle. His deepest concern was that he might be obliged to

Nelson in 1781, the year he was
given command of the *Albemarle*,
in the uniform of a post-captain, by
J F Rigaud. (National Maritime
Museum, London)

put to sea short of the proper complement of men and therefore have to sail
undermanned or worse, not be able to set sail at all.

The 'Eggs-and-Bacon'

The muster of the 'Eggs-and-Bacon', as the *Agamemnon* was affectionately
called by her crew, to Nelson's delight began to fill with a high proportion of
volunteers with Norfolk and Suffolk names. Several of the officers were old
friends or the sons of friends. Locker, who was Commander-in-Chief at the
Nore, flying his pendant on board the *Sandwich*, discharged Lieutenants Maurice Suckling and George Andrews into the *Agamemnon* and he brought
Joseph King, once boatswain of the *Boreas*, from the *Valiant*. King, according
to Nelson, was 'one of the best boatswains I have ever seen in His Majesty's
service.'[17] All his neighbours in Norfolk seemed to have youngsters to offer,
when what he really needed was a pair of strong and steel-nerved surgeon's
mates. The Reverend Bolton, his sister Susanna's brother-in-law, sent his son,
and Fanny was fitting out hers, Josiah Nisbet, as a midshipman.

Nelson was jubilant. 'On January 30th, 1793,' he proudly wrote, 'I was
commissioned in the very handsomest way for the *Agamemnon*, 64; and was
put under the command of that great man and excellent officer, Lord Hood.'

His opening statement in the *Agamemnon*'s log was to note that on 7 February 1793, he went on board to put the ship in commission, and found the carpenter and joiner at work.

The captain's cabin on the *Agamemnon* was comfortable with its elegant wide row of windows giving onto its private gallery with a sweeping view of the sea. It was low ceilinged but as Nelson was a mere sparrow of a man, only 5 feet 6 inches tall, it was not much of an inconvenience.[18] It was furnished comfortably with pictures, curtains, a writing desk, bookshelves, a dining table with chairs, his swinging sleeping cot and a carpet on the deck, all of which could be cleared for action in 6 minutes. When that happened, the captain's gear was stowed below and the bulkheads separating him from the quarter-deck swung up and fastened to the deckhead, opening up the deck from bow to stern. Nelson had been able to secure as his steward his old servant on a previous ship. A sort of sea-going valet, Frank took care of his stateroom and wardrobe and served his meals. Nelson had his own galley, his own cook, his own provisions, including wine, and candle lanterns to light the cabin at night. He had a charcoal brazier for warmth in lieu of a fireplace. Prone to feeling cold, he kept the brazier lit even in the Mediterranean summer. To one side there was a rack for sword, pistols, and telescope, and behind it, a locker covered by a leather mattress. While the amenities were undeniably designed for service and not for show, it was comfortable enough to entertain guests in style.

On 7 February, in the company of his First Lieutenant Mr Hinton and the Master, John Lisbon, Nelson strode out on his quarterdeck for the first time and, unfolding his papers, read aloud to his assembled officers his commission.[19] He then shook hands all round and had a private word with the Purser, Mr Fellows. He told him that he would not fail a person called upon to perform many duties necessarily odious, provided that he was careful. 'I daresay we will do very well together,' Nelson concluded, seeing that Mr Fellows understood his instructions.[20]

Four days later men from the guardship *Sandwich* were sent on board by Locker to complete the ship's company. They were passed in review by the Surgeon, the Purser, and the Boatswain. The Scots doctor, Mr Roxburgh, made only a cursory physical examination of them, since crew was hard to come by and he could not be too choosy; Joseph King, the Boatswain, singled out those recruits who were not presentable in their own clothes and sent them on to Mr Fellows to be outfitted from the slop chest. Uniforms did not exist in those days, but old hands knew what was expected of them in the matter of dress, and keen volunteers copied them. Furthermore, the Purser's slops had really only one sort of clothing, so in the end, the men of the *Agamemnon* presented a fairly uniform appearance. Check shirts were quite common, and white or buff trousers cut short in the leg and loose at the ankle, instead of the breeches and stockings worn by landmen, who were often subject to derisory comments about their clothes when they first they

A typical seaman of Nelson's day, by Rowlandson. Features of his dress
include the round hat with a small brim, less likely to be knocked or
blown off, and trousers, in an age where most landsmen wore breeches
and stockings. (National Maritime Museum, London)

appeared on board. Seamen wore blue jackets that were cut short at the waist
and had no collars, and had buttoned cuffs so that the sleeves could be rolled up
easily while working. A handkerchief knotted round the neck protected the
jacket from the grease of the pigtail, or queue, until in battle when it was wound
around the head to protect the eardrums from the noise of the explosions of the
guns. Headgear consisted usually of a hat with a small brim (to minimise the

chances of it getting knocked off or blowing away) or a woollen or fur cap. Captains sometimes kitted out the crews of their personal gigs or barges with more resplendent uniforms for special occasions. Then they might wear a straw boater painted with black enamel, or japanned, occasionally turned up on the side, to show a coloured lining. The ship's name was often either painted on the hat's ribbon, or engraved on a small copper plate attached to it.[21]

To Cadiz

The *Agamemnon*, now 12 years old, sailed down the river from Chatham on 24 April 1793, and proceeded to the Nore. Delighted with the ship's performance, Nelson wrote, 'We appear to sail very fast; we went, coming out, nearly as fast, without any sail, as the *Robust* did under her top sails.' The 74-gun *Robust*, commanded by George Keith Elphinstone, was a ship with which the *Agamemnon* was often in company. Strong gales followed, and upon arrival at Spithead, Nelson was signalled to take the ship to sea for a week on a shakedown cruise, but 'for two days it blew so strong we could not get up our anchors'. Finally, she sailed as one of five of the line under the command of Admiral Hotham and met up with the main force under Hood off the Scilly Isles. After keeping the Channel clear for a homeward bound convoy of East Indiamen, the fleet sailed for the Straits of Gibraltar. Off Cape St Vincent Nelson had a boat hoisted out and had himself rowed to the *Victory* to pay his respects to the Commander-in-Chief. Lord Hood was civil but businesslike, as was his way.

At a time when nations in Europe changed their alliances with dramatic suddenness, Spain was now temporarily Britain's ally. Hood took advantage of this and ordered six of his ships to water at Cadiz, among them the *Agamemnon*. Cadiz was then the finest marine city of the world, the wealthiest port of western Europe, and the headquarters of the Spanish treasure fleets. After obtaining provisions for their ships, the visiting captains were permitted to see the dockyards, the naval arsenal of the Isla de León, and the bastion of Cortadura. The captain of the *Agamemnon* obtained a cask of the celebrated sherry from Jerez to send as a gift to his friend Captain Locker. While there, he was entertained, together with the other British captains, by the Spanish Admiral on board the 112-gun *Concepción*. There were four magnificent First Rate ships in Cadiz, beautifully built but manned by inexperienced and undisciplined crews. Nelson remarked disparagingly, 'The Dons may make fine ships; they cannot, however, make men . . . Long may they remain in their present state.'

Nelson sat with the five other British captains dining in the splendour of the great stern cabin of the *Concepción* without understanding a word of Spanish. The sun was waning over the bay of Cadiz, highlighting in a golden glow the walls and turrets of the great walled city of the five gates, famed since the days of Ancient Rome. Sitting silently pensive, Nelson could not help reflecting that with his five British companions and a boarding party of not more than their ships' barges they could have taken this Spanish First Rate. When they stood up to leave, they discovered the party was not over. The Spanish Admiral stated that the day would be incomplete without some additional entertainment that translated as the 'Bull Feast'. Disembarking and walking through the noisy crowds, they made their way to an amphitheatre said to hold up to 16,000 and were given prominent seats. In the audience were many well-dressed women wearing mantillas with statuesque tortoiseshell combs in their hair. The beauty of some bore witness to the fact that Cadiz had, in years gone by, experienced over 500 years of Moorish occupation.

The Bullfight, by Goya. Nelson and the other captains of Hood's squadron witnessed similar scenes in Cadiz, as guests of the Spanish in 1793. Nelson did not enjoy it. (New York Metropolitan Museum of Art)

The Spanish hosts explained the ritual of the bullfight and how the ladies often would choose their lovers — 'husbands' wrote Nelson to Fanny — from the more daring and dexterous of the matadors.

Ten bulls were selected for the afternoon's entertainment. A half-dozen men on foot entered first, dressed in sky blue jackets hung with tassels, close fitting knee breeches with gold embroidery down the sides, and pink cotton stockings. They wore brimless hats of astrakhan and carried scarlet cloaks over their arms. Three cavaliers on horseback followed the procession. When the first bull was let into the ring, the arena was transformed into a canvas of colour and thundered with applause. One of the men on foot stood out from the rest and pierced the beast's neck with coloured darts; the horsemen, with spears capable of penetrating six inches, spurred their steeds into action to infuriate the timid bull. This was followed by the bewildering magic of the twirling scarlet cape that hypnotized the beast into submission before the kill. It was a pageant of machismo, sexuality, and blood.

'It turned us sick', Nelson wrote to Fanny, 'and we could hardly go through with it: the dead mangled horses with entrails torn out, and the bulls covered with blood, were too much. However we have seen our bull-feast, and agree that nothing shall tempt us to see another. Ten bulls and five horses were killed and two toreadors badly hurt. Had they been killed, it would have been quite complete,' Nelson growled. 'We felt for the bulls and horses and I own it would not have displeased me to have had some of the Dons tossed by the enraged animal. How women can ever sit, much more applaud, such sights is astonishing.' However displeasing the bull ring, it was a suitable overture to what awaited them in the Mediterranean.

On Sunday 7 July, Nelson called out the ship's company and conducted a religious service on deck. As a clergyman's son he did not forget the spiritual welfare of those under his care, and he presented them with a Psalm Book and a Seamen's Monitor. The next morning, the Spanish fleet joined Lord Hood's contingent off Alicante. After several hours of manoeuvring, to Nelson's amusement, they did not 'form anything which could be called a Line of Battle ahead.' A short time later, a Spanish frigate came with the message that as their vessels had many sick, they were returning to Cartagena, adding that ill health was no wonder, as they had been 60 days at sea. Nelson commented: 'This speech was to us ridiculous, for from the circumstance of having been longer than that time at sea, do we attribute our getting healthy. It has stamped with me the extent of their nautical abilities'. He ended saying, 'I really never expect to see them again.'

A few days later, Hood offered the captain of the *Agamemnon* a 74-gun ship, as the First Lord had originally promised, to which Nelson replied, 'As the Admiralty chose to put me in a 64, there I stay . . . I cannot give up my officers.' Nelson told Fanny 'Lord Hood approved of my reasons: so far well.' Clearly, loyalty to both his ship and men had by this time taken root.

Toulon

Hopes were raised in London by the French Royalists' daring scheme to impede the Revolution by proclaiming civil war in France. They seized Toulon with its great naval base in which there were seventeen French battleships ready for sea, amongst them the 120-gun *Commerce de Marseilles*, Rear Admiral Trogoff's flagship. 'Seventeen ports on each deck, the *Victory* looks nothing like her,' wrote Nelson. Besides these there were one 120, one 80, and two 74s repairing, and one 74 building: a total of thirty-one ships-of-the-line, in addition to twenty-seven frigates and corvettes.

The French naval commander, Rear Admiral the Comte de Trogoff, was a staunch Royalist, as were many of his officers and much of the population. Hood's fleet stood close in to Toulon, and on 22 August two envoys from Marseilles, also a royalist bastion, ventured out to Hood's flagship, the *Victory*, to treat for the surrender to the British of the port and the fleet at Toulon. They said the surrender would aid them in the re-establishment of the monarchical system in France. They told Hood that the inhabitants of Toulon agreed with their views, and they, in turn, would send their own delegates to the *Victory* to talk to Lord Hood. Subsequently, it appeared that they had overstated the case, because the delegates never arrived. Rear Admiral Saint Julien, second-in-command of the French fleet and a republican, had replaced Trogoff by force and prevented the delegates from going on board.

Had Britain sent troops to hold Toulon, a vital base for future invasion might have been secured, but Henry Dundas, the British Secretary of State for War, had made the mistake of assigning all available troops to the West Indies. Hood's immediate needs were men and ammunition to hold the citadel against the attack of the advancing republicans. He therefore chose the *Agamemnon*, a very fast sailer, for a special mission. Nelson was to sail without an instant's delay, carrying dispatches to be delivered to the British Envoy and Minister Plenipotentiary to the Court of the Two Sicilies at Naples, urging him to beseech King Ferdinand for Neapolitan troops. Forces were required immediately to help the Allies to hold Toulon.[22]

Vedere Napoli . . .

On 11 September 1793, Nelson wrote that the *Agamemnon* was 'now in sight of Mount Vesuvius, which shows a fine light to us in Naples Bay, where we are lying-to for the night, and hope to anchor early tomorrow.'[23] He was in sight of the city that mortals are advised to see before they die — '*vedere Napoli e puoi morire*'. Viewing the city from *Agamemnon*'s quarterdeck, with the last rays of sun shimmering on the windowpanes and the slopes of the twin peaked Mount Vesuvius in the background, he admitted he was not dissapointed. 'We are in the Bay all night, becalmed, and nothing could be finer than the view of Mount Vesuvius,' he recorded. The fatigue of the past 5 months had worn him down: 'My poor fellows have not had a morsel of fresh meat or vegetables for near nineteen weeks, and in that time I have only had my foot twice on shore, at Cadiz. We are absolutely sick with fatigue . . . I have only to hope I shall succeed with the King of Naples.'

Nelson called his servant Frank and instructed him to prepare his full dress uniform for the following morning, which might involve a royal audience. He ordered Josiah to turn out in his best uniform as he was to go ashore with him in the morning. The importance of the mission concerned Nelson greatly. Would it bring a chilling repulse or a generous response? He must not fail. After a long anxious look from the quarterdeck across the peaceful bay, Nelson retired to bed.

NOTES

1. Carola Oman, *Nelson* (London: Hodder & Stoughton, 1947), p 9.
2. Tom Pocock, *Nelson and His World* (London: Thames & Hudson, 1974), p 16.
3. Ibid, p 16.
4. Ibid, p 19.
5. Ibid, p 26.
6. The name given to the island by Columbus was 'Nieves', as the shape of the island reminded him of the snow-capped mountain of that name in Spain.
7. Son of George III, Prince William Henry, Duke of Clarence, was later to be crowned William IV after the death of his elder brother George IV.
8. Pocock, p 33.
9. A *pterygium* is a benign tumour of the conjunctiva which can grow over the cornea and impair vision. Nowadays it can be easily removed surgically by an ophthalmologist and is a fairly common condition.
10. Carola Oman, p 91.
11. Ibid, p 91.
12. Warner, p 76.
13. Winston Churchill, *A History of the English Speaking Peoples* (London: Cassell, 1957) Vol. 3, p 229.
14. Ibid, p 231.
15. Ibid.
16. Warner, p 77.
17. Carola Oman, p 97.
18. Although even his contemporaries thought him shorter, his true height is attested by his uniforms and skeletal remains.
19. Carola Oman, pp 102–103.
20. Ibid, p 103.
21. Carola Oman, p 103; Lavery, pp 203–204.
22. Carola Oman, p 107.
23. Warner, p 82.

CHAPTER 5

Toulon, San Fiorenza and Bastia
1793–1794

A fellow has now no chance of promotion unless
he jumps into the muzzle of a gun and crawls out
of the touch-hole.

One of Nelson's midshipmen.

The twin kingdoms of Naples and Sicily were ruled by an exotic and flamboyant couple. King Ferdinand IV was an ungainly Spanish Bourbon who had been a king since he was a boy and remained one in most respects even at forty-two.[1] A licentious extrovert, whose principal interests were hunting, cooking, and whoring in his capital, Ferdinand was loved for all of these traits by the Neapolitan masses who affectionately nicknamed him *Il Nasone*, 'Old Nosey', because of his bulbous nose and *Il Lazzarone* ('the Scoundrel') because of his dissipated ways. His queen, Maria Carolina, was the daughter of the Empress Maria Theresa of Austria and a sister of the unhappy Marie Antoinette, soon to be taken from imprisonment in the Conciergerie to the guillotine. In accordance with her marriage treaty, Maria Carolina had a voice in the Neapolitan Councils of State, so her influence was great. It also went without saying that she, as well as Ferdinand, was fiercely opposed to Revolutionary France. The most powerful man in the Neapolitan government owed his position to the Queen's influence. A French-born Englishman and a former sea officer in the Tuscan navy, Sir John Acton, although technically only Secretary for War and Minister of the Marine, had become the universal channel for affairs of state.

Nelson's introduction to this eccentric court was by way of the British Envoy and Minister Plenipotentiary, Sir William Hamilton. A vigorous and sophisticated aristocrat of sixty-three, Hamilton was a collector of classical antiquities, an amateur archaeologist and an expert on subjects that varied from volcanic eruptions to antique coins.[2] He also knew beauty when he saw it. Two years before he had married Emma, who had been his mistress and companion at the Embassy for the previous five years.

The Divine Emma

Emma Hamilton, formerly Emy Lyon, was twenty-eight at the time. The daughter of a Welsh country blacksmith, she had been brought to London where her startling beauty and her youthful enthusiasm became an effective means of improving her status.

According to an anonymous source,[3] after working as maidservant in successive London households, Emma lost her virginity to a friend of the Prince of Wales, one Rear Admiral Willet-Payne. The story goes that, during the early part of the American War of Independence, Emma went to Willet-Payne to plead for the release of a cousin who had been pressed into service on the vessel which Willet-Payne commanded. Emma later admitted that 'she soon became the mistress of her new admirer' and later wrote: 'Oh, my dear friend, for a time I own through distress my virtue was vanquished, but my sense of virtue was not overcome.'[4]

Legend has it that she had worked at age thirteen for a procuress until she made the acquaintance of a young aristocrat, Sir Harry Fetherstonehaugh. Sir Harry took Emma to live with him at Uppark, his family mansion in Sussex, where shortly after settling into one of the cottages on the estate, she discovered that she was pregnant.[5]

One of the many visitors to Uppark was the Honourable Charles Greville, second son of the Earl of Warwick and nephew of Sir William Hamilton. Emma took a liking to Charles and they engaged in a surreptitious affair during the summer of 1781, with Emma travelling by coach to London to sleep with him. Late in autumn she confided to Greville the problem of her pregnancy and he advised her to confront Sir Harry. Emma tracked Sir Harry down to Leicestershire where he had gone on a shooting trip. She faced him with the news but the dissolute baronet, tired of what he called her 'giddy ways', dismissed her and gave her hardly enough money for the fare to get back to her lodgings.

Emma gave birth to her child sometime before March 1782, when she sat for the artist George Romney. The child was a healthy girl whom she named Emma. Shortly after giving birth, she placed 'little Emma', as she called her daughter, in the care of her grandmother Mrs Kidd who lived in Wales.[6] Soon after this she agreed to terms set out in a letter of contract by Greville, in which he agreed to maintain Emma and become her protector while she, to use her own words, became his property. A few days later she moved into the house he had rented for her in London, together with her mother, who took on the household responsibilities of cook and housekeeper.

Emma was to spend four years with Greville, a time she later referred to as 'years of poverty and distress'. Greville occasionally held some minor government appointment but was always in financial difficulties. When his father, the Earl of Warwick, died nine years before, he had left Charles only £100 to buy a mourning ring, virtually disinheriting him.[7] Strapped for cash in 1785, Greville concluded that the best and simplest solution to his problems would be to marry an heiress. To do so he needed to prove some source of wealth, as what family of position would consider a suitor with only £500 a year? He would also have to divest himself of Emma. To accomplish both objectives, he focused upon his wealthy and recently widowed uncle, Sir William Hamilton. Greville extracted a letter from Sir William to show to Lord Middleton,

A portrait of Emma Hamilton personifying Nature, one of the many painted of her by the artist George Romney in the early 1780s, when she was the mistress of the Honourable Charles Greville, nephew of her future husband Sir William Hamilton. (The Frick Collection, New York)

whose eighteen-year-old daughter he had chosen as the object of his marital ambition. The letter announced that he had been named the heir to the Hamilton estates in Pembrokeshire. With that part of his plan fulfilled, Greville proceeded to use his guile to foist Emma upon Sir William.[8]

Sir William did not entirely dislike the idea of taking Emma as his mistress, though he showed some reluctance at the outset. He had met her several times at his nephew's house when visiting England and been captivated by her 'exquisite beauty', her ability to move gracefully and to pose for portrait painters in a whole range of postures and expressions. Her deep violet eyes beneath strong eyebrows set in a faunlike face, the whole effect set off the more by being surrounded by a head of thick auburn hair, were but part of her compelling beauty. She was tall, with well-developed breasts widely set, and her broad thighs were like those of a goddess of fertility. George Romney was captivated by her. During her four years with Greville, she posed for him for over 300 hours, for portraits that mainly depicted idealised classical subjects.

After meeting her for the first time, Sir William commissioned Sir Joshua Reynolds to paint her picture as a Bacchante to take back with him to Italy. Most of the great artists of the day felt impelled to draw or paint her. Sir Thomas Lawrence, Angelica Kauffman, Benjamin West, Madame Vigée-Le Brun and J H Schmidt were among the many. Each in their own style tried to outdo the others, knowing that Emma's beauty on canvas attracted all eyes, as indeed it did in the flesh.

Sir William finally succumbed to Greville's constant prodding and reluctantly agreed to take on Emma as his mistress. Dispatched by Greville, Emma and her mother left England on the Dover packet and thence by coach through France, across the Alps, and down through Italy. The trip had taken 43 days by the time the travellers alighted in the courtyard of the Palazzo Sessa, Sir William's home in Naples. It was Emma's twenty-first birthday.

Being a good-natured extrovert, Emma flourished in the hothouse of Neapolitan society. Her beauty made her a celebrity and, as Sir William entertained on a grand scale, she often danced, sang and performed her classical impersonations, her 'Attitudes', before the assembled congregation. An example of contemporary opinion of her performances, put forward by Johann Wolfgang von Goethe, ran as follows:

> Sir William Hamilton . . . has now, after many years of devotion to the arts and the study of nature, found the acme of these delights in the person of an English girl of twenty with a beautiful face and a perfect figure. He has had a Greek costume made for her which becomes her extremely. Dressed in this, she lets down her hair and, with a few shawls, gives so much variety to her poses, gestures, expressions, etc., that the spectator can hardly believe his eyes. He sees what thousands of artists would have liked to express realised before him in movements and surprising transformations — standing, kneeling, sitting, reclining, serious, sad, playful, ecstatic, contrite, alluring, threatening, anxious, one pose follows another without a break. She knows how to arrange the folds of her veil to match each mood, and has a hundred ways of turning it into a head dress. The old knight idolises her and is quite enthusiastic about everything she does. In her he has found all the antiquities, all the profiles of Sicilian coins, even the Apollo Belvedere. This much is certain: as a performance it's like nothing you ever saw before in your life. We have already enjoyed it on two evenings.[9]

Illusion soon became reality when Sir William, during a short spell of leave in England, made Emma his Lady Hamilton. When we consider that the marriage took place in an age when few men of breeding, and fewer still of diplomatic rank, ever married their mistresses, it is a tribute to the extent of Emma's achievement. She had also made a place for herself in the Neapolitan court by becoming the established favourite of the Queen, her confidante and, some even said, her lesbian lover, although this was never confirmed. Whatever the reason, Emma had become a political force to be reckoned with in Naples.

Agamemnon *in Naples*

The sudden appearance in the Bay of Naples of HMS *Agamemnon* on 11th September 1793 caused considerable excitement. Sir William had cleverly devised a policy of substituting British influence for that of Spain and had negotiated a treaty with Sir John Acton. By its terms, the Royal Navy undertook the protection of the Neapolitan merchant fleet, provided that Naples did not conclude any private peace agreement with the French or trade with them without Britain's consent. Thus the powerful presence of the *Agamemnon* anchored in full sight of the city became the symbol of the recently signed treaty and the proof of British naval power in the Mediterranean.[10]

When Nelson disembarked with his wife's son Josiah he was welcomed at the dockside by Sir William, who took him to a formal audience with the King. Ferdinand had heard rumours of the fall of Toulon, which he took to be the result of the combined efforts of the Spanish and English fleets. Nelson put him right on this point, explaining that Lord Hood had decided to enter the port of Toulon long before the Spanish fleet sailed into view. The King registered surprise, then added, as Nelson recorded in his journal later, that 'we were the saviours of Italie and of his Kingdom in particular.'[11]

Following the meeting with the King, Sir William took Nelson to call on Sir John Acton to convince him that Neapolitan troops were urgently needed to help the allies hold Toulon. Acton assured his visitor that King Ferdinand would indeed supply the manpower but he suggested delaying a week or two until provisions could be collected to embark with them. Sir William countered saying that due to the urgency of the situation, it would be preferable to send 2,000 men in three or four days rather than a larger force in several weeks. He won his point. At dinner that night, Acton stressed that the Neapolitan troops should serve only under Lord Hood and not under either Spanish or Sardinian commanders.[12]

While Josiah was shown the sights of Naples by Emma, who had taken the rather awkward boy under her wing, Nelson was treated with exceptional courtesy by Sir William Hamilton. He took Nelson to his leased home, the Palazzo Sessa, and gave him a very comfortable set of rooms on the second floor to use for the length of his stay. The apartment had recently been redecorated in preparation for the visit of Prince Augustus, the Duke of Sussex. The rooms offered a beautiful view of the Bay through windows that in the evening glowed with diffused southern sunlight. Nelson had hardly been able to enjoy the comfort of this setting, so busy was he with official business. Except for two nights, he had only snatched a few hours of rest between appointments.

Nelson and Sir William took to one another. 'You do business in my own way! I am, now, only a captain; but I will, if I live, be at the top of the tree,' Nelson, rarely modest, told him. An account is given of the first meeting of the two men:

> On Sir William Hamilton's returning home, after he first beheld Captain Nelson, he told his lady that he was about to introduce a little man to her acquaintance, who could not boast of being very handsome: 'but' added Sir William, 'this man, who is an English naval officer, Captain Nelson, will become the greatest man that ever England produced . . . he will one day astonish the world. I have never entertained any officer in my house, but I am

determined to bring him here. Let him be put in the room prepared for Prince Augustus.'[13]

This account by Harrison is suspect on two counts. In the first place, Sir William, himself the son of a naval man, had certainly entertained other officers at his home in the past. Secondly, but more importantly, Harrison's biography was written 'under the immediate dictation of Lady Hamilton', which perhaps accounts for such high-flown sentiments, wise after the event. However, it was plain fact that Nelson's visit was fruitful and that he had personally been a success. In four days he had been with the King three times and dined with him once. He had obtained the 4,000 Neapolitan troops from Acton, having pursued his purpose 'with a zeal which no one could exceed'.

To celebrate his successful mission, Nelson personally invited the King to dine aboard the *Agamemnon*. The Queen, 8 months with child, could not attend. The festivities began early. At 10am Sir William and Lady Hamilton arrived on board with other members of the English colony. They included, among other notables, the Bishop of Winchester, his wife and family, Lord and Lady Plymouth, Viscount Grandison, and Lady Gertrude Villiers. 'I gave them breakfast', Nelson recorded later.

According to the arrangements, the King was to board at 1pm when his Royal Standard was to be hoisted and he was to be entertained with a display of gunnery. Because the *Agamemnon* was not provisioned for entertainment on so lavish a scale, catering for the event was provided from the kitchens and cellars of the British Embassy, as were also the glass, silver and china.[14]

Before the King's arrival, while all awaited the royal barge, Nelson received a note from Sir John Acton informing him that a French corvette was anchored off Sardinia with a small English ship as her prize, together with two ships under her convoy. The note added that the Neapolitan fleet could have sent their own ships after them, but they were 'otherwise employed'. Nelson, casting his gaze around the harbour, counted seven Neapolitan men-of-war and a Spanish 40-gun frigate 'otherwise employed', showing no inclination whatever to weigh anchor and go after the enemy.

'So', he wrote later to his brother William in Norfolk, 'unfit as my ship was' (he had a sick list of nearly a hundred on board), 'I had nothing left for the honour of our country but to sail, which I did in two hours afterwards,' the guests having been courteously put ashore.[15]

Nelson concluded that Naples entries in his journal with interesting comments on the people he had met:

I believe we carry with us the good wishes of Naples and of Sir William and Lady Hamilton in particular, which I esteem more than all the rest. Farewell Naples, may those that were kind to me be repaid tenfold. If I am successful I return, if otherwise go to Toulon. I should be wanting did I not say how active Sir William Hamilton has been in getting these troops sent off, for left to themselves I am sure they would not have sailed these three weeks, the Vanity of the [King] is such that he wish'd to cut a great figure by sending his stipulated force all at the same time, and to that vanity we are now indebted for the 4,000 instead of the 2,000 at first promised.[16]

During his brief visit, Lady Hamilton left an enduring impression. Naturally good-natured, Emma had exerted herself, and her efforts and her beauty did not go unnoticed by the admiring guest. 'Lady Hamilton', wrote Nelson to his wife, 'has been wonderfully kind and good to Josiah. She is a young woman of amiable manners and who does honour to the station to which she is raised.'

Nelson was not forgotten by the Hamiltons when he left. He corresponded fairly regularly with them and they with him. His first letter to Sir William was sent from Livorno 12 days after leaving Naples. It enclosed a butter dish borrowed from Palazzo Sessa for the party on board, which he had omitted to return before he sailed. Nelson was not to return to Naples for 5 years, until after his victory at the Battle of the Nile in Abourkir Bay on 1 August 1798.[17]

The *Agamemnon* never caught up with her prey. The French corvette had either made for Livorno or some Corsican port. Having surmised as much, Nelson decided to make for Livorno himself. His ship had only been at anchor for 20 days in the last 5 months and he felt it necessary to make for a friendly port 'absolutely to save my poor fellows'. It was too late to save his surgeon's second mate, however, who was buried at sea with the usual sad naval ceremony off the northern tip of Corsica.[18]

Sailing off of Livorno before entering port, Nelson spied a French frigate lying at anchor. Hoping the *Agamemnon* had not been seen, he decided to wait for her outside the port and ride out the night of 27 September in a gale and with lumping seas. The frigate, which had been ready to weigh anchor just when the *Agamemnon* hove in sight, thought better of it and patiently waited to sail out under cover of darkness. Nelson thought she might prove an easy prize, as he had received a report that her men 'had deposed their captain, made the Lieutenant of Marines Captain of the ship, the Sergeant of Marines Lieutenant of Marines and their former Captain, Sergeant of Marines. What a state!' wrote Nelson in his journal. Having no way to entice her to leave neutral waters, Nelson abandoned the idea of entering Livorno and instead steered a course for Sardinia and then Toulon.[19]

The Corsican Soldier

The *Agamemnon* arrived at Toulon on 5 October just as the second division of troops sent by Acton from Naples was disembarking. Nelson wrote to Fanny to say that it had made 'no difference' to a court martial on which he had sat, that cannon shot had whistled overhead. 'Such is the force of habit, we seem to feel no danger.'[20] The shots were fired from batteries on shore under the direction of a young lieutenant in the French Army. Sprung from a leading Corsican family, and well-versed in gunnery and other military matters, he happened to be on leave from his regiment. Looking in on the camp of General Dugommier who commanded the Jacobin besieging army of 45,000 men, the lieutenant walked along the line of batteries and announced that their shot would not reach halfway. This error was adjusted, and the upstart soldier began to earn a degree of admiration at Dugommier's headquarters.

Meanwhile, orders arrived from the fearsome Committee of Public Safety in Paris, laying down the methods of siege the army should adopt even though most of the material resources were lacking. At a council of war held in daylight on a parade ground, the skilled lieutenant spoke up. The orders were foolish, and all there knew it, or so he was to claim later. Nevertheless, there was a way of capturing Toulon. Jabbing his finger at Fort L'Aiguillet on the map, a promontory commanding the entrance to the harbour, he said 'There is Toulon!' Having convinced the surrounding group of officers that their only road to success lay in defying the orders from Paris, he led the assault on the fort. After a hot fight, it fell. The Jacobins could now look down upon the whole wide front of the Royalist defences, as well as the battleships in the port. The morning after Fort L'Aiguillet fell, the ships of the allied British and Spanish fleets weighed anchor and moved out of range of the shore batteries. The allies had decided to evacuate Toulon, taking with them as many French ships loaded with Royalist troops as they could. Then they proceeded to destroy the arsenal and magazine of the city. They managed to save 14,877 Royalists. Sadly, more did not fit on board their ships. Of thirty-one French ships of the line in port, nine were burned or sunk. Only four were carried off. Of the twenty-seven frigates and corvettes, five were destroyed, fifteen escaped, and seven left to the Republicans.

Once the British-Spanish fleet had departed, all resistance ended. There was a stampede to escape upon the vessels that remained. Many rushed frantically into the water and were drowned. The French government had deliberately decreed the death of all surviving Royalists, as well as the demolition of the town. General Dugommier protested in vain. The Republican deputies, not content with the slaughter of the Royalist troops, wreaked horrible vengeance on 6,000 helpless civilian captives who were guillotined to prevent them from being the vanguard of a counter-revolution.

Notified of these matters, Robespierre, his brother, and the Committee in Paris, thought they would like to know more about the competent and apparently well-disposed artillery lieutenant who had brought about the victory. Their enquiries must have told them that the officer was a native of Ajaccio, the capital of the island of Corsica. He was born on 15 August 1769 to Carlo and Letizia Buonaparte, 15 months after the island had been ceded to France by Genoa. In recognition of his Greek origins, he had been named Napoleone — pronounced 'Nabulione' in the Corsican dialect — after a Greek saint. At the age of nine, he had been sent to mainland France on a scholarship to study the French language, of which he could hardly speak a word, and from there, a year later, he was sent on to the royal military academy at Brienne in north central France. The following five and a half years forged his military career, as he devoted special efforts to learning geography, history, and mathematics. Shy, introverted, and provincial, with a thick Italian/Corsican accent and little money, the lonely boy shared classes with the sophisticated sons of the French nobility. By dedicating himself single-mindedly to his studies, his examination grades won him a scholarship to the École Militaire in Paris. He graduated the following year as a sub-lieutenant and was assigned garrison duty in several inland towns from 1785 to 1787. During that time he also shouldered responsibility for his family, since his father had died leaving his mother, Letizia, with eight surviving children.

Napoleone, whose name means 'lion of the valley' was the second born, Joseph being the eldest. But he was to prove the only lion of his family, the others behaving no better than a pack of howling, snarling jackals, fighting and tearing at each other over his kingdoms, the loot and titles of his triumphs and conquests.

The victory at Toulon, his very first, brought glowing recommendations from his superior officers to the newly organised War Office in Paris, which passed them on to Robespierre. Extolled in writing were 'the virtues of this exceptional officer', his 'great intelligence and scientific knowledge', even his 'perhaps overly great personal courage'. Though his career could not be said to be assured as yet, since officers were being demoted or promoted as fast as others lost their heads — a fate he was narrowly to escape — he was promoted to Brigadier General after Toulon at the age of twenty-four. His meteoric military career had started, a career that would not end until his final defeat at Waterloo 21 years later.[21]

The action with the Melpomène

Only three days after she arrived back at Toulon, Lord Hood, pleased with Nelson's efficiency and success at the court of Naples, dispatched the *Agamemnon* to sea again, considering her one of the fastest ships of his fleet. This time, Nelson's orders were to join Commodore Robert Linzee's squadron at Cagliari in Sardinia. As many of her men were sick, the *Agamemnon* was undermanned. With a complement of only 345 at quarters, she could not man all her guns. A twelve year-old midshipman on the *Agamemnon*, William Hoste, provided an account of what happened as the ship sailed southwards in the darkness. In a letter to his father, a Norfolk parson like Nelson's, he wrote:

> On the 22nd of October, when running down the island of Sardinia, about two o'clock in the morning, being off Monte Santo, twenty leagues to the northward of Cagliari, we saw five sail of ships standing to the NW. On observing us, they tacked and stood to the eastward. Captain Nelson, suspecting them to be a French convoy, immediately stood after them. About three o'clock we were

HMS *Agamemnon* engaging the *Melpomène* and four other French frigates off
Sardinia on 22 October 1793. The damage she sustained to her masts and
rigging, particularly the loss of her main topmast, was the principle cause of
Nelson's breaking off the action. (National Maritime Museum, London)

very near up with the hindermost; and at four got within gunshot. We hailed
her in French, but receiving no answer, fired a gun for her to bring-to, and
shorten sail; when we observed her making signals with sky-rockets to her
consorts, who were at some distance to windward. After we had repeatedly
hailed her to no purpose, we fired one of our eighteen-pounders at her, to
oblige them to shorten sail.

When Nelson saw that the frigate had instead set all sail to make away, he
decided to chase after her and gave the order to open the ports and run out the
guns. The *Agamemnon* engaged the frigate for 3 hours with the other four
French ships on the weather side following but out of range. As the frigate was
smaller and faster, she was able to yaw and deliver broadsides, while the
Agamemnon could only bring her bow guns to bear. At daybreak, identifying
the frigate as the *Melpomène*, William Hoste pays tribute to her fighting spirit:

She bravely engaged us in this manner for three hours, both ships sailing at the
rate of six knots an hour . . . The other frigates were coming after us with a
fresh breeze; consequently we expected to have warm work, and were therefore

anxious to dispatch this gentleman before they arrived: but, about eight o'clock, by an alteration of the wind our antagonist got out of the reach of our guns. Our last broadside did infinite damage; nor was what we had received inconsiderable, as our rigging was shot away, and our main top-mast broken, which prevented us from going after the frigate.[22]

The *Melpomène* had taken such a pounding that had not the other French ships gone to her rescue, she would have had to surrender or sink. She had lost twenty-four men and many had been wounded. On board the *Agamemnon*, only one man was killed and six wounded, but her topmast, mainmast, and mizzenmast had been shot to pieces, her foreyard shattered into fragments, and her sails and rigging so badly damaged that with the little wind there was, she could not close to board her adversary.

Before breaking off the action, Nelson was careful to summon his officers to ask their opinion. He asked if they thought the *Agamemnon* was fit to continue the action, given the superior force against them, without first repairing the damage and nourishing the men. It was a rare occurrence in those days for a commanding officer to place such trust in the opinion of his subordinates, but it was characteristic of Nelson to do so even when he became an admiral. By unanimous opinion, his officers felt the ship needed a respite. After accepting their counsel to withdraw, Nelson ordered:

> Veer the ship, and lay her head to the westward; let some of the best men be employed refitting the rigging, and the carpenters getting crows and capstan bars to prevent our wounded spars from coming down, and get the wine up for the people, with some bread; for it may be half an hour good before we are again in action.

The enemy, instead of pressing their advantage, contented themselves with carrying off the *Melpomène*. In a sinking condition, it eventually reached Calvi in Corsica.

Nelson was pleased and relieved at the outcome of the encounter. His simple trust in Providence, which was never to forsake him throughout his life, is expressed in the following passage from his journal written on board the *Agamemnon*, at anchor in Cagliari.

> When I lay me down to sleep I recommend myself to the care of Almighty God, when I awake I give myself up to His direction, amidst all the evils that threaten me, I will look up to Him for help, and question not but that He will either avert them or turn them to my advantage though I know neither the time nor the manner of my death, I am not at all solicitous about it because I am sure that He knows them both, and that He will not fail to support and comfort me.[23]

When the *Agamemnon* joined Commodore Linzee's squadron at Cagliari, not only was she long overdue for a refit but her state had worsened considerably after her crippling action with the *Melpomène*. Shattered she might be, but 'I would not say *Agamemnon* was ever unable to go in search of the enemy', wrote Nelson. 'We worked all night fixing our masts and yards and stopping shot holes, mending sails and splicing our rigging.' According to his report to Lord Hood, the ship was 'after a very few hours at anchor, in many respects fitter for service than before'. In the report, he pays tribute to his officers and the ship's company, saying they had 'conducted themselves entirely to my satisfaction'. That the satisfaction aboard *Agamemnon* was mutual is proven by the conclusion to William Hoste's letter to his father: 'Captain Nelson is acknowledged one of the first characters in the Service, and is universally beloved by his men and officers.'[24]

Expedition to Tunis

Linzee's orders from Hood sent the squadron immediately to Tunis to complain to the Bey about his obvious display of favouritism towards the French. Since the early sixteenth century when the brothers Barbarossa, of Turkish origin, had established a string of ports on the North African coast dedicated to piracy in the Mediterranean, their successors, the Bey of Tunis and the Dey of Algiers, had followed their example. The city states of Algeria and Tunisia, though nominally part of the Ottoman empire, were in fact anarchic military republics that chose their own rulers and lived by plunder. In the first half of the seventeenth century, more than 20,000 captives were said to have been imprisoned in Algiers alone. Holding victims to ransom was a lucrative business, as was selling into slavery those who could not redeem themselves or arrange for their release. The naval activity of this ancient brigandage was conducted by the captains or *reises* of their armed cruisers. These men were prominent in the social hierarchy, since they made a valuable contribution to the wealth of the country. The pasha, who bore the titles of Agha, Dey, or Bey, received into his treasury 10 per cent of the value of all prizes taken. Furthermore, what was fast becoming the most profitable of the Bey's source of revenue in the late eighteenth century was the extortion of vast sums of money from powers willing to pay for 'protection' on the sea lanes of the Mediterranean. That France was one of these nations few had any doubt. The government of France paid the Bey regularly to assure safe passage for her merchant ships. As proof of this point, the five ships with which Nelson had recently tangled had left Tunis unharmed. Not only that, upon arrival at Tunis, the British squadron had found a large French convoy escorted by a frigate and a ship of the line at anchor beneath the white turrets of the town.[25]

Commodore Linzee and his captains, dressed in their formal blue and white gold-trimmed uniforms, with cocked hats placed squarely on their heads, and the single thick braid of their queues hanging beneath, ascended the winding street from Bab el Marsa, the gate of the port, towards the Bey's palace of green tiled domes which was itself a fortress deep within the Casbah. Passing beneath Bab el Suk, the gate of the market place, they entered a narrow tortuous cobbled street roofed by planks and slimy with filth. Fighting against

One of the Bey of Tunis' Nubian guards,
painted by Ludwig Deutsch. (The J Paul
Getty Museum)

the crowd amidst camels laden with charcoal and water, and pavement
vendors selling everything from carpets to hashish, as well as the occasional
snake charmer that lined the route, they picked their way forward with care.
The great doors of the palace were opened to them by an impressive Nubian
guard who stood imperiously in the shadow of the archway, long lance in
hand. Elaborately dressed, he wore a mail shirt with a scarlet cloak draped
regally across one shoulder. A green silk scarf flowed from his neck and the
handles of a pistol and scimitar protruded from the rich gold cummerbund
that circled his waist. Tall, erect, and with an air of solemn authority, he led
the British naval officers into the enthroned presence of the Bey, to whom he
bowed low before retiring from the room.

Commodore Linzee's instructions from his brother-in-law Lord Hood had
commenced: 'You are to expostulate with His Excellency, the Bey, in the
strongest and most impressive manner, on the impolicy of his giving countenance and support to so heterogeneous a government as the present one of
France, composed of murderers and assassins, who have recently beheaded
their Queen in a manner that would disgrace the most barbarous savages . . .'

It was Nelson who voiced this complaint, but the reply of His Excellency,
the Bey, well versed in cunning, was exasperating. On being reminded of the

hideous excesses of the French Revolutionary government, including the murder of their King and Queen, the Bey through his interpreter soberly observed that while nothing could be more heinous than the murder of sovereigns by their subjects, yet, if the historians of the great country represented by his naval visitors were to be believed, the subjects of a King of England had once arisen and beheaded their own sovereign.[26] Nelson was irked by the cleverness of the answer and refers in his journal to the negotiations as that 'damn'd Palaver' that spread over the first five days of November. Fire-eating man of action that he was, Nelson was all for attacking the French ships in the port. He wrote: 'The English seldom get much by negotiation except the being laughed at, which we have been; and I don't like it. Had we taken, which in my opinion we ought to have done, the men-of-war and convoy, worth at least £300,000, how much better we could have negotiated. [Had we] given the Bey £50,000 [of that sum], he would have been glad to have put up with the insult offered to his dignity.'[27]

That the French had expected Linzee to attack was proved by their moving their ships very close to shore under the protection of the Ottoman batteries. Linzee, however, had received from Hood orders only to negotiate, and he was not intrepid enough to disobey. He had patiently sent to Toulon for further orders as his did not include the use of force. Had he done so, it is quite likely that he would have achieved success, but the consequences of attacking enemy ships in a neutral port, and by so doing making an enemy of the piratical stronghold of Tunis when the British fleet was engaged further north, might not have been tactically sensible.

Fed up with it all, Nelson was glad to receive new orders. In his journal he wrote:

> The English never yet succeeded in a negotiation against the French, and we have not set the example at Tunis. Thank God! Lord Hood, whom Linzee sent to for orders how to act after having negotiated, has ordered me from under his command, and to command a Squadron of Frigates off Corsica, and the Coast of Italy, to protect our trade and that of our new Ally, the Grand Duke of Tuscany, and to prevent any Ship or Vessel, of whatever Nation, from going into the port of Genoa. I consider this command as a very high compliment. There being five older Captains in the Fleet . . . Lord Hood is certainly the best officer I ever saw. Every order from him is so clear, it is impossible to misunderstand him.[28]

Nelson felt exhilarated to be given an independent command and the chance to go after the frigates that had escaped him. He learned that two of them were at San Fiorenza and one at Bastia, while the badly damaged *Melpomène* was moored in Calvi.

The *Agamemnon*'s condition once again had deteriorated. She badly needed repairs, as did her officers and men a respite from the monotony of shipboard life. Nelson wrote to Locker, 'We have only had our anchor down thirty-four times since we sailed from the Nore, and then only to get water and provisions'.

The *Agamemnon* had arrived in Leghorn (Livorno) roads and was actively involved in provisioning ship when the bad news arrived that Toulon had fallen to the French Revolutionary army. Leghorn was in confusion as vessel after vessel arrived packed with exhausted refugees and wounded soldiers. Rumours spread that the city was already short of food and that it was likely that the authorities would refuse further admittance except to those ships carrying only wounded. Nelson was never to forget the tales of horror that he heard following the fall of Toulon. He wrote home: 'One family of a wife and five children are just arrived, the husband shot himself . . . Fathers are here without families, families without fathers . . . I cannot write all . . . My mind is deeply impressed with grief. Each teller makes the scene more horrible.' That Napoleon, another eyewitness, saw the horrifying scene in a different heroic light was to be proven in later years. He would captivate audiences during his imprisonment on St Helena with descriptions of his feelings as ship after ship exploded into red flames matching the tide of blood running in the gutters as the guillotine took possession of Toulon. In one way or another, he would say, over 6,000 Toulonaises had paid the penalty for resisting the Revolution.

The Corsican campaign: attack on San Fiorenza

After being forced to retreat from Toulon, Hood decided to make Corsica his base of operations. He had been in touch with the Royalist General Pasquale de Paoli, a Corsican patriot who had recently seen his island ceded to France by the Genoese. With deep bitterness over this, Paoli promised Hood that if he attacked San Fiorenza by sea, he, Paoli, would move upon it by land. He was anxious to see the French evicted and the island placed under British rule. Unfortunately, Paoli was unable to comply with his part of the bargain, and Commodore Linzee, who conducted the naval operation, was repulsed, sustaining considerable losses.

Hood had moved the main body of his fleet to Hyères Bay, a short distance to the east of Toulon. Hearing that the Republican troops in Corsica were short of provisions, he dispatched several of his ships to prevent supplies reaching the island as well as to harass the French shore batteries. Nelson was one of the few given this task. Leaving Leghorn on 28 January, the *Agamemnon* was blown off the Corsican station:

> By the hardest gale of wind almost ever remembered here. The *Agamemnon* did well but lost every sail in her. Lord Hood had joined me off Corsica the day before and would have landed the troops but the gale has dispersed them over the face of the waters. The *Victory* was very near lost . . .

At the end of the same letter to Fanny, Nelson described his first brush with the French forces on the island as follows:

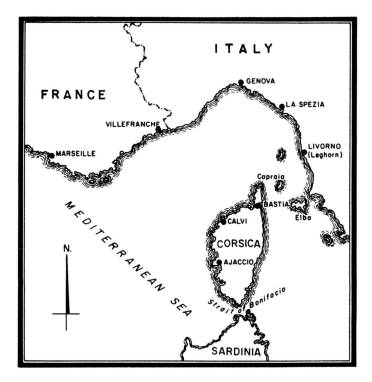

Map of the Corsican theatre of operations 1794.

A thing happened a few days past which gave me great satisfaction. The 21st January the French had their store house of flour near a water mill close to St Fiorenza. I seized a happy moment, landed sixty soldiers and seamen. In spite of opposition at landing the sailors threw all the flour into the sea, burned the mill the only one they have, and returned on board without the loss of a man. The French sent 1,000 men at least against them in gunboats etc, but as the French shot went over them they were just within reach of my guns. It has pleased the Lord [Hood], if this dreadful gale has not blown it out of his memory.

These attacks were in essence guerrilla warfare, and Nelson kept up these acts of harassment against the coastal shipping and defences. Twelve vessels loaded with wine were attacked and set on fire, and four others were taken as prizes. At L'Avisena a fort was reduced and its garrison forced to withdraw. Further down the coast, Nelson put himself at the head of a landing party which seized a small castle. Fighting his way to the flagpole, he struck the French colours with his own hands. Later, a courier boat was apprehended and carried in 'high style'. 'My ship's company behaved most amazingly well; they begin to look upon themselves as invincible, almost invulnerable . . . They really mind shot no more than peas.' Everywhere down the length of the Corsican coast Nelson's 'Agamemnons' inflicted damage on the French intruders and convinced them that Bastia was the British objective.[29] This deception was what

Hood wanted, as he really had his eye on San Fiorenza. On 7 February, he detached to Mortella Bay in front of San Fiorenza three ships of the line, two frigates, and transports carrying troops commanded by Major General Dundas. The troops landed that evening and a combined attack by land and sea was made on the Tower of Mortella, which surrendered to the British after its little garrison had defended it magnificently for 26 hours. After several days' bombardment, San Fiorenza fell to the British with the French troops retreating to Bastia.

Hood's next scheme was to reduce Bastia but General Dundas, much to Hood's annoyance and Nelson's fury, considered the plan impracticable without reinforcements. Hood, who in the meantime had moved the body of his fleet to San Fiorenza, made a demonstration off Bastia, cruising there for a fortnight and gathering intelligence. He then returned to San Fiorenza and as Dundas still declined to act pending the arrival of 2,000 troops from Gibraltar, he embarked a few soldiers and marines and, with a handful of artillerymen, sailed on 2 April. Daring as always, when Nelson heard of Dundas' refusal to act, he was incensed. 'What would the immortal Wolfe have done?' he wrote. 'A thousand men would to a certainty take Bastia. With 500 and the *Agamemnon* I would attempt it . . .'

Bastia

Nelson had made himself thoroughly familiar with the appearance of Bastia long before he landed, running so close inshore with two of the frigates under his command that they had been fired upon by the enemy from the batteries beyond, below, and from, the very port of the citadel. That same afternoon, during a third run through the bay, all three ships had been hit, but fortunately suffered no casualties, whereas a Danish ship that had left the port told them that their own salvoes had destroyed six French guns and killed several gunners.[30]

Nelson knew that his reports had influenced Hood to attempt to take Bastia, and therefore he felt that his reputation depended upon the result. At his request, an artillery officer and an engineer, both of them young and enthusiastic, were landed under cover of darkness, to survey his choice of sites on shore for a battery and a landing place. He then sent a fast frigate to Naples, with Lieutenant Duncan, the artillery officer, as envoy, to petition Sir William Hamilton to plead with the King and Sir John Acton for mortars, shells, field pieces and stores. Nelson was delighted to learn how successful his bombardment of Bastia had been. He heard it had shaken morale to the point that General Lacombe Saint Michel, the French Commissioner, had felt bound to hide from the townspeople's fury, and he had only restrained them from going out in a boat to treat for peace by threatening them that he would blow up the town.

By the end of March, the *Agamemnon* had been at sea for 3 months. Nelson explained to Hood in a letter that they had no fuel left for the galley and that

A view of Bastia painted in 1794. (National Maritime Museum, London)

due to the decks being in dire need of caulking, 'not a man has slept dry for many months'. He also admitted they were out of 'wine, beef, pork, flour and almost without water: not a rope, canvas, twine or nail in the Ship. The Ship is so light, she cannot hold her side to the wind'. He added that if he were given permission to sail to Porto Ferraio and Leghorn to get water and stores, he could be back on station within 24 hours. As for refitting, he could postpone that a little longer, as he was determined to be present at the attack on Bastia.

The British military hierarchy at San Fiorenza had sarcastically nicknamed Nelson 'The Brigadier' because he had voiced his opinion that the taking of Bastia was feasible, while their own generals, first Dundas and later D'Aubant who had succeeded him, refused to attempt it without reinforcements from Gibraltar. Who was this thirty-five year old naval upstart, they asked, who dared dispute military strategy with professionals such as themselves? Nelson was about to prove to them that he deserved the military title they had given him in sarcasm and that he could mete out punishment to the enemy on land in the same measure that he could at sea.[31]

On the night of 3 April, a force of 1,248 officers and men under the command of Lieutenant-Colonel Vilettes and Captain Horatio Nelson landed at a spot a little to the north of the town. Hood moored his fleet in crescent formation round the harbour, just out of reach of the batteries, and protected the inshore activity with a flotilla of gunboats and armed launches.

So efficient was the small invading force that by noon on 4 April, Nelson's 'Agamemnons' had landed eight 24-pounders from the gun deck of the ship and had brought them up to their lines together with eight 13-inch mortars supplied by the Kingdom of Naples. Colonel Vilettes and Captain Nelson had encamped under a rocky promontory only 2,500 yards from the citadel. Both the Corsican patriots who had occupied the neighbouring tower of Torga, as well as Sir Gilbert Elliot, the future British Viceroy of the island, watched amazed while the versatile seamen from the *Agamemnon* made roads, hauled up guns and sandbags, cut down undergrowth, and cleared platforms on the mountainside to mount the cannon. Sir Gilbert, who was an admiring spectator of the efficiency of the Blue Jackets, said that the face of the mountainside was steeper than Minto Crags at home, and regardless of that:

> They fastened great straps round the rocks, and then fastened to the straps the largest and most powerful purchases, or pullies, and tackle, that are used on board a man-of-war. The cannon were placed on a sledge at one end of the tackle, the men walked down hill with the other end of the tackle. The surprise of our friends the Corsicans, and our enemies the French, was equal to the occasion.

Day after day the log of the *Agamemnon* recorded the intense activity of setting up the batteries on shore.[32]

> Saturday 5 April: Landed the troops equipage & 2 days provisions. Left on shore several sail for tents for the officers and seamen. People employed making sandbags for the batteries. Empd getting into launch two 24-pounders, sent them on shore with sundry other stores.
> Wednesday 9 April: Landed 150 barrels of powder with a quantity of grape & canister shot.

Then at last on Friday 11 April, eight days after the landing, the log records: 'At ½ past 9 our Batteries opened upon the Enemy's Redoubts, the Mortars upon the Town. Weather inclinable to calm.'

In the middle distance, from the heights above, Nelson and his sweating seamen had the comforting vision of the *Agamemnon* at anchor in the bay, and further out towards the south of the town, Lord Hood was lying at anchor in the *Victory*. Nelson's batteries had been under heavy fire for the last two days, and the French Commissioner had a blind belief in the strength of his position. When Lord Hood sent a flag of truce before the batteries opened fire, the Frenchman audaciously replied: 'I have hot shot for your ships, and bayonets for your men', whereupon Lord Hood ordered a red flag hoisted at the main-topgallant masthead of HMS *Victory*, to which Nelson answered by hoisting the English colours on the rock above his ragged tent as he gave the order for his

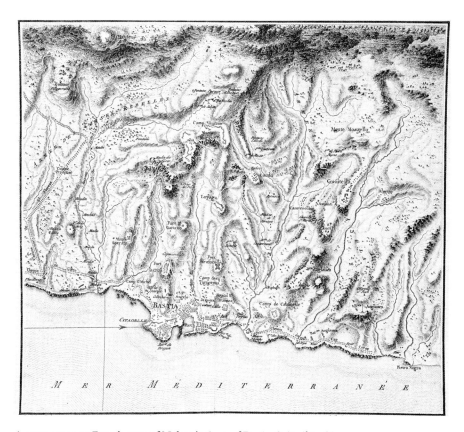

A contemporary French map of Nelson's siege of Bastia, 3 April to 21
May 1794, showing the town's defences and the British batteries
established by the *Agamemnon*'s bluejackets, mounting 24-pounders from
the ship and 13in mortars brought from Naples. (National Maritime
Museum, London)

battery to open fire upon the town. The 'Agamemnons' present are recorded
as having bellowed three cheers. The batteries fired throughout the night.
During the afternoon of the next day, Colonel Vilettes, Nelson, Duncan of
the artillery (back safely from Naples with the necessary mortars), as well as
two other military officers and a Corsican guide, went to survey a ridge a
thousand yards closer to the citadel. At the same time, the enemy were firing
muskets and grape shot at their camp. The guide was killed, a brigade major
was fatally wounded and Nelson received 'a sharp cut in the back'. Next
morning, regardless of his wound, he was building two more batteries to
mount mortars and more guns from the *Agamemnon*. The pounding continued
from both sides day after day with losses mounting. Five 'Agamemnons' had
been killed, 'not men to keep out of the way' of shot.

The need for more British troops was urgent, but General D'Aubant continued firm in his resolve not to cooperate. 'It is enough to make any lover of

his Country run distracted,' wrote Nelson, who suspected however, that as soon as Bastia was ready to surrender, they would march and try to take any glory for themselves.

The enemy stepped up their fire after getting their batteries into 'a tolerable state', and one of the best of the 'Agamemnons' died while working on repairs during the night. Nelson despatched a note of condolence to a humble home in Swansea:

> From the nature of our profession, we ever hold life by a more precarious tenure than many others, but when we fall, we trust it is to benefit our Country. So fell your Son, by a cannon-ball, under my immediate command, at the Siege of Bastia. I had taken him on shore with me, from his abilities and attention to his duty.[33]

In a letter to Fanny written in early May, Nelson told her, 'As a secret, Bastia will be ours between the 20th and 24th of this month, if succours do not get in. Our Ships are moored across the harbour's mouth and three boats from each ship row guard every night'. On 21 May, short of food and ammunition, after a siege lasting for thirty-seven days, and negotiations lasting for four, the town and citadel of Bastia surrendered unconditionally. The British army, as Nelson had predicted, made its timely appearance. At 6pm on 23 May the troops, knowing it was about to capitulate, took possession of the town gates. Fanny's son Josiah, whom Nelson had prudently kept safe aboard the *Agamemnon*, was given the honour the next morning of marching at the head of the grenadiers into Bastia to the strains of the National Anthem.

As a result of the victory, the island's allegiance was transferred by General Paoli from France to Great Britain. The formalities took place on 19 June, when Sir Gilbert Elliot assumed the position of Viceroy and the members of the new Assembly took the oath of allegiance to King George. The British forces had lost nineteen dead and thirty-seven wounded, the enemy over 200 dead and 540 wounded, most of whom died shortly afterwards. It had been a stunning and well deserved victory for a mixed force of 1,248 troops and seamen over an enemy of 4,500 men who were well trained and entrenched in their own strongholds. It certainly reinforced, almost mathematically, Nelson's long established opinion that one Englishman was equal to three Frenchmen:

> Had this been an English town, I am sure it would not have been taken by them. They have allowed us to batter it without once making an effort to drive us away. I may truly say that this has been a Naval Expedition; our boats prevented anything from getting in by sea and our sailors hauling up great guns, and then fighting them on shore.[34]

Long overdue, the *Agamemnon* was at last sent to Gibraltar for an emergency refit before entering once again upon a series of combined land-sea operations in the Mediterranean.[35] Before leaving, Nelson sent a brief triumphant letter to Sir William Hamilton, enclosing a note for Emma. In it he pledged, 'We shall now join heart and hand against Calvi.' With San Fiorenza and Bastia under British authority, all Hood needed to control Corsica was precisely Calvi, on the north western side of the island. With the whole of Corsica in his grasp he would have a bastion, with ports for his fleet from which to keep watch on the coast of southern France and its principal naval base, Toulon.

NOTES

1. Carola Oman, *Nelson* (London: Hodder & Stoughton, 1947), p 109.
2. Ibid. Sir William Hamilton was cousin of the Duke of Hamilton, cousin of Lord Abercorn, uncle of the Duchess of Atholl and of Elizabeth Hamilton, married to the Earl of Warwick. His first marriage was to Miss Barlow, who died in 1782, leaving him a fortune but he, having known many great fortunes, mentioned it as having afforded him merely 'a little independence'.
3. *Memoires of Lady Hamilton* (1815), p 2.
4. Flora Fraser, *Emma, Lady Hamilton* (New York, Alfred A Knopf, 1987), pp 8–10.
5. Ibid, p 10.
6. Ibid, p 17.
7. Ibid, p 19.
8. Ibid, p 58.
9. Ibid, p 105.
10. Ernle Bradford, *Nelson: The Essential Hero* (London: Macmillan, 1977), pp 93–94.
11. Oliver Warner, *A Portrait of Lord Nelson* (London: Penguin Books, 1987), p 84.
12. Ibid, p 84.
13. Flora Fraser, *Emma, Lady Hamilton* (New York, Alfred A Knopf, 1987), pp 166–167, quoting Harrison, *Life of Lord Nelson*, (1806) Vol. 1, pp 108–109.
14. Ibid, p 168.
15. Warner, p 84.
16. Ibid, p 85.
17. When he did return to Naples, Nelson was a sorry figure. He had lost his right arm and also the vision of his right eye, and he had a gash on his face received during the battle. He convalesced at the Palazzo Sessa in the arms of Lady Hamilton with whom he was to fall desperately in love.
18. Carola Oman, p 114.
19. Warner, p 86.
20. Ibid.
21. Frances Mossiker, *Napoleon and Josephine: The Biography of a Marriage* (London: Victor Gollancz, 1965), pp 80–82.
22. Bradford, p 97.
23. Warner, p 87.
24. Carola Oman, p 116.
25. Bradford, pp 98–99.
26. Carola Oman, p 117.
27. Ernle Bradford, p 99.
28. Carola Oman, pp 117–118.
29. Bradford, p 102.
30. Carola Oman, p 122.
31. Bradford, p 104.
32. Admiralty: Captains' Logs (ADM 51): ADM 51/1104, HMS *Agamemnon*.
33. Carola Oman, p 126.
34. Bradford, p 106.
35. Carola Oman, p 127.

CHAPTER 6

Calvi, Genoa and Hyères 1794–1796

Lay a Frenchman close and you will beat him.

Said by Lord Hawke and used by Nelson
as his favourite fighting signal.

The small town of Calvi was as strongly fortified by human ingenuity as it was by nature. Placed in inhospitable rocky territory on the north-western side of the island, it was going to prove more challenging to the invaders than Bastia had been. This time, however, there was no question about the army refusing to cooperate. It was to be a combined operation with Lieutenant General the Hon Charles Stuart in charge of the military and Captain Horatio Nelson in charge of the naval forces. From the moment that Stuart came on board the *Agamemnon* and expressed his eagerness to proceed with the attack, affairs moved swiftly and efficiently.

Preparations for the siege of Calvi

In the early afternoon of 18 June 1794, HM ships *Agamemnon*, *Dolphin* and *Lutine*, together with fifteen sail of transports, stood in for the anchorage in Porto Galere a little to the south of Calvi. The *Agamemnon* hoisted out its boats to tow the ship into the bay where she anchored in 53 fathoms of water at 8pm. Very deep water with dangerous uncharted rocks extended to within 20 feet of the beach. The weather had turned stormy and heavy squalls blew in from the sea, causing a swell dangerous to boats attempting to land.[1]

Very early next morning, Nelson and General Stuart went ashore to survey the coast and pick out the best place for landing guns and stores. After a thorough reconnaissance they decided on Porto Agro, a small cove 3 miles from Calvi. From this distance they examined the enemy's defences: Fort Muzello to the west of the town, Fort Monteciusco to the south, the Fountain Battery on a rocky peninsula and finally Fort San Francesco tucked behind an outcrop of the mountain side. All were strategically placed to defend the town, which appeared well fortified though it had no surrounding trench.

At 3am the following day, troops and seamen began to disembark, together with the necessary provisions and stores including sails and spars, a 4-pounder field piece, ninety-one hammocks, five casks of beef, six casks of pork, twenty-five bags of bread, three pipes of wine, and 2,400 sandbags.[2]

The operation of getting men, provisions, and armament ashore continued for 2 days in worsening weather. On Sunday 22 June, with the work still in progress, a howling gale blew and a heavy sea set into the bay from an opening to the southwest. The danger of being driven aground obliged the three ships to put to sea. After unfurling the fore and mizzen topsails and hoisting the staysails in haste to escape being trapped on the lee shore,[3] the *Agamemnon*'s crew buoyed the anchor hawser and cut it with an axe before making for the open sea.

Anxious that the worst possible fate might have befallen his force during the gale, Lord Hood wrote a worried note to Nelson from the *Victory*, anchored off San Fiorenza: 'I tremble for what may have happened from last night's wind.' However, despite the lack of proper shelter or protective clothing, Nelson's 'Agamemnons' were on shore and had begun to make a road for their guns.[4]

Four days later, the *Agamemnon* returned to Porto Galere, shortened sail, and hove to beside the buoy she had left tied to the anchor cable. The cable was picked up from the sea and slowly hauled aboard. All went well until 7 fathoms from the anchor, where, possibly due to having been chafed on a sharp rock, the rope stranded in two places. Before a 'preventor' could be tied beneath and above the broken strands, the rope parted, and the ship's best bower anchor disappeared into 53 fathoms of water. However, the *Agamemnon* was safe, as she was moored by two hawsers to another anchor.

Nelson proceeded to land more armament for the shore batteries: one 24-pounder, two 18-pounders, two howitzers and two mortars, complete with mortar beds and gun carriages. During the next few days larger quantities of ammunition and more guns were sent ashore, as well as much-needed rations for the men.[5] Hood contributed a detachment of seamen from the *Victory* as well as guns from the flagship under the command of Captain Hallowell and Commander Serocold, a friend of Nelson's. On 27 June, Hood himself arrived before the beleaguered town and landed more guns, seamen and provisions.

Nelson was proud of the remarkable performance of his men on shore: 'By computation we may be supposed to have dragged one 24-pounder with its ammunition and every requisite for making a battery upwards of 80 miles, 17 of which were up a very steep mountain.'[6] The 'Royal Louis', the first of the batteries completed, came into action early in the morning on 4 July, two more following suit within the next three days. Amongst the first casualties was Commander Serocold: 'by grape-shot passing through his head as he cheered the people who were dragging the gun', Nelson reported in his journal.

Walter Serocold had been an enthusiastic supporter of Nelson's daring schemes. During the siege of Bastia he had commanded the *Proselyte*, a bomb-brig captured at Toulon. He had anchored it close to shore and had courageously fired round after round of shells at the French batteries. The French, in turn, had trained their guns on the bomb-brig and by firing red-hot shot set her on fire. Serocold and his sailors were taken off by the boats of the squadron moments before his vessel burned to the waterline. It was also Serocold who had stood up for Nelson when Hood, for reasons best known to himself, had in dispatches given most of the credit for the command of the batteries at Bastia to Captain Anthony Hunt and had merely mentioned Nelson as 'commanding and directing the seamen, landing guns, mortars and stores.' Serocold had been so incensed at this injustice that he had said that Hunt 'never was on a battery, or even rendered any service during the siege . . . if any person says he did, then I submit to the character of a story-teller', and he had hotly announced his intention of 'publishing an advertisement' with the truth.

The Dog Days and the Lion Sun

The siege of Calvi proceeded according to plan. The guns of the huge *Commerce de Marseille*, Rear-Admiral Trogoff's flagship taken at Toulon, had been landed and the carpenter of the *Agamemnon*, who had proved himself expert at making gun platforms, now set to the task of constructing siege ladders in anticipation of assaults on the enemy battlements. However, the news was not entirely good, as each day Nelson received increasing lists of men who had succumbed to 'the fever'. He noted sombrely in his journal: 'We have far more to fear from the climate than the enemy.' In the intolerable heat of the Corsican summer and with malaria rampant, conditions were ominously similar to those he had experienced on the Mosquito Coast of Nicaragua. In one of his letters to Prince William Henry, Duke of Clarence, with whom he kept up regular correspondence, Nelson described the situation:

> It is now what we call the dog-days, here it is termed the Lion-Sun; no person can endure it: we have upwards of one thousand sick out of two thousand, and others not much better than so many phantoms. We have lost many men from the season, very few from the enemy. I am here the reed among the oaks: all the prevailing disorders have attacked me, but I have not strength for them to fasten upon. I bow before the storm, while the sturdy oak is laid low.[7]

Nelson's eye is injured

The enemy's astonishment turned to consternation when they discovered that the British had not only brought their guns over terrain considered inaccessible, but had also erected gun batteries that were now in position and ready to fire. Realising their plight, the French opened heavy and concentrated fire upon the British works, destroying two 24-pounders from the *Agamemnon* and a 32-pounder from the *Victory*.

In the early morning on 10 July, Nelson was hit in the face and chest by splinters, stones and sand which were thrown up when an enemy shell hit the earthen battlement. Blood poured from a wound over his right eyebrow, and after examining this it was discovered that the eye itself had been damaged through a cut that had penetrated the eyelid. The surgeons that attended him and performed the first dressing held out hope that his sight might recover over the next few days. Unfortunately, they were wrong. The sight of his right eye was lost to him for the rest of his life. He did not wear an eye-patch as was often supposed. Instead he had made and attached to his hat a green shade to protect

On 10 July 1794, during the siege of Calvi, Nelson was hit in the face by sand and fragments thrown up by the explosion of a French shell against a British earthwork. It was later found that he had lost the sight in his right eye, the first of his famous injuries (both, coincidentally, suffered when he was in action on land). (National Maritime Museum, London)

his good eye, and later a wider shade to protect both eyes, as can be seen on a hat preserved at Westminster Abbey.[8] Considering the pain he was in, Nelson showed remarkable courage and self control after the accident. In spite of his throbbing head and bandaged eye, he wrote to Lord Hood: 'I got a little hurt this morning; not much, as you may judge from my writing.' Hood showed immediate concern and replied saying he would send a person next morning 'to know how you are, and whether you would not have assistance,' to which Nelson answered that his eye was better and that he would be able to continue at his post.

The surrender of Calvi

Fort Muzello was taken on 19 July. The British then turned the might of their thirty-five guns upon the town. The next day the French Governor negoti-ated a 25-day truce, pledging to surrender if he did not receive reinforcements by then. He had learned of the sickness that had taken hold of the British forces and was drawing out the issue. His own position, however, was unsus-tainable. British troops and batteries ringed the city, his garrison's magazines were almost empty and his provisions nearly spent. On 10 August, he hung out the white flag. It was none too soon for the British. Lord Hood was reported unwell, General Stuart was visibly sick, and the half-blind Nelson was once more feeling the sickening symptoms of malaria. He kept on his feet hoping that an 'active scene' would cure his shivering. Perhaps malaria both-ered him less than it did others who were new to the disease.

An entry in the ship's log for Tuesday 12 August, states briefly that Captain Nelson, with his officers and seamen, returned from the shore batteries and boarded the *Agamemnon*.[9]

Back in his familiar cabin, Nelson stared into his small mirror. He covered each eye in turn. He had totally lost the ability to see objects with his right eye, and could barely distinguish light from darkness.

While waiting for the *Agamemnon*'s guns to be brought back and shipped, Nelson went for a medical consultation on board the *Victory*. In the hospital on the orlop deck of the flagship Dr Harness, Physician to the Fleet, con-firmed the previous diagnosis. He stated in his written report that it was 'a wound of the iris of the right eye, which has occasioned an unnatural dilation of the pupil, and a material defect of sight'. Nelson enclosed both medical certificates to Lord Hood. 'As to all purposes of use', he wrote, his eye was gone. 'I feel the Want of it but such is the chance of War, it was within a hair's breadth of taking off my head.' He wrote to Fanny the extent of the damage a month after the incident: 'The blemish is nothing, not to be perceived unless told.' He also assured her that the wound had not kept him from his duty. This was true. His name had never even appeared in the Calvi casualty list.

A diplomatic visit to Genoa

One of the last duties Hood assigned to Nelson before he retired from the Mediterranean was a diplomatic errand. Since his success at Naples, Nelson was now required to sail the *Agamemnon* to Genoa to interview the Doge and request docking facilities for British ships of war. After his arrival on 20 September 1794, he wrote to Fanny: 'This city is, without exception, the most magnificent I ever beheld, superior in many respects to Naples, although it does not appear quite so fine from the sea, yet on shore it is far beyond it. All the houses are palaces on the grandest scale. However, I trust we shall soon quit these magnificent scenes, and retire to England, where all that I admire is placed.' Later he informed Lord Hood: 'I was received in some state, the Doge advancing to the middle of the room to receive me, and I had the honours of a Senator.' He left the meeting having achieved his mission and parted from the Doge with mutual assurances of friendship.[10]

Lord Hood sailed for Gibraltar and Portsmouth on 12 October 1794 in the *Victory*. He was succeeded by the elderly Admiral Sir William Hotham, who with his lethargic mind was hardly a man of action in comparison with his predecessor. He had hoisted his flag in the *Britannia*. The endless blockade of Toulon wore on day after day, as the ships of the British squadron stood out at sea very much worse for wear, with patched sails and hulls battered by the waves of winter storms.

'The gale moderates, and I am just going to get under way again', wrote Nelson to his uncle William Suckling from Livorno (usually called 'Leghorn' by the English) in October. The *Agamemnon* was undermanned. She had lost six of her best men during the siege of Calvi, and since then over fifty more to malaria. Nelson sailed her into the Bay of Hyères and from there past the entrance to Toulon, where he made a rapid count of the enemy vessels assembled in the port. 'Twenty-two sail of ships in the inner Harbour', he reported to the recently appointed Viceroy of Corsica, Sir Gilbert Elliot. He added in his letter some personal suggestions for the defence of Ajaccio, the birthplace of Napoleon, should the enemy attempt to attack it.

Livorno

Towards the end of November the weary *Agamemnon* was taken to the neutral port of Livorno to undergo a rapid refit. Used by the Mediterranean fleet for refitting and victualling, 'Leghorn', on the Tuscan coast, was well known for licentiousness. It attracted flocks of women who sold their favours to officers and sailors, many of whom contracted venereal diseases and landed in the recently opened British hospital at Ajaccio. Parson's son though he was, Nelson enjoyed the pleasures of female company in a foreign port, as his friend Captain Thomas Fremantle recorded in his journal about this particular visit:

> December 1794. Wed. 3. Dined at Nelson's and his Dolly, called on old Udney (the British Consul), went to the opera with him. He introduced me to a very handsome Greek woman.[11]

Among Nelson's female friends in Livorno was a certain Adela Correglia. However, it is unlikely that she was the Dolly that Fremantle mentions, whose full name is unknown.

James Harrison's posthumous biography of Nelson has often been labelled fictitious and inaccurate. He wrote, however, on Lady Hamilton's authority and no one could have known more about Nelson's amorous affairs than she. Dealing with the human weaknesses of a national hero, the author went as far as propriety permitted in this account:

. . . though by no means ever an unprincipled seducer of the wives and daughters of his friends, he was always well known to maintain rather more partiality
for the fair sex than is quite consistent with the highest degree of Christian
purity. Such improper indulgences, with some slight addiction to that other
vicious habit of British seamen, the occasional use of a few thoughtlessly profane
expletives, form the only dark specks ever yet discovered in the bright blaze of
his moral character.[12]

For two years Nelson had been away from home. It was understandable that
he should seek the pleasures and comforts of a friendly port in the company of
brother officers. Apropos of women in his life, Nelson wrote cheerfully to
another naval officer: 'they always will do as they please. Orders are not for
them — at least I never knew one who obeyed, your most faithful Horatio
Nelson.'[13]

The action off Genoa

When the *Agamemnon* put to sea again in mid-January 1795, the weather
continued to be intolerable: 'We have had three gales of wind in thirteen days.
Neither sails, ships, or men can stand it.' Despite his discomfort, Nelson
continued to be in love with his ship. 'We have had nothing but gales of wind
and a heavy sea,' he wrote to Fanny, 'so much so that one of the ships lost all
her masts last night. In *Agamemnon* we mind nothing. She is the finest ship I
ever sailed in and was she a 74 nothing should induce me to leave her while
the war lasted'.

Lord Hood maintained an uneasy watch on Toulon. Intelligence reports
stated that the French were rapidly refitting the ships left to them after the
evacuation of the port, with the purpose of invading Corsica and re-
establishing their control over the island. They had put to sea on 5 June 1794
with seven sail-of-the-line and five frigates under Rear Admiral Pierre Martin.
Hood had chased them into Gourjean Bay, but they managed to escape
during a spell of bad weather and sailed back to Toulon.

Pierre Martin was a typical early product of the French Revolution, when
many senior officers lost their heads to the guillotine. Due to the shortage of
senior naval officers, Martin had ascended the ladder of promotion from
lieutenant in 1792 to rear admiral in 1794, with only a brief stop as captain on
the way. It was hardly surprising that he lacked the knowledge and the
necessary experience to conduct a fleet in battle, especially against the well-
trained and seasoned British. To add to his difficulties, it was said that out of
the 12,000 men that made up his ships' companies, some 7,000 of them were
landsmen who had never been to sea before.

On 8 March 1795, Hotham received news via Genoa that Pierre Martin
had led his fleet of seventeen sail-of-the-line out of Toulon on a course for
Corsica. The ships had been sighted at 10am. Hotham, with fourteen British
line-of-battle ships, and one Neapolitan, hoisted the signal for a general chase.

It was a mild day with light, variable winds and morning mists, typical of the early Mediterranean spring. The enemy could barely be seen on the horizon, and the chance of catching up with them seemed remote. Nelson was concerned that the *Agamemnon* might not acquit herself worthily in battle; she was undermanned due to sickness, as indeed were all the vessels of the British fleet. However, he was quite cheerful when he wrote to Fanny on 10 March: 'I shall commence a letter at this moment to assure you, although I flatter myself that no assurance is necessary, of my constant love and affection. We are just in sight of the French fleet and a signal is out for a general chase.' The following day he added to the letter: 'Did not get sight of the French fleet this morning. I suppose they stood to the westward all night. The admiral has just got information that the French . . . on the 8th off Cape Corse took the *Berwick* of 74 guns.' The *Berwick*, which had been refitting in the Bay of San Fiorenza, had been caught in a heavy cross swell that had rolled the three masts out of her. She was rigged with jury masts and was struggling along on a course for Livorno, when the French engaged and captured her.

On 10 March, British lookout vessels sighted the French fleet standing towards Toulon against a southwest wind. At midnight, Hotham hoisted the signal for battle formation but by next morning the enemy were over the horizon. Toward evening a fresh breeze sprang up and the British fleet closed and formed in line of battle heading to the westward. Nelson saw the Genoa lighthouse about five leagues to the northeast with the lights of Columbus' birthplace twinkling behind it.

During the night the weather became squally and the French started to show their lack of seamanship. The 74-gun *Mercure* lost her topmast and was escorted by a frigate to Gourjean Bay. At 8am the next day the 80-gun *Ça Ira* (named after the savage battle hymn of the French Republic) collided with the 80-gun *Victoire*, and lost her fore and main topmasts. Captain Thomas Fremantle, in the leading British frigate *Inconstant,* of only 36 guns, came up fast and with great resolution fired a broadside at the *Ça Ira*. The *Vestale*, a French 36, bore down to protect the larger ship, firing at the *Inconstant* and taking the disabled *Ça Ira* in tow. The *Inconstant*, after tacking again, passed under the large ship's lee and again fired a broadside at her. She received such heavy punishment in return that she was forced to retire. Nelson, who had as usual outdistanced the fleet in the *Agamemnon*, bore down upon the crippled *Ça Ira*, protected now by Rear Admiral Pierre Martin's flagship the *Sans Culotte* of 120 guns and the *Jean Bart* (which Nelson wrote down as *Jean Barras*, being more familiar with the names of the members of the French Directory than with French naval heroes of an earlier age).

To the dramatic sound of the drummers beating to quarters, the *Agamemnon* cleared for action. There was a scurrying patter of bare feet on hollow decks as every man hurried to his pre-assigned duty. Almost like magic the wooden bulkheads on the main and quarterdecks vanished and the furniture in the captain's and officers' quarters went into the hold. Hammocks, neatly rolled

HMS *Agamemnon* engaging the dismasted *Ça Ira*, 11 March 1795. The
French ship suffered nearly 100 casualties from the *Agamemnon*'s fire, due
to Nelson being able to rake the disabled ship's stern with virtual
impunity. She was taken next day after further attacks by HMS *Captain*
and *Bedford*. (National Maritime Museum, London)

and lashed, were packed into the troughs around the upper deck. The galley
fire was quenched with water and the sails were doused aloft. The fighting
decks were dressed with wet sand to lessen fire risk and to provide better
footing. The ship's company tied their neckerchiefs around their heads and
cast off their footwear and all clothing except their trousers. Surgeons preferred to operate on wounds uninfected by dirty clothes. The officers changed
into clean linen, breeches and silk stockings for the same reason. The gun
crews stood ready at their stations with the ports open, flint-locks ready, and
slow-matches burning in the tubs. Powder monkeys ran to bring up cartridges
to the guns. Nets were spread between the main and mizzenmasts to repel
boarders and to catch falling men, as well as any broken spars which might
drop from aloft.

Mr Roxburgh, the surgeon, repaired to the cockpit with his mates. They
rolled up their shirt-sleeves as they went and proceeded to lay out their
instruments in readiness for the first casualties. The carpenter and his men
gathered in a group below the waterline with their tools, lengths of timber and
wooden plugs ready to deal with any underwater damage to the hull. Marines
armed with pistols took up positions at the hatches to keep passage free for the

powder-boys and designated messengers, while the formidable figure of the master-at-arms, familiarly known as 'Jaunty' and responsible for discipline, made his round of the decks. In action, 'Jaunty's' specific duty was to keep a record of the fighting ability of the ship by itemising guns out of action and human losses at each station. Six minutes was the allotted time for the ship's total transformation from cruising state to fighting fortress. Once accomplished, the first lieutenant descended from the quarterdeck to make a complete inspection of the ship and issue final orders.

Refusing battle, the French were sailing as fast as they could for the security of Toulon with the British in hot pursuit. Due to her speed, the *Agamemnon* had gained so much on the rest of the fleet that she was now alone and close to the French. At 10:45am, with a squally wind blowing out of the southwest, Nelson bore down upon the *Ça Ira*'s quarter while the *Jean Bart* and the *Sans Culotte* dropped back to protect their dismasted consort. As the *Agamemnon* approached the stricken 80-gun vessel Nelson lightened ship. With great regret he hove overboard seven live bullocks; the purchase of a captain with strong views on the importance of nutrition.[14]

Nelson wrote later, 'We could have fetched the *Sans Culotte* by passing the *Ça Ira* to windward, but, on looking round, I saw no ship of the line within several miles to support me.' The frigate *Vestale*, having passed the *Ça Ira* a tow, was making a valiant attempt to get her under way when Nelson skilfully manoeuvred the *Agamemnon* behind the enemy's stern. While this brought her under the accurate fire of the Frenchman's stern guns, the huge ship, 'absolutely large enough to have taken the *Agamemnon* in her hold', could not bring her broadside to bear, which at close quarters would have been devastating. 'Seeing plainly from the situation of the two Fleets the impossibility of being supported, and in case any accident happened to our masts, the certainty of being severely cut up, I resolved to fire as soon as I thought we had a certainty of hitting.' Nelson continued to manoeuvre for over 3 hours, tacking the *Agamemnon* back and forth under the huge stern of the *Ça Ira* and pouring broadsides through her stern windows along the length of her decks. He wrote later of his satisfaction in observing 'my poor brave fellows' carrying out orders with as much calm and precision as if they had been working the *Agamemnon* into Spithead. 'Scarcely a shot seemed to miss: the instant all were fired, [we] braced up our after-yards, put the helm a-port and stood after her again . . . never allowing the *Ça Ira* to get a single gun from either side to fire on us.' By 1pm the *Ça Ira* was a wreck. Her commander, albeit too late, ordered the towing frigate to pull the ship around so he could bring her broadside to bear, but the shots passed over the *Agamemnon*. All firing ceased when, instead of hurrying ships to Nelson's assistance, Hotham hoisted the signal of recall. The *Agamemnon* had seven wounded as compared to an estimated one hundred casualties aboard the *Ça Ira* when Nelson broke off the action and dropped into his station in the line.[15] During the night, the 74-gun *Censeur* relieved the *Vestale* from towing the *Ça Ira* and with her fell astern and to leeward of the French line.

At sunrise the following morning, the *Captain* and the *Bedford* bore down upon the stricken ship and her assistant. They sustained such heavy broadsides from both French ships that after an hour and a half of action, they signalled for assistance and had to be towed out of range of the enemy's guns. The *Ça Ira* had been completely dismasted and the *Censeur* had lost her mainmast. 'Our fleet', wrote Nelson to his friend the Duke of Clarence, 'closed with *Ça Ira* and *Censeur*, who defended themselves in the most gallant manner; the former lost four hundred, the latter three hundred and fifty men.'[16]

At 8pm the British ship *Illustrious* engaged in succession the *Duquesne* and the *Victoire* at a distance of a quarter of a mile. The *Illustrious*, however, took a pounding, losing her fore-topmast and later her mainmast, which also brought down her mizzen.

After some more firing in which the *Agamemnon* again engaged the enemy, the French fleet abandoned its crippled ships and stood away under all sail towards the security of the French coastline. As the two fleets lost sight of one another, the *Ça Ira* and *Censeur*, which between them were to show a casualty list of some 750, were taken by the British. It was later stated in French accounts of the battle, that when Captain Coude of the *Ça Ira* surrendered his sword to Vice Admiral Goodall, the latter said, 'Sir, I will keep this glorious sword for myself, but I beg you to accept mine in recognition of your noble courage.'[17]

In essence, it was an unsatisfactory victory. Two French ships of the line had been taken, but Hotham could and should have done much more. Nelson himself went on board the admiral's flagship to urge him to leave the prizes in the care of the two damaged English ships and some frigates and continue the chase with the rest of the fleet in the hopes of bringing the French to battle. Hotham's reply was almost identical to Rodney's in the previous war: 'We must be contented,' he said, 'we have done very well'. Nelson, as enraged as Hood had been 13 years before, did not agree: 'Now, had we taken ten sail, and allowed the eleventh to escape, when it had been possible to have got at her, I could never have called it well done. We should have had such a day as, I believe, the annals of England never produced. Nothing can stop the courage of English seamen . . .'[18]

In an indignant and smouldering mood Nelson went on board the 98-gun *Princess Royal* taking with him, on Hotham's orders, the captains of the two French prizes. There in the aft cabin he met with Vice Admiral Goodall who shared his views. Goodall, also incensed by Hotham's lack of initiative, wrote a letter to his commander-in-chief backing Nelson's opinion and saying: 'if they could get close enough, they might have [taken] the whole enemy fleet'. 'Sure I am,' Nelson confided privately in a letter to Fanny soon after the battle, 'had I commanded our Fleet on the 14th, that either the whole French Fleet would have graced my triumph, or I should have been in a confounded scrape.' It was precisely the possibility of a scrape that had deterred Hotham. Nevertheless, he had achieved his main objectives. The French fleet had been chased back to Toulon, Corsica was temporarily saved, and two French sail-of-the-line had been captured. To Nelson the outcome of the engagement proved several things. It confirmed his opinion of Hotham, who, as he wrote to Locker, is 'very well, but I believe heartily tires of his temporary command; nor do I think he is intended by nature for a Commander-in-Chief, which requires a man of more active turn of mind.' It reinforced his belief that a ship's fighting potential depended in great measure on how she was handled; and it defined his personal ambition: 'I wish to be Admiral, and in command of the English fleet,' he wrote to Fanny. 'I should very soon either do much, or be ruined. My disposition cannot bear tame or slow measures.'[19]

Though contemporary comment did not criticise Hotham too severely, Nelson and Goodall were not alone in their condemnation of him. 'I can *entre nous* perceive,' wrote Sir William Hamilton from the Palazzo Sessa in Naples, 'that my old friend Hotham is not quite awake enough for such a command as that of the King's Fleet in the Mediterranean; although he appears the best creature imaginable.'[20] A further shadow was cast on the outcome of the engagement when the *Illustrious* was wrecked. She was driven ashore in Valence Bay between La Spezia and Livorno, adding to the misfortune of the *Berwick*'s seizure by the French prior to the engagement.

Contemporary statistics regarding the relative strength of the two fleets on 14 March 1795 are interesting. They are given as follows: Royal Navy: fourteen sail-of-the-line; 8,810 men; 557 guns that fired broadsides weighing 12,711lbs. French Navy: thirteen sail-of-the-line; 9,520 men; 490 guns that fired broadsides weighing 12,307lbs. (The last figure in each case is meaningless unless taken comparatively as it was at that time. It refers to the possible total weight of iron shot fired at one discharge from each cannon in the fleet.)

British losses were given as follows: *Agamemnon*, 0 killed, 13 wounded; *Captain*, 3 killed, 19 wounded; *Bedford*, 7 killed, 18 wounded; *Princess Royal*, 3 killed, 8 wounded; *Illustrious*, 20 killed, 70 wounded; *Courageux*, 15 killed, 33 wounded; *Britannia*, 1 killed, 18 wounded; *Egmont*, 7 killed, 21 wounded; *Windsor Castle*, 6 killed, 31 wounded; *Diadem*, 3 killed, 7 wounded; *St George*, 4 killed, 13 wounded; *Terrible*, 0 killed, 6 wounded; *Fortitude*, 1 killed, 4 wounded; *Inconstant*, 3 killed, 14 wounded; *Minerva*, 0 killed, 4 wounded; and *Tancredi*, 7 killed, 5 wounded. Total 74 killed and 284 wounded. Losses in the French ships were stated by the British as unknown.[21]

On 25 March, after the damaged ships had been partially repaired, the British fleet weighed anchor from La Spezia Bay and sailed to San Fiorenza. There the ships lay refitting until 18 April when Hotham, now promoted to Admiral of the Blue, left the French prizes behind and proceeded to Livorno.

Lord Hood strikes his flag in the *Victory*

It has been said that grumbling is the Englishman's privilege. It has also been said that at sea some growling is occasionally necessary to give vent to an officer's pent-up feelings. Nelson growled at Hotham's lethargy. Thoroughly exasperated at the prospect that the French might attack the English convoy they were eagerly awaiting at Livorno, or worse, that they might attempt to regain Corsica while Hotham frittered the days away with the fleet at anchor, he could hardly contain himself:

> I am absolutely, at this moment in the horrors, fearing from our idling here, that the active Enemy may send out two or three Sail-of-the-line, and some frigates, to intercept our convoy, which is momently expected . . .

The news of the appointment of Lord Spencer to succeed Lord Chatham as First Lord of the Admiralty was a further setback: 'Now he is out, all hopes will be done away', Nelson wrote, refering to compensation for the loss of his eye. Nelson's anxiety and depression deepened further with news that Lord Hood, who had been expected back in the Mediterranean aboard the *Victory* to resume his command, had fallen out with the new Board of Admiralty. While at Spithead aboard the *Victory*, ready to return, Hood had felt it his duty to argue with their Lordships. In his fierce, impatient and implacable manner, he criticised the inadequacy of the reinforcements that they intended to send to the Mediterranean station. As was his way, he stated his arguments with such vehemence that their Lordships took offence. He was consequently ordered to strike his flag and come on shore, which he did accordingly, never to be employed at sea again. 'Oh, miserable Board of Admiralty,' wrote Nelson. 'They have forced the first officer in the Service away from his command. His zeal, his activity for the honour and benefit of his King and Country are not abated. Upward of 70, he possesses the mind of 40 . . .'[22]

Reinforcements to both fleets

In early May, Hotham sailed from Livorno. On reaching the southwest tip of Minorca, he was joined by the long-awaited reinforcements from England, about which Hood had been so vociferous. They numbered nine sail-of-the-line: HM ships *Victory*, *Barfleur*, *Gibraltar*, *Bombay Castle*, *Saturn*, *Cumberland*, *Defence*, *Culloden* and *Audacious* under Rear Admiral Robert Man. With these additions the British fleet in the Mediterranean increased to twenty-three line-of-battle ships, six frigates and two brigs. Also, the long awaited convoy from Gibraltar had arrived safely at Livorno loaded with desperately needed powder and ammunition. 'Had we lost them the game was up,' wrote Nelson. Nevertheless, most captains in the fleet felt indignation that the merchant vessels had undergone such unnecessary risk of capture. Hotham continued cruising until the end of the month when he bore up eastward, reaching port at San Fiorenza on 29 May.

At this time Nelson was granted a request he had made in writing to the Secretary at War. He had asked for the equivalent allowance of a land officer, because of his services on shore during the Corsican campaign. By return mail he received a chilly answer: 'No pay has ever been issued under the direction, or to the knowledge of this Office, to Officers of the Navy, serving with the Army on shore.'[23] But then, in a surprising reversal of attitude, due to the intervention of the new First Lord of the Admiralty, Earl Spencer, he was granted an honorary command as Colonel of Marines, which carried with it a salary but no duties. While the extra pay was a welcome reward, it was the recognition of his services that pleased him most, especially after having been the target of the sardonic comments of the army during the siege of Bastia.

During April Rear Admiral Pierre Martin's fleet had also increased in number due to Rear Admiral Renaudin's safe arrival in Toulon from Brest, with six sail-of-the-line, three frigates, and three corvettes. Martin now had twenty-three serviceable line-of-battle ships. After anchoring in Hyères Bay, he moved to Toulon where the crews of his ships became mutinous. It took a republican deputy named Niou, working on the mutineers' patriotism, to reverse the situation. The men repented and pledged themselves 'to purge their offence in the blood of the enemies of the state'. Knowing such sentiments would not last, Martin put to sea.

On 4 July, Hotham detached the *Agamemnon* from the fleet at anchor in San Fiorenza Bay and sent her, together with the *Meleager*, *Ariadne*, *Moselle* and *Mutine*, with orders to proceed to Genoa and from there to sail westward to reconnoitre the French coast. During the afternoon of 7 July, while midway between Genoa and Nice, Nelson sighted Martin's fleet.

Nelson's small squadron was chased as soon as it was seen, and during the night the French nearly captured the *Moselle*. It was a harrowing 24 hours aboard the *Agamemnon*, running before a northerly wind back towards San Fiorenza. As dawn broke Nelson ordered the guns to be fired intermittently to alert Hotham of the proximity of the enemy. But as they approached the coast the French saw the masts of the twenty-three British ships at anchor in the bay and gave up the chase.

The action off Hyères

Hotham's fleet was neither fit nor able to set sail at once. Many of his ships were in the process of refitting or watering and the wind was blowing straight into the bay from the sea. At nightfall, however, he took advantage of a breeze from shore and succeeded in getting under way. As the British ships left the anchorage and sailed west under all sail, the French had vanished over the horizon several hours before.

Off the Isle du Levant, Hotham learned that the French had been sighted a few hours earlier to the south of Hyères. He immediately gave the signal to prepare for action and make all haste. However, during the night a heavy gale from the northwest had split the main topsails on several British ships. At dawn, while the vessels were bending on new ones, and with the wind still fresh and a heavy swell, the French were sighted 5 miles to leeward. As the weather favoured the British, Hotham made the signal for a general chase, directing his ships to take stations for mutual support and to engage the enemy as soon as they were within range. By noon the *Agamemnon*, in company with the *Victory*, *Culloden*, and *Cumberland*, came up with the French rear. As the *Victory* opened fire the wind shifted, giving the three rear French ships an opportunity of bringing their broadsides to bear. In the following action the French 74-gun *Alcide* was so badly damaged that she struck her colours to the *Culloden,* which, not stopping to take possession of her, passed on to engage another ship in French rear. As she did so, the *Alcide*'s foretop caught fire. The fire spread throughout the ship, reaching the main magazine, and at 3:45pm the vessel blew up, killing over half her crew. As the sun struggled to shine through clouds of smoke, the British lowered their boats and were able to save some 200 men. Nearly all the prisoners declared themselves Royalists and, when Nelson eyed them on the *Agamemnon*'s deck, he decided that upon the whole he found French Republicans better specimens.[24]

With the smoke from the gunfire lying heavy in the windless air, the *Agamemnon* and the *Cumberland* struggled to get into action. 'It was impossible

The aftermath of Hotham's battle off Genoa. Two French ships of the line were taken, but Nelson, like Hood after The Saintes thirteen years earlier, felt more could have been done had his commander-in-chief allowed a pursuit of the remaining enemy ships. (National Maritime Museum, London)

for us to close with them,' Nelson wrote to the Duke of Clarence later, 'the smoke from their Ships and our own made a perfect calm; whilst they, being to windward, drew in shore.' As the two ships attempted to get closer to the enemy, Hotham, who was 8 miles astern, signalled: 'The whole Fleet will now retire.' Captain Nelson of the *Agamemnon* and Captain Rowley of the *Cumberland* did their best to avoid seeing the unwelcome signal, but as the *Victory* repeated it, hoisting the *Cumberland*'s distinguishing pendant, they were obliged to obey just as they were getting into range. Hotham gave the usual lame excuse for calling off the action: 'Those of our ships which were engaged had approached so near to the shore, that I judged it proper to call them off.'

The French fleet had escaped destruction once again due to the lack of British naval leadership. The eventual consequences, of what was later called 'this miserable action' were to include the abandonment of the Mediterranean by the British Fleet, the loss of Corsica, and the alliance of Spain with France.[25] Nelson summed it up in his letter to the Duke of Clarence:

> Thus has ended our second meeting with these gentry. In the forenoon we had every prospect of taking every Ship in the Fleet, and at noon it was almost certain we should have had the six rear Ships. The French Admiral, I am sure, is not a wise man, nor an Officer: he was undetermined whether to fight or run away: however, I must do him the justice to say, he took the wisest step at last . . . To say how we wanted Lord Hood at that time is to say, "Will you have all the French Fleet, or no Action?" but the subject is unpleasant and I shall have done with it. I am now cooperating with the Austrian Army, under General de Vins, and hope we shall do better there.

The French returned to Toulon. The British went first to San Fiorenza and then to Livorno. Hotham sailed again on 6 August, and looking into Toulon saw the French fleet safely anchored. Reassured, he appointed Nelson to command a squadron of eight frigates; his orders being to cooperate with the army under the old Austrian cavalry general, Baron de Vins. The *Agamemnon* proceeded to Genoa in company with HM ships *Speedy*, *Tartar*, *Inconstant*, *Southampton*, *Lowestoffe*, *Meleager*, *Romulus* and *Ariadne*. Three of their captains, Fremantle, Hallowell and Cockburn, were Nelson's old friends.

With General de Vins

Baron de Vins, whose motto was 'All War or all Peace', espoused the glorious but impossible plan of advancing on Nice within 6 weeks, sweeping the enemy before him. He maintained that once he was across the Var, all Provence would rise and unite under his flag. The object of the British squadron was to stop trade and communications between Genoa and France. Nelson soon found out that the only efficient action was displayed by his own blockading squadron. As an exasperated Napoleon exclaimed: 'They have suspended our commerce, stopped the arrival of provisions, and obliged us to supply Toulon from the interior of the Republic.'[26]

Nelson knew well from his previous experience in the West Indies that he could be sued for damages by the owners of vessels that he delayed or detained. The Genoese merchants became furious: 'But that does not matter . . . It seems almost a trial between us who shall be first tired — they of complaining, or me of answering them.'

The boarding and detention of merchant vessels from Algiers caused a furore in London where it was thought that the age-old pirates of the Mediterranean sea lanes might retaliate and attack British shipping. 'But, Sir,' Nelson wrote to Sir Gilbert Elliot, 'is England to give up the almost certainty of finishing this war with honour, to the fear of offence to such beings?' The same clarity of purpose and moral obligation that in the West Indies had been seen as the self-assertive uppishness of a young naval officer had now been tempered by experience. Nelson's new approach required that the British representative on shore appoint agents to pay the freight, sell the cargo, and hold the amount until a decision was reached in a court of law. He wrote to Fanny from the *Agamemnon*, 'Political courage in an Officer abroad is as highly necessary as military courage. I am acting not only without the orders of my commander-in-chief, but in some measure contrary to them. However, I have not only the support of his Majesty's Ministers, both at Turin and Genoa, but a consciousness that I am doing right and proper for the service of our King and Country.'

Nelson had other problems. The glare of the summer sun on the sea day after day affected his 'good' left eye. For 10 days in August he was in great pain and became almost totally blind. He also complained of waking suddenly in the night with an uncomfortable feeling 'as if a girth were buckled taut over my breast', and not being able to get to sleep again. It is likely that his problems would be associated today with stress caused by wretched food, irregular meals, lack of sleep, accumulated fatigue, worry and anxiety. Doctors that attended him were not far off the mark in prescribing shore leave for a month or two 'without thoughts of service', but because of his sense of duty he would not follow their advice.[27] He was further disappointed to discover that General de Vins, who at first evaluation he had thought reliable, turned out to be hopelessly inadequate before the resourceful and aggressive French.

To make matters worse Nelson's servant, Frank Lepee, who had been at his side during the expedition up the San Juan river on the Mosquito Coast of Nicaragua, had to be dismissed. Nelson wrote in his journal: 'Parted with Frank for drunkenness, and when so mad; never will keep a drunkard another hour.' Tom Allen, a boy that had volunteered from Burnham Thorpe for the *Agamemnon*, was given the post instead. He was black-haired, stunted, uncouth, entirely illiterate, and, of course, he was never wrong. However, he knew his place as well as his limitations, and Nelson was to endure him for 7 years, until after the Baltic campaign: 'That beast Allen has left behind, or lost all my papers . . . I asked him in the boat for my red case, as I did not see it. His answer was, "Sir I put it in the stern locker". I then desired him to take particular care in handling the case up the side, when he knew perfectly well he had not put it in the boat . . . Huzza! Huzza! P.S. Allen is returned with my case.'

Nelson had, however, one small successful action during this time to make him feel 'better every way'. On 26 August, the *Agamemnon* and six of his eight frigates raided the small port of Alessio occupied by the French. Under Nelson's personal direction his squadron cut out of the bay and captured a corvette, two gun brigs, and two 5-gun galleys, as well as five vessels laden with stores. They then destroyed another two vessels, all without losing a man. The sole casualty was young William Hoste, son of another Norfolk clergyman and a kinsman of Nelson's, who, in charge of a small boat, cut out a vessel loaded with ammunition and broke a leg falling down her scuttle.[28] He rather enjoyed his spell in the *Agamemnon*'s sick-bay, as Captain Nelson, 'whom I may say has been a second father to me', came down freqently to see him. He was soon getting about on crutches and the ship's company, concluding he was born lucky, harboured a superstitious affection for him.

Nelson's account of the action, in a letter he sent to Hotham, is an example not only of his ability to express himself but also of the considerate way in which he spoke of his subordinates, giving to each due recognition of his efforts. It also serves to illustrate the manoeuvrability of the *Agamemnon*, which handled more like a frigate than a ship of the line:[29]

Agamemnon, Vado Bay
27 August 1795

Sir,
Having received information from General de Vins, that a Convoy of provisions and ammunition was arrived at Alassio, a place in the possession of the French Army, I yesterday proceeded with the Ships named in the margin★ to that place, where, within an hour, we took the Vessels named in the enclosed list.† There was but a very feeble opposition from some of the Enemy's cavalry, who fired on our boats after Boarding the Vessels near the shore, but I have the pleasure to say no man was killed or wounded. The Enemy had two thousand horse and foot soldiers in the Town, which prevented my landing and destroying their magazines of provisions and ammunition. I sent Captain Fremantle in the *Inconstant*, with the *Tartar*, to Languelia, Town on the west side of the Bay of Alassio, where he executed my orders in the most officer-like manner; and I am indebted to every Captain and Officer of the Squadron for their activity, but most particularly so to Lieutenant George Andrews, first lieutenant of the *Agamemnon*, who by his spirited and officer-like conduct saved the French corvette from going on shore.

I have the honour to be, Sir
With the highest respect
Your most obedient Servant

★ HM ships *Inconstant*; *Meleager*; *Southampton*; *Tartar*; *Ariadne*; *Speedy*.
† *La Resolve*, corvette; *La Republique*, gunboat; *La Constitution*, galley; *La Vigilante*, galley; two brigs; three barks; one galley unnamed and a tartane.

Nelson's raid on the Italian port of Alessio, 26 August 1795, in which ten French vessels were taken. *Agamemnon* is in the foreground. This success went some way to ease his frustration at Hotham's lack of initiative, which he felt had cost the British fleet great successes. (National Maritime Museum, London)

The next expedition did not end quite so well. Attempting to cut off a ship from Oneglia, Lieutenants Spicer and Andrews were confronted by three armed Turkish merchantmen who opened fire. One of the Turkish ships was captured, but the other two escaped to Genoa with £6 million in hard cash. Nelson regretfully noted in his journal: 'My gallant Officers and men, after a long contest, were obliged to retreat; and it is with the greatest pain that I have to render so long a list of killed and wounded.'[30]

On the bitterly cold night of 10 November, while the *Agamemnon* rode to a single anchor in Vado Bay, ready to weigh at short notice, a French frigate in the company of several privateers crept out of Genoa harbour. An Austrian messenger carrying £10,000 for de Vins' troops had carelessly mentioned that he would spend the night in the small town of Voltri, 9 miles to the east of Genoa. That night, a landing party of some 300 from the French frigate took the neutral town unopposed, robbed the messenger, and seized stores of corn and wheat which they loaded onto their ships. The next day the French captain, flushed with triumph, was brazenly enlisting men in the streets of Genoa. He collected some 700 who were to sail under his command to raid another town between Voltri and Savona. The plan involved joining forces on shore with a detachment of the French army, and the Genoese peasantry were to be incited into insurrection to swell their ranks.

The British Minister at Genoa, Francis Drake, sent urgent messages to Nelson pleading for the *Agamemnon*'s return to Genoa. Deprived of all but one of his frigates, Nelson regretted that the *Agamemnon* could not be cut in two. Her presence was needed in Vado to prevent the enemy gunboats from harassing the Austrian left flank. However, after consideration, Drake's plea seemed more urgent. Nelson weighed anchor and sailed east along the coast to Genoa. Arriving at night, he laid the *Agamemnon* across the harbour entrance so that no French ship could leave port. The ship's log now became a record of what sailors called 'boisterous' or 'dusty' weather: 'so very bad that neither sails, nor ships, nor people could remain at sea very long.' In the Alps, Austrian soldiers were dying of cold at their posts and in the French lines General Kellerman, their commander, was reported to be moving from one post to another, attempting to encourage his troops.

On 23 November, Nelson's worst fears about the war on the continent were confirmed. Massena, who was to become one of the greatest of Napoleon's marshals, had routed the Austrians and their allies at Loano. On 4 December, with this bitter truth fresh in mind, Nelson wrote a chilling entry in his journal:

> The Austrians, by all accounts, did not stand firm. The French, half naked, were determined to conquer or die. General de Vins, from ill health, as he says, gave up the command in the middle of the Battle, and from that moment not a soldier stayed at his post . . . It was "Devil take the hindmost" . . . The Austrians ran eighteen miles without stopping, The Men without soldiers, Women without assistance. Thus has ended my campaign.

Sir John Jervis relieves Hotham

Nelson had heard that the French fleet in Toulon was ready to sail loaded with troops. He feared that if the *Agamemnon* were sighted at sea, her situation would be extremely dangerous. Adding a postscript in a letter to his brother William, which he had begun a fortnight earlier, he remarked: 'I am on my way to Livorno to refit. The campaign is finished by the defeat of the Austrians, and the French are in possession of Vado Bay. My Ship and Ship's Company are worn out, but the folks at Home do not feel for us.'[31] The inactivity of the British fleet under Hotham was not material for the British newspapers. However, there was an exception: a short article in *The Gentleman's Magazine* mentioned that men of a certain 64 on the Mediterranean station, disliking the classical names given to HM ships, had renamed the *Bellerophon* the 'Bully Ruffian', the *Polyphemus*, 'Polly Infamous', and their own *Agamemnon*, 'Eggs and Bacon'.

The 'Eggs and Bacon' arrived without incident at Livorno, where Nelson learned to his delight that Sir John Jervis had arrived in San Fiorenza from Spithead to relieve Hotham as commander-in-chief of the Mediterranean station.

Sir John Jervis was 63 at the time. Nicknamed 'Hanging Jervis', he had the reputation of a stern disciplinarian with a nose for inefficiency, a heart of stone and a phenomenal temper. He believed that men must be made to fear their officers more than danger: 'the slightest loosening of discipline,' he said, 'will lead to barbarization'. He had, nevertheless, an excellent professional record and was looked up to by his peers in the Navy. His taking over from Hotham as commander-in-chief was greeted with well-founded apprehension by the majority of the captains in the Mediterranean fleet.[32] Without delay, Jervis curtailed the privileges that had become custom. There was to be no more peaceful lying at anchor in San Fiorenza Bay or socialising on the wharf at Livorno. His measures became so resented that even 4 years later the ward-room toast: 'May the discipline of the Mediterranean never be introduced into the Channel Fleet', was expanded by a naval wife with the rider: 'May his next glass of wine choke the Wretch!'[33]

'His tastes were cultivated', wrote Lord Charles Beresford, who later became an admiral himself, 'his conversation charming, his table well-appointed and yet he was not liked.' 'Where I should take a penknife,' said Nelson, 'he takes a hatchet.'

After going aboard the *Victory* to visit Sir John Jervis on 19 January 1796, Nelson found the old man amenable. He offered Nelson a change of ship, the *St George* of 98 guns, or the *Zealous* of 74. Nelson respectfully declined, whereupon Sir John dropped the subject abruptly and began to plunder Nelson's knowledge and even ask his advice on matters relating to the fleet. After a long and interesting talk, Jervis enquired if Nelson would mind serving under him when promoted. Nelson replied that if the *Agamemnon* were ordered home before his flag arrived, he had many reasons to return to England. But should his flag arrive and the war continue, he would be proud to hoist it under the command of Sir John Jervis. Later in February, Nelson had a second interview with Sir John in a blizzard off Toulon, after which he sounded more confident:

> Sir John Jervis, from his manner, as I plainly perceive, does not wish me to leave this station. He seems at present to regard me more as an associate than a subordinate Officer; for I am acting without orders . . . He asked me if I had heard any more of my promotion. I told him "No". His answer was, "You must have a larger Ship, for we cannot spare you, either as Captain or Admiral."

On 9 March, Nelson, feeling more ill at sea than he could ever remember, sailed the *Agamemnon* to Livorno for repairs. Worn out by continual active service and now 15 years old, she had to be frapped with cables (thick hemp hawsers passed around her hull) to keep her frame together. There was hardly a patch of paint left on her, and the worst north-westerly gale Nelson had ever experienced in the Mediterranean had stove in her stern, carried away her starboard quarter gallery, and sprung her main topmast.

Nelson strikes his flag in Agamemnon

On 11 March 1796 Nelson received the long-awaited order from Admiral Jervis to hoist his Commodore's broad pennant aboard the *Agamemnon*. Midshipman William Hoste, now fifteen, celebrated Nelson's promotion in a letter he wrote to his family:

> Our Squadron at present consists of two sail-of-the-Line and four Frigates, but is to be increased in the summer, when we shall not want for amusement, I make no doubt, as our Commodore does not like to be idle.
>
> I suppose your curiosity is excited by the word Commodore Nelson. It gives me infinite pleasure to be able to relieve it by informing you that our good Captain has had this additional mark of distinction conferred upon him, which I daresay you will agree with me, his merit richly deserves. His Broad Pendant is now flying; therefore I must beg my dear father to draw an additional cork.

Nelson had one last successful action with the *Agamemnon* before leaving her. Cruising off Oneglia on 31 May he chased six French vessels under the battery of the port. The *Agamemnon*, *Meleager*, *Petrel*, and *Speedy* anchored close in, with only a few inches of water under them. They silenced the battery and captured four French transports full of guns and ammunition destined for Napoleon's siege of Mantua. (Later it was said that this siege had failed because the supplies did not arrive.) The British lost one man and three were wounded.

On 11 June 1796, the *Agamemnon*, by far most in need of repair of all the ships in the Mediterranean fleet, was ordered to return to England for a thorough refitting. For a week it seemed likely that Nelson would go with her but the health of a brother officer, Captain J S Smith of the *Captain*, was even worse than his own. He told Sir John Jervis in a letter, that he was 'not so bad . . . indeed, I cannot bear the thoughts of leaving your command.'

Nelson had been aboard *Agamemnon* for over three years, and during that time he had experienced with her every kind of weather that the unpredictable Mediterranean could unleash. The paint-blistering heat of summer calms, the winds of the Levant and the sand-laden Sirocco, the howling gales off Corsica and the freezing winter squalls off Toulon, all had left their scars on the Homeric *Agamemnon*. Her ground tier was giving way and not an ounce of paint had been sent on board for many months. The last rope sent to Nelson had been an insult: 'without exception the worst I ever saw. The twice-laid we make on board is far preferable; indeed, I never saw any so bad in my life.' She might have stood another month without a refit but never another winter. 'A tub floating on water' was Nelson's description of her when on 13 June 1796 his broad pennant was transferred to the 74-gun *Captain* at anchor in San Fiorenza Bay. As he stood on the quarterdeck with his new first lieutenant Mr Edward Berry by his side, he watched the *Agamemnon* until the grand old ship faded slowly from view over the horizon.

Towards an alien sea with hostile ports

Bonaparte had led his ragged and famished troops in 1796 through the passes of the Alps into the smiling, fertile land of Italy. He initiated his campaign against the Austrians there in mid-April in a series of battles won against the odds. He fought by new rules, marching at night, fighting in the rain and even on Sundays, gambling boldly and baffling the opposing generals. Victory followed victory as he conquered the broad base of the Italian peninsula: Montenotte, Dego, Lodi, Castiglione, Arcola, Rivoli, Mantua. At Arcola there was a wooden bridge blocked by the Austrian rear guard. Napoleon rode into the centre of the fighting, personally aimed twenty-four cannon, then with a stirring speech sent a column of grenadiers charging across the bridge. The Austrians broke and fled. This was the battle that established Napoleon's reputation with his troops and they dubbed him *le petit caporal*, to distinguish him from the usual generals who rarely fought alongside their men. By showing his courage and by winning each battle in turn, he bound his men to him as Nelson did.

In a matter of months, Napoleon had driven the Austrians out of Italy to within sight of Vienna. As he conquered, he sent back to Paris cargoes of treasure: Caravaggios, Botticellis, Bellinis, and Tintorettos, even the 'Mona Lisa' and the four bronze horses from above the portico of the Basilica of San Marco in Venice.

Livorno fell in July and Genoa was closed to the British. Seeing that Corsica would become untenable, Nelson was dispatched to take Elba. The island's harbours of Porto Ferraio and Porto Azzurro were reasonable alternatives to those lost to the French forces. Nelson thought that 'for its size' Porto Ferraio was 'the most complete harbour of the world.'

By autumn, Spain and Holland had joined France in alliance against Britain, and in December, the British government reluctantly took the decision to evacuate the fleet entirely from the Mediterranean. All Britain's hard-won possessions there were given up, except for Gibraltar which stood a lonely sentinel at the entrance to what had now become an alien sea with hostile ports.

NOTES

1. Admiralty: Masters' Logs (ADM 51): ADM 51/1104, HMS *Agamemnon*.
2. Ibid.
3. Ibid.

4. Carola Oman, p 128.

5. Admiralty: Masters' Logs (ADM 51): ADM 51/1104, HMS *Agamemnon*.

6. Ernle Bradford, *Nelson: The Essential Hero* (London: Macmillan 1977) p 108.

7. Ibid, p 108.

8. Ibid, p 110. The hat kept at Westminster Abbey was made by James Lock, the famous hatter on St James' Street in London. Nelson is correctly depicted on his column in Trafalgar Square with no eye-patch.

9. Admiralty: Masters' Logs (ADM 51): ADM 51/1104, HMS *Agamemnon*.

10. Oliver Warner, *A Portrait of Lord Nelson* (London: Penguin Books, 1987), p 95.

11. Ernle Bradford, p 113.

12. Ibid, p 112.

13. Oliver Warner, p 98.

14. Carola Oman, p 139.

15. Ernle Bradford, p 116.

16. Ibid, p 116.

17. William Laird Clowes, *The Royal Navy, a History from Earliest Time to the Present* (London: Sampson Low, Marston, 1898), Vol 5, p 272.

18. Oliver Warner, pp 100–101.

19. Ibid, p 101.

20. Carola Oman, p 140.

21. Laird Clowes, Vol 5, p 272.

22. This grand old seaman, one of the greatest in the annals of British naval history, ended his days as Governor of Greenwich Hospital, a post he held for 20 years. He performed his duties there with the same efficiency and resolve as he had done everything else throughout his life.

23. Carola Oman, p 144.

24. Ibid, p 146.

25. William James, *The Naval History of Great Britain* (1822).

26. Ernle Bradford, p 119.

27. Carola Oman, p 150.

28. William Hoste, victor of the Battle of Lissa in 1811, became Admiral Sir William Hoste and for his valiant exploits was made a baronet and a Knight of the Bath in 1815.

29. Oliver Warner, p 103.

30. Carola Oman, p 151.

31. Ibid, p 154.

32. John Jervis, first Earl St Vincent, had run away to sea as a boy. After he was brought back, his father told him that if he wished to make the Navy his career, he would get nothing from him except a suit of clothes and £20, which the boy accepted. His naval career is one of the longest on record, 1735 to 1823 when he resigned. Nelson and Collingwood expressed admiration and gratitude to him for his leadership and George III referred to him as 'my old oak'. Jervis once said that 1782 had been a memorable year for him because in it he committed three great faults: 'I got knighted, I got married and I got into parliament'. But he had his softer side. When a child asked him what was the Star of the Order of the Bath he was wearing, and where he had found it, he said: 'I found it upon the sea; and if you become a sailor, and search diligently, perhaps you will find just such another'. Grant Uden & Richard Cooper, *A Dictionary of British Ships & Seamen* (London: Allen Lane, 1980), p 235.

33. Carola Oman, p 155.

CHAPTER 7

The Naval Mutinies of 1797

For a few terrible weeks till discipline was restored
England seemed doomed. With invasion threatening
her from every side it was the ultimate disaster.

Nelson[1]
SIR ARTHUR BRYANT

The reluctance of the British Board of Admiralty to improve the appalling conditions imposed upon its rank and file finally led to the unprecedented mutinies of 1797. Insubordination became so widespread that it imperiled national security.

At first the outbreaks were isolated events and occurred regardless of whether the captains of the ships involved had good or bad reputations. There were abundant practical reasons for discontent on the lower decks, but the naval authorities chose to believe that the insurrections stemmed from the epidemic of unrest rife in Europe at the time. Britain had not succumbed to the revolt against authority which had ravaged France but nevertheless conditions in the Navy fostered a climate of dissent that made its seamen as susceptible to insurrection as the most revolutionary Frenchman. By not recognising their own role in causing the problem, the Admiralty contributed to the escalation of events and fuelled the rebellion.

Trouble arose soon after the beginning of the war. In November 1794 mutiny broke out aboard HMS *Windsor Castle* at San Fiorenza. In this case, the crew simply stated their dislike of certain officers aboard the ship instead of pointing to poor conditions as reason for their action. Whether symptomatic or not, their discontent heralded the painful events to come.

Mutiny at Spithead

Barely a month later, while the *Culloden* was anchored at Spithead, her company mutinied and refused to proceed to sea. Acting with firmness, Captain Thomas Troubridge seized the ringleaders and brought them to trial by court-martial. Eight were sentenced to death. On 13 January, five of these were hanged from the yardarm of their ship with all hands present. The remaining three received His Majesty's pardon.

Discontent festered during 1796 and finally flared up the following year with a virulence that had never before been experienced. In February 1797, petitions from each of the ships of the line at Portsmouth were forwarded to Lord Howe at the Admiralty. No attention was paid to them. In early March,

HMS *Queen Charlotte*, flagship of the Channel Fleet, on board which the
Spithead Mutiny broke out on 15 April 1797. She is shown here at a review
of the fleet at Spithead in 1790. (National Maritime Museum, London)

the Channel Fleet put to sea for a cruise. On their return to port, finding their
petitions had been ignored, the seamen began to correspond among themselves. Throughout the fleet a general agreement was reached that no ship
should weigh anchor while the seamen's grievances remained unresolved. The
first test came on 15 April. Admiral Lord Bridport, commander of the Channel Fleet, ordered his ships to prepare for sea. On being notified, the crew of
the *Queen Charlotte* ran up the shrouds. They gave three cheers, the signal for
mutiny, and were answered in a similar manner by the crew of every other
ship.[2] Attempts were made to persuade the men to return to their duties, but
all was in vain. The next day, two delegates selected from each ship met in the
admiral's cabin on the *Queen Charlotte*. The delegates arrived at an agreement
and every man in the fleet was solemnly sworn to adhere to the cause.
Unpopular officers were set on shore, and nooses were reeved at the fore-
yardarm of each vessel to show the mutineers' determination to proceed or die
in the attempt.

On 21 April, a committee of the Board of Admiralty, headed by Vice
Admiral Sir Alan Gardner, was rowed out to the *Queen Charlotte* to interview

the delegates. The seamen informed the committee that no conclusive arrangement would be accepted unless it were duly sanctioned by Parliament and the King, and accompanied by a general pardon. Sir Alan Gardner lost his temper. Grabbing hold of one of the delegates, he declared that this man and all his associates, together with every fifth seaman throughout the fleet, would be hanged. After this provocative action the Vice Admiral barely escaped with his life. When the delegates returned to their ships and reported what had taken place it was decided that a council of leaders of the insurrection would convene aboard the *Royal George*. At the appointed time, those wishing to attend would hoist the red flag of mutiny on their ships.

Frustrated by the conduct of the fleet under his command, Lord Bridport struck his flag and stated he had no intention of ever hoisting it again. In the meantime, the mutineers took desperate measures. They loaded every gun in the fleet, confined all remaining officers to their respective ships, ordered watches on board as if the fleet were at sea, and despatched an explanatory letter to the Admiralty. On 23 April, a more confident Lord Bridport rehoisted his flag on the *Royal George*, and addressing his ship's company from the quarterdeck he informed the mutineers that he had with him the King's pardon for the offenders and that a redress of all their grievances had been granted.

The seamen's complaints, set out in their petition, included the following points:

1. Wages had not been raised since the time of Charles II (1630–1685), when the necessities of life were at least 30 per cent cheaper. Wages of the army had been increased but not those of the navy.
2. Provisions were inferior and served out short of weight. In port, vegetables should be issued and flour should not be substituted for fresh beef, as too often had been the custom.
3. The sick were inadequately treated and any luxuries intended for them were embezzled.
4. Insufficient shore leave was granted when a ship reached harbour.
5. Men wounded in action were deprived of their wages, pending either their cure or discharge.

The commissioners of the Admiralty finally conceded most of these points. Wages were raised; it was promised that the correct weight of provisions would be issued in future at the rate of 16 ounces to the pound; and payment of full wages would be granted to the wounded. A full pardon was promised to every man who, within the hour of being notified of their Lordships' resolution, returned to his duties and ceased all communication with the ringleaders of the mutiny.

These concessions went to the mutineers' heads, and not content with what they had gained, they demanded more. This is the closing statement of their response:

We beg to remind your Lordships that it is a firm resolution that, until the flour in port be removed, the vegetables and pensions augmented, the grievances of private ships redressed, an Act passed, and his Majesty's most gracious pardon for the fleet now lying at Spithead granted, the fleet will not lift an anchor; and this is the total and final answer.

Due perhaps to pride and to wishful thinking, the Board of Admiralty did not take the threat seriously. Content with proclaiming the pardon of the mutineers they declared that the unpleasantness was over.

On 7 May, Lord Bridport (whom the Spithead mutineers would later call their 'father and friend') signalled from the *Royal George* to weigh anchor and put to sea, but not a single ship obeyed. The seamen, believing that the lack of reply to their letter meant rejection and disdain, resolved to hold another meeting, this time on board the *London*. But when their boats rowed alongside, Vice Admiral Colpoys, who was in command of the *London*, refused to allow them on board. He declared that if they persisted, he would order the marines to fire. The delegates did persist, and a scuffle ensued in which one mutineer fired and wounded a marine. The First Lieutenant ordered the marines to fire, and five seamen, including two delegates, were killed. Active mutiny followed on board the *London* as its infuriated crew overran the ship, obliging the officers and marines to surrender. The seamen had every intention of hanging the First Lieutenant but Vice Admiral Colpoys persuaded them that the officer had acted on specific instructions from the Admiralty. All the officers were confined to their cabins. Those that were strict disciplinarians were sent ashore, and the marines were made prisoners. Similar violence broke out on other ships.

The revolt continued until the middle of May when Lord Howe, armed with plenary powers, arrived from London. He brought an Act of Parliament passed in accordance with the seamen's demands and a new proclamation of pardon for all men who returned to their duties. The Act, the proclamation, and Lord Howe's diplomacy restored order. On 15 May 1797, the mutiny ceased, and on the following day, the Channel Fleet put to sea.[3]

Mutiny at the Nore and in the North Sea

Barely a day or two after the fleet had sailed, mutiny again broke out, this time in the ships at the Nore[4] and on those in the North Sea. As before, the mutineers chose two delegates from each ship and elected a committee of twelve to manage the affairs of each vessel. In addition they appointed as their president a man named Richard Parker, a bluejacket on HMS *Sandwich*.[5]

The men at Spithead pointed out that most of Parker's demands had already been met by their own settlement, but Parker pushed ahead. On 20 May, he sent Vice Admiral Charles Buckner, commander-in-chief at the Nore, a statement of demands (see Appendix 3), which Buckner in turn forwarded to the Admiralty. Two days later the authorities replied,

A contemporary illustration showing Richard Parker, leader of the Nore mutiny, handing the sailors' list of grievances to Vice Admiral Buckner aboard HMS *Sandwich*. After the collapse of the mutiny, Parker was court-martialled and hanged from the topgallant yardarm of the same ship. (National Maritime Museum, London)

RICHARD PARKER,
President of the Committee of Delegates, tendering the List of Grievances, to Vice Admiral Buckner, on Board the Sandwich at the Nore .

refusing some of the demands but promising forgiveness to any men who returned to duty.

Vice Admiral Buckner personally delivered the answer to the delegates, allowing them ten minutes to make up their minds. Instead of submitting, the mutineers rowed to the harbour in their ships' boats and commandeered all the gunboats lying at anchor. They sailed these small, heavily-armed vessels to the Nore, and as they passed the fort at Sheerness, each in turn fired at it in defiance. On arrival at the Nore, the delegates informed Vice Admiral Buckner 'that nothing could be settled until three of the Board of Admiralty came down to Sheerness.' The mutineers added a further insult by striking Buckner's flag on board the *Sandwich*, Parker's headquarters, and hoisting instead the red flag of mutiny. Finally, they obliged every ship lying near Sheerness to sail to the Nore, where they concentrated their forces.[6]

The delegates adopted the habit of landing daily at Sheerness to hold meetings. They drew attention to themselves by parading on the wharves with flags and with music. The arrival of Lord Keith and General Sir Charles Grey, who had orders to enforce naval and military measures of repression, soon put a stop to the ribald behaviour. In future, the mutineers visited the shore at their peril.[7] Towards the end of May, Richard Parker again refused a conditional pardon by the Admiralty.

Mutiny on the Agamemnon

After her adventures with Nelson in the Mediterranean, the *Agamemnon*, sadly in need of repair, had been completely refitted from the bottom up at Chatham. Entering active service again, she was ordered to join Admiral Duncan's squadron off Yarmouth, which was keeping watch on the coast of Holland.

After dinner on the evening of the ship's arrival on station, the men refused to answer the call of the boatswain's mate. Fourth Lieutenant Brenton reported the sequence of events in a letter he wrote home:

> We went forward on the lower deck, and found the men had made a barricade of hammocks from one side of the ship to the other, just before the fore hatchway, and had left an embrasure on each side, through which they had pointed two 24-pounders; these they had loaded, and threatened to fire in case of resistance on the part of the officers. The captain spoke to them but, being treated with much contempt, returned to the quarter-deck. A few minutes after a number of people came up; some seized the wheel, while others rounded the weather braces and wore the ship, passing under the stern of the *Venerable*. The admiral made our signal to come to the wind on the larboard tack, the same as he was on himself. We answered with what was then called the signal of inability, being a flag half white and red over half blue and yellow, both horizontally divided. When the sails were trimmed on the starboard tack, and the course had been shaped by the delegates for Yarmouth roads, the captain went to his dinner with the officers, whom he had, according to the usual custom, previously invited, leaving me in charge of the deck, though, without the smallest authority, if such an anomaly can be conceived. About half-past three, Axle, the master-at-arms, came to me, and openly, in the presence of others, said, "Mr. Brenton, you have given the ship away; the best part of the men and all the marines are in your favour." I replied that I could not act by myself; that the captain had decided, and I feared there was no remedy. I, however, went into the cabin, and in a very clear and distinct manner told Captain Fancourt what the master-at-arms had said, and added my firm conviction that he was right, advising immediate measures to retake the ship and join the admiral. His answer I shall never forget. "Mr. Brenton, if we call out the marines some of the men will be shot, and I could not bear to see them lying in convulsions on the deck; no, no, a little patience and we shall all hail unanimity again." I quitted the cabin and walked the deck until my watch was out, too much irritated to say a word more.
>
> On the following morning we reached Yarmouth roads, and joined three other ships, each having a red flag flying at her foretopgallant masthead; the *Agamemnon* hoisted one also, which was called by the delegates the flag of defiance. During the whole of this time the officers kept charge of their watches, the seamen obeying them in any order for the safety of the ship, but no farther. A meeting of the delegates was immediately called, at which it was decided that the *Agamemnon* and [her sister ship] *Ardent*, of 64 guns, and the *Leopard* and *Isis*, of 50 guns, would go to the Nore, to augment the number of ships at that anchorage in a state little short of open rebellion, but not with any view to assisting them or being assisted by the enemies of their country; and it is

certain that, had these put to sea, we should have gone in pursuit of them with the same zeal and loyalty as at the beginning of the war.[8]

By the end of May, Admiral Duncan had been deserted by all his vessels except the *Adamant* of 50 guns and his own flagship, the *Venerable*. Mutiny did break out on the *Venerable*, but due to his strength of character and determination Duncan succeeded in repressing it. In spite of his isolation, he managed to keep on station until reinforcements finally arrived.

On 6 June, after the mutineers had been joined by the last deserting vessels from Admiral Duncan's fleet, their total force had risen to twelve ships of the line together with two ships of 50 guns, six frigates, and six smaller craft.[9] That same day two Acts of Parliament were hastily introduced and passed. One was to bring about 'the better prevention and punishment of those enticing others to mutiny and disobedience', and the other granted ample powers for suppressing the mutiny. The fate of the rebellion was sealed.

The situation of the mutineers became desperate. Success was hopeless, punishment was almost certain, and flight with or without the ships seemed the sole chance of saving their skins. In retrospect, it is astonishing that the fleet did not desert to France. Instead, they tried to force the authorities to give in to their demands. They moored the *Standard*, *Brilliant*, *Inspector*, and

Admiral Duncan, commander of the squadron to which *Agamemnon* was attached during the 1797 mutinies. The *Agamemnon* was in the hands of mutineers until 13 June 1797, but the majority of the crew had opposed the insurrection and no-one from the ship was hanged after the ship surrendered. (National Maritime Museum, London)

Swan across the entrance to the Thames and allowed no vessels to pass them without a signed order from Richard Parker. Then they turned pirates, helping themselves to provisions and water from merchant vessels, carrying off sheep from the Isle of Grain, and plundering the storeship *Grampus*, recently fitted out for service in the West Indies.

The final days

The two emergency Acts of Parliament enabled the authorities to crush the mutiny without regard to cost. New batteries were erected on both sides of the Thames and the buoys at its mouth were removed. Furnaces for heating shot were prepared at various points, and three ships of the line and several gunboats under the command of Commodore Sir Erasmus Gower were directed to attack the insurgents. Realising that the end was near, the mutineers attempted to enter into negotiations by approaching the captain of the *Monmouth*. Their overtures were rejected. Preparations to reduce them by force were almost complete on 9 June, when the mutinous vessels began to abandon their anchorage. The first two to escape from the fleet were the *Repulse* and the *Leopard*. The *Repulse* grounded and was fired on by the mutineers. Several of her men were killed. The *Leopard* entered the Thames. The following night the *Ardent* made off, though she was fired at and also lost several of her men. As traffic was reopened on the Thames the following day, more vessels hauled down the red flag. Early on 13 June, the *Agamemnon* and her sister ship the *Nassau*, after some bloody struggles aboard, shipped their anchors, hoisted their sails, and sailed into Sheerness to surrender. They were immediately sent to Gravesend under guard. The majority of the *Agamemnon*'s crew, as well as the marines, had not been in favour of the mutiny. They had been forced to conform by the twelve desperate delegates. As the *Agamemnon* was considered untrustworthy by Richard Parker, she had had the guns of three other line-of-battle ships trained on her while she was anchored at the Nore to make certain she did not 'blackleg'.[10] In the proceedings that followed, all thirteen of the *Agamemnon*'s men who were tried were pardoned.

On the same day that the *Agamemnon* turned herself in at Sheerness, the majority of the rebels, including the crew of Parker's ship the *Sandwich*, announced they would surrender if they were granted a general pardon. Soon after this the *Sandwich* acknowledged defeat and moored under the guns of Sheerness. Vice Admiral Buckner sent a boat full of soldiers to board her. Richard Parker, the ringleader, was arrested together with a man named Davis who had acted as his flag captain and about thirty of the delegates. One of them, named Wallace, committed suicide. Parker's trial by court-martial aboard the *Sandwich* lasted several days. He was, of course, sentenced to death.

The *Agamemnon* was brought from Gravesend to Sheerness to witness the hangings, as were all the other scattered ships of the fleet. Parker was hanged from the topgallant yardarm of the *Sandwich* on 29 June. It is said that he

In the first major defection from the Nore Mutiny, the crew of HMS *Clyde*
(38), accepting the offer of a pardon that Parker had refused, sailed their ship
into Sheerness on the night of 31 May 1797. Admiral Buckner, who had
been forced to strike his flag in HMS *Sandwich*, made her his flagship after she
escaped from the mutinous fleet. (National Maritime Museum, London)

acknowledged the justice of his sentence. Many other mutineers were executed; several were flogged from ship to ship; some were imprisoned in the
Marshalsea prison and a number remained under sentence on board the prison
ship *Eagle*.

The mutineers retrieved their honour off Camperdown shortly afterwards
in a handsome victory over Holland, now a satellite of France. At the petition
of Admiral Duncan, who commanded the British fleet during the battle, the
King was pleased to grant his pardon to the surviving mutineers.[11]

The aftermath

The mutinies did not cease with the failure of the outbreak at the Nore and
the execution of Richard Parker. Further incidents occurred in the 80-gun
Pompée; the 100-gun *Sovereign*; the 74-gun *Saturn*; the 74-gun *Mars*; the 74-
gun *Marlborough*; the 74-gun *Bedford*; the 64-gun *Ardent*; the storeship
Grampus; the 36-gun frigate *Beaulieu*; the frigates *Phoenix* and *Hermione*, as well

as the 16-gun *Calypso* and a few other vessels. The whole summer of 1797 was taken up with courts-martial. Many offenders were condemned to death and many more received floggings so severe as to be barely preferable to the death sentence.

Three interesting descriptions of these events are given here:

The *Beaulieu* was a 36-gun frigate launched at Buckler's Hard in 1790. Her crew took part in the aftermath of the mutiny in the Nore. The incident is described in a letter written by one of her officers, Mr John Burn:

Beaulieu in the Downs
June 26th 1797

My dear Father
In consequence of order as it was supposed being restored on board the *Beaulieu* — rejoined according to order from the Admiralty the 24th inst a Captain Fayerman now commands the ship — I had not been on board above five hours when they mutinously demanded the release of two men from Irons who had been confined for improper conduct — with this improper demand I absolutely refused to comply — the Captain being on shore I immediately assembled the officers who readily agreed with me that should they persist — force should be used — about nine at night they assembled and were proceeding to liberate their friends. I immediately armed the officers and as many marines as from situation could join. I expostulated with them on the impropriety of their conduct and exhorted them to go quietly to bed and that I was determin'd to put the Fiend to death that attempted to approach near the Prisoners. They mouthed contempt — one ran with a Cutlass in his hand rushed forward and was instantly shot through the Neck by the Purser and through the body by me — this checked them for a moment when they made a second attempt and had so far succeeded as to run one of the sentinels through and seize some cutlasses. We fired again when two dropp't — they fled to the forecastle and pointed the Guns aft but before they could get them primed we attacked them so close that they fled all but one Villain who told us to shoot and be damned. I put a ball through his shoulder which quieted him — on our return to the Quarter Deck one of them who is now in Irons, hid himself behind a gun and aimed a blow at me with a Cutlass which brought me down but luckily a piece of wood turned the cutlass and the flat of it only struck me across the belly — so that I am only a little blue without being lame. At half-past ten they were entirely subdued and 13 of the Principals put in Irons. Thirteen were wounded on both sides, four of the Mutineers desperately so — the first who had the two balls lodged in him only died this morning — the others cannot live long — but above all I am concerned for the poor Sentinel who cannot live — The Officers all behaved nobly as did the Marines
Remember me to all and believe me
Yours J Burn[12]

The *Marlborough* had been part of the mutiny at Spithead. Subsequently, while lying in Bantry Bay in southwestern Ireland, she had given plenty of trouble to her officers. Despatched to join the Mediterranean fleet commanded by Admiral John Jervis (created Earl St Vincent after his victory over the Spanish fleet five months before) some of her crew again became mutinous. Aware of her rebellious state, the commander-in-chief ordered her to anchor between the lines of the fleet. Immediately upon arrival, her captain applied to Admiral Jervis for a court-martial to try the leader of the insurrection. Tucker, in his *Memories of St Vincent*, relates the events that followed:

A court-martial on the principal mutineers was immediately assembled, and one was no sooner sentenced to die than the Commander-in-Chief ordered him to be executed on the following morning, 'and by the crew of the *Marlborough* alone, no part of the boats' crews from the other ships, as had been usual on similar occasions, to assist in the punishment' — his Lordship's invariable order on the execution of mutineers. On the receipt of the necessary commands for this execution, captain of the *Marlborough*, Captain Ellison, waited upon the Commander-in-Chief, and, reminding his lordship that a determination that their shipmates should not suffer capital punishment had been the very cause of the ship's company mutiny, expressed his conviction that the *Marlborough*'s crew would never permit the man to be hanged on board that ship.

Receiving the Captain on the *Ville de Paris*'s quarter-deck, before the officers and ship's company, hearkening in breathless silence to what passed, and standing with his hat in his hand over his head, as was his Lordship's invariable custom during the whole time that any person, whatever were his rank, even a common seaman, addressed him on service, Lord St Vincent listened very attentively till the Captain ceased to speak; and then, after a pause, replied: 'What; do you mean to tell me, Captain Ellison, that you cannot command his Majesty's ship the *Marlborough*? For, if that is the case, sir, I will immediately send on board an officer who can.'

The Captain then requested that, at all events, the boats' crews from the rest of the fleet might, as always had been customary in the service, on executions, attend at this also, to haul the man up; for he really did not expect the *Marlborough* would do it. Lord St Vincent sternly answered: 'Captain Ellison; you are an old officer, sir; have served long, suffered severely in the service, and have lost an arm in action; and I should be very sorry that any advantage should be now taken of your advanced years. That man shall be hanged, at eight o'clock to-morrow morning, and by his own ship's company; for not a hand from any other ship in the fleet shall touch the rope. You will now return on board, sir; and, lest you should not prove able to command your ship, an officer will be at hand to you who can'.

Without another word Captain Ellison instantly retired. After he had reached his ship, he received orders to cause her guns to be housed and secured, and that at daybreak in the morning her ports should be lowered. A general order was then issued to the fleet for all launches to rendezvous under the *Prince* at seven o'clock on the following morning, armed with carronades and twelve rounds of ammunition for service; each launch to be commanded by a Lieutenant, having an expert and trusty gunner's mate and four quarter-gunners, exclusive of the launch's crew; the whole to be under the command of Captain Campbell, of the *Blenheim*. The written orders to the Captain will appear in their place. On presenting them, Lord St Vincent said, 'he was to attend the execution, and, if any symptoms of mutiny appeared in the *Marlborough*, any attempt to open her

Admiral John Jervis, 1st Earl St Vincent, whose enforcement of discipline in his command made the Mediterranean Fleet a byword for severity in the Royal Navy, as the crew of HMS *Marlborough* found out. (National Maritime Museum, London)

ports, or any resistance to the hanging of the prisoner, he was to proceed close touching the ship, and to fire into her, and to continue to fire until all mutiny or resistance should cease; and that, should it become absolutely necessary, he should even sink the ship in face of the fleet.'

Accordingly, at seven the next morning, all the launches, thus armed, proceeded from the *Prince* to the *Blenheim*, and thence, Captain Campbell having assumed the command, to the *Marlborough*. Having lain on his oars a short time alongside, the Captain formed his force in a line athwart her bows, at rather less than pistol-shot distance off; and then he ordered the tompions to be taken out of the carronades, and to load.

At half-past seven, the hands throughout the fleet having turned up to witness punishment, the eyes of all were bent upon a powerfully armed boat as it quitted the flag ship; every one knowing that there went the provost-marshal conducting his prisoner to the *Marlborough* for execution. The crisis was come; now was to be seen whether the *Marlborough*'s crew would hang one of their own men.

The ship being in the centre between the two lines of the fleet, the boat was soon alongside, and the man was speedily placed on the cathead and haltered. A few awful minutes of universal silence followed, which was at last broken by the watch-bells of the fleet striking eight o'clock. Instantly the flagship's gun fired, and, at the sound, the man was lifted well up; but then, and visibly to all, he dropped back again at the sound, and the sensation throughout the fleet was intense. For, at this dreadful moment, when the eyes of every man in every ship were straining upon this execution, as the decisive struggle between authority and mutiny, as if it were destined that the whole fleet should see the hesitating unwillingness of the *Marlborough*'s crew to hang their rebel, and the efficacy of the means taken to enforce obedience, by an accident on board the ship the men at the yard-rope unintentionally let it slip, and the turn of the balance seemed calamitously lost; but then they hauled him up to the yard-arm with a run, the law was satisfied, and, said Lord St Vincent at the moment, perhaps one of the greatest of his life, 'Discipline is preserved, sir.'

When the sentence was executed, and not any disturbance appeared, that it might be again made perceptible to all the fleet that abundant force had been provided to overpower any resistance which a line-of-battle-ship could offer, Captain Campbell broke his line, and, rowing down, placed his launches as close alongside the *Marlborough* as their oars could permit; and then, re-forming them, resumed his station across her bows, continuing there until, the time for the body's hanging having expired, it was taken down, sewed up as usual in its own hammock with a shot, and carried in one of the *Marlborough*'s boats to half a mile from the ship, and sunk; upon which Captain Campbell withdrew his force, and the *Marlborough*'s signal was made to take her station in the line . . . The dreadful sentence was again and again inflicted, and, in all cases of insubordination, the crews were invariably the executioners of their own rebels; but never again was the power of the law doubted by anyone.[13]

The *Hermione*, a frigate of 32 guns, was commanded by a courageous but tyrannical officer named Captain Hugh Pigot. Part of his crew mutinied in the night while sailing off Jamaica. They imprisoned those seamen who were not parties to their plot, and savagely murdered Captain Pigot, two lieutenants, the purser, the surgeon, the captain's clerk, a midshipman, the boatswain and a lieutenant of the Marines, disfiguring their dead bodies. To complete their crime, they sailed the ship to La Guayra and handed her over to the Spaniards. When they were recaptured by Captain Edward Hamilton of the *Surprise*, many of these mutineers were tried and hanged for their villainy.

For several years after, mutiny was fairly common in the Royal Navy, though it never again reached the height attained in 1797. In September 1798 nineteen seamen of the *Defence* were sentenced to death and six to flogging and imprisonment. In October eight seamen of the *Glory* were sentenced to death, one man to 200 lashes and two men to 100 lashes each. These men were also docked of their pay and sentenced to 12 months' solitary confinement.

As the seaman's lot gradually improved cases of this kind became fewer. However, the main deterrent to insubordination in the Royal Navy remained fear of iron-fisted discipline and severe punishment for the slightest indications of mutiny. The officers of the Royal Navy had become hypersensitive, and for many years they lived in dread of a recurrence of the events of Spithead and the Nore, and it was a long time before the naval system was able to relax. During 1839, 42 years after these events took place, 2,007 men were flogged in the Navy. Six years later the number dropped to 860, a sign that flogging was at last on its way out. In 1866 a new Naval Discipline Act limited the

The recapture of HMS *Hermione*, the frigate handed over by her
mutinous crew to the Spanish in La Guayra, Puerto Rico, by boats from
HMS *Surprise* in 1799. Her crew were relentlessly pursued by the Royal
Navy and in all twenty-four of them were hanged. (National Maritime
Museum, London)

punishment to forty-eight lashes. Oddly enough, flogging has not been formally abolished to this day, although it has been 'suspended' first in peace
time, and then in time of war.[14]

NOTES

1. Sir Arthur Bryant, *Nelson* (London: Collins, 1970), p 27.
2. The ships involved in the mutiny of 15 April were: *Royal George, Queen Charlotte, Royal
   Sovereign, London, Glory, Duke, Mars, Marlborough, Ramillies, Robust, Impétueux, Defence,
   Pompée, Minotaur* and *Defiance.*
3. Clowes, Vol 4, p 172.
4. The Nore is a sand-bank in the Thames estuary lying off the approach to the River
   Medway. It was also the name given to the area of naval command of ships based on

Chatham and Sheerness that used the sand-bank as an anchorage. Joseph Conrad, in *The Mirror of the Sea* (1906) wrote: 'The Nore sand remains covered at low-water, and never seen by human eye; but the Nore is a name to conjure with visions of historical events, of battles, of fleets, of mutinies, of watch and ward kept upon the great throbbing heart of the State.'

5. Having been imprisoned for debt, Richard Parker obtained his release by volunteering for service in the Navy as a midshipman. It is hard to understand why he was in the service at the time of the mutiny as he had been court-martialled, reduced for misbehaviour in 1793 and discharged from the service as insane in 1794.

6. Among these ships was the frigate *San Fiorenzo*, which had been fitted to convey the Princess of Württemburg to Germany. Her crew was loyal and although she was ordered to anchor close under the stern of the *Sandwich* her captain was able, a few days later, to sail her unmolested into Harwich.

7. Laird Clowes, Vol 4, p 173.

8. A J Holland, *Buckler's Hard, A Rural Shipbuilding Centre* (Emsworth, Hampshire: Kenneth Mason, 1985), p 128.

9. The total force of ships controlled by the mutineers at that point were: *Sandwich*, 90 guns; *Montagu*, 74; *Agamemnon*, 64; *Ardent*, 64; *Inflexible*, 64; *Monmouth*, 64; *Director*, 64; *Nassau*, 64; *Repulse*, 64; *Belliqueux*, 64; *Standard*, 64; *Lion*, 64; *Leopard*, 50; *Isis*, 50; *Terpsichore*, 32; *Iris*, 32; *Brilliant*, 28; *Vestal*, 28; *Proserpine*, 28; *Champion*, 20; *Pylades*, 16; *Inspector*, 16; *Swan*, 16; *Comet*, fireship; *Grampus*, storeship and *Serapis*, storeship.

10. A J Holland, p 128.

11. Laird Clowes, Vol 4, p 176.

12. Letter addressed to Alexander Burn, Bonnington, North Berwick. A J Holland, p 129.

13. Jedediah Stevens Tucker, *Memoirs of Admiral the Right Honourable the Earl of Vincent*, (London: R Bentley, 1844), Vol 2, p 303.

14. Grant Uden & Richard Cooper, *A Dictionary of British Ships and Seamen* (London: Allen Lane, 1980), p 162.

CHAPTER 8

The Battle of Copenhagen 1801

Nothing except a battle lost can be half so
melancholy as a battle won.

WELLINGTON

With trouble brewing from within and with the fortunes of war stacked against her, Britain was in a difficult position. Without allies apart from Portugal, she stood alone. At home, the government took repressive measures against those who were sympathetic to the French revolutionaries and who professed the republican philosophy. Distinguished writers were prosecuted for treason, although juries would not convict them. The slightest criticism of the constitution became potential grounds for treason.

Ireland was on the verge of open rebellion. Largely Catholic but governed by a Protestant parliament since 1782, Ireland was a puppet of British authority. The eloquent Irish leader, Henry Grattan, who had tried so hard to win a semblance of freedom for his countrymen, urged that Catholics be given both the vote and the right to sit in Parliament and hold office. While the right to vote was granted, seats in Parliament were denied. The country simmered with discontent.

The European scene

On the continent the French army was triumphant. Having conquered Northern Italy, Bonaparte prepared to strike at Austria through the Alpine passes. Proving that his political skills matched his military talents, he signed the Preliminaries of Leoben with Austria, which were later formalised as the treaty of Campo Formio. The Republic of Venice became a province of Austria. The small principalities of Northern Italy, including Milan and Piedmont, were moulded by force into a new Cisalpine Republic. After the annexation of Belgium there was some speculation as to where France would prevail next. One option was to move against England by way of Ireland, but Napoleon felt his destiny lay in a broader field. He put his plan to the Directory: attack Britain's commercial lifeline to the east starting with Malta and Egypt as a preliminary to his vaster scheme of conquering Constantinople, India and, like Alexander the Great, all of Asia.

Napoleon's invasion of Egypt and the Battle of the Nile

In May 1798 detailed reports of massive military and naval preparations at Toulon reached Nelson, who had recently lost his right arm in a failed attack on Tenerife. Nelson had been chosen by Lord St Vincent to command the fleet in the Mediterranean with orders to proceed 'in quest of the Armament preparing by the enemy at Toulon and Genoa . . . On falling in with the said Armament, or any part thereof, you are to use your utmost endeavours to take, sink, burn or destroy it.'

In June 1798 Napoleon sailed for Egypt. Nelson sailed after him in hot pursuit. With a head start over the British fleet of only three days, Bonaparte landed 40,000 men in Alexandria on 1 July. Having moored his transports snugly under the guns of Alexandria and his battleships 15 miles to the east in a supposedly impregnable position in the bay of Aboukir (an anchorage chosen by his naval commander Admiral de Brueys), Napoleon marched on Cairo. Among his entourage were archaeologists, scientists, lawyers, administrators and specialists in almost every field. In 15 days he would be twenty-nine years old and with a highly developed sense of history, speaking from the saddle before facing the enemy he refered to the distant pyramids as he told his men: 'Soldiers, from the tops of these monuments, forty centuries look down!'

The ensuing battle at Chebreiss was fought against the Mameluke cavalry, who although gorgeously enrobed, were armed in mediaeval fashion with sabres and lances. It was a massacre. Thousands of Mamelukes died. The French lost thirty men.

It was not until after this victory and his triumphant entry into Cairo that Napoleon felt secure enough to send a message to Admiral de Brueys ordering him to withdraw his ships to Corfu. Until then he had felt it wise to keep the fleet at hand. The messenger was ambushed and killed as he rode through the desert night with Napoleon's letter in his pouch. Unaware of any danger the French fleet remained snugly at anchor in Aboukir Bay.

During the afternoon of 1 August the masthead lookout of HMS *Zealous* called down to the deck that he had sighted the topmasts of the French fleet. The message was immediately signalled to Nelson aboard the *Vanguard*.[1] Nelson, who was pacing the quarterdeck, exclaimed with a smile and a wry chuckle to Edward Berry his flag captain (and later a member of his Band of Brothers): 'Before this time tomorrow, I shall have gained a Peerage, or Westminster Abbey.'[2]

De Brueys had anchored his thirteen ships in a line nearly two miles long. There were nine of 74 guns, three of 80 guns and in the centre of the line was his own flagship *L'Orient* of 120 guns. Pointing west, they lay close together in shallow water with dangerous shoals to port. De Brueys was convinced that even Nelson would not risk sailing his ships between the shoals and the French line. But the French admiral was wrong. Once Nelson had made the signal for close action his captains needed no further orders.

Towards evening the *Zealous*, followed by the *Goliath*, cautiously crept to landward of the French van. Captain Foley in the *Goliath* fired the opening broadside of the great battle a few minutes before sundown. Then five British ships stealthily passed to landward of the enemy, while Nelson led the rest of his fleet to seaward of the French line.

Many of the French sailors were on shore and the decks of their vessels were cluttered with gear. Admiral de Brueys had not even thought it necessary to keep the gun ports clear on the landward side as he believed it impregnable. By the time darkness had fallen total confusion had seized the French fleet. The British had hoisted four lanterns in a horizontal pattern from their mizzen-peaks to distinguish one another in the darkness. Then relentlessly and with mathematical precision they pounded the enemy with their broadsides. Ship after ship was disabled as the British passed down the French line.

While Nelson stood with Edward Berry on the quarterdeck of the *Vanguard* he was hit on the forehead above the blind eye by a piece of chainshot. It cut him to the bone and the blood and the flap of skin resulting from the injury temporarily blinded his good eye. He was carried by Berry down to the cockpit.

De Brueys suffered a worse fate. He had fought his flagship *L'Orient* gallantly throughout the action despite the fact that both his legs had been blown

The French flagship *L'Orient* explodes at the climax of the Battle of the Nile, 1 August 1798. Nelson's destruction of the French fleet at Aboukir Bay marooned Napoleon and his army in Egypt and fatally damaged his ambitions in the east. (National Maritime Museum, London)

off by a cannon ball. He ordered the ship's surgeon to apply tourniquets to the stumps to stem the haemorrhages and carried on conducting operations from an armchair he had had placed on his quarterdeck. A fire had started at the stern of the ship and as De Brueys sat giving orders for putting it out, a shot from the *Swiftsure* nearly cut him in two. His men attempted to carry him below but he refused and is said to have exclaimed: 'A French Admiral must die on his quarterdeck.' He was dead before his ship blew up under him. The explosion lit up the sky as red as the fires of hell and was heard 10 miles away by Napoleon's troops at Rosetta.

The five ships ahead of the *L'Orient* had already surrendered; others with their cables cut by shot and drifting helplessly, desperately attempted to avoid the inferno. Stunned men, many of whom were wounded, clung to wreckage in the water. Some went under, never to reappear, while others struggled to keep afloat, crying out for help. It was said that not more than seventy of the 400 or so men seen in the water before the explosion were rescued. In the silence of the morning hours three French ships ran ashore and surrendered. A fourth was burned by her officers. Of the great fleet that had conveyed Napoleon's army to Egypt only two ships of the line and two frigates were saved. Seeing all was lost their captains had cut their cables and stood for the open sea. The tired and spent British did not pursue them.

Having lost his fleet as well as some 5,000 men, Napoleon and his army were stranded in Egypt. His communications and supply lines with France were cut. Nevertheless, he carried on with his plan. At Jaffa he exhibited ruthlessness by killing 3,000 prisoners before retreating.

Return to Paris

During the spring of 1799 Napoleon seemed hopelessly marooned as Nelson's victory at the Nile had cut his communications with France. Not one to give in meekly, he thought of an alternative plan. He told Bourrienne that since Nelson blockaded the Mediterranean he would march along its edge: 'through Syria, to Damascus, Aleppo, to Constantinople! I shall over-throw the Ottoman Empire, found a great new Eastern dominion to assure my place in the records of posterity. It may be that I shall return to Paris through Adrianople, or even through Vienna, annihilating the house of Hapsburg en route.' Napoleon might have done this, had it not been for the stubborn resistance he encountered outside the walls of Acre, in Syria. The defence of Acre was conducted by Captain Sir William Sidney Smith who with Syrian troops and a force of English seamen eventually caused Napoleon to lift his costly blockade. He reluctantly returned to Cairo, arriving in time to put down an insurrection and to defeat a powerful Turkish invasion force near Alexandria.

On 18 August 1799 Napoleon entrusted his army to General Kleber and embarked for France. With him went some 500 men, as well as his personal staff which now included Roustam, a former Mameluke slave. This man would serve as his personal bodyguard and ride beside him in every battle for the next 16 years, stretching out at night to his full 6 feets and more in front of his master's door. 'Loyal until death', it was said of Roustam. Not, however, loyal into exile as was proved later.

Back in France, Napoleon's trip by carriage from the coast to Paris was one long triumph. Local citizens with torches in their hands lined the route to get a glimpse of him and to light his way to the capital.

First Consul

National events were moving quickly. The Napoleonic epic was mounting to the climax of the *coup d'état* from which Napoleon emerged holding the reins of power as First Consul. It was a source of intense irritation to him that since his departure for Egypt the Austrians had made steady advances in Italy. There he had gradually lost his earlier conquests to them one by one. 'My power depends on my glory and my glory on my victories', he told his friend Bourrienne. Crossing the Alps in a logistical manoeuvre as courageous and daring as Hannibal's 2,000 years before, he took charge of the army in Italy. On 16 June 1800 he resoundingly defeated the Austrians at Marengo. France

Bonaparte as First Consul, by Ingres. Although seemingly invincible on land in 1800, he was never able to overcome British sea power. (Musée des Beaux Artes, Liege)

was once again mistress of Europe. In one bold stroke Napoleon had shown the world that even if the British were masters of the sea, he was unmatched on land and that, he said, was where it counted.[3]

The Baltic controversy

Britain's insistence on boarding vessels to search for arms and other contraband goods and if need be seize them at sea, meant that she was now at loggerheads with the very countries she wished to keep as allies. The Danes had particular cause for complaint when the *Freja*, one of their frigates, and her convoy of merchant vessels had been fired on and captured by the British. In this instance war was averted by a hasty diplomatic settlement between the two countries whereby it was agreed that the *Freja* and her merchantmen would be repaired at British expense.

Just as the difficulty with Denmark seemed to be resolved, the demented Tsar Paul I of Russia entered the quarrel. Offended because the British had prevented him from annexing Malta, in a fit of pique he transferred his allegiance to France and placed an embargo on all British shipping in Russian ports. He then revived an old alliance hostile to Britain, the Armed Neutrality of the North; and induced Denmark, Sweden, Norway and Prussia to adhere to it. This treaty denied Britain access to the Baltic, the source of essential materials for shipbuilding such as timber, cordage and canvas. Napoleon naturally was delighted and declared that France was proud to be at peace with the Tsar, though there had been no time to sign a treaty officially.

The Tsar pressed on, with designs on India at the back of his mind. He now suggested to the First Consul that diplomatic pressure be brought to bear on Portugal and the United States of America to join the Alliance. The Danes then made a provocative move. Copying the Russians they recklessly placed an embargo on all British merchantmen in their ports, sent forces to Hamburg and declared the Elbe closed to British shipping. Britain struck back. William Pitt spoke in ringing tones to his opponents in the House of Commons: 'He [Mr Fox of the opposition] defies me to state in one sentence, what is the object of the war. I know not whether I can do it in one sentence, but in one word I can tell him that it is security; security against a danger, the greatest that ever threatened the world.'[4] Pitt decided to send a powerful fleet to the Baltic to bring the signatories of the Alliance to their senses and obtain the surrender of the Danish fleet, if necessary by bombarding Copenhagen.

The British fleet was put under the command of Admiral Sir Hyde Parker and Nelson was appointed second-in-command. The hero of the Nile, discredited for having abandoned his post in the Mediterranean to travel with the Hamiltons overland to England, had been subjected since his arrival there to outspoken disapproval, both socially and professionally, because of his affair with Emma. Little more than a month before, Emma had secretly given birth to his daughter, the survivor of twins, to be christened Horatia.

Sir Hyde Parker, a man of more than sixty, was one of the many who disapproved of Nelson's conduct. Nelson, on the other hand, thought Parker a prude as well as professionally slack. He had good reason since when he joined the fleet in Yarmouth Roads he found the elderly admiral living ashore with his new wife of eighteen, known as 'Batter Pudding' by the wags of the fleet. 'Consider how nice it must be laying in bed with a young wife, compared to a damned cold raw wind,' snapped Nelson, impatient to weigh anchor and be off, since he could not be snugly in bed with his own voluptuous Emma.

Moving the Fleet to battle positions

Entry in Captain Fancourt's log on HMS *Agamemnon*:

> Thursday 12th
> Bearing & distance at Noon Lowestoft N W by W 5 Leagues
>
> Do Wr [Ditto Weather] Empd accordingly
>
> AM Wr Modte & hazy At 2 unmoored Ship & hove to half a cable on the Best Bower at 5 hove short, up Top Gallant Yards quarter past 6 weighed & through St Nicholas Gatt under the Command of Admiral Sir Hyde Parker & Vice-Admiral Lord Nelson in Company with 23 Sail of the Line & 20 Sail Frigates, Bombs, & Gun Vessels at 8 shortened Sail & hove to at noon.[5]

The progress of the fleet was delayed by bad weather. It took six days to reach the Continent during which the North Sea lived up to its inhospitable winter reputation. As the fleet sailed northwards the dismal rainy weather gave way to snow and then ice. The *Agamemnon*'s log records fresh gales with snow in squalls, close reefed topsails, downed topgallants and yards with halyards breaking. At daylight on 19 March they sighted Scaw Lighthouse on the northernmost part of Jutland. On the evening of 20 March they anchored with 'the Small Bower in forty-five fathoms' in the Kattegat, 18 miles north of Hamlet's Elsinore. A British diplomatic envoy, Nicholas Vansittart, had been sent ahead to Copenhagen with an ultimatum that Denmark either withdraw from the Alliance or face the guns of the British fleet. Three days later the diplomat returned with the Danes' rejection of the offer. He reported feverish preparations for defence at Copenhagen.

Sir Hyde Parker conferred with Nelson aboard his flagship the *London*. 'Now we are sure of fighting, I am sent for,' Nelson wrote briefly to Emma. 'When it was a joke, I was kept in the background; tomorrow will, I hope, be a proud day for England.' Pacing up and down the flagship's stateroom before the great stern windows, Nelson listened to Vansittart's appraisement of the strength of the Danish defences. While Parker sat in gloomy silence, appalled by the picture of the Danish fleet moored bow to stern amongst floating batteries, all in a solid line before the capital, Nelson quietly and persuasively gave his reasons for attacking. Asking Vansittart how the Danish fleet was formed and learning that their most powerful ships were at the head of the line, as well as the formidable batteries of the Trekroner forts, he immediately proposed that the British fleet should sail down the Great Belt around Zealand and fall on the enemy from the rear. The element of surprise was all-important. 'Go by the Sound or by the Belt or anyhow,' he said, 'only lose not an hour.' As soon as he returned to his ship he put his ideas in writing, emphasising his strategy and showing how it could be done. On reading it Parker argued no more, though he wished that all could be resolved without action.

On 26 March, as soon as the wind allowed, the fleet was ordered to weigh anchor and with shortened sails moved to the entrance of the Sound. Even when the weather improved Parker delayed. He listened to pilots who magnified the dangers of the channel ahead and he even sent a messenger under a flag of truce to Elsinore (Helsingør) Castle to inquire if the governor of the fortress would oppose the passage of the British fleet. The answer was emphatic, that indeed he would. Due to head winds the fleet remained immobile off the entrance to the Sound. On 30 March the ships set sail to enter the dreaded Strait of Elsinore, only three miles wide and dominated on opposite sides by Danish and Swedish forts. Surprisingly, the passage proved easy. The Swedes held their fire while the Danish shot aimed from the imposing fortress of Cronenburg (Kronborg) splashed harmlessly short of the British ships. The entry in the *Agamemnon*'s log gives the sequence of events during the passage.[6]

> Monday 30th. March 1801
> At Single Anchor in Copenhagen Roads.
> PM Fresh Breezes & cloudy half past 2 weighed & made sail Fleet in Company half past 4 shortened Sail & came to in 19 Fathoms veered to ½ Cable.
> AM Do Wr half past 5 answered Signal to weigh Weighed & made Sail at 6 answered Signal to form Line quarter past 7 answered No.15 General [Signal] Cronburg Castle passing at 11 shortened Sail & came to in the Line of Battle with the Small Bower in 7 Fathoms veered to ½ a Cable Blowed overboard off the Poop a Spanish Ensign Jack clearing Ship for Action[7]

While clearing for battle, the *Agamemnon* had lost one of its own jacks, a Spanish ensign, which was part of a collection of different flags kept on British ships so that they could fly false colours if necessary. The loss had to be reported in the log, otherwise the flag would have to be paid for. Later on that day Nelson wrote to Emma:

> We this morning passed the fancied tremendous fortress of Cronenburg, mounted with 270 pieces of cannon. More powder and shot, I believe, never were thrown away, for not one shot struck a single ship of the British fleet. Some of our ships fired; but the *Elephant* did not return a single shot. I hope to reserve them for a better occasion.

The British fleet forcing the Straits of Elsinore on the approach to Copenhagen, 30 March 1801. Elsinore castle is shown on the left of the picture. Despite the powerful Danish batteries guarding the Straits, *Agamemnon* and the rest of the British fleet passed through undamaged. (National Maritime Museum, London)

Soon after midday the fleet anchored about 15 miles from Copenhagen, above the Swedish island of Hveen. In the afternoon the commander-in-chief, accompanied by Lord Nelson, boarded a frigate to reconnoitre. They found that the defences of Copenhagen had been made even more formidable during their days of waiting and that all buoys marking the channel had been removed. At a council of war held in the evening, Nelson offered to undertake the attack with ten sail-of-the-line and the small craft attached to the fleet. Parker gave him twelve, two more than he had asked for. Among the twelve was the *Agamemnon*.

As soon as the council of war was over Nelson went in a boat to sound and re-buoy the Outer Channel. From the boat he could quietly survey the defences of the city which consisted of hulks and floating batteries which though old, were well-armed and manned and could be easily supplied from the shore. Between them were the eighteen Danish men-of-war moored north to south over a distance of about a mile and a half along the edge of the shoal, so there was absolutely no chance of getting inshore of them as there had been in Aboukir Bay.

On the morning of 1 April 1801 Parker ordered the fleet to weigh. It moved to the northwest point of the Middle Ground and anchored six miles from the threatened city. Nelson left his ship the *Elephant* and went on board Captain Riou's frigate the *Amazon*, which was of shallower draught, to make a final inspection of the channel. At 1pm having returned to the *Elephant* he signalled to his squadron to weigh anchors. The order was received with cheers. Sir Hyde Parker remained at the anchorage to the north of Copenhagen facing the Trekroner batteries and guarding the exit of the King's Channel. Nelson's squadron, piloted by the *Amazon*, entered the Outer Channel and sailing down it anchored late that evening at the southern end of the Middle Ground. There they had to wait until the wind shifted south to move into the King's Channel and thus into the firing range of the Danish ships. Under cover of darkness Captain Thomas Hardy put off in a small boat and using a pole to avoid the noise of the splash of the lead, courageously sounded to within yards of the first Danish ships. His discovery that the water was deeper near the Danish line could have prevented the *Russell* and *Bellona* grounding later next day.

The Battle of Copenhagen

At 7 o'clock on the morning of 2 April a favourable wind blew from the southeast. Nelson signalled for his captains to come on board the *Elephant* to receive instructions. Leaving nothing to chance he also met with the pilots and masters of the vessels. An hour later the signal was given to weigh anchors in succession. Nelson flying his flag in the *Elephant* had as flag captain Thomas Foley, who commanding the *Goliath* had led the English line into action at the Nile. On board the *Elephant* also was Thomas Hardy, captain of the *St George*. Other distinguished captains were Fremantle in the *Ganges*, Sir Thomas Thompson in the *Bellona* and the misanthropic William Bligh, survivor of the famous mutiny on the *Bounty* and the longest trip (4,000 miles) ever sailed in an open boat, commanding the *Glatton*.

The *Edgar* led the squadron. The *Agamemnon* followed. She weighed anchor, made sail with reefed topsails, foresail, jib, main, staysail, spanker and mizzen staysail and was in the act of setting her topgallants when Fancourt, her captain, found himself hemmed in by a shoal in the Middle Ground. There was simply no way he could clear it and he had to anchor again. After furling all sails the stream and kedge anchors were put into the launch with cables and attempts were made to warp the ship to windward. The method consisted in rowing for a distance, throwing the anchors and attached hawsers overboard and once they had firmly gripped the bottom, hauling the cable in using the capstan. This would normally have moved a floating ship to a new position, in this case, as Fancourt hoped, away from the shoal. But they made little progress owing to the strength of the current and hardness of the ground so were out of action for most of the day.

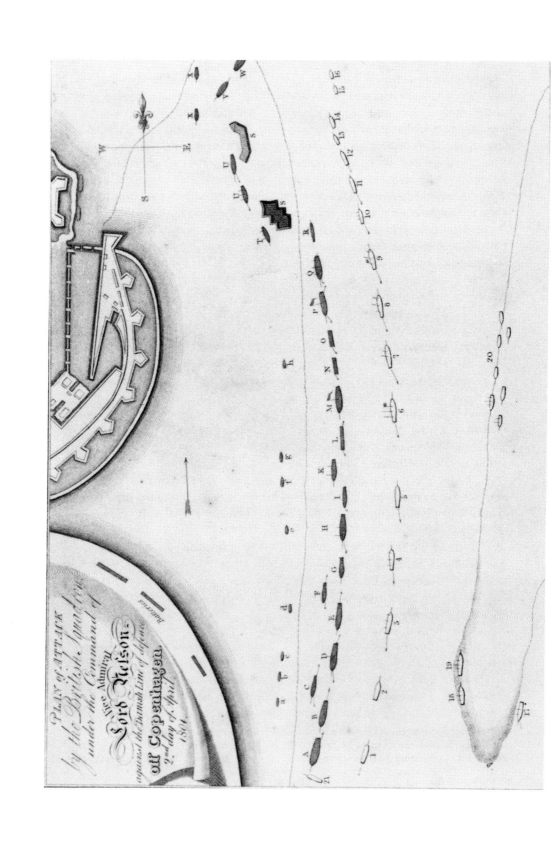

PLAN of the Attack
by the British Squadron
under the Command of
Vice Admiral
Lord Nelson
against the Danish Line of defence
off Copenhagen,
2nd day of April
1801.

In the meantime the *Polyphemus* had been signalled to take the *Agamemnon*'s place. She and the *Edgar* remained unsupported for a considerable time owing to the *Agamemnon*'s misfortune. They received such a heavy weight of fire from the enemy that they had to anchor further from their designated opponents than the 250 yards given by Nelson in his instructions. This caused all the other ships that were following to anchor at a less effective distance than Nelson had intended.

There was further misfortune in store. The *Isis* followed the *Polyphemus*. Then the *Bellona* and the *Russell*, in trying to overtake the *Isis*, came too close to the western edge of the Middle Ground and ran onto the bank. While both kept firing their guns throughout the battle, the distance from their objectives considerably diminished their efficiency. As well as losing the *Agamemnon*, Nelson was deprived of a quarter of his squadron very early in the battle. He soon managed to anchor each of the remaining nine ships opposite an opponent but owing to the absence of the *Agamemnon*, the *Bellona* and the *Russell*, they were overburdened by having to take on more adversaries than intended for them. This was especially true at the northern end where Captain Edward Riou on the little *Amazon* of 38 guns and his small squadron courageously opposed the Trekroner forts.

Nelson, aboard the *Elephant*, took up his position opposite the *Dannebrog*, the Danish flagship. This position had originally been assigned for the *Bellona*. Fremantle in the *Ganges* was anchored in front of him and Captain James Mosse in the *Monarch*, one ship beyond. Mosse was killed moments after the action began at 10:05am. By 10:30am about half the British squadron was engaged and after 11:30am the battle became general. From that moment on, in the arctic winter light, the adversaries settled down to pounding each other to death. As Nelson put it, 'Here was no manoeuvring. It was downright fighting.'

When Nelson had weighed anchor to move his squadron into battle position, Sir Hyde Parker had done the same. His intention was to add the weight of his guns to those of Riou's squadron against the Trekroner and the Danish ships defending the harbour's mouth. With the wind and current against him, however, his progress was very slow. It was only towards the end of the battle that a few of his ships were able to enter the action.

For three hours the cannonade was furious. Parker watching from the quarterdeck of his flagship, the *London*, could see the *Bellona* and *Russell* flying signals of distress and the *Agamemnon* the signal of inability. Furthermore, Parker had at his elbow Captain William Domett, who instilled in him his

(*left*) A contemporary plan of Nelson's attack on Copenhagen 2 April 1801. Nelson's flagship *Elephant* is at the centre of the British line (No.6). *Agamemnon* can be seen at the bottom left of the picture (No.17), where she had been forced to anchor, being hemmed in by a shoal, taking no further part in the action. Above her are *Russell* (No.18) and *Bellona* (No.19), both aground. A quarter of Nelson's force was therefore unable to engage the enemy from the outset. (National Maritime Museum, London)

own insecurities by insinuating that not only was disaster possible, but imminent and inevitable. Seeing that few of the Danish guns had been silenced after three hours of action and prompted by his flag captain, Parker turned to him and said, 'I will make the signal for recall for Nelson's sake. If he is in a position to continue the action successfully, he will disregard it; if he is not, it will be an excuse for a retreat, and no blame imputed to him.' Robert Southey, whose brother Thomas was present at the battle, gives us his brother's narration of the famous event:

> 'The fire' [said Parker], 'was too hot for Nelson to oppose; a retreat he thought must be made; he was aware of the consequences to his own personal reputation, but it would be cowardly in him to leave Nelson to bear the whole shame of the failure, if shame it should be deemed.' Under a mistaken judgement therefore, with this disinterested and generous feeling he made the signal for retreat.

It was 1:30pm. Aboard the *Elephant* Nelson walked the starboard side of his quarterdeck with Colonel William Stuart. Anchored by the stern and presenting her broadside to the enemy, the *Elephant* was hotly engaging the Danish flagship *Dannebrog* as well as two floating batteries ahead of her. A shot from the *Dannebrog* passed through the mainmast of the *Elephant* sending wood and splinters flying. Nelson remarked with a smile to Colonel Stuart, 'warm work!', then stopping at the gangway for a moment he turned and said quite seriously, 'But, mark you, I would not be elsewhere for thousands.'

As soon as signal No. 39, 'the recall', was made from the *London* on the orders of the commander-in-chief, Nelson's signal lieutenant reported it. Colonel Stuart vividly paints the scene in his narration of the historical moments that followed:

> He continued his walk, and did not appear to take notice of it. The Lieutenant, meeting his Lordship at the next turn, asked 'whether he should repeat it?' Lord Nelson answered, 'No, acknowledge it.' On the Officer returning to the poop, his Lordship called after him, 'Is No. 16, for close action, still hoisted?' The lieutenant answering in the affirmative, Lord Nelson said, 'Mind you keep it so.' He now walked the deck considerably agitated, which was always known by his moving the stump of his right arm. After a turn or two he said to me, in a quick manner, 'Do you know what's shown on board of the Commander-in-Chief? No. 39!' On asking him what he meant, he answered, 'Why, to leave off action. 'Leave off action!' he repeated, and then added with a shrug, 'Now damn me if I do!' He also observed, I believe to Captain Foley, 'You know, Foley, I have only one eye — I have a right to be blind sometimes;' and then, with an archness peculiar to his character, putting his glass to his blind eye, he exclaimed, 'I really do not see the signal!'

There is conflicting evidence as to which ships actually repeated signal 39, which meant they tacitly agreed to obey it (see Appendix 4). However, seeing that Nelson kept No 16 flying 'for close action', most acted as did Rear

Admiral Graves on board the *Defiance*. He repeated the commander-in-chief's signal but hoisted it only at the yardarm while keeping Nelson's signal flying at the main truck. As the higher message was apparently the more important it could be said that the lower one had been cancelled.

On seeing Parker's signal Graves had asked if it had been repeated by Nelson, and on being told it had not said: 'Then we have nothing to do with it.' The only ships to obey Parker were the frigates of Captain Riou's squadron which had they not, would probably have been destroyed. As he retired from the battle scene Riou is said to have remarked: 'What will Nelson think of us.' On seeing Riou's ships retreat the Danes stepped up their fire and more of his men were killed. Above the sound of destruction on board the *Amazon*, Riou was heard to yell: 'Come, then, my boys, let us all die together!' Moments later he was cut in two by a roundshot. Before 2pm the Danish fire ceased along the greater part of the line, though it was still very active near the Trekroner forts.

The superior British rate of fire finally decided the battle in their favour since each side had approximately the same number of guns. The British had slightly over 400 and the Danes 380. Many of the Danish gunners were inexperienced volunteers who were no match for the hardened veterans on the gundecks of the British men-of-war. As has often been the case, greater experience can give the edge over an opponent and can change the course of history.

Robert Southey mentions that:

> Between one and two the fire of the Danes slackened; about two it ceased from the greater part of the line; and some of their lighter ships were adrift. It was, however, difficult to take possession of those which struck, because the batteries on Amager Island protected them, and because an irregular fire was kept up from the ships themselves as the boats approached. This arose from the nature of the action: the crews were continually reinforced from the shore: and fresh men coming aboard did not inquire whether the flag had been struck, or perhaps did not heed it, many or most of them never having been engaged in war before . . .

It had infuriated Nelson that the *Dannebrog*, the great Danish flagship, continued to fire after she had struck her colours. As a result of this behaviour the *Elephant* and *Ganges* trained their guns on her until she caught fire and drifted off before the wind to blow up later that afternoon.

Nelson was anxious to stop the fighting. He turned to Fremantle, who had come on board from his ship the *Ganges* and asked his opinion of a message that he had scribbled resting his notebook on the casing of the rudder head:

> To the Brothers of Englishmen, the Danes. Lord Nelson has directions to spare Denmark, when no longer resisting; but if the firing be continued on the part of Denmark, Lord Nelson will be obliged to set on fire all the Floating-batteries he has taken, without having the power to saving the brave Danes who have

defended them. Dated on board His Britannic Majesty's ship *Elephant*, Copenhagen Roads, April 2nd, 1801.

Fremantle approved the draft. It was written as a formal letter, signed and sealed with an impression of Nelson's own coat of arms and sent under a flag of truce to the mainland with Captain Sir Frederick Thesiger (an *aide-de-camp* who was fluent in Danish and Russian). Thesiger personally delivered it to the Prince Regent whom he found near the sally port.

In the meantime, the two leading ships of Sir Hyde Parker's squadron had arrived on the scene after working their way against the wind and current. Their arrival caused the Danish ships ahead of the *Elephant* to strike their colours. The Danish commander Commodore Fischer had shifted his flag first from the *Dannebrog* to the *Holstein* and finally to the Trekroner forts. The forts had been reinforced and were still firing as well as the four Danish ships that were still intact. Nelson wanted to concentrate all of his ships' guns on them

A rare view of the Battle of Copenhagen from the Danish side, showing the British fleet engaging the Danish ships and floating batteries. It was a very hard-fought action, the Danes being able to send supplies and fresh gun-crews to their fleet from shore, and at one point the British commander Hyde Parker signalled Nelson to withdraw. But Nelson famously ignored the signal and after 6 hours of fierce fighting the Danes accepted his offer of an armistice. (National Maritime Museum, London)

but Fremantle and Foley wisely advised him against this. They argued that it would be difficult enough to manoeuvre the severely-damaged ships to safety, even with the wind in their favour, not to mention what might happen if it shifted against them. They also reminded him that they were three vessels short of their full squadron.

The *Agamemnon* had never been able to join the action. Her officers and crew had spent the day of battle trying to warp the ship free from the shoal, some distance from the engagement. Her launch and flat boat had been sent to the Middle Ground to assist the grounded *Bellona* and *Russell*, and she had spent all the time of the battle as a reluctant spectator.

At 4pm the battle was over. The Danish Prince Regent sent Nelson a message asking the immediate object of Nelson's letter. Nelson sent the messenger back with a written reply stating that his object was purely humanitarian, that he proposed to put an end to hostilities and suggesting that the wounded Danes be taken ashore. He ended the note saying that he would 'esteem it the greatest Victory he ever has gain'd if this flag of truce may be the happy forerunner of a lasting and happy Union between my most Gracious Sovereign and His Majesty the King of Denmark.' Not long after the Trekroner forts ceased firing.

The Danish Adjutant-General Hans Lindholm was sent with a flag of truce to see Sir Hyde Parker aboard the *London*. Parker was the only British flag officer with sufficient authority to negotiate a peace settlement. While this was going on Nelson took the opportunity to retire his badly-battered squadron. He at once signalled for his ships to weigh anchor and proceed. The *Monarch* immediately grounded. She was pushed off again by the *Ganges*. The *Glatton* sailed out in safety. The *Defiance* and *Elephant*, both of deeper draught, piled up on the shoal about a mile from the Trekroner forts and would have been in a very dangerous position had it not been for the ceasefire. Both were stuck hard and fast until 10pm when a rise of the tide floated them off.

During the night the British got their grounded ships away except for the 40-gun *Désirée*. They also took possession of all the prizes that could be moved. The *Agamemnon* floated free at last and took aboard 182 prisoners. She then sent men to help warp the *Désirée* off the bank. Her log at this time is a litany of continual bad weather. It dismally records snow storms and heavy squalls of sleet and rain. On the fourth day after the battle it reports that the *Désirée* floated free after much effort and that the *Agamemnon* sailed with her to join the fleet. The log also mentions sending carpenters to help repair the captured 60-gun *Holstein*. Food and victuals were taken on, crew members were punished with the cat-o'-nine-tails and one seaman had to run the gauntlet. There was never an idle moment on a ship of the line, whatever might befall it.

Nelson ordered his gig to row him to the meeting with Sir Hyde Parker and Hans Lindholm aboard the *London*. As he left he was heard to remark: 'Well, I have fought contrary to orders, and perhaps I shall be hanged. Never mind, let them!' He need not have been concerned. It was quite evident to Parker and to everyone else that Nelson's decision to sail his squadron around the Middle Ground so as to come upon the weaker end of the Danish line from the south, when they were expected from the opposite direction, had won the battle. Now Nelson's immediate concern was to try and secure by negotiation what he had won by force. He did not rate his own diplomatic talents highly: 'A negotiator is certainly out of my line,' he had been known to say. By the time the Danish representative took his leave that night all that had been achieved was a 24-hour truce and an agreement that the British should take possession of their prizes as well as some other Danish ships which had not formally surrendered. At the suggestion of Sir Hyde Parker, it had also been agreed at the meeting that Nelson would go ashore to discuss terms of an armistice with the Prince Regent.

That night Nelson slept aboard the *St George*, his permanent flagship. Before he climbed into his cot he noted in his journal:

> April 2. Moderate breezes southerly, at 9 [really 10] made the signal to engage the Danish line; the action began at 5 min, and lasted about 4 hours, when 17 out of 18 of the Danish line were taken, burned or sunk. Our ships suffered a great deal. At night went on board the *St George* very unwell.

The weight of responsibility, the uncertainty and exhaustion due to lack of sleep for several days had taken an emotional as well as a physical toll. It was almost too much for Nelson's frail frame to bear. He was forty-two, with only one arm and nearly blind. Picking up his pen by candlelight he wrote to Emma: 'St George, April 2nd, 1801, at 9 o'clock at night very tired after a hard fought battle . . .'

The casualties

Including killed and wounded the losses in the British ships were calculated at upwards of 1,200. Of this figure those killed and mortally wounded numbered over 350. It was hard to assess the casualties in the Danish fleet due to a disparity of figures. By British account the Danes had lost, including killed, wounded and prisoners, about 6,000 men while the Danish commander Commodore Fischer assessed the number between 1,600 and 1,800. In the *Dannebrog* alone 270 men were killed when she exploded.[8]

The British ships had been badly damaged in the action but none had been completely disabled. Most of them had been badly hit about the hull and lower rigging due to the Danes firing low. Numerous guns on the British ships were disabled, some by enemy shot, some by their own recoil and several of them had burst while being fired. Cast iron guns of the period became very dangerous when they heated up and were subjected to the violent shocks of continual firing. More than half of all the Danish craft that formed the line in front of Copenhagen were a total loss. But one ship, the

74-gun *Syaelland*, which had anchored under the guns of the Trekroner Forts, refused to surrender to anyone except Lord Nelson personally. Next day, an early morning visitor climbed from his gig up the side of the *Syaelland* and throwing back his old green boat cloak revealed his jacket with the three stars and the empty sleeve, symbols of an unmistakable identity. The *Syaelland* surrendered and was taken in tow as a prize though her captain said he would have preferred the guns of the Trekroner to have opened fire and sunk her.

Negotiating for peace

It is curious that Parker himself did not undertake the negotiations with the Prince Regent of Denmark. His nomination by the Admiralty as commander-in-chief of the Baltic fleet pointed to the role of the diplomat; while his fiery second-in-command provided the leadership in battle. One can only suppose that Parker, recognising Nelson's fame, reasoned that he would be more likely to impress and to attain success than Parker himself with his less significant personality.

There was considerable nervousness ashore when Nelson disembarked for the meeting. No little hostility could be expected from the citizens of Copenhagen towards their principal aggressor. Guards had been posted along the route and Nelson arrived at the palace unharmed. Later, during the state dinner he became an object of curiosity to the townsfolk who were given permission to enter the palace to watch the proceedings but it did not bother him in the least. 'The people,' he recorded later, 'received me as they have always done.' With a mixture of curiosity and awe, he might have added.

At the interview that followed, the Prince, who spoke English as also did the Adjutant-General Hans Lindholm, made the opening remarks. The meeting wore on. Nelson brought up the crucial matters of freedom of navigation, liberty for British vessels to enter Danish ports, trading rights and the perennial thorny question of neutral ships being stopped by the British and searched for arms and ammunition. Nothing was concluded until 9 April when an armistice of only 14 weeks was agreed upon. Meanwhile, it was arranged that Denmark would take no action under the Treaty of Armed Neutrality. It irked Nelson that so much time had been spent negotiating after the power of Denmark had been crippled. In a letter to Lord St Vincent he wrote that if he had been in command, he would have hurried to Reval and destroyed the Russian fleet, as a further measure.

On 16 April, Sir Hyde Parker sent home the *Monarch*, *Isis* and *Holstein* with most of the wounded. He had left the roadstead of Copenhagen on 12 April with his fleet except for the *St George*, the *Agamemnon* and some frigates that followed a week later. His objective this time was to intimidate the Swedes and Russians.

The Baltic and the Gulf of Finland

The fleet entered the Baltic between the islands of Amag and Saltholm. The heavier ships had to hoist some of their guns into merchantmen to get over the shallows and then hoist them back in again once across. In spite of these precautions several were unable to avoid grounding. Fremantle, who had lightened the 74-gun *Ganges* to draw only 22 feet 2 inches led the fleet through 4½ fathoms of water and frequently less, for over 4 miles.[9] The *Agamemnon* sailed over the Grounds, a few days later, in the illustrious company of the *St George* with Nelson and his flag captain Thomas Hardy on board. With them also went the *Désirée* and some smaller craft. The *Agamemnon* had hoisted out her boats and had trimmed ship by shifting the water and ammunition in her holds. This enabled her to cross the shoals but it was another matter for the *St George* whose progress was slow as she had to have her guns removed to get through. Consequently, they trailed the rest of the fleet by some 24 miles.

The Russian fleet was anchored in the ice-bound harbour of Reval while the Swedish squadron was thought to be at Karlskroner. The intention of the British was to attack the Russian ships before they could join the Swedes and become a formidable opponent. On his way to Reval, Parker learned from one of his look-out frigates that the Swedish fleet was at sea. He immediately sent the news to Nelson, who, scenting the possibility of battle, became so impatient that he ordered a boat to be lowered and jumped into it. He forgot to take even his boat cloak, an unfortunate mistake in the bitterly cold weather. As the boat pulled away from the *St George* he asked Alexander Briarly, Master of the *Bellona*, who was with him, 'Do you think the Fleet has sailed?' 'I should suppose not, my Lord,' Briarly answered. Nelson thought for a bit and then growled: 'If they are, we shall follow them to Karlskroner in the boat, by God!' Fortunately, it was not necessary to cover the 150 miles to the Swedish anchorage in the six-oared cutter. The British fleet was still at anchor and Nelson stepped aboard the *Elephant* some 6 hours after he had left the *St George*. He was greeted by his old friend Foley who responded warmly to the enquiry 'in true Norfolk drawl' as to whether Captain Foley could be so good as to be plagued again by Admiral Nelson.[10]

Nelson suggested sailing the British ships into the Gulf of Finland to prevent the Russian fleets from Reval and Kronstadt joining forces after the thaw. Parker, however, true to temperament, wasted his time blockading the small Swedish fleet of eight sail-of-the-line and two frigates snugly at anchor in the 'Swedish Portsmouth', as it was called.

All at once the futility of the whole campaign became apparent. Thousands of lives had been lost, ships and property damaged, an unfair war had been waged against a traditional ally, and finally, with a great deal of effort, a precarious armistice had been achieved. All had been in vain since the mad Tsar Paul I of Russia had been murdered on 23 March, ten days before the

Battle of Copenhagen. Neither side knew this and had carried on fighting each other on the Tsar's account. A group of patriotic noblemen had murdered him, ashamed of his policies and alarmed at the increasing evidence of his insanity. It was his intimidating influence that had pushed his weaker neighbours into joining the Alliance. Later, fear of his retaliation had restrained the Danish Regent from signing an armistice for a longer period than 14 weeks. Robert Southey gives the following account of Nelson's own feelings of remorse:

> The fate of these men [the 270 men that were killed when the flagship *Dannebrog* blew up] after the gallantry which they had displayed, particularly affected Nelson: for there was nothing in this action of that indignation against the enemy and that impression of retributive justice, which at the Nile had given a sterner temper to his mind, and a sense of austere delight in beholding the vengeance of which he was the appointed minister. The Danes were an honourable foe; they were of English mould as well as English blood; and now that the battle had ceased, he regarded them rather as brethren than as enemies.

The British fleet was sailing from Karlskroner to Reval on 23 April when Parker received dispatches from the Russian ambassador at Copenhagen indicating that the new Tsar, Alexander I, had reversed his father's pro-French policies and in future would consider Britain a friendly nation. St Vincent, now First Lord of the Admiralty, had decided to abruptly recall Parker. He sailed for England on board the frigate *Blanche*, and Nelson took over the command of the fleet.

Nelson did not share Parker's optimism about Russia's peaceful intentions. He thought that the presence of the British fleet could do no harm in the Gulf of Finland. Therefore, leaving the *Agamemnon* to watch Karlskroner with the *Edgar, Saturn, Russell, Raisonnable, Glatton* and a frigate off Bornholm Island, he sent word to the Swedish admiral that if his ships put to sea they would be treated as enemies and fired upon. With his remaining eleven line-of-battle ships Nelson sailed for Reval only to find that the Russians had gone up to Cronstadt. The authorities in Reval were alarmed at the arrival of the British squadron and Nelson was officially informed that the Tsar had expressed astonishment that the fleet of a nation that openly declared its friendship should anchor uninvited on the threshold of their naval base. The only guarantee of loyalty which Russia could accept, said the message, was the instant withdrawal of the British fleet. Knowing when to step down in the interests of diplomacy, Nelson sent a letter to the Tsar saying that his visit to Reval was intended solely to pay his respects to the new sovereign of Russia and that he would withdraw his fleet immediately to the Baltic. He sailed from Reval on 17 May and two days later, both Russia and Sweden released all British merchant vessels impounded in their ports. The Armed Neutrality of the North was dissolved and the threat to British trade was over. Friendly relations were at last restored.

During this period, there is an interesting entry in the *Agamemnon*'s log in which sugar and lime juice are mentioned for the first time. The supply of this aboard Royal Navy ships had been made compulsory some years earlier in order to combat scurvy. The disease was largely eradicated by 1797, and by the time of the Battle of Copenhagen in 1801, the officers and crews were well aware of the preventative qualities of the lime juice they received aboard. The following entries are taken from the captain's log for two successive days while the ship was at anchor in Kjoge Bay on the west coast of Sjaelland, Denmark:

> Sunday 14th June
> At single Anchor in Kioge Bay
> PM Light Breezes & Squally with Flying Showers of Rain Recd flour from HMS *Defiance*
> AM Strong Breezes & Do Recd Sugar & Lime Juice from HM Ships *Ardent* & *Glatton* and from the latter 1 Fore-Topsail & Main Do, 1 Jib & 2 Puncheons Rum ½ past 11 fired a Salute of 21 Guns on Rear Admiral Graves being Knighted Mustered Ships Company Recd 10 Officers & 39 Privates of the 49th Regt from HMS *Ardent*.

> Monday 15th June
> PM Do Wr & Cloudy Received flour from HMS *Glatton*
> AM Do Wr Sent the Flat Boat & Launch for Water sett up Main Topmast rigging Read the Articles of War & punished Samuel Berryman by Running the Gauntlett for Theft, and William Foley (M) with 12 Lashes for Drunkenness & Neglect of Duty

The aftermath

Nelson's requests to be relieved of his command had been granted and he sailed for Yarmouth on 19 June in a small naval brig, the *Kite*, so as not to deprive the fleet of a larger ship. Four days later his old friend Sir Charles Pole arrived in HMS *Aeolus* to take command of the fleet. Forming part of Rear Admiral Sir Thomas Graves' squadron, the *Agamemnon* remained on station until 11 July when she sailed for Yarmouth. After provisioning, she left again for the Baltic. There she cruised in company with the other ships of the fleet until late October when they all returned to England. On 18 April 1802 the *Agamemnon* finally moored at Chatham Dockyard to undergo another complete and much-needed refit.

The rewards for the victory of Copenhagen were grudgingly bestowed. The admirals, captains, officers and men of Parker's fleet received the thanks of the House of Commons and the House of Lords. Nelson was given the title of Viscount when what he had expected was an Earldom and Rear Admiral Graves was invested with the Order of the Bath. The usual gold medals which flag officers and captains had come to look upon as prestigious awards were not forthcoming. The ordinary seamen who had survived the slaughter of the gun decks and had provided the muscle power to win the battle got nothing at all. Their small share of prize money went up in smoke when Sir Hyde Parker ordered all prizes to be burned, with the exception of one which was used as a hospital ship.

Most in Britain felt embarrassment at the heavy-handed way in which their Government and the Royal Navy had acted against the smallest nation of the Alliance of the North. In the people's minds, the true enemy was France and Denmark had been intimidated into joining Russia. Even so, the Danes did not abide by the armistice. Passing by Denmark on his return from the Baltic, Nelson observed that a French officer had become a counsellor and a constant companion to the Prince and that much was going on in violation of the peace treaty. It was beginning to look as if a second display of force might be necessary. 'I see everything which is dirty and mean going on, and the Prince-Royal at the head of it. Ships have been masted, guns taken on board, floating batteries prepared, and except for hauling out and completing their rigging, everything is done in defiance of the treaty,' wrote Nelson, and his judgement was shrewd. It was confirmed by Napoleon many years later when talking to Admiral Cockburn, that Denmark was supplying France with timber and cordage soon after the battle. This conduct eventually led to another expedition in which the *Agamemnon* took part seven years later, an expedition which was to cause further bloodshed and damage to Copenhagen and to the Danish Fleet.[11]

NOTES

1. Ernle Bradford, *Nelson: The Essential Hero* (London: Macmillan, 1977), p 198.
2. Ibid.
3. It was while in Italy that Napoleon began to put into practice his ideas of restructuring the French government. Stripping it down and organising it like an army he demonstrated his extraordinary talent for administration. He reorganised the central government, stabilised the currency and established a system of education. Working furiously, calling on his experts, sleeping little and dictating to four secretaries at once, he drew up the famous Code Napoleon which gave the country a greatly improved legal system. This period of prosperity and stability was to become one of France's golden ages.
4. Winston Churchill, *A History of the English Speaking Peoples* (London: Cassell, 1957) Vol III, p 239.
5. Admiralty: Masters' Logs (ADM 51): ADM 51/1361, HMS *Agamemnon*.
6. In early logs the Admiralty 'day' ran from noon to noon, so the entries start with PM and end with AM. This was rescinded by Admiralty order on 15 December 1805, after which the logs were to run from midnight to midnight. It took some years for commanders to get used to this change and there were invariably errors some of which were noticed during research for this book.
7. Admiralty: Masters' Logs (ADM 51): ADM 51/1361, HMS *Agamemnon*.
8. Clowes, *The Royal Navy, a History from Earliest Time to the Present* (London: Sampson Low, Marston, 1898), Vol 5, p 438.
9. Fathom: Originally the width of the outstretched arms, it became standardised at six feet and was used to measure the depth of water. Admiralty charts showed the depth in fathoms until the recent change over to the metric system. Grant Uden & Richard Cooper, *A Dictionary of British Ships and Seamen* (London: Allen Lane, 1980), p 150.
10. Carola Oman, *Nelson* (London: Hodder & Stoughton, 1947), p 401.
11. Clowes, Vol 4, p 176.
11. Oliver Warner, *A Portrait of Lord Nelson* (London: Penguin Books, 1987), p 270.

CHAPTER 9

Trafalgar 21 October 1805

Oh, the bellowing thunders! The shudders, the
  shocks!
When thousands 'gainst thousands come clashing
  like rocks.
When the rain is all scarlet; the clouds are half fire;
And men's sinews are snapped like threads of a lyre!
When each litter's a hearse, and each bullet a knell;
When each breath is a curse, and each bosom a hell!

Barry Cornwall
BRIAN WALTER PROCTER

William Pitt, the British Prime Minister, had pledged freedom for Irish
Catholics without the King's written consent. When George III went back on
his word and refused his support for the cause, Pitt saw no alternative but to
resign. His successor was Henry Addington, a former Speaker of the House of
Commons. He was an amiable man, but with few gifts as a statesman.

On 23 March 1802 Addington's government came to terms with Napoleon
and signed the Treaty of Amiens. For 14 months there was a pause in the
fighting, but the treaty was not advantageous to Britain. She relinquished to
France, Holland and Spain all the territory she had gained in the war except
for Trinidad and Ceylon. Malta was handed back to the Knights of St John,
Minorca to Spain, the Cape Colony to the Dutch and Martinique and Guadaloupe to France. As a further concession to French pride, George III renounced the ancient but empty title 'King of France' which had been borne
by English sovereigns since 1340. France's part of the bargain included the
evacuation of Egypt, Naples and the Papal States, and recognition of the
sovereignty of Turkey and Portugal. British tourists flocked to France to see
for themselves the changes brought about by the Revolution and also, if luck
permitted, to get a glimpse of the dynamic little man, now known by the
formidable title of First Consul, who in such a short time had changed the face
of Europe. The period of peace was sadly short as in May the following year
hostilities were renewed. However, since Napoleon had been heard to say
that 'every peace treaty means no more than a brief armistice', no one should
have been surprised.

Addington had failed to use the breathing-space to build up England's
defences. Napoleon had successfully tricked him into believing that after
nearly 10 years of war he wanted a long period of peace, while at the same
time he assembled his forces at Boulogne, Brest and Toulon, intent upon
seizing England by the throat.

The rising hopes of the Tories were young George Canning and Lord Castlereagh who had served under Pitt. They were among the most critical of Addington's incapable government. It was a government that not only lacked administrative experience but had no influence or authority over its military and naval leaders. Canning wrote in despair, voicing the thoughts of many fellow citizens: 'Whether Pitt *will* save us I do not know, but surely he is the only man that *can*.'

Pitt had retired to Walmer, in Kent. When Prime Minister he had been criticised, and rightly so, for preferring to borrow money rather than increase taxation, thereby burdening posterity with gigantic debts. In other respects he was head and shoulders above any other contemporary British statesman. He was an eloquent speaker who had the added qualities of perseverance and courage. He also had the confidence of the British public. In retirement he seemed a broken and lonely man, prematurely aged by the strains and disappointments of his years in government. During this short period in which he was out of office, he is depicted by historians as fulfilling his duties as Warden of the Cinque Ports astride his horse at the head of a rustic assortment of yokels armed with sporting guns and with pitchforks. He drilled these men as local militia against the threat of invasion. Ironically, barely 20 miles away across the Channel 130,000 men of Napoleon's Grand Armée were waiting only for orders to embark and cross the Straits of Dover.

Addington's government fell after three years in power and Pitt was recalled to office. He immediately devoted all his efforts to reorganising England's armed forces and to encouraging likely allies on the continent. The results of this were not immediate, although a coalition with Austria and Russia was eventually set up. In the meantime, Bonaparte set himself the task of drawing up the final plans for the crushing of Britain. On 2 December 1804 he accepted the Imperial Crown from the Senate and, to the utter amazement of all Europe and much of France, he summoned the Pope to preside at his coronation, as Charlemagne had done. The aged Pope, Pius VII, officiated in Notre Dame cathedral on 2 December 1804. On that day the wheel had turned its full ironic circle. The most ambitious and militant son of the Revolution had assumed the very throne that had cost so many lives to overthrow.

Napoleon naïvely thought that becoming Emperor would gain him admittance in the exclusive world of legitimate monarchs. Understandably, the opposite proved true. The crowned heads of Europe became so infuriated by his arrogant behaviour that they determined to make every effort to drive France back to its original frontiers and break this upstart soldier in the process. By taking the Imperial wreath in Notre Dame and placing it upon his own head Napoleon had played into the very hands of William Pitt who urgently sought to form an association of allied nations.

Napoleon's Grand Scheme

To subdue the stubborn islanders of Britain, Napoleon had temporarily suspended any other military activities and thrown the whole weight of his armed forces into the enterprise. The huge army of trained troops was concentrated around Boulogne for the invasion and was to be carried by a fleet of over 2,000 flat-bottomed boats built for the purpose. For the plan to be successful it was essential for the French to obtain control of the Channel. Before this could be achieved a problem had to be overcome: the Channel ports on the French side were not large or deep enough to take large ships of the line, so the fleets in the Atlantic and Mediterranean harbours would have to join up elsewhere. The Emperor envisioned concentrating his scattered squadrons somewhere in the West Indies, where they would rendezvous with the Spaniards (who had been drawn into the scheme because their fleet was needed). Napoleon hoped that this strategy would draw the British away from their stations and into the western Atlantic. Once this was accomplished, the combined French and Spanish fleets would double back to Europe, secure command of the Channel and assure the crossing from Boulogne. The strategy seemed brilliantly simple, at least on paper, but a lot was taken for granted. It was a totally different matter to plan a vast manoeuvre with ships than with an army on land.

For instance, what were constant factors on land became variable ones at sea, such as distance and speed, which in the age of sail depended on the elements of wind, weather and currents, difficult to predict with accuracy. Furthermore, the plan failed to take into account the superiority of British seamanship and gunnery.

Earl St Vincent, when First Lord of the Admiralty, had divided the fleet in the following manner: eleven sail-of-the-line were under the command of Lord Keith at the Downs; Sir William Cornwallis held the Channel with seventeen ships against the massive French preparations at Boulogne; Sir Robert Calder had eight, among them the *Agamemnon*, stationed off Ferrol; Sir John Orde had six guarding Cádiz, and Nelson was given eleven sail-of-the-line and the Mediterranean Command. His main task was to keep watch on Admiral Pierre Charles de Villeneuve's fleet in Toulon.

The situation can be better understood as shown opposite.[1]

Napoleon issued his final orders to Villeneuve and Ganteaume on 2 March 1805. Villeneuve was to sail for Cádiz where he would be joined by the ships already there and proceed to Martinique. At Martinique he was to wait up to thirty days for Ganteaume who would be the commander-in-chief after they had joined forces. Ganteaume's orders were to sail immediately to Ferrol, evade the blockading squadron and with the Spanish ships in port, sail for the West Indies to join Villeneuve. The united force was then to steer for the Channel and appear off Boulogne between 10 June and 10 July.

When Ganteaume arrived off Ferrol and saw Calder's small squadron he sent word to Napoleon that if he faced the British force he would be certain of

Franco-Spanish		British	
Port, etc.	Ready for service in March	Station	Ready for service in March
The Texel	9 ships of the line[1] 80 transports 25,000 troops	The Downs	11 sail of the line (Keith)
Boulogne, etc.	950 transports 1300 armed small craft 130,000 troops		
Brest	21 ships of the line (Ganteaume) Transports 3600 troops (embarked)	The Channel	17 sail of the line[2] (Cornwallis and others)
Rochefort	2 ships of the line (Magon and later Allemand)		
Lorient	1 ship of the line		
Ferrol	12 sail of the line[3] (Grandallana and Gourdon)	Off Ferrol	8 ships of the line (Calder)
Cadiz	7 sail of the line[4] (Graviña)	Off Cadiz	6 ships of the line (Orde)
Cartagena	6 sail of the line[1] (Salcedo)	Mediterranean	11 ships of the line[5] (Nelson)
Toulon	11 sail of the line (Villeneuve) 3500 troops (embarked)		

1. Took no part in the campaign.
2. Increased, by April 1st to 21.
3. Besides 3 not ready for sea.
4. Besides 8 or 9 not ready for sea.
5. Of which 1 was stationed at Naples.

In addition, the allies had 5, and Great Britain had 10 ships of the line in the West Indies; while Great Britain had about 9 ships of the line in the East Indies; and 2 British ships of the line were on their way from England to join Nelson in the Mediterranean. In the above summary, no mention is made of frigates.

victory. Napoleon sent the following answer: 'A naval victory at this time would produce no results. Keep a single object before you. Fulfill your commission. Go to sea without fighting.'

It is curious that this brilliant military strategist misunderstood the basic elements of naval warfare. He was all for evasion, and for not risking a ship. He believed that his entire fleet could vanish into thin air and appear again on a certain date at a given time from out of the blue, as it were, in the English Channel. Perhaps if he had realised that squadrons or fleets, unlike regiments, could not be moved like pieces on a chess-board, his plans might have ended differently. For instance, if he had understood that in order to achieve his ultimate objective he must annihilate the British fleet piecemeal and therefore if he had allowed Ganteaume to face Cornwallis's inferior force the end result might have been very different. It is easy to surmise what the outcome would have been if Villeneuve, after leaving Toulon, had picked up the six ships from Cartagena and the seven from Cádiz and then with twenty-four ships had faced Nelson with his eleven ships of the line. As Laird Clowes puts it:

> The British naval leaders of that day were giants; but they were not almighty; and it is well for the Britons of today [Laird Clowes was writing in 1898] and of tomorrow to remember that, although they triumphed in that decisive campaign of 1805, they owed their victory as much to the errors of the enemy as to the skill and bravery of themselves.

The pursuit of Villeneuve

After a false start in January, Villeneuve finally left Toulon on the night of 29 March. Nelson was waiting off the Sardinian coast when the news reached him. Unfortunately, his frigates soon lost touch with Villeneuve. Very anxious, Nelson made certain that he was not heading for Sicily or the Near East. Having ascertained this he turned round and set all sail for Gibraltar. His squadron consisted of eleven sail-of-the-line, four frigates and two corvettes. Fierce head winds prevented him from reaching the Straits for a week and *en route* he learned that the French had passed The Rock on a course for Cádiz more than three weeks before. The wind continued to blow with such intensity from the west that the squadron could not make the passage through the Straits, whereupon Nelson took the decision to anchor in Mazari Bay on the African coast for water, and then go on to Gibraltar to provision. Piecing together scattered reports from frigates and merchantmen he fathomed the French plan. He knew that when Villeneuve passed Cádiz six Spanish naval vessels had come out to join him under the command of Admiral Federico Carlos de Graviña. But where had they headed thereafter? It is known that an old friend of Nelson's from his Naples days, Rear Admiral John Campbell of the Portuguese navy, went on board the *Victory* at Gibraltar and had a private talk with him. It is almost certain that in the privacy of the great stern cabin Campbell told Nelson Villeneuve's destination.[2] Whether true or not it is significant that on the morning after this visit Nelson wrote: 'My lot is cast, and I am going to the West Indies, where, although I am late, yet chance may have given them a bad passage, and me a good one: I must hope the best.' The fox was out and the chase began. Newbolt put it into verse:

> The wind was rising easterly, the morning sky was blue,
> The Straits before us opened wide and free;
> We looked towards the Admiral where high the Peter flew,
> And all our hearts were dancing like the sea.
> The French are gone to Martinique with four-and-twenty sail.

The old *Superb* is old and frail and slow,
But the French are gone to Martinique
and Nelson's on the trail.
And where he goes the old *Superb* must go!

At an average speed of 5½ knots Nelson pursued his quarry across the Atlantic. He left Gibraltar under full sail on the night of 11 May and made his landfall at Barbados on 4 June. Villeneuve and his Spanish allies had reached Martinique 21 days before. They received the news of Nelson's arrival with alarm and made for the Atlantic on an easterly course. Arriving at Antigua where Villeneuve had called only 4 days earlier, Nelson began to piece together his enemy's itinerary in the West Indies. Villeneuve's fleet, carrying 3,000 French and 1,500 Spanish troops, had arrived at Martinique with over 1,000 sick men and had buried almost that number during their stay. Villeneuve had taken under his command two French line-of-battle ships which he had found at Martinique, raising his force to twenty. Then he had recaptured the Diamond Rock, a small pinnacled island at the entrance to Fort Royal (called Fort de France today) which had been taken and fortified by an intrepid party of British bluejackets the year before. While anchored at Fort Royal a frigate had arrived from France and from that moment events accelerated. Nelson guessed that the frigate was the unidentified sail his squadron had sighted in mid-Atlantic. He surmised that the frigate had outdistanced him and had given the news of his approach to Villeneuve and Graviña, hastening their departure. With these and a few other pieces of information Nelson had to make another crucial decision. Was he right in believing that Villeneuve and Graviña were sailing for Europe? He ruled out attacks on Trinidad, Tobago, Barbados, St Lucia or Grenada. Jamaica seemed a possibility but the enemy would have approached it directly from Martinique. After making up his mind that Europe must have been their destination he wrote in a dispatch, 'So far from being infallible, like the Pope, I believe my opinions to be very fallible, and therefore I may be mistaken that the enemy's fleet has gone to Europe; but I cannot think myself otherwise, not withstanding the variety of opinions which a number of good people have formed.'

The day before Nelson sailed from the islands he sent Captain Bettesworth in the *Curieux* to England with dispatches. Bettesworth caught up with Villeneuve and, at a distance, kept in company long enough to ascertain the number of enemy ships, their course and position. He then raced home to England with the news that the combined enemy fleet was on a course for the Bay of Biscay.

Bettesworth arrived at the Admiralty in London close on midnight. Lord Barham, the new First Lord, who was nearly eighty, had gone to bed. No one cared to disturb him and he did not see Bettesworth's dispatches until the following morning. He was furious at the waste of time and without even waiting to dress he wrote to Admiral Cornwallis ordering him to detach

Admiral Charles Stirling, who was blockading Rochefort with his five line-of-battle ships, to join Vice Admiral Sir Robert Calder. Calder was directed to station himself westwards of Cape Finisterre, while Cornwallis, in the *Ville de Paris*, was to cruise with his squadron between Finisterre and Ushant. Calder had recently been detached from the Channel fleet to command the blockade of Ferrol, covering for Rear Admiral Cochrane who had also sailed to the West Indies in pursuit of the French. With his flag hoisted in the *Prince of Wales*, Calder reached his station and found that the squadron there was made up of six sail-of-the-line including the *Agamemnon*, commanded by Captain John Harvey.

Villeneuve, in the meantime, intended to break the blockade at Ferrol and release the twelve Spanish ships trapped in port. Thus reinforced he would join up with Ganteaume at Brest. Ganteaume, however, was hemmed in by Cornwallis's fleet and failed to break out despite insistent orders from Napoleon.

On 18 July 1805, with the *Victory* heading the squadron, Nelson recorded in his journal: 'Cape Spartel [off Tangier] in sight, but no French fleet, nor any information about them. How sorrowful this makes me, but I cannot help myself.' The next day they rounded Cape St Vincent which heralds the approaches to Gibraltar. After covering some seven thousand miles Nelson's pursuit of Villeneuve and Graviña was temporarily over. He had missed them by only two days and only 360 miles, having relied on guesswork alone. After anchoring in Rosia Bay, Gibraltar, he noted in his diary, 'I went on shore for the first time since the 16th of June, 1803; and from having my foot out of the *Victory*, two years, wanting ten days.' The unfairness of it was that after so much effort and preparation the battle had ultimately fallen to Calder.

Calder's Action

Two days after Nelson set foot in Gibraltar, the enemy was sighted through the fog by the *Defiance*, a ship of Calder's squadron, sailing on a course for Ferrol some one hundred miles west of Cape Finisterre. Here on 22 July 1805, the campaign of Trafalgar opened.

The enemy fleet numbered twenty sail-of-the-line, seven frigates, two brigs and the Spanish galleon *Matilda*. Including the ships dispatched by Cornwallis, Sir Robert Calder now had fifteen ships of the line, two frigates, a small lugger and a cutter. At 3pm the 74-gun *Defiance*, which had sighted the enemy sailed back and took up her station in the line.[3] The *Agamemnon* stood fifth in the line, behind the *Barfleur* and ahead of the *Windsor Castle*. The wind being very light they had set their topgallant sails and were sailing parallel to the enemy. At a distance of some 7 miles the Franco-Spanish fleet moved under topsails in a well-formed line with the frigate *Sirène* towing the treasure galleon *Matilda*. Captain Prowse of the British frigate *Sirius* thought he saw his opportunity

Calder's action off Cape Finisterre, 23 July 1805, by William Anderson.
Agamemnon was fifth in the British line in this battle. (National Maritime
Museum, London)

and working his ship sufficiently to windward prepared to place her alongside
the galleon to board her on the next tack. Just as he was ready to commence
the manoeuvre, he suddenly saw through the fog the Spanish flagship *Argonauta* bearing down upon him. Realising the danger of his position, Prowse
instantly changed course and broke away. 'With a forbearance highly honourable to Admiral Graviña, the *Argonauta* passed the British frigate without
firing.'[4] Shortly after, the Spanish ships hoisted their colours and commenced
the action. The *Argonauta* fired her guns at the *Hero* and the *España* at the little
Sirius, killing two men and wounding three. By 5:50pm the *Agamemnon*,
Triumph, *Barfleur*, *Windsor Castle* and *Defiance* had tacked in succession and
found opponents and the flagship followed. As darkness fell the smoke of the
guns mixed with the fog and the battle became a game of blind man's buff.
Vessels often found themselves surrounded by several of the enemy and had to
shoot their way out. On the British side those that suffered worst were the
Windsor Castle, the *Malta* and the *Ajax*; while of the enemy, the *San Rafael*, the
Firme and *España* were badly mauled by overwhelming British fire. After 8pm
the *Firme* was almost mastless. She struck her colours and the *San Rafael*, a little
later, followed suit. After this, Calder signalled to discontinue the action. Due
to greatly diminished visibility, many of the British ships did not see the

admiral's signal and carried on firing their guns at the enemy for over an hour. The *Windsor Castle* which had lost her fore topmast was taken in tow by the *Dragon*. The *Agamemnon* had lost her mizzen topmast and her fore topsail yard. Other ships lost yards and had their rigging cut to pieces but only in a few cases was there serious damage. For such a short and indecisive action, however, casualties were severe. When they boarded the two prizes, the *Firme* and the *San Rafael*, the British discovered 476 killed and wounded. According to the enemy they had a further 171 casualties on other vessels, which made a total of 647 against 198 casualties on the British side.

By the following morning the centres of the two fleets were 17 miles from each other and making very little progress. There was still some fog and a light breeze from the northwest. Calder signalled for his scattered ships to gather around him to protect his crippled vessels. When Villeneuve saw them slowly move towards the flagship he thought the British were taking flight. Annoyed at the loss of two of his ships and forgetting the Emperor's instructions, he sent some frigates to inform his captains that he intended to continue the battle and destroy the British fleet. Towards noon, with a light breeze from the north, the Franco-Spanish fleet formed a line of battle and bore down upon the British ships. Seeing the threat, the British hoisted their colours and hauled closer to the wind awaiting battle. To their astonishment Villeneuve called off the attack. The reason given later was that due to light airs his ships would not get within gunshot of the British before nightfall. It was more likely, however, that Villeneuve recollected Napoleon's orders to unite with Ganteaume off Brest without fighting. After the battle the wind brought Villeneuve's and Graviña's ships almost astern of Calder's, who could have faced the enemy again if he had wished but he made no attempt to do so. By midday on 24 July the Franco-Spanish fleet edged away to the southeast and by evening the two fleets were out of sight of one another. Villeneuve steered course for Vigo where he left three ships and then sailed into Ferrol.

Calder had won a victory of sorts. With a numerically inferior force he had captured two enemy ships but he had not shown the initiative expected of a British commander since Nelson had come on the scene and set new standards. The English public was outraged and the newspapers reflected the general feeling that had Calder possessed half Nelson's qualities the combined enemy fleet would have been destroyed and the campaign ended. Due to the adverse opinions stated in the press Calder demanded a court-martial that was later held on board the *Prince of Wales* at Portsmouth. He was acquitted of cowardice in the presence of the enemy but he was severely reprimanded for not having done his utmost to renew the engagement. The verdict clearly stated that his foremost objective should have been to annihilate the Franco-Spanish fleet. To all in Britain Sir Robert Calder simply had not lived up to expectations.

Meanwhile, Nelson sailed towards Cádiz where he found Collingwood on guard but no sign of the enemy. Suspecting Villeneuve had gone north he had replenished his fleet in Morocco and sailed north himself. That same day, Napoleon reached Boulogne and the crisis was at hand. The outlying British squadrons were now concentrated at the entrance to the Channel for the defence of their Island. Calder and Cornwallis met off Brest on 14 August and Nelson, who had been delayed by northerly winds since leaving The Rock, arrived the following day bringing the fleet to a total of thirty-four ships. On the way, he had received news from a frigate that there had been no sign of the enemy either in the Bay of Biscay, or off the Irish coast.

The *Victory* saluted Cornwallis's flagship, the *Ville de Paris*, hove to for a while and at sundown, leaving his squadron to Cornwallis, Nelson sailed for Portsmouth in the lonely company of the *Superb*. As his barge pulled up to the Portsmouth shore Nelson received the most enthusiastic greeting of his career. In spite of the rain the streets leading to Portsmouth harbour had been thronged as soon as news of his arrival had reached the town. He went first to pay his respects to the commissioner of the port and then on to London in a post-chaise. At 6pm on 20 August 1805 he reached the comforts of Merton, his new home in Surrey, where Emma, now a widow, and their daughter Horatia anxiously awaited him.

Cornwallis's blunder

During the following days the campaign came to a climax. Napoleon, believing the British were still dispersed and that the moment had come for the invasion of England, pressed Villeneuve to leave Ferrol, join up with Ganteaume and enter the English Channel. Cornwallis received intelligence of this and dispatched Calder with the *Agamemnon* and another seventeen line-of-battle ships to guard Ferrol.

This was an unpardonable strategic blunder for an officer of Cornwallis's calibre to make. An *insigne bétise*, as Napoleon called it when he heard of the separation of the Channel fleet. The detachment of Calder was an invitation to Villeneuve and his vastly superior force to leave port and crush half the British fleet at a time. Another alternative would have been for him to have evaded Calder altogether and sailed to Brest where he could have placed Cornwallis and his remaining seventeen ships between his own twenty-eight on one side and Ganteaume's twenty-one on the other. Had he chosen to do this Cornwallis would have either had to flee or be crushed. Either way, the Franco-Spanish fleet would have been able to concentrate about fifty ships of the line off the entrance to the Channel and Napoleon's dream of invading England could have become reality.

Villeneuve missed his chance. Ganteaume was ready to cooperate with him as soon as he was sighted off Brest but Villeneuve never went near the port. Having edged out into the Atlantic he had changed his mind. After touching Ferrol and later Vigo he sped south to Cádiz, stopping to burn three British merchantmen on the way. Collingwood followed the French fleet keeping just out of gunshot. He tacked whenever they tacked and finally followed them to Cádiz. Meanwhile, Calder learned from a frigate that Villeneuve had left Ferrol with thirty men-of-war and he too gave chase southwards and joined Collingwood off Cádiz.

The threat of invasion was over. After 7 months Napoleon's Grand Design had ended in frustration. He was angered because Villeneuve had not followed his instructions and he thought this had caused his elaborate scheme to collapse. The failure was irreversible. The French fleet had suffered severely during the long chase, the Spaniards had lost faith in their ally, the season was already advanced and it was no longer possible to take the British by surprise. The invasion was abandoned. Due to his prudence as well as his lack of boldness Villeneuve had saved Napoleon's fleet from a fate worse than that of the Spanish Armada in 1588. Like the Duke of Parma who had waited in the Netherlands with an army to be ferried to England, Napoleon's Grande Armée was marooned at Boulogne with all hopes of crossing the Channel gone. The French and Spanish squadrons were back in the ports of Cádiz, Ferrol, and Toulon, and the Royal Navy had resumed their blockade. The initiative was back in British hands after an extremely perilous period.

Activities before Trafalgar

On the evening of 2 September 1805, the frigate *Euryalus* hove to off the Needles. Her commander, Captain Henry Blackwood, was rowed ashore and, hiring a chaise and four in Lymington, set off towards the Admiralty in London. He brought the news that Villeneuve and Gravina had at last been sighted entering Cádiz. At five o'clock in the morning he stopped on the way for a few minutes at Merton, Nelson's home. He found the master of the house already up and dressed and after showing his visitor in, Nelson exclaimed: 'I am sure that you bring me news of the French and Spanish fleets . . .' Blackwood concurred and Nelson turned to his visitor and exclaimed: 'Depend on it Blackwood, I shall yet give Mr Villeneuve a drubbing.' Nelson eagerly accompanied Blackwood to Whitehall and arriving at the Admiralty he was ushered into the presence of the First Lord.

Lord Barham, who scarcely knew the Vice Admiral, was slightly distrustful of Nelson's colourful reputation. He sent for Nelson's personal file and after looking through it became convinced that even if his behaviour had at times been unorthodox he was a master of his calling, and had clearly demonstrated this throughout his career. He might be a junior admiral but his right to command the fleet was indisputable. Old Lord Barham requested that Nelson resume his command as soon as possible and gave him a free hand to choose his own officers.

After an emotional departure from Merton, Nelson went to a meeting with Pitt in London. After the interview the Prime Minister walked him to his carriage, a compliment which Nelson thought would not have been granted

Nelson being rowed out to HMS *Victory* at Portsmouth on 14 September 1805, on his way to join the fleet off Cadiz. From a painting by B F Gribble (1873–1962). (National Maritime Museum, London)

to even a Prince of the Blood. In his private diary, while the horses were being changed at Guildford, he wrote the following prayer:

> Friday Night at half-past Ten drove from dear, dear Merton, where I left all which I hold dear in this World, to go to serve my King & Country. May the Great God Whom I adore enable me to fulfill the expectations of my Country, and if it is his good pleasure that I should return, my thanks will never cease being offered up to the Throne of his Mercy. If it is His good providence to cut short my days upon Earth, I bow with the greatest submission, relying that He will protect those so dear to me that I may leave behind. His Will be done. Amen. Amen. Amen.

Nelson arrived at the familiar George Inn at Portsmouth, at 6am on 14 September. There was a carriage drawn up at the door belonging to the vicar of Merton who was delivering his fourteen-year-old son to join the *Victory* as a volunteer, first class. Within, Nelson found his friend George Rose, Vice-President of the Board of Trade, and George Canning, Treasurer of the Navy, who had come to pay their respects and see him off. Nelson invited them to dine with him on board the *Victory*. After breakfast, he walked to the Dock-yard to pay his old friend Commissioner Saxton a visit. He learned from the captains of the *Royal Sovereign*, *Defiance* and *Agamemnon* who had come to see him, that their ships were at Spithead under repairs. He instructed them to follow him speedily to a secret rendezvous as soon as they provisioned and were ready for sea. A frigate, he said, stationed off Cape St Vincent, would tell them where he was. If, by chance, after cruising for 24 hours they failed to find her, they were to call at Cape St Mary's and Cádiz with equal caution. At 2pm the Vice Admiral left the inn for the *Victory*, in the company of Canning and Rose who were to have dinner with him on board.

> Nelson, [said Southey] endeavoured to elude the populace by taking a bye-way to the beach; but a crowd collected in his train, pressing forward to obtain sight of his face; many were in tears, and many knelt down before him, and blessed him as he passed. England has many heroes; but never one so entirely possessed the love of his fellow-countrymen as Nelson. All men knew that his heart was as humane as it was fearless: that there was not in his nature the slightest alloy of selfishness or cupidity; but that, with perfect and entire devotion, he served his country with all his heart, and with all his soul, and with all his strength; and, therefore, they loved him as truly and as fervently as he loved England.

It was as if all England realised that her fate lay in the hands of this small, frail man.

On the following morning, Sunday 15 September, the *Victory* weighed anchor with light airs and steered a course SSE with Blackwood's frigate the *Euryalus* in company. The wind turned against them, however, and only 6 days later did they clear the Soundings. Then fortunately the wind veered north and carried them swiftly across the Bay of Biscay and down the Portuguese coast. Nelson sent urgent messages ahead on the *Euryalus* to the British consul at Lisbon and to Admiral Collingwood, telling them that on no account should they 'mention Lord Nelson's approach or acknowledge his arrival'. To Collingwood he added: 'I would not have you salute even if you are out of sight of land.' At dawn on 28 September with the scent of Spanish orange groves wafting from the shore, the *Victory* joined the fleet off Cádiz. It was the eve of Nelson's forty-seventh birthday.

The Agamemnon *and the 'Stormy Petrel'*

Sir Edward Berry, at thirty-seven, was a feisty little man full of lively aggressiveness, not unlike Nelson himself. The son of a London merchant, Berry had entered the service as a volunteer when only eleven. He became a midshipman during the American War of Independence and saw five fleet actions before his fifteenth birthday. Promoted to lieutenant as a reward for his bravery in boarding a French ship of war, he distinguished himself again in the battle of the Glorious First of June in 1794. Berry was first lieutenant of the

Agamemnon under Nelson in 1795 and followed him into the *Captain*. During the battle of St Vincent he was the first man to board the *San Nicolás* and assisted Nelson to board the *San José*. He was Nelson's flag captain in the *Vanguard* at the battle of the Nile. When Nelson was wounded he caught him in his arms and carried him below. He was sent to England with dispaches after the battle but was captured in the *Leander* by the French ship *Généreux* after much resistance. Severely wounded, he was later released on parole from prison in France. Upon arrival in England he was knighted and presented with a gold medal and the freedom of the City of London. As captain of the *Foudroyant* he pursued and captured his old enemy the *Généreux* in 1799. Present at the blockade of Malta in 1800, he helped to take the *Guillaume Tell*. Later the same year he conveyed the Queen of Naples from Palermo to Livorno for which he was presented with a gold box set with diamonds and a diamond ring. He had taken part in no less than seven naval engagements prior to Trafalgar.

Often called the 'Stormy Petrel' of the service, this was the man that on 17 September 1805 became commander of the *Agamemnon*. Striding onto the quarterdeck of the famous old ship in his dress uniform of blue and gold, white breeches and cocked hat, with his sword hanging at his left side, he unfolded his papers and with a firm voice read his commission to the officers gathered around him. He then shook hands and had a word with each of them in turn. They were Hugh Cook, Samuel Clark, William Coot, Thomas Pinto and Stewart Blacker. The master was Thomas Webb and the surgeon John Jameson.

The ship was anchored at Spithead undergoing repairs. Carpenters had been working on her for several days patching up her many battle scars and replacing timbers, while riggers were working aloft with their ropes and cordage. Twenty-four active years was a long life for a wooden-walled ship of the line and the years had taken their toll in many ways. One major problem was the corrosion of the fittings due to the electrolytic action of different metals being submerged in salt water.

On 3 October, with 6 months provisions on board, the *Agamemnon* weighed anchor and ran through the Needles on a southeasterly course. The log records 'Punished James Mounslow, seaman for deserting. Several sails in sight.'[5] The next day found her sailing past Brest where only three ships could be seen at anchor in the port. During their run across the Bay, Berry exercised the great guns and the small arms and warded off idleness by employing the seamen in 'working up junk'. This involved cutting old rope into short pieces out of which 'baggywrinkles' or 'bag'o'wrinkles' were woven. These short hairy strands of rope were useful on board to wrap around certain parts of the standing rigging to prevent chafing.

A week out of Portsmouth found the *Agamemnon* sailing into gales and squalls off Cape Finisterre. Through the rain Berry could see strange ships ahead which did not acknowledge his private signal. Unknowingly, he was sailing towards the French squadron out of Rochefort, commanded by

Captain (later Sir) Edward Berry (1768–1831), by J S Copley. Becoming captain of the *Agamemnon* on 17 September 1805, he was to command her at Trafalgar just over a month later and the next year at Santo Domingo. (National Maritime Museum, London)

Admiral Allemand. The squadron consisted of six sail-of-the-line, two frigates, a brig and four small vessels in tow. As soon as he realised the danger Berry tried to escape but the *Agamemnon* had been seen and a French three-decker and an 80-gun ship detached themselves from the squadron and steered towards her. Berry ordered thirty casks of water to be thrown overboard to lighten ship and the guns to be fired continuously to alert any British ships that the enemy were on the prowl. An hour later, the French were gaining on them and the situation became very serious indeed when fortunately a convoy came into sight. This distracted the pursuers who gave up the chase to bear down upon the convoy. It had been a very close call in which the *Agamemnon* narrowly escaped falling into enemy hands.

At daylight on Sunday 13 October the lookout in the *Agamemnon*'s foretop called down to the deck that the British fleet was in sight. The fleet was composed of several divisions but Berry was able to get close enough to the *Victory* to be rowed over and pay his respects to the commander-in-chief.

Every day brought new additions to the British fleet stationed off Cádiz, but frigates were in short supply. Nelson dictated letters incessantly to Lord Barham, to the Secretary of the Admiralty, to Lord Castlereagh, asking for 'more eyes . . . The last fleet was lost to me for want of Frigates; God forbid this should,' he wrote privately to Rose. In the letter he asked if Mr Pitt could be prevailed upon to pass the word on to the First Lord that he would be uneasy until the necessary ships reached him. In the meantime, he told Blackwood: 'Let me know every movement. I rely on you that we can't miss getting hold of them. Watch all points, and all winds and weather, for I shall depend upon you.'

When his favourite ship the *Agamemnon* hove in sight at dawn that Sunday morning with none other than his old friend Sir Edward Berry in command Nelson was delighted. 'Here comes that damned fool Berry!' he exclaimed rubbing his 'fin'. 'Now we shall have a battle!'

Our only object is to annihilate the enemy!

On 14 October the enemy were seen at the entrance to Cádiz harbour and Nelson knew that there was not long to wait before the battle. 'Placed *Defence* and *Agamemnon* from seven to ten leagues West of Cádiz,' he noted in his journal, 'and *Mars* and *Colossus* five leagues East from the Fleet, whose station will be from 15 leagues to 20 West of Cádiz, and by this chain I hope to have a constant communication with the frigates off Cádiz.' Then, as today, communication was an important element of success. No one was more aware of this than Nelson who had waged his own personal battle for more frigates in every fleet he had commanded.

Apart from the lack of frigates, Nelson was also anxious about Hardy. Hardy was his friend, one of the great 'Band of Brothers', the distinguished group of captains who had fought with him at the Battle of the Nile. He had been Nelson's flag captain for seven years prior to being with him on the *Victory*. Six feet four inches in height, he had been a lieutenant aboard the *Agamemnon* when the ship was first commissioned under Captain Caldwell. Aboard the *Victory* his health had been poor for a long time and many of his administrative duties had fallen upon Nelson's shoulders. Nelson also missed his flag captain at table as Hardy usually cut up his meat for him and in his absence Nelson had fallen back on a softer diet. Quite often he refused to eat at all.

'We have only one great object in view,' Nelson wrote to Collingwood, his second-in-command, 'that of annihilating our enemies.' His intention was to starve the enemy fleet which was concentrated in Cádiz harbour and force it out to sea and to battle. To tempt the enemy out he withdrew his fleet approximately 50 miles from shore. His force consisted of twenty-seven sail-of-the-line besides the two frigates. The combined French and Spanish fleet, on the other hand, consisted of thirty-three ships of the line. Among these were four three-deckers mounting 100 to 130 guns, five frigates and two gun brigs. A force of twenty-seven ships was not in theory adequate to take on a force of thirty-three and to make matters worse some of the British vessels were running short of water. Nelson had detatched five of the most needy under Rear-Admiral Louis to sail to Gibraltar to take on provisions. This left

Nelson with an inadequate force not only to keep watch on Cádiz but to defend itself if the Brest fleet, having evaded Cornwallis, took the blockaders in the rear. Shortly after, however, two 74s arrived from England, and the small frigate force was gradually strengthened by the arrival of five more ships, as well as some smaller vessels. Nelson's pleas had been heard.

Nelson's energy and inspiration roused the spirit of his captains to the highest pitch. On 10 October he outlined a new and daring plan of action, ignoring the Admiralty's 'Fighting Instructions'. He had resolved to abandon the old formal line of battle technique, that stipulated sailing parallel to the enemy's fleet. His new strategy consisted in breaking Villeneuve's line as soon as he left port by boldly sailing at right angles into it with his own fleet divided into two main divisions. The enemy van would be cut away from the centre and rear which the British would then attempt to destroy. After the meeting with his captains Nelson wrote: 'All approved. It was new, it was singular, it was simple. It must succeed.' In a mood of confidence and elation the fleet prepared for the trial ahead.

A discerning and shrewd Villeneuve sensed that Nelson would not form a line parallel to his own in the conventional way. He committed his thoughts to paper, just as Nelson had done, for the benefit of his captains. 'He will try,' he wrote, 'to double our rear, cut through the line, and bring against the ships thus isolated groups of his own, to surround and capture them. Captains must rely upon their courage and love of glory, rather than upon the signals of the admiral, who may already be engaged and wrapped in smoke. The Captain who is not in action is not at his post.'[6]

Manoeuvring before the battle

Villeneuve had received new instructions from Napoleon written on 17 September, instructing him to enter the Mediterranean and sail for Naples in support of the Emperor's new military plans. Furthermore, learning of the arrival in Madrid of Admiral Rosily sent by Napoleon to supersede him, Villeneuve resolved to try his luck one last time before his successor arrived. On 18 October 1805, he informed Graviña that he would sail the following day.

Their movements were first noted by the inshore squadron who reported: 'Enemy has their topsail yards hoisted,' and some time later, 'Enemy ships are coming out of port.' On receiving these signals Nelson, who was 50 miles to the west, led his fleet to the southeast to cut the enemy off from the Straits of Gibraltar and force them into battle in the open sea. At daybreak, having arrived in sight of The Rock without sighting the enemy, he put his fleet about and made sail to the northwest under a fresh southwest breeze.

On 20 October, the *Agamemnon*, which was one of the inshore communications squadron, sighted a vessel through the mist. Berry hove to and seeing a chance to take a prize, sent a party of men to board what turned out to be a large merchant brig flying an American flag. The boarding party captured it and took it in tow. Shortly after, Blackwood's frigate the *Euryalus* came sailing down with signals flying to warn the *Agamemnon* that she was running straight towards some thirty enemy ships from Cádiz. Berry immediately ordered that the tow rope be cut and put the *Agamemnon* about. The activity on board became intense. Men climbed the rigging to shorten sails, the guns were fired in warning and signals were hoisted saying the enemy was close at hand. The *Agamemnon* moved swiftly out of danger. It was the second time in 10 days that she had miraculously escaped from a hazardous situation. In the course of the morning the *Sirius* also narrowly escaped falling among the enemy due to the prevailing mist.

The Franco-Spanish fleet formed in three columns and cleared for action as soon as their advance frigates signalled that eighteen British sail-of-the-line were in sight. They stood south until about 5pm and then steered for the mouth of the Straits. The news was at once conveyed to Nelson who signalled that he relied on Captain Blackwood to keep sight of the enemy during the night.

Just before dawn on the day of the battle, Villeneuve discovered that the British were in an advantageous position to windward of him, instead of to leeward as he had supposed. He also discovered that Nelson had a larger force than he had suspected. He had thought the British had only twenty-one ships of the line. Villeneuve, with his fleet of thirty-three ships divided into three columns, was in a situation where only the outside column could fire without danger to the rest. He therefore made the signal to form a single line of battle with the *Principe de Asturias* heading the van and the *Neptuno* bringing up the rear.

Nelson had ordered his four frigate captains to meet with him at dawn on the *Victory*. After the meeting, he kept Blackwood with him until as long as possible and did not dismiss him until the enemy's shot whistled overhead. Blackwood, with Captain Hardy, had early that morning witnessed the will in which Nelson recommended Lady Hamilton and little Horatia to the care of his country. He left the following memories of these last hours:

> He seemed very much to regret, and with reason, that the enemy tacked to the northward, and formed their line on the larboard instead of the starboard tack, which latter line of bearing would have kept the Strait's mouth open. Instead of which, by forming to the northward, they brought the shoals of Trafalgar and St Pedro under our lee; and also, with the existing wind, kept open the port of Cadiz, which was of infinite consequence to them. This movement was in a great degree the cause of Nelson's making the signal to prepare to anchor, the necessity of which was impressed on his mind to the last moment of his life . . . He frequently asked me what I should consider as a victory? — the certainty of which he never for an instant seemed to doubt, although, from the situation of the land, he questioned the possibility of the subsequent preservation of the prizes. My answer was that, 'considering the handsome way in which battle was

offered by the enemy, their apparent determination for a fair trial of strength, and the proximity of the land, I thought, if fourteen ships were captured it would be a glorious result'; to which he always replied: 'I shall not, Blackwood, be satisfied with anything short of twenty.' . . . About 10 o'clock his Lordship's anxiety to close with the enemy became very apparent. He frequently remarked to me that they put a good face upon it; but always quickly added, 'I'll give them such a dressing as they never had before.' . . . As we were standing on the front of the poop, I took his hand, and said, 'I trust, my Lord, that on my return to the *Victory*, which will be as soon as possible, I shall find your Lordship well, and in possession of twenty prizes:' on which he made his reply: 'God bless you, Blackwood; I shall never speak to you again.'

Trafalgar, 21 October 1805

Lord Nelson was on his quarterdeck with first light of dawn, wearing the undress uniform jacket with its four decorations that he had used every day since he left Portsmouth. He had taken his sword from its rack but then had left it forgotten on the table of his cabin. One of the officers thought Nelson's jacket would make him too conspicuous and was tempted to suggest that he cover his decorations with a handkerchief. The enemy were known to have Tyrolean riflemen dispersed among their ships and sharpshooters in the rigging. The officer never found an opportunity to speak. However, Hardy had been approached about this matter and as he paced by Nelson's side he mentioned that his jacket might draw attention to his figure. Nelson agreed that perhaps it might but said, 'it was now too late to be shifting a coat.' Blackwood introduced another note of caution, suggesting that Nelson should shift his flag to the *Euryalus* and conduct the battle from a safe distance, but he would not hear of it. The only visible result of that suggestion was an order to crowd more sail onto the *Victory*.

After receiving their instructions, the four frigate captains accompanied Nelson and Hardy on the rounds of the ship. The commander-in-chief praised the way the hawse holes had been barricaded, he reminded the gun crews to take careful aim and not to waste shot, and stopped often to exchange cheerful words with the men. Despite the press gangs and the fact that Nelson's name had brought nearly 200 volunteers, the ship was undermanned. Her ship's company, however, was a veritable Tower of Babel as it included Frenchmen, Spaniards, Germans, Scandinavians, Dutch, Portuguese, Swiss, Kanakas, Italians, Hindus and Americans.

At about 9:30am, Blackwood, having failed to persuade Nelson to transfer to his frigate, suggested that another ship should lead the weather column into

(*right*) A plan of Nelson's attack at Trafalgar 21 October 1805. *Agamemnon* was the eighth ship in the column lead by Nelson in the *Victory* (on the left in this picture). The approach at right-angles to the enemy's line had the desired effect of disrupting his formation and reducing the battle to a series of ship-to-ship encounters in which superior British gunnery would be decisive. (National Maritime Museum, London)

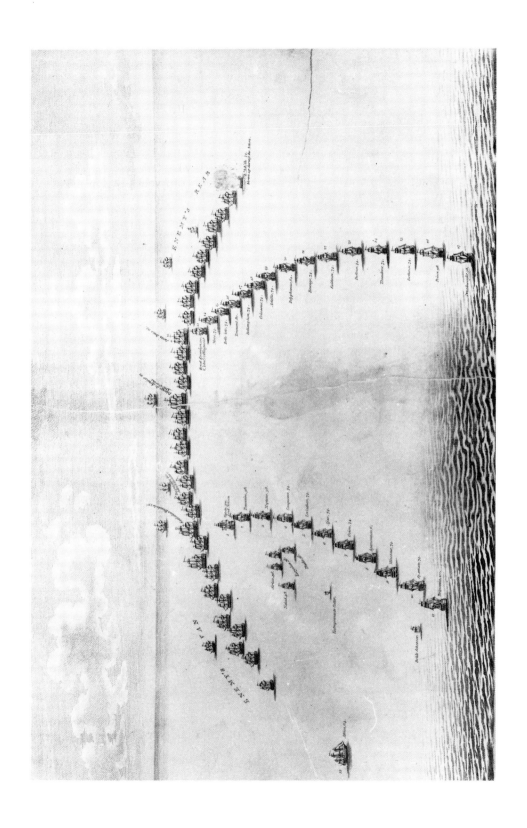

action. Both Blackwood and Hardy thought it would be sensible to keep the admiral out of battle as long as possible. Nelson consented to let the 98-gun *Téméraire* take the lead, but then regretted the decision. The swift-sailing *Victory* did not give way. As the *Téméraire*'s bowsprit ranged upon the flagship's quarter, Nelson hailed her with his slight nasal intonation saying: 'I'll thank you, Captain Harvey, to keep your proper station which is astern of the *Victory*.'

The Admiralty Pilot tells that 'Cabo Trafalgar, called by the Romans Promontorium Junonis, and by the Arabs Taraf El Agar (promontory of caves) is a small peninsula, about 66 foot high, and is uneven and sandy.' A rocky shoal runs from it into the sea. The French fleet were some 8 miles from this obstacle and the British about ten miles west of them to windward. At around 10am Nelson signalled his ships to steer ENE for an attack in two columns as he had planned. To Collingwood, who led the southern column in the *Royal Sovereign*, he signalled: 'I intend to pass through the van of the enemy's line, to prevent him from getting into Cádiz.'

Early in the morning, before the sun cast its first rays, Collingwood's steward had entered his master's cabin with a light. He found the admiral already up and shaving. Brushing his face with shaving soap, Collingwood asked if his servant had seen the enemy. The startled man looked out of the gun port and saw the 'crowd of great ships' 10 miles to leeward. Continuing his shaving with face askew, Nelson's second-in-command murmured: 'In a short time we shall see a great deal more of them'. The steward was the only one of Collingwood's personal servants to survive the day. His ablutions over, Collingwood walked out onto the quarterdeck, and seeing his First Lieutenant Mr Clarel in boots, he advised him to change them for shoes and silk stockings, 'so much more manageable for the surgeon' he said. Sir Edward Rotherham, the flag captain, resplendent in his full dress uniform with his telescope under his right arm, stopped and nodded to Admiral Collingwood as he paced the quarterdeck. Rotherham said that he had always fought in his cocked hat and full dress uniform and always would.

Berry had manoeuvred the *Agamemnon* into her position seventh in the line of the weather division. The *Africa* had lost touch with the fleet during the night. She was 10 miles away at dawn and unable to take up her position ahead of the *Agamemnon*. Down in the half light of the gun decks and in the 'slaughterhouses' near the main mast, the gun crews waited in silence. The ports were open, the slow matches lighted in case the flintlocks missed fire when the guns were run out. The *Agamemnon* rolled heavily in the swell. Suddenly cheering could be heard, which spread like a tidal wave from the other ships to their own. It was caused by Nelson's signal to the fleet. On the *Victory*, 3 minutes earlier, the admiral had turned to his signal lieutenant John Pasco and said he would amuse the fleet with a signal. 'I wish to say . . . "England Confides that Every Man will do his Duty." You must be quick', he added, 'for I have one more to make which is for Close Action.' Pasco suggested he substitute 'expects' for 'confides'. 'Expects' was in the book as a combination signal on a single hoist, whereas 'confides' would have had to be spelled out letter by letter using several hoists, as indeed 'duty' had to be. 'That will do, Pasco,' said Nelson, 'make it directly.' The first reaction was one of irritation. 'What is Nelson signalling about?' muttered Collingwood irascibly. 'We all know what we have to do.' Between decks the reaction was pretty much the same. 'Do your duty! Of course we'll do our duty. I've always done mine, haven't you?' Nevertheless, the men cheered, more perhaps from love and admiration for their admiral than in appreciation of this now legendary signal.

When Villeneuve saw the British fleet coming towards his own at right angles and in two divisions, he confessed he could no longer prevent the impending battle by reaching safety in Cádiz. Gathering his officers around him on the quarterdeck of the *Bucentaure* and pointing towards the British fleet, he spoke of the manner in which the two columns descending upon him were being led in perfect formation, and he is said to have exclaimed in admiration, 'Nothing but victory can attend such gallant conduct.' Due to the disorderly manoeuvring of his ships, Villeneuve had been unable to form a proper line of battle. Assembled helter-skelter, his line looked more like a crescent and had taken over 2 hours to turn northward. As the signals for battle were hoisted, Commodore Don Cosme Churruca in command of the *San Juan de Nepomuceno*, closing his telescope with a click, turned to one of his officers and said: 'This fleet is doomed. The French admiral does not know his profession. He has compromised us all!' Soon after, sensing catastrophe, he summoned his crew to prayers.

A deathly silence fell upon the ships as the two fleets drew nearer. Two towering clouds of sail advanced resolutely against each other, wielding the combined might of 5,000 guns.[7] Nelson in the *Victory* led the weather division and Collingwood in the *Royal Sovereign* with her new copper sheathing was sailing well ahead in the leeward division. Each captain marked down his adversary as the two English columns thundered into action.

It was noon when the first shot of the great battle was fired by the *Fougueux* at the *Royal Sovereign*. Seconds later the huge 112-gun *Santa Ana* joined in with direct fire. Collingwood had broken the enemy line astern of Vice Admiral Alava's flagship. The *Belleisle* came to help relieve the *Royal Sovereign*. Then the whole of the British lee division burst through between the fifth and sixth ships of the enemy's rear. The air was rent with the roar of the broadsides, the crashing of falling spars, the rattle of musketry at close range. On the *Victory*'s quarterdeck Lieutenant Pasco, looking through his glass, exclaimed, 'There is a topgallant yard gone!' 'Whose topgallant yard is that gone?' asked Nelson briskly. 'Is it the *Royal Sovereign*?' 'No, my Lord, an enemy's.' The admiral smiled. 'Collingwood is doing well.' He pulled out his watch, and called the officers about him to set theirs by it.

To avoid any possible confusion in the heat and smoke of battle, the commander-in-chief had given the order that every ship of the British fleet hoist the white ensign. In addition, they had been ordered to fly the Union flag from both the fore and main topgallant mast so as to easily identify each other.

Nelson had ordered the *Victory* to be steered towards the bow of the *Santísima Trinidad*. He was searching for the ship in which Villeneuve was present. He had not long to wait for an answer to his unspoken challenge as the French flagship the *Bucentaure* opened fire with all its guns. The *Victory*'s speed as she headed for the gap between the *Bucentaure* and the *Santísima Trinidad* became slower than ever as the wind had almost disappeared. During the long approach she suffered terribly. One shot cut her mizzen topmast in two and another knocked her wheel to pieces so that from then on she had to be steered from the gunroom. Every sail she carried was cut to threads and all her foremast studding sail booms had been shot away.

Hardy said to Nelson that the *Victory* could not pass through the French line without running on board one of their ships. The French were sailing very close together with bows and sterns almost touching. 'It does not signify which we run on board of. Go on board which you please. Take your choice.' Whereupon Hardy made for the *Redoutable*. As the *Victory* passed astern of the *Bucentaure* she fired every one of her port side guns, all loaded with double shot, and some with treble shot, into the cabin windows of Villeneuve's

A painting by Thomas Buttersworth showing the leading British ships breaking through the Franco-Spanish line at Trafalgar. This allowed them to fire their broadsides into the enemy's unprotected stern as they passed, shot sweeping the open decks from end to end. One broadside from HMS *Victory* in these circumstances killed or wounded 400 men aboard the French *Bucentaure*. (National Maritime Museum, London)

flagship. The range was so close that as the *Victory* rolled, her main yardarm struck the vangs of the *Bucentaure*'s gaff and the Frenchman's ensign caught in the *Victory*'s rigging. The broadside wrecked the stern of the French flagship, destroyed twenty of her guns and, as was later said, killed and wounded nearly 400 of her men.

Hardy was still intent on running down the *Redoutable* which was on his starboard bow. He fired a broadside into her as soon as the *Victory*'s guns would bear and putting the helm hard a-port made straight for her. At the same time, the captain of the *Redoutable* put her helm down and the two great ships met sideways on and locked their topmasts together in a savage tangle of spars, canvas and cordage. Both ships fired at each other with their muzzles almost touching the other's hull. The *Redoutable* also fired muskets with great accuracy from her decks and her topmasts. The *Victory* countered by firing her 68-pounder carronades to good effect, but her upper deck guns were silenced by the deadly small-arms fire from sharpshooters in the rigging of the *Redoutable*.

Launched in 1769, *Santisima Trinidad* was the largest warship in the world, carrying 130 guns on four decks. *Agamemnon*, together with HMS *Neptune* and *Conqueror*, dismasted her completely at Trafalgar and forced her to surrender. She was scuttled by the British three days after the battle. (National Maritime Museum, London)

In the meantime, the *Agamemnon* had come through the French line and firing both her broadsides took on first the *Héros* to larboard and then the *Santísima Trinidad* on her starboard side. Moving closer in, she joined with the *Neptune* and *Conqueror* to take on the huge Spanish four-decker, the largest fighting ship in the world, which mounted 130 guns. With her hull glowing vermilion and white with a magnificent white figurehead above her bows she stood out like a beacon from the rest of the fleet. Berry, who like Nelson was full of courage, nervous energy and ambition, was drawn to the target presented by the *Santísima Trinidad* like a moth to a flame. Getting under her guns, the *Agamemnon*, *Conqueror* and *Neptune* fought like pitbull terriers around their quarry, keeping up an unrelenting barrage until, at 2:30pm they dismasted the great ship completely, having brought down her fore, main, and mizzen masts. Ten minutes later, the *Santísima Trinidad* struck her colours but Berry, who was anxious to board her and hoist the Union flag, was prevented by four enemy ships which kept up a heavy fire upon him to ward him off. The *Colossus* was so heavily damaged that the *Agamemnon* later had to take her in tow. This was no small undertaking since the *Agamemnon* herself was badly damaged. She had received one shot hole in the upper counter, one in the stern and six under her waterline which kept the pumps going constantly. In addition she had received three shots in the port side, one in the starboard side, six in the fore yard and one had carried away the cheek of the mainmast. She had lost two men killed and eight had been wounded.

In the meantime, Nelson and Hardy had been pacing the quarterdeck of the *Victory* as if on parade. At 1:15pm Nelson was wounded in the shoulder by a bullet aimed from the masthead of the *Redoutable*. He sank to his knees supporting himself with his hand for a moment and then fell to the deck. 'They have done for me at last Hardy,' he said, 'my backbone is shot through.' The bullet had been fired at him from the mizzen top of the enemy ship some 15 yards away. Striking him in front of his left epaulette, it entered his shoulder, fractured the second and third ribs and penetrated the left lung severing a branch of the pulmonary artery on its way. The bullet passed through his spine and finally lodged in the muscles below his right scapular. He was carried below amid the thunder of the *Victory*'s guns. The battle was still raging. The log of the *Victory* reports: 'Partial firing continued until 4–30pm, when a victory having been reported to the Right Hon Lord Viscount Nelson, KB and Commander-in-Chief, he then died of his wound.' It was 4:40pm.

Five minutes later the *Bucentaure*'s last mast came crashing down. Villeneuve, a tranquil, placid Frenchman, English in appearance and wearing a long tailed uniform coat and green corduroy pantaloons, looked for someone to whom he could surrender. Finally a marine officer with five men from the *Conqueror* went on board the French flagship to take him and his two captains prisoner. Of the foremost group of the Franco-Spanish line, six had been captured. Of the rearmost group twelve had been taken or destroyed. In total,

'Hero of Trafalgar' by William Heysman Overend (1851–1898), showing
Nelson on the quarterdeck of HMS *Victory* at the height of the battle. His
many decorations made him an obvious target for the French marksmen in
the fighting tops of the *Redoutable*. (National Maritime Museum, London)

nine were French and another nine Spanish. Fifteen French ships under Rear-
Admiral Dumanoir Le Pelley had escaped southward. Admiral Don Federico
Graviña had been mortally wounded on board the *Principe de Asturias*. He
ordered that the signal to retire be hoisted. Then he withdrew towards Cádiz
taking with him ten crippled ships. The *Victory* in the meantime had managed
to untangle herself from the *Redoutable*'s rigging and the *Redoutable* was
boarded and taken.

Nelson and Collingwood had been close friends ever since they had been
lieutenants. To spare Collingwood's feelings as much as possible Hardy sent
the *Victory*'s only remaining boat to the *Royal Sovereign* with the news that
Nelson had been dangerously wounded. When Captain Blackwood came
alongside the *Victory* in his own boat after the battle and learned the truth,
both he and Hardy went together to break the full news to Collingwood.
They told him that Nelson's last order was to anchor the fleet and the prizes as
soon as possible to protect them from the dangers of a lee shore and a probable
gale. 'Anchor the fleet! Why, it is the last thing I should have thought of,'

answered Collingwood, and, in spite of his old friend's dying request, he thought better. During the following afternoon, the gale foreseen by Nelson came up from the southwest accompanied by torrential rain. Codrington of the *Orion* said years later that he had never been so glad to see the stars as after Trafalgar, as for four days after Nelson's death no one in the fleet saw the sun, the moon or the constellations.

With the shoals of Cape Trafalgar threatening to leeward the *Victory* was taken in tow by the *Polyphemus*. Later, due to the bad weather, the *Polyphemus* was obliged to cut the towing hawser to prevent the *Victory* riding forward onto her stern, but in spite of the *Victory* burning blue lights the flagship was lost from sight for 48 hours. On 26 October the storm finally abated and Captain Fremantle with HMS *Neptune* came to her aid.

On 24 October the senior French officer in Cádiz put to sea to try and retake some of the prizes. At noon he was close to the British ships, ten of which, casting off their tow lines, formed a line to protect their captives. He managed to retake two of them and make off. Due to the storm, the French 80-gun *Indomptable* grounded and went to pieces; the *San Francisco de Asís* was driven ashore in Cádiz Bay; the *Rayo* and the *Monarca* were wrecked; the *Aigle*, the *Intrepide* and the *San Augustín* were burned; the *Argonauta* was scuttled as it seemed impossible to save her, and the *Berwick*, which had been captured by the French in 1795 off Corsica, grounded and went to pieces off San Lucar. The *Santísima Trinidad* was scuttled by Collingwood's order three days after the battle. Of the numerous prizes only four remained. They were those which had been anchored after the battle. (For Collingwood's account of the battle and its aftermath, as well as his orders to the fleet, see Appendix 5.)

The *Victory*, in tow of the *Neptune*, reached Gibraltar where she was partially refitted. She sailed for England on 3 November, arriving at Plymouth harbour on 4 December with Nelson's flag still flying from the masthead. The body of the dead admiral, preserved in spirits, was on board, later to be buried with all the pomp and ceremony Nelson deserved, directly under the cupola in the crypt of St Paul's Cathedral.

Of all the epitaphs which were composed for him none is more fitting than the one written by Joseph Conrad, another seaman:

> Not the least glory of the Navy is that it understood Nelson. In a few short years he revolutionised not the strategy or tactics of sea warfare, but the very conception of victory itself. He brought heroism into the line of duty. Verily he is a terrible ancestor.

To the British people Nelson had become simply The Hero and is so still to many until this day. Every year on the anniversary of Trafalgar naval officers on whatever station they may be, stand and lift their glasses to the toast: 'Gentlemen! The Immortal Memory.'

'The battle of Trafalgar: prizes in a gale the day after the action' after the style of the Tudgay family. In the storms following Trafalgar, many of the French and Spanish ships captured in the battle were either lost or abandoned by the British ships which had them in tow. (National Maritime Museum, London)

The aftermath

On the day after the battle the badly damaged *Agamemnon* limped along towards Gibraltar 55 miles away, with the dismasted HMS *Colossus* in tow. Taking in water from her wounds below the waterline at the rate of 3 feet per hour, her pumps were manned around the clock. The bad weather after the battle, with constant rain, added to the discomfort of the men, who were already exhausted. Knowing that their fatigue was only equalled by his own, Berry ordered a gill of spirits per man to be measured out every day of the trip. The *Agamemnon* took six days to reach her destination. Upon arrival, she anchored in 20 fathoms in Gibraltar Bay, cast off the *Colossus*, sent her wounded to the hospital and then set about moving her stores to make the shot holes under her waterline accessible to her carpenters. Other ships that had been badly damaged in the battle arrived in ones and twos. The *Thunderer* arrived towing a Spanish prize on the same day as *Agamemnon*, then came the *Revenge*, followed by the *Tonnant* and the *Victory* herself with Nelson's body on board. Ships of the fleet towing French and Spanish prizes continued to arrive until 3 November. On 30 October the brig *Beagle* ran foul of the *Agamemnon* and carried away one of her chainplates. Carpenters from the dockyard repaired the damage to the hull, while onshore in the workshops, new masts and spars were made.

The man who shot and killed Nelson seems to have been shot himself by John Pollard, midshipman of the *Victory*. It is said that Pollard seized a musket and was supplied with cartridges by the quartermaster, Mr King, from two barrels kept on the poop for the use of the marines. Thus armed, he fired at the sharpshooters in the rigging of the *Redoutable* until none were left alive. Years later Pollard would relate that after the action Captain Hardy congratulated him upon having avenged the death of Vice Admiral Nelson.

Admiral Collingwood, who was now commander-in-chief of the Mediterranean fleet, continued on station to watch what was left of the enemy fleet in Cádiz. The enemy, however, did not venture out to sea. Four days after the battle, on 25 October, Vice Admiral François Étienne Rosily arrived from Paris by way of Madrid to supersede Vice Admiral Villeneuve. Villeneuve had been released six months after being taken prisoner by the British and had landed at Morlaix in France on 22 April 1806. While he awaited Napoleon's instructions in Rennes, he was found dead in his hotel room, stabbed five times. Officially it was said he had perished by his own hand but it was generally believed he had been assassinated. On St Helena years later, Napoleon related to his physician not only how the unfortunate naval officer had killed himself but emphasised that he had disobeyed his orders. It was likely, though, that the one was consequence of the other. It is interesting to note that regardless of Napoleon professing Villeneuve's gallantry, the officer was buried without honours.

> Villeneuve, [said Napoleon,] when prisoner in England, was so much affected by his defeat that he studied anatomy with a view to taking his own life. To that end, he purchased several anatomical engravings of the heart, and compared them with his own body in order to make certain of the exact position of that organ. Upon his arrival in France, I ordered him to remain at Rennes, and not to come to Paris. Villeneuve, fearing to be convicted by a council of war of having disobeyed my orders, and of having lost the fleet in consequence (for I had directed him not to put to sea, and not to engage the English), determined to put an end to himself. He took his engravings of the heart, again compared them with his breast, made a deep prick with a long pin in the centre of the picture, and then, applying the same pin as nearly as possible to the corresponding place in his own body, drove it in up to the head, pierced his heart, and so died. When they opened his room they found him dead, the pin being in his breast, and the mark on the picture corresponding with the wound on his body. He should not have acted that way. He was a gallant man, although he had no talent.

Nelson was barely forty-seven when he died. As he and Fanny had not had any children, his honours and titles were inherited by his eldest brother, the

Rev William Nelson. William, quite undeservedly, was made an Earl and granted a pension of £6,000 a year that went with the Nelson peerage. He was also presented with £108,000 to purchase an estate. To each of Nelson's sisters, Susannah Bolton and Catherine Matcham, Parliament voted £10,000. A pension of £2,000 per annum was assigned to his wife Fanny, Lady Nelson. Fanny, who was never strong and who was constantly on the move, lived to be seventy-three. There are glimpses of her in a hotel in Lyons and, surprisingly, on a boating trip on Lake Geneva with Lord Byron in company with her daughter-in-law, Josiah's wife, as well as a grandchild and her nurse.

If she had been less of a spendthrift, Emma, Lady Hamilton, might have lived quietly and survived on the annuity of £500 left her by Nelson. But the Bronté estate in Sicily given to Nelson by King Ferdinand of Naples produced nothing for three years and even after that the funds were remitted irregularly. The British government provided nothing for the woman and child entrusted by the admiral to his King and country before the Battle of Trafalgar. George Rose, Nelson's friend, tried using his influence but William Grenville, the new Prime Minister, gave him a chilly response. Rose proceeded to tackle the Foreign Secretary, George Canning, who turned him down saying that he could not help either.

The fabulously wealthy Abraham Goldsmith, who had been a friend of Nelson's, paid nearly £13,000 to Emma for the purchase of Merton. This money slipped through her fingers, spent on extravagant living as all her other funds had been. One by one she parted with her Nelson relics. The death of her mother, the shrewd old Mrs Cadogan, removed the last brake on her irresponsibility. Emma was detained and cast into a debtors' prison. 1813 found her huddled in sordid rooms in London's Temple district, where she was permitted to reside 'within the rules of the King's Bench', as long as she did not attempt to escape.[8]

All Emma's personal effects had been seized and sold. Finally she was re-arrested and put back into jail. After another nine months in prison she was rescued by a friend who had known Nelson in the West Indies. She obtained her discharge during the first week of July 1814, and sailed for Calais in France with Horatia on a vessel called the *Little Tom* with less than £50.

For a while she seemed in better health due perhaps to the country air, the exercise and above all to having her freedom. The jaundice which had afflicted her had not recurred, 'but my broken heart does not leave me,' she wrote. Horatia takes up the sad story of her last few months:

> At the time of her death she was in great distress, and had I not, unknown to her, written to Lord Nelson to ask the loan of £10, and to another kind friend of hers, who immediately sent her £20, she would not literally have had one shilling till her next allowance became due. Latterly she was scarcely sensible. I imagine that her illness originally began by being bled whilst labouring under an attack of jaundice whilst she lived at Richmond. From that time she was never well, and added to this, the baneful habit she had of taking wine and spirits to a

fearful degree, brought on water on the chest. She died in January, 1815, and was buried in the burying ground attached to the town. That was a sad miserable time to me.

The service was read over the body by a Roman Catholic priest who had attended her at her request during her illness. Lady H. had, ever since she had been in Calais, professed herself a Catholic.

Latterly her mind became so irritable by drinking that I had written to Mr Matcham, and he had desired that I would lose no time in getting some respectable person to take me over and that I was to come to them, where I should always find a home. After her death, as soon as he heard of it, he came to Dover to fetch me.

With all Lady H.'s faults, — and she had *many*, — she had many fine qualities, which, had [she] been placed early in better hands, would have made her a very superior woman. It is but justice on my part to say that through *all her* difficulties, she *invariably* till the last few months, expended on my education etc., the whole of the *interest* of the sum left me by Lord Nelson, and which was left entirely at her control.

Fortunately, Nelson's prayers for Horatia were answered. Her life was full and happy and reached into old age. She married and, surrounded by peace in a rural community, bore a child almost every year. Her only worries seem to have been caused by the usual epidemics common to children. One of her children also contracted cholera. She never learned her true parentage though as early as her fourteenth year she asked her mother the question. 'On her death-bed at Calais I earnestly prayed her to tell me who my father was but she would not, influenced then, I think, by the fear that I might leave her.'

It is unlikely that Horatia ever inherited anything material. She received only the slightest recognition from those in power of her father's great services to the nation. However, from her mother she inherited the gift of kindness, a love of animals and a cheerful disposition. Furthermore, Horatia inherited the genes of her long-living, county clerical forbears. The child conceived aboard HMS *Foudroyant* in April 1801, and born in the year of Copenhagen, was a faithful likeness of her solid Norfolk ancestors. She lived to be eighty-one.

NOTES

1. William Laird Clowes, *The Royal Navy, a History from Earliest Time to the Present* (London: Sampson Low, Marston, 1898), Vol 5, p 95.
2. This officer's visit to the *Victory* could not remain a secret and within four months at the instigation of the French Ambassador to Lisbon, Donald Campbell lost his command. One of two reasons given was that he had given the English admiral the destination of the combined fleets.
3. Laird Clowes, Vol 5, p 112.
4. Ibid, Vol 5, p 114, quoting James.
5. Admiralty: Masters' Logs (ADM 51): ADM 51/5176, HMS *Agamemnon*.
6. Laird Clowes, Vol 5, p 130.
7. The Franco-Spanish fleet had a total of 2,874 guns and the British fleet had 2,232.
8. Carola Oman, *Nelson* (London: Hodder & Stoughton, 1947), p 569.

CHAPTER 10

Santo Domingo, *La Dame Ernouf* and *La Lutine* 1806

In Torrid Climes, where Nature pants for Breath,
Or tainted Gales bring Pestilence and Death;
Where Hurricanes are born, and Whirlwinds
    sweep
The raging Billows of th'Atlantic Deep.

Ballad of the West Indies. ANONYMOUS

Two months before Trafalgar Napoleon had suddenly changed his plans. He decided to attack the coalition of European states that had been welded together by Pitt. In August 1805, the French army around Boulogne, which was preparing for the invasion of England, was disbanded and the troops under Marshals Ney, Soult, Lannes and Davout set out instead on a long march towards the Danube.

Napoleon victorious

During the month of the battle of Trafalgar the Austrian army under Baron Karl Mack von Leiberich surrendered to Napoleon at Ulm, on the eastern edge of the Black Forest. Two months later, at Austerlitz[1] the Grand Armée of 68,000 men, faced a force of 85,000 fielded by Tsar Alexander I and the Austrian Emperor Francis I. In the ensuing confrontation, which came to be known as the Battle of the Three Emperors, a total of 153,000 men and 400 cannon confronted each other. By the time the sun had set on that terrible day, 11,000 Russian, 2,000 Austrian and 1,300 French soldiers lay dead upon the cold earth of the battlefield. The Tsar prepared to retreat towards Russia and the Austrian Emperor attempted to seek a treaty with Napoleon.

Acclaimed by military strategists as a perfect victory, the Battle of the Three Emperors sent tremors throughout Europe. Napoleon's star was in the ascendant and England was plunged into gloom. It seemed as if everything had failed and had to be re-attempted; the boulder of Sisyphus was rolling down the hill again despite attempts to push it to the summit.

Pitt was sorely stricken by the events at Austerlitz. This news, coupled with the sadness of seeing his lifelong friend and political colleague Henry Dundas in disgrace and impeached in the House of Commons for mismanagement in the Admiralty, probably broke Pitt's spirit and brought about his death in January 1806.[2]

Leissegues and Willaumez

The French fleet at Brest had not taken part in the Trafalgar campaign. For two months after the battle it remained in the security of its home port. Then on 14 December, having divided into two squadrons, it slipped out into the Atlantic. Cornwallis, whose ships stood guard outside the port, did not see the French fleet leaving as he had been driven off station by bad weather.

One squadron, under the command of Vice Admiral Leissegues, was ordered to carry 1,000 troops to reinforce the garrison of Santo Domingo and then to show its colours off Jamaica and Newfoundland before returning to the port of L'Orient. The other squadron under Vice Admiral Willaumez was given a choice of orders. They should either sail to the Dutch colony of the Cape of Good Hope, or to St Helena. In either case, the final destination was Cayenne and Martinique.

On 15 December 1805, before they separated, both squadrons were sighted by Captain Charles Brisbane whose frigate *Arethusa* was protecting a convoy of twenty-three merchant ships sailing from Cork to the West Indies. Quite by chance, a week later, the *Arethusa* encountered a British squadron at sea. It was the squadron hastily put together by Collingwood after Trafalgar to guard

Vice Admiral Sir John Thomas Duckworth, commander of the British squadron blockading Cadiz in December 1805, of which *Agamemnon* was part. He pursued the French squadron under Leissegues to the West Indies and engaged it off Santo Domingo. (National Maritime Museum, London)

the port of Cádiz and it included the *Agamemnon*. This squadron was under the orders of Vice Admiral Sir John Duckworth who had been sent from England in HMS *Superb* to take over command from Rear Admiral Sir Thomas Louis.

Shortly after his arrival on station, Duckworth was tempted out to sea by a rumour that some French ships of the line had attacked a British convoy off the island of Madeira. Leaving Cádiz unblockaded, he sailed with his squadron in pursuit.[3] Not finding the enemy, Duckworth was returning to Cádiz when he fell in with the *Arethusa* and received the news from Captain Brisbane that the French were just over the horizon ahead of him.

Three days later, Duckworth's frigates sighted nine unidentified sail. The British squadron tacked after them with every rag of canvas set. At dawn the following day Duckworth saw through his telescope that his quarry consisted of six French sail-of-the-line. By noon, Duckworth's flagship, the famous old *Superb*, had gained on the French and was only 7 miles from their rearmost ship. The rest of his squadron was spread out over 50 miles. With the wind in his favour, Duckworth concluded that he would probably catch up with the French within a couple of hours and that if this was the case the *Superb* would be overwhelmed before he could be assisted by the other ships of his squadron. He called off the chase. It was an unfortunate decision. The French were not superior in numbers and were not a concentrated force able to crush the British. Had Duckworth pressed on, the rest of his ships would have arrived on the scene in succession and Willaumez would have been forced either to flee and abandon his rearmost vessels, or shorten sail to protect them and face the British. Duckworth hesitated and then took the easy option. Gathering his squadron he sent the frigate *Amethyst* to England with details of the size, strength and supposed destination of the French. Duckworth then bore away for the Leeward Islands, to replenish his stock of water which was running low.

On 2 January 1806 Duckworth anchored his squadron in Carlisle Bay, Barbados. He sent the frigate *Acasta* ahead to St Kitts to make arrangements for watering the vessels. They arrived a week later and were surprised to find Rear Admiral Alexander Cochrane in the 74-gun *Northumberland* and Captain Samuel Pym in the 74-gun *Atlas* at anchor there. Neither of these men had any particular news of the enemy, so Duckworth in a leisurely manner carried on watering and refitting his ships in preparation for the return trip to Cádiz.

The Battle of Santo Domingo, 6 February 1806

On 1 February the British brig *Kingfisher* sailed into Bass Terre harbour, St Kitts, with news that three French line-of-battle ships had been sighted on a course for Santo Domingo. At once Duckworth gave the order to weigh anchor and made all sail to find them. Off the island of St Thomas the squadron was joined by two other British frigates whose captains confirmed the previous news. As proof, they had with them a Danish schooner whose captain had sailed from Santo Domingo after the French had arrived there. At dawn the following morning, abreast now of Santo Domingo, the British squadron spied no less than nine ships at anchor in the port. Eight of the vessels belonged to Vice Admiral Leissegues' squadron, comprising five sail-of-the-line, two frigates and a sloop. The other ship was a merchantman.

Leissegues, after chasing the *Arethusa* and her convoy on 15 December, had encountered bad weather off the Azores which had damaged some of his ships and delayed his arrival. After disembarking the 1,000 troops and stores he carried for the relief of the garrison at Santo Domingo, he was about to put to sea when he was discovered.

Knowing the audacity of the British and thinking that they might attack his ships in port, Leissegues ordered his squadron to weigh anchor and make for the open sea, taking advantage of the light northwesterly wind in his favour. Approaching Punta Palenque, some 20 miles southwest of the port, Leissegues formed his squadron in line of battle. The 80-gun *Alexandre* was followed in succession by the flagship *Impérial*, the *Diomede*, *Jupiter* and *Brave*.

The famous painting of the Battle of Santo Domingo, 6 February 1806, by Nicholas Pocock. *Agamemnon* is the third ship from the left in this picture. In the foreground, Duckworth's *Superb* has just brought down *Impérial*'s mainmast. (National Maritime Museum, London)

The frigates *Félicité* and *Comète* and the sloop *Diligente* formed a parallel line closer inshore.

Seeing the French in battle order, Duckworth formed his own squadron in two lines and steered to cross the bows of the leading French vessels, while signalling that the main object of his attack would be the first three ships of the enemy. His starboard or weather line consisted of the *Superb*, the *Northumberland*, the *Spencer* and the *Agamemnon*, while his port or leeward line was made up of the *Canopus*, *Donegal* and *Atlas*. By 8am both lines were sailing close abeam of one another. The smaller vessels, the *Acasta*, *Magicienne*, *Kingfisher* and *Épervier* had taken stations to windward of the ships of the line.

The three leading ships of the British weather line were bow to stern of one another and gaining fast on the French squadron, which at about 9:45am hoisted its battle colours. The *Agamemnon* and the *Canopus* had dropped somewhat astern of the rest when the *Superb*, having shortened sail, opened fire with her starboard guns upon the *Alexandre*. The *Northumberland* sailed in close upon the three-decker *Impérial*, firing her broadsides in quick succession. Five minutes later, the *Spencer* which was close to the *Northumberland*'s starboard quarter also began firing at the *Diomede* and occasionally fired at the three-decker ahead of her as well. Both squadrons kept running almost before the wind at a speed of nearly 8 knots.

Due to her age and poor condition, *Agamemnon* had difficulty getting into the action, no longer the excellent sailer Nelson had so admired. However, according to the *Agamemnon*'s log, Berry, true to his courageous and fearless nature, engaged the French flagship, the *Impérial*. Coupled with the heavy firing from *Superb*, the *Imperial* lost her main and then her mizzenmast. With only her foremast standing the French admiral, very confused, headed directly for the shore. It was noon precisely when the ship ran aground. Her foremast fell directly backwards upon her deck and she was wrecked, her hull imprisoned among the rocks that jutted out to sea. The *Superb*, now in only 17 fathoms of water, was forced to put about in haste and steer for the open channel just as the *Diomede*, hoping to aid her admiral by coming up behind, ran aground as well. As she hit the rocks her masts fell down upon her. The *Diomede* kept on firing but she soon filled with water, her bottom being stove in upon the rocks just like the *Impérial*'s.

The *Agamemnon* lost seaman James Cavenough in the action and three officers, two marines and sixteen other seamen were wounded. The ship received seven shot holes in the hull, two in the foremast and one in the main topmast. There was also considerable damage to sails and rigging. But losses were even higher in the other ships of the fleet: on the *Northumberland* twenty-one were killed and seventy-nine wounded; on the *Canopus* eight were killed and twenty-two wounded; on the *Spencer* eighteen were killed and fifty wounded; on the *Donegal* twelve were killed and thirty-eight wounded; on the *Atlas* eight were killed and eleven wounded and on the flagship, the *Superb*, six had been killed and thirty wounded.

This painting by Robert Dodd shows *Impérial* aground (left), a dismasted wreck. Soon after, *Diomede* shared the flagship's fate and *Superb* only narrowly avoided grounding herself. Three more French ships of the line were captured at Santo Domingo. (National Maritime Museum, London)

French losses were much more severe. They amounted on the *Alexandre* to 300; on the *Brave* to 260; on the *Jupiter* to 200; on the *Diomede* to 250 and on the *Impérial* to nearly 500, including both killed and wounded. Of the prizes taken, the *Alexandre* and the *Brave* were badly cut up; the *Brave* sank on her way to England and on arrival the *Alexandre* was found to be too shattered to be worth repairing for service. Only the *Jupiter*, hardly damaged and renamed *Maida*, was added to the Royal Navy.

La Dame Ernouf and La Lutine

Two days after the battle the *Agamemnon* was sailing in company with the flagship and a diminished squadron, since the *Spencer*, *Donegal* and *Atlas* had left for England with the prizes. Berry sent Lieutenant Clark in the cutter to reconnoitre the two French ships driven on shore in the action. The few sailors still on board struck their ship's colours in submission. After an hour's reconnaissance the cutter returned to the ship and the *Agamemnon* made all sail in company with HMS *Northumberland*.

During the next few days the *Agamemnon* was involved in chasing ships and checking their identities. Sometimes they turned out to be British, once an

American schooner was spotted, then an American brig from St Thomas bound for New Orleans and a Danish ship sailing from Antigua to Santa Cruz. From 2 March until 7 March 1806, the *Agamemnon* was moored in English Harbour, Antigua. Her activities between 2 March and 30 March are detailed in the captain's log book. The *Agamemnon* sailed southeast to Barbados and the surrounding seas of the Windward Islands and captured a French privateer, the notorious *La Dame Ernouf*, of 19 guns, and later *La Lutine*, an armed brig of 16 guns.[4] (See Appendix 6.)

What happened to Willaumez?

Rear Admiral Willaumez, who had escaped on 26 December 1805 due to Duckworth's misjudgement, in due course reached the Cape of Good Hope where he heard from the commander of a merchantman that the Dutch colony had fallen into British hands. The naval part of the British expedition had been led by Commodore Sir Home Popham with the military contingent under the command of Brigadier-General W C Beresford. Having subdued the Cape Colony with singular ease, these gentlemen were preparing to pounce upon the Spanish provinces of the Río de la Plata. Willaumez put to sea again and reached San Salvador on the Brazilian coast. He then sailed north to Cayenne. There he divided his squadron into three divisions which fanned out as far south as Brazil to prey on merchant shipping. As previously agreed the squadrons reassembled in the month of June at Fort Royal, Martinique.

Fort Royal was watched by Rear Admiral Sir A F Cochrane, whose squadron consisted of the *Northumberland*, the *Elephant*, the *Canada*, the *Agamemnon* and the frigates *Ethalion*, *Seine*, *Galatea* and *Circe*. Sir Edward Berry left for England on 29 June and provisional command of the *Agamemnon* was entrusted to Captain S Searle until 8 July when Captain Jonas Rose arrived from England to take permanent command of her.

Bad weather prevented the British from keeping a continuous watch on the port and this enabled Willaumez to put to sea. Like a fox on the prowl he preyed upon the merchant vessels plying between the British islands. His squadron seized three merchantmen lying at anchor in Montserrat and then captured three ships and a brig off Nevis. Willaumez also made an abortive attempt to attack a convoy anchored under the protective guns of Brimstone Hill, St Kitts. After learning of another much larger British convoy assembling at Tortola and bound for England, he hurried there. Sailing past St Thomas his ships were sighted by Cochrane's squadron and, not wishing to stand and fight, Willaumez bore off and ran through the Leeward Passage between St Thomas and Thatch Cay with Cochrane in pursuit. As the French squadron outdistanced him Cochrane altered course that afternoon and made for Tortola. Entering Drake's Bay he found no less than 280 sail of West Indiamen anchored, all desperately waiting for the protection of his squadron.

The French privateer *La Dame Ernouf* (right). This picture shows her
earlier capture by HMS *Curieux* in February 1805. She was re-taken by
the French shortly afterwards and resumed her privateering career until
she was again taken by the *Agamemnon*. (National Maritime Museum,
London)

Willaumez thought it wise to shorten his stay in the Antilles as by then the
British were alerted to his presence. After provisioning and watering his
vessels in Martinique he made for the Bahama Bank to lie in wait for the
homeward-bound Jamaican convoy. To keep his presence secret, he seized
every neutral vessel that came within sight of him. It is more than likely that
he would have been successful had it not been for an act of insubordination of
one of his captains.

The commander of the 74-gun *Veteran* was Jerome Bonaparte, the youngest brother of the Emperor. Born in 1784 he had chosen the navy as a career
and ascended the hierarchical ladder in record time. He was made an *enseigne
de vaisseau* on 25 January 1802, a *lieutenant de vaisseau* on 14 January 1803, a
capitaine de frégate on 1 November 1804 and in 1805, after attempting to confer
the rank upon himself, he was appointed *capitaine de vaisseau*. Arrogant, frivo-
lous and headstrong, he soon decided that cruising off the Bahama Bank was
not to his liking and on the night of 31 July he secretly parted company with
the squadron setting all sail for Europe. When early next morning Willaumez

saw that a ship of his squadron was missing and that it was none other than the *Veteran* commanded by the Emperor's unruly brother, he became very uneasy. Cruising in all directions in search of the *Veteran*, he missed the Jamaica fleet of 109 sail.

Giving up his search after several frustrating days Willaumez returned to the Bahama Bank and again waited for the convoy until he learned from a neutral ship that it had passed and was now beyond his reach. Despondent at having missed such an opportunity for reward he decided to cruise the coast of North America in hope of better luck, but his ships were caught in a hurricane. Using jury masts and a jury rudder he barely reached Havana in his flagship the *Foudroyant*.[5]

Jerome Bonaparte fell in with a British convoy on his way home and was fortunate to capture and burn six of the merchantmen. He was sighted in mid-Atlantic by HMS *Gibraltar* but the capable officers who had been sent to sea with him succeeded in getting the ship to a safe anchorage in the Baie de La Fôret in Brittany where no British ship of the line would venture. In spite of this escapade Prince Jerome was shortly afterwards made a Rear Admiral, but the following year he finally abandoned the sea for the army.[6]

The Agamemnon *returns to England*

In early October the *Agamemnon* and her squadron escorted a convoy of merchant ships from the Leeward Islands to England. Having seen them safely home she moved from Sheerness to the Downs where she bided her time before the dockyard at Chatham could take her for refitting. There she underwent repairs. Many of her problems, especially those of her hull, went unnoticed while she was moored in the calm waters of the dockyard, only to become increasingly evident again when she was under canvas. However, short of rebuilding her from the bottom up there was little any dockyard could do for her. She was now 26 years old and the destructive erosion of her iron and copper fittings had diminished their power to hold the woodwork of her hull tightly together. From then on, her pumps would have to be worked on a twice-daily basis.

NOTES

1. Now Slavkov U Brna, Czech Republic.
2. The inscription on Pitt's monument at the Guildhall in London reads: 'In an age when the contagion of ideals threatened to dissolve the forms of civil society he rallied the loyal, the sober-minded, and the good around the venerable structure of the English monarchy.' As Winston Churchill proclaimed later: 'it is a just and fitting epitaph!'
3. Duckworth was afterwards severely reprimanded by Collingwood for leaving his station unprotected. For many years after Trafalgar the attitude of naval commanders acting *à la* Nelson, on their impulses and disobeying orders, had become a thorn in the side of the British naval authorities. It took years for commanders to realise that there would never be another Nelson.
4. Admiralty: Masters' Logs (ADM 51): ADM 51/1576 HMS *Agamemnon*.

5. After refitting, Willaumez returned to Brest in February 1807. As for the other ships of his squadron, the *Valeureuse* reached the Delaware and was broken up at Philadelphia, the *Patriote* and *Eole* reached the Chesapeake but were blockaded there by the British. After a long delay the *Patriote* found her way back to France but the *Eole* never again left the river. The *Cassard* headed for Rochefort as soon as the gale abated but the *Impetueux*, which was crippled, never made port. Under jury rig she ran aground and surrendered to the British who burned her.

6. After his naval experiences, Jerome was named King of Westphalia in 1807 only to be expelled in 1813. He fought at Waterloo, was granted the title of Comte de Montfort, returned to France in 1847, was created Marshal of the Empire in 1850 and died in 1860. Laird Clowes, Vol 5, p 194.

CHAPTER 11

The Siege of Copenhagen 1807

Something is rotten in the state of Denmark
Heaven will direct it.

Hamlet, Act 1 Scene 4
WILLIAM SHAKESPEARE

By the Treaty of Pressburg, signed on 26 December 1805, Austria renounced her claims upon the Venetian states and agreed to them being annexed to the kingdom of Italy, retaining Trieste as its only port onto the Mediterranean. Prussia had also made temporary peace with Napoleon after her defeat at Jena. These agreements freed the Emperor of France sufficiently to enable him to devote his attention to other causes. Heading his list was the punishment of King Ferdinand for having allowed British and Russian troops to land in the Bay of Naples and harrass the French army in defiance of a treaty of neutrality signed in October 1805. He decreed the deposition of Ferdinand and his dynasty, who with his family and court hurriedly fled Naples for Palermo aboard the British 74 HMS *Excellent*. As the French army began to advance the Russian troops embarked for Corfu and the British forces, about 10,000 strong, transferred from Naples to Messina in Sicily. Soon after, Napoleon's troops were in possession of the whole Kingdom of Naples.

Napoleon plots with Tsar Alexander

The reconciliation of Napoleon and Tsar Alexander after Austerlitz took place on a raft upon the River Niemen. With their armies gathered on either bank the two emperors met and embraced. Then, with the map of Europe spread out between them they planned each country's boundaries according to their personal interests. Estranged from England for what he saw as a lack of support Alexander yielded to Napoleon's spell. There were some sombre moments of remorse, however, as when he reviewed the French troops with Napoleon by his side. As the veterans of the Old Guard marched past them with their scars and wounds very much in evidence, Alexander turned to Marshal Ney and asked 'And where are the soldiers who have given these wounds?' Ney solemnly replied, 'Sire, they are dead.'[1]

More than a Franco-Russian peace, it was an alliance signed at Tilsit on 7 July 1807 that marked the culmination of Napoleon's power. His brothers reigned as kings at Naples, in Westphalia and at The Hague. His step-son Eugène de Beauharnais ruled Northern Italy as viceroy for his step-father.

Spain had joined the alliance and Denmark and Scandinavia, fearing the worst, made haste to obey. Russia, when allied to Britain, had helped equal the balance of power, but now in a moment of fickle sentiment had swung over to Napoleon's side. Only Britain stood implacable and unconquered. Ruled by her stubborn aristocracy she faced Napoleon's might alone, fierce and cooly unperturbed. Mistress of the seas, she had isolated the French Empire within the iron grip of her blockade. In France supplies from abroad dwindled: there was no coffee or sugar, a lack of many raw materials, and little chance of bringing the problem to an end.

Napoleon thought that with the whole of Europe behind him, England would come to terms. But no sound came from the island. There they continued to thrive on their seaborne trade, more interested in fox-hunting than matters on the Continent. Alarm was sounded, however, when grave news was conveyed to London of the agreements reached by the two emperors upon the raft anchored in the river Niemen. A British spy had reported that there had been secret understandings between them, that Napoleon was to seize the Danish fleet and gain control of the entrance to the Baltic. This strategy was to precede a joint invasion of England with the help of Russian forces.

To put his scheme into practice Napoleon needed a sizeable fleet, if for no other reason than to distract the British long enough to accomplish his plan of invasion. In theory, the number of ships he could count on were numerous and well-equipped at the conclusion of the Treaty of Tilsit. Between the French and Spanish navies he had forty-five sail-of-the-line ready for sea, spread between the ports of Brest, L'Orient, Rochefort, Ferrol, Vigo, Cadiz, Cartagena, and Toulon, apart from those on station in the West Indies and North America. In addition, by the secret articles of the treaty, twenty-five new ships which the Tsar had ready for sea were at his disposal in the ports of Reval and Kronstadt, as well as five other Russian vessels in the Mediterranean. He also counted on obtaining by fair means or foul, the Dutch fleet of fourteen line-of-battle-ships, the Danish fleet of sixteen and eleven belonging to Sweden. Privately, he boasted that soon he would also have the added weight of nine Portuguese vessels lying in the Tagus.

The British react to the threat

Facing imminent danger the British Cabinet acted with resolution. On 19 July 1807 they presented Denmark with the ultimatum that she either hand over her fleet, with the promise that it would be restored at the conclusion of the war, or have it seized by force. Had the British government not acted with speed it was evident that the French would have been in possession of the Danish navy in a matter of days. Wasting no time, Admiral James Gambier sailed from Yarmouth roads for the Baltic on 26 July with seventeen ships of the line (subsequently his fleet was increased to twenty-five and later to forty) with orders to procure by force the surrender of the Danish fleet.

Admiral James Gambier, British naval commander at the siege of
Copenhagen 1807. He was awarded a peerage for his successful
prosecution of the operation. (National Maritime Museum, London)

During the second week of August the *Agamemnon* with another seven
ships of the line sailed for the Baltic protecting a large number of transports.
Rounding the Skaw on the northern tip of Denmark the convoy sailed down
the Kattegat. On passing they saluted a squadron of six British ships sent to
occupy the passage of the Great Belt so as to prevent Copenhagen being
reinforced from its territories of Jutland and Funen. Two days later, with
Cronenburg Castle visible to the southeast the convoy came to anchor in the
roads of Copenhagen.

The anchorage was abustle with transports unloading troops and war
materials. The *Agamemnon* landed General McFarlane and his retinue who had
boarded in England. During the night the ship grounded by the stern, almost a
repeat performance of what had happened during the Battle of Copenhagen six
years before. But by evening she was free on the rising tide, having moved her
heavy guns forward and heaved off on the two anchors she had cast astern.

In the meantime, the British diplomatic envoy Mr Jackson had conferred
with the Danish Crown Prince at Kiel and had stated the British demands.
These had been politely rejected by the Prince who then sent urgent orders by
messenger to Copenhagen for the city to prepare for the inevitable British
bombardment. The Crown Prince sped back to the capital. The next day the

King departed it for Kolding in Jutland leaving the defence of Copenhagen in the hands of General Peyman, the governor.

The defence of the capital was no easy matter as the bulk of the Danish army was stationed far from the city at the time. Some 5,000 troops were all the governor could muster besides 3,000 armed civilians and 4,000 seamen. The city's defences were basically the same as those in Nelson's day. The famous Trekroner batteries mounted sixty-eight guns besides mortars. The citadel had another twenty, as well as three or four mortars. An additional battery to one side of it had thirty-six guns and nine mortars and the batteries of the arsenal mounted another fifty guns and twelve mortars. The guns themselves were long-barrelled 36 and 24-pounders and the mortars all of large calibre. As to floating defences, they were also similar to those of 1801. This time they consisted of the mastless 64-gun *Mars*, the 22-gun *St Thomas*, three 20-gun ships and about thirty gunboats mounting two guns each. They were strategically positioned in the vicinity of the Trekroner and moored bow to stern down the waterfront. Inside the port proper there were several sail-of-the-line, some frigates and sloops, besides three two-deckers on the stocks.[2]

During August the British had mobilized 377 transports. Divided into convoys they carried some 27,000 troops to the battle scene. Less than half of these troops were British, the majority being German mercenaries embarked on the island of Rugen in the Baltic Sea on the northwest German coast.

On 12 August the British military commander-in-chief, Lieutenant-General Lord Cathcart arrived from England aboard the *Africaine* and the landing of the troops began in earnest. The greater part of the fleet moved into Wedbeck Bay while a squadron anchored closer to the city. The troops disembarked without opposition.

'How to Start a Conflict in One Easy Lesson'

Feeling supremely confident of his position the British Commander-in-Chief addressed a proclamation to the inhabitants of Copenhagen. The king from his temporary residence in Jutland, and General Peyman from the capital, countered by issuing an edict for the detention of all British vessels and property. Following this, Danish gunboats left the harbour, seized and burned a British merchantman and fired at the pickets of the British army. They were fired at in turn by the British vessels whereupon they withdrew into the harbour. That same day Admiral Gambier with sixteen sail-of-the-line and several frigates anchored some four miles northeast of the Trekroner, at the same spot where Parker had anchored in 1801, and ordered his vessels to detain all Danish ships.

More British troops were disembarked this time at Kjoge Bay, to the southwest of the capital. They immediately set about building a battery on the outskirts of the city. The *Agamemnon* contributed four of her 18-pounders and three 24-pounders complete with carriages, as well as 200 rounds of ammunition. All these were towed ashore by the ship's boats.[3]

While the battery was being mounted, three Danish vessels of 20 guns each and other smaller ones tried to interrupt the construction. The British sent a flotilla to repel them but were furiously attacked not only by the Danish vessels but by the Trekroner as well. Overpowered, they managed to retire their heavily damaged ships, having lost one officer and three seamen as well as thirteen wounded. The British shore batteries drove off the Danish vessels eventually, but also sustained heavy losses. During the day they had fired upon the city and, as noted in the *Agamemnon's* log, due to the bombardment, they 'perceived [from on board] a great fire in Copenhagen', that lit up the evening sky like the devil's torch.[4]

The Siege of Copenhagen

The Danish vessels near the harbour's mouth began a fresh attack upon the British shore batteries to the north of Copenhagen and the flotilla that supported them. During this attack a British armed transport, the *Charles* of London, blew up having received a shell from the Trekroner directly in her magazine. Her master as well as seven seamen were killed in the explosion, besides two men of HMS *Valiant* anchored alongside of her. She also sustained twenty-one wounded. That same evening the *Agamemnon* took on board 106 Danish prisoners and sent an officer and twenty men on shore to assist in building yet another battery.[5]

In the meantime Stralsund, on the German Baltic coast, had fallen into French hands as Napoleon desperately rushed his troops to help his ally Denmark. The British countered by detaching a squadron to blockade that port to prevent reinforcements reaching Copenhagen. That was also the day the British finally completed their preparations to batter the city into submission.

The British commander-in-chief, Lord Cathcart, summoned General Peyman to surrender the Danish fleet assuring him, in carrot and stick fashion, that it would be restored, as well as other captured Danish property, upon signing a peace treaty according to British conditions. General Peyman declined, and asked for time to consult his sovereign. Lord Cathcart refused the request and at 7:15pm the British land batteries and ships opened fire upon the town. Under their systematic barrage the beautiful citadel of Copenhagen was set on fire within a matter of minutes.

The bombardment lasted until the following dawn. It was resumed with fury the next evening and continued throughout the night. On 5 September Jonas Rose recorded the scene in the *Agamemnon's* log:

> AM at 6 observed Copenhagen on fire whilst our Batteries Bombarding the Town . . . Copenhagen High Steeple burned down . . . PM the fire in Copenhagen apparently increasing . . .

British troops enter Copenhagen after the surrender on 7 September
1807. On the left of the picture, part of the city is still burning, set alight
by the shells and Congreve rockets of the British bombardment. On the
right can be seen part of the Danish fleet moored in the harbour. It was to
deny the use of these ships to Napoleon that the whole expedition was
undertaken. (National Maritime Museum, London)

Enormous conflagrations raged and enveloped the town but the Danes still
remained obstinate. The city's firemen, many of whom had fallen, proved
unable to cope with the task as the flames threatened the entire destruction of
Copenhagen. That was when General Peyman sent an officer, under a flag of
truce, to beg for a 24 hours' armistice in which to discuss terms. The request
was refused but the firing was ordered to cease. In short order the Governor
agreed to accept the surrender of the fleet as a basis for negotiation. However,
prior to this the Crown Prince had sent General Peyman an order to burn all
the Danish battleships but, as luck would have it, the messenger was captured
by a British patrol and his dispatches destroyed.

The articles were drawn up by the victors on 6 September and on the
morning of the following day they were signed and ratified. The Danes gave
up their citadel to the British as well as all their ships and stores. Hostilities
ceased, prisoners exchanged and property promised to be restored.[6]

British troops immediately marched into the town to take possession of it
while Captain Rose sent a party of fifty-eight men from the *Agamemnon* to

board the *Prindsesse Caroline*, a Danish 74. They brought her out of harbour and anchored her close to their own ship. During the next few days the *Agamemnon*'s carpenters and some of her seamen were employed repairing the damage to the *Prindsesse Caroline*'s hull caused by the bombardment as well as repairing her rigging. One of *Agamemnon*'s sailors, John Newhouse, fell to the deck from the captured vessel's yard and was killed instantly. His body was sewn in canvas and weighted with shot before being committed to the deep. By Thursday 17 September the ship's company aboard the *Agamemnon* had become so attached to the *Prindsesse Caroline* that they began to call her the *Young Agamemnon*. Even Captain Rose refers to her under that alias when writing entries in his log book after the siege.[7] It seems a curious breach of custom in an era when rigorous ground rules applied to almost every task aboard a ship of the Royal Navy.

Thirty-one Danish ships surrendered under the terms of the capitulation. They ranged from the 84-gun *Christian VII* to the 20-gun *Fylla*, as well as thirty-nine vessels of lesser importance. There were also three 74s on the stocks which were taken to pieces. Four vessels, their timbers rotten, were destroyed. As a safety measure the others were moved out of the harbour to anchor in the roads.

The arrival of Sir Samuel Hood

On 10 October Jonas Rose records in his log that Sir Samuel Hood arrived off Copenhagen and hoisted his flag as Rear Admiral of the Blue, on board HMS *Centaur*. The entry states that the *Centaur* fired a salute of eleven guns in greeting which was formally returned by the flagship, the *Prince of Wales*.[8]

Sir Samuel was one of the 'Band of Brothers', the distinguished group of captains, trained under Admiral Sir John Jervis (later Earl St Vincent), that had fought with Nelson at the Battle of the Nile in 1798. He was member of a famous naval family that has often confused naval historians, since there were two Alexanders and two Samuels serving at approximately the same period. Three of them became admirals. This Sir Samuel was a cousin of Vice Admiral Sir Samuel Hood (first Viscount Hood, 1762–1814), who fought with Rodney at the Battle of the Saintes in 1782, became a Lord of the Admiralty and finally Governor of Greenwich Hospital.[9]

The damage and the casualties

The damage to Copenhagen was extreme as whole sections of the city were burned to the ground. It would take years to rebuild those devastated areas. The Danes lost at least 250 men of their armed forces as well as 24 that were missing from sorties undertaken against the British batteries. Unfortunately, a considerable number of civilians also perished including women and children

When the British captured Copenhagen, there were three 74-gun ships of
the line under construction in the shipyards, which were broken up on
the stocks by the victors. (National Maritime Museum, London)

unable to leave the city prior to the bombardment. The British sustained 42
deaths, 145 wounded and 24 missing.

On 14 October Vice Admiral Stanhope left for England with some of the
prizes. A week later, when the army had been re-embarked the huge fleet of
British transports, the remaining warships as well as the surrendered Danish
vessels, weighed anchors and made sail for England. The *Agamemnon* had
General McFarlane and his retinue once again on board, this time for the
return passage.

The second day out, the 80-gun *Neptunus* of the Danish navy grounded
near the island of Hveen and had to be destroyed. In the Kattegat worse
happened when, owing to very rough weather, all the captured gunboats
except three were dashed upon the rocks. They had not been designed to
withstand the gales of the northern seas.

By the end of the month, without further casualties, the expedition reached
Yarmouth and the Downs. Admiral Gambier then made the pompous announce-
ment that his success had 'added the navy of Denmark to that of the United
Kingdom'. It was not even a half-truth as of the many Danish warships brought to
England, only four were found to be worth refitting for the British navy. These
were the 84-gun *Christian VII*, the 74-gun *Denmark*, the 74-gun *Norge* and the
74-gun *Prindsesse Caroline* (alias *Young Agamemnon*). The *Christian VII*,

One of the Danish ships brought back to England after the campaign, *Odin* was not taken into British service. (National Maritime Museum, London)

of advanced design, was to serve as model for the *Cambridge*, laid down at Deptford and launched in 1815.

The aftermath and brief evaluation

Admiral Gambier was given a peerage and Lord Cathcart who already had a Scottish title was knighted again by the English realm.

The siege provoked a formal declaration of war by Denmark. Great Britain replied by ordering reprisals, but the harshness of the northern winter came upon them and hostilities came to an abrupt halt. The British left only a skeleton force cruising in the Belt as protection for their merchant shipping.

The merciless attack on Copenhagen in 1807 was as tragic as Nelson's bombardment of the city six years earlier. In either case, the Danes had no alternative but to submit to British demands or be crushed. Denmark's only importance was strategic, since whoever commanded her territory controlled the entrance to the Baltic. A weak power, she held no hope of preserving her neutrality. The British, on the other hand, believed Napoleon must be destroyed at any cost, and it was this principle that justified for them both attacks on the all-but-defenceless city. Nevertheless, it seems there was a hint of remorse at Whitehall after the event. Though a subdued Parliament voted its thanks to both branches of the service, it is significant that there were none of the customary celebrations nor were any medals struck to commemorate the victorious outcome of the operation.

NOTES

1. Winston S Churchill, Vol 3, p 254.
2. Laird Clowes, Vol 5, p 211.
3. Admiralty: Captains' Logs (ADM 51): ADM 51/1855, HMS *Agamemnon*.
4. Ibid.
5. Ibid.
6. Laird Clowes, Vol 5, 215.
7. Admiralty: Captains' Logs (ADM 51): ADM 51/1855, HMS *Agamemnon*.
8. Ibid.
9. For more information, see Chapter 3, and Chapter 6.

CHAPTER 12

From Portugal to Brazil

*My affection hath an unknown bottom, like the
bay of Portugal.*

As You Like It, IV, i, 219
WILLIAM SHAKESPEARE

Upon return from her mission to the Baltic and the Siege of Copenhagen, the *Agamemnon* came to anchor in Margate Roads on 11 November 1807. Two days later she moved on to the Downs, that famous old anchorage in the Straights of Dover tucked behind the Goodwin Sands. From there she moved to Spithead to provision and on 6 December 1807, she sailed in company with the *Elizabeth*, *Foudroyant*, and *Plantagenet*, to join in the blockade of Lisbon.

While on patrol duty, after her arrival, she captured a Portuguese ship. A few days later, she chased another, the *Comerciante*, bound for the Tagus, which she boarded and towed to Lisbon Rock. Her log records taking still another Portuguese prize, the *Europa*, on 29 December, and yet a fourth, on the last day of the year.[1]

While it relieved the tension and boredom of standing out at sea, day after day, in all weather, detaining and boarding merchant vessels was not a pleasant task. Regardless of the prize money that might accrue, an officer had to have the stomach for it. The looks of disdain, the rudeness it invited, and the danger of 'accidentally' falling down a hatch, made the job objectionable.

This tedious occupation continued with little respite during harsh winter weather well into February when at last, on the 16th of that month, to the delight of everyone on board, orders were given for the *Agamemnon* to water at Casçais Bay, slightly west of Estoril, and sail south to provision at Gibraltar. She accomplished this without incident and then crossed the Straights of Tangier in Northern Africa to join the *Foudroyant* and the *Pitt*, as previously arranged by the Admiralty.

Aboard the *Foudroyant* was Rear Admiral Sir William Sidney Smith, the intrepid naval officer who, with a handful of British seamen, had repelled Napoleon's troops at the siege of Acre in 1799. He was on his way to take up his post at Río de Janeiro as commander of the Brazil Squadron. The 80-gun *Foudroyant* was a relatively new ship having been built in 1798, and she was larger and faster than the *Agamemnon*.[2] She was also the ship on which Nelson and Lady Hamilton had conceived Horatia in April 1801.

Napoleon's Continental System

Powerless at sea, Napoleon concluded that to conquer his last important rival, he had to turn the British blockade against itself. Britain, in the process of transformation from an agricultural economy to an industrial one, depended entirely upon seaborne trade. Napoleon's strategy, to which he directed all his strength, consisted in a continental exclusion of British shipping. English merchandise was banned from European markets by armed customs guards and French troops at every port, forming an impenetrable barrier along the Mediterranean coastline, from the Dardanelles up through western France, and from northern Europe to the borders of Russia. The critical points of the barrier were Spain and particularly Portugal, Britain's traditional ally, since Lisbon offered a safe haven to the British Fleet. For Napoleon's plan to work, it was crucial for him to take over the Iberian Peninsula.[3]

The invasion of the Iberian Peninsula

The young George Canning, trained by William Pitt in the artful business of government, directed the Foreign Office. Guessing Napoleon's intentions, he had wasted no time in dispatching a naval squadron to the Tagus under the command of Sir William Sidney Smith. Next, the British government declared the total blockade of all French ports, including those of her allies. The measure involved nearly all the ports of Europe. In a short time, commerce froze, the old question of freedom of the seas a bone of contention once again, as British ships intercepted neutral vessels attempting to trade with countries on the continent.

Napoleon, meanwhile, in his effort to seize the Spanish crown, lured the old and senile King Carlos IV of Spain[4] and his son Fernando, Prince of Asturias, who had plotted against his father, into a trap at Bayonne. Threatening them with execution before a firing squad, he induced Carlos to abdicate and Fernando, the heir-apparent, to renounce his claim to the Spanish throne.

Fernando, that ill-mannered royal oaf so mercilessly portrayed by Goya, who would be proclaimed King Fernando VII by the Spanish *Junta*, was taken and imprisoned. Such was the outrage at Napoleon's bullying behaviour, however, that young Fernando was seen as a romantic and pathetic figure by his people, who labelled him 'the well-beloved'.[5] Even those in the Indies who harboured feelings for independence joined in the chorus of kindly and sympathetic expressions of loyalty towards him.[6] Napoleon, oblivious to their complaints, replaced Fernando on the throne with his own elder brother Joseph.

Writing to his friend the eminent jurist, Regis de Cambacérès, Napoleon boasted, 'Spanish opinion bends to my will. Tranquility is everywhere re-established.' It had not dawned upon him yet that he had committed the greatest error of judgement thenceforth of his career.

Overture to disaster

It took little time for the Spaniards to become aware that their country had been virtually annexed to France. When they did, towards the end of May 1807, they rose in spontaneous revolt. Taking whatever arms that came to hand, they silently converged on their local centres and provincial capitals, where a battalion was galvanised on a large scale by the local *juntas*. The local *juntas* in turn obeyed the Central or national *junta*, first at Aranjuez, then at Seville, where a Council of Regency was formed to govern on behalf of the now exiled Fernando.

Nothing like it had ever happened before. A ragged mass of furious peasants, unified by one thought and one purpose, sullenly confronted the usurper. For the first time, Napoleon faced an adversary that was neither king nor emperor but everyday citizens, inflamed by patriotism and indignation. The very nature of warfare changed. In Austria, Italy, and Germany there had been the usual excesses, pillaging and cruelty, but it was nothing to what the French encountered on their march through Spain and Portugal. Here were people brought up in the shadow of the bull ring, to whom the loss of a leg or an arm meant little, people who had manned the ships of Columbus, Magellan, and the great Vasco da Gama, to whom hardship was a way of life. These were people, as Napoleon found daily, who neither gave nor sought mercy. As they marched down the Peninsula, the French discovered with a chill that the corpses of their stragglers and wounded were often horribly mutilated, showing signs of torture. Furthermore, the foe was everywhere, in the hedgerows, behind the wall, lurking in the shadows.

In July, brother Joseph, the *de facto* ruler of Spain, derisively called 'Pepe the Bottle' by the locals for obvious reasons, wrote to Napoleon from Madrid. 'No one has told the truth so far. The fact is that there is not a single Spaniard who is for me except the few who came here with me. All are terrorised by the unanimous feelings of their compatriots.' He closed the letter requesting 'plenty of troops and money'.

The revolt in Asturias

On the northern coast of Spain, onto the Bay of Biscay, lies the diminutive province of Asturias. Isolated by mountains from the rest of the country and with little chance of communicating with Madrid, the people rose unprompted, banished the French governor, and seized the arsenal with over 100,000 muskets. With the help of army officers, they organised a militia. Then, joining forces with regiments of their regular army under generals Barcena and Woster, they drove out the French troops, commanded by no less figures than Marshal Ney and Generals Kellerman and Bossnet.

The Asturians sent envoys to England to appeal for aid. They landed at Falmouth and were immediately taken to see George Canning at the Foreign Office. Canning listened attentively and saw an opportunity. Without further ado, he resolved to send an army to the Peninsula to tie down Napoleon's armies and aid the Spanish partisans. It is said that was the moment the Iberian war began.

Because the *juntas* of Galicia and Andalucia were nervous about accepting foreign troops, Canning sent them to Portugal instead, where they disembarked on the banks of the Mondego River north of Lisbon in July 1808. Consisting of 30,000 men, they were led by Sir Arthur Wellesly, the future Duke of Wellington, who had recently distinguished himself in the war in India.[7]

Day after day the spirit of patriotism among the partisans rose up to baffle and defeat Napoleon's armies. General Dupont, forced to withdraw from Córdoba towards Madrid, was brought to a halt at Baylen, in Andalucia, where he fought for water in the scorching heat. Finding none, he surrendered with 20,000 French troops to an inferior Spanish army.[8]

The capitulation at Baylen forced the French to evacuate Madrid. Bundling off King Joseph with them, the French retreated to safer territory in the northwest, beyong the river Ebro.

The Portuguese royal family flees Lisbon

As early as the autumn of 1806, Napoleon had put pressure on Portugal to turn against Britain, her oldest ally. On 8 November, Dom Joâo, Portugal's

Dom Joâo, Prince Regent of Portugal in 1807, and later Emperor of Brazil and King of Portugal. (Author)

prince regent, was persuaded to detain a few British citizens and confiscate some British property in Lisbon. In answer, Britain's diplomatic minister Lord Percy Strangford demanded his passport while lodging a formal protest with the Portuguese government. Then, closing the ministry, Strangford boarded HMS *Confiance*, a vessel of the British squadron. On being notified of the affront to British citizens and property, Sir William Sidney Smith tightened his blockade of the Tagus.

Information had reached Lisbon that Junot had entered Portugal through Spain and was swiftly marching on the city. Lord Strangford let sufficient days slip by for the perilous news to have its effect. He then returned to Lisbon under a flag of truce and met with the Portuguese minister of foreign affairs. Strangford informed the minister that the blockade would be raised if the Portuguese navy surrendered to Great Britain. He suggested that it would be far more sensible, however, if their ships were used to transport the royal family to Brazil and stay there until the end of the war. He emphasised his government's wish that the Portuguese fleet not fall into Napoleon's hands. Dom João needed little convincing that Britain was a better friend than France and that Napoleon's aim was to depose the House of Braganza. He hastened preparations for the immediate withdrawal of the royal family to their South American domain.

The following eye witness account of their flight is a translated excerpt from *Historia de El Rey D. João VI*, by an anonymous author 'S L', published in Lisbon in 1866.[9] The scene is the hurried departure of some 15,000 frightened members of the royal household, court, and government:

Forced by the circumstances, Dom João became aware of the necessity to move his government across the sea. Consequently, the date of embarkation was fixed for the early morning of 27 November. It was none too soon, as the vanguard of the invading French army might reach Lisbon on the 29th or 30th. With a series of forced marches, the French had covered over 200 leagues strewn with every obstacle the terrain could offer, particularly since entering Portugal, where rain had swelled the rivers and made the roads all but impassable. Thus, it is easy to imagine the confusion on embarkation day. Servants, soldiers, women, trunks full of precious objects, and furniture (some the most useless and ordinary imaginable) lined the wharf. It gave the piers of Belém an appearance both melancholy and grotesque.

There was not a single official to greet the Prince Regent when he arrived in his carriage, accompanied by [his second son] the Infante de Espanha and one servant. A couple of policemen standing there put some planks over the muddy ground for them to step down onto. Then he and the Infante were lifted in their arms and carried the short distance to the landing stage.

Next to arrive was the Princess Dona Carlota [the regent's wife] with her other children and afterwards the queen herself, accompanied by her lady-in-waiting. Helped into a sedan-chair, she screamed obscenities at those around her, as was her custom [she was mentally deranged which was the reason her son Dom João had been named regent[10]]. The two princesses, her sisters, were the last members of the royal family to arrive, followed by an immense retinue of courtiers.

Attempts were made to embark various regiments; however, the 13th Infantry Batallion had to be disbanded after discovering there was not room enough in the transports allotted to them. At midnight of the 28th, the hatches aboard some ships had to be unbattened to load some indispensable items that had been forgotten during the confusion of the day.

On the 29th, the wind, which had been blowing unfavourably from the southwest, at last turned north, and the squadron took advantage of the opportunity to set sail [down the Tagus]. On the 30th, the wind veered again to the southwest, but the ships had already crossed the bar and were in the open sea. At seven that very morning Junot entered Lisbon.

Had the wind not veered favourably when it did, the Regent and the whole squadron would have fallen into the enemies' hands. In barely 3 days and 3 hours, the French had covered a distance of 22 Portuguese leagues between Abrantes and Lisbon on terribly muddy roads, leaving their artillery bogged down by the wayside. Such was the speed of their approach that the king's ministers learned of the arrival of the French at Abrantes only on the 26th [4 days before they entered Lisbon]. The poor [meaning the people] were profoundly dismayed at the fate that awaited them. They viewed with displeasure how the court had taken with them considerable riches in gold and diamonds calculated at over 80 million cruzados, having emptied the coffers of the realm and left the unhappy creditors of the state without any hope of payment whatever!

Before setting sail, the prince named a regency [to run the country in his stead], presided over by the elderly Marqués de Abrantes, and he issued a proclamation to the poor, ordering them to accept the French as friends . . .

The Regent Dom João, the Queen, Maria I, and Dom Pedro, Dom João's eldest son, as well as his second son Dom Pedro Carlos, Infante de Espanha, sailed aboard the *Principe Real*. The Princess Dona Carlota Joaquina [Dom João's wife] and the royal children were aboard the *Rainha de Portugal*. The *Principe de Brazil* was graced by the presence of the princesses, sisters to Queen Maria. The ships *Medusa, Dom João de Castro, Alfonso de Albuquerque, Conde Dom Henrique* and the *Martin de Freitas* were occupied by the court and the ministers of state. Aboard the smaller naval vessels and the many armed merchantmen travelled businessmen and merchants bringing the total to over 15,000 persons and carrying as well half the money of the realm that was in circulation at the time. It was precisely predicting such a catastrophe as this one [the invasion of Portugal by a foreign power] that the government had stuffed the pockets of the Regent with gold, to the extent that on the day of departure what money remained in the state coffers barely amounted to 10,000 cruzados . . .

The ships of the Portuguese navy left the Tagus accompanied by a fleet of twenty armed merchantmen. They were met at sea by the British squadron, which welcomed them with a salvo of twenty-one guns which the Portuguese returned in similar fashion. Sir William Sidney Smith escorted the royal family as far as latitude 37° 47'N and longitude 14° 17'W. Believing it safe from there on he detached Captain Graham Moore with the *Marlborough, London, Monarch* and *Bedford* to see them to Bahia and on to Río de Janeiro. He then turned about and returned with the rest of the squadron including the *Agamemnon*, to look for Russian ships which had been seen entering the Atlantic from the Mediterranean on their way to the Baltic.[11]

Queen Maria I of Portugal, in a
portrait painted before madness
overtook her. (Author)

The Portuguese fleet arrived at Sâo Salvador, Bahia, on 21 January 1808.
S L's chronicle states that:

> Among the more prominent passengers to disembark and stretch their legs upon
> arrival, after almost two months' confinement aboard ship were the nobility, the
> hierarchical members of the church, army generals, court justices and business-
> men of note. They comprised an elite that had shared a common feeling of
> terror for Junot and the invading French Army.[12]

After a short sojourn at Bahia, the operation of embarking was carried out
again and the fleet, forty-six ships in all,[13] sailed southward down the coast to
Río de Janeiro arriving on 7 March 1808.

The Agamemnon, Foudroyant, Confounder *and* Pitt *sail for the Cape Verde Islands*

On 14 March 1808 the *Agamemnon* and the *Foudroyant* set sail from Tangier
Bay in company with the armed brig *Pitt* of 12 guns under the command of
Lieutenant William Perkins and the gun brig *Confounder*. While the *Confounder* parted company the next day, the remaining ships sailed on covering
the 700 miles between Tangier and Madeira in 13 days at a leisurely average

speed of 3½ knots. They came to anchor in Funchal bay on 27 March. Fruit and vegetables were taken on board, and presumably the ships' captains bought for their private use, as most captains did, a keg or two of the coveted dark and syrupy Malmsey wine, as well as the usual boxes of sun-dried dates and figs.

For three days the British ships patrolled the clear blue waters around Grand Canary and Tenerife, finding the area free of enemy vessels. They then steered a course for the Cape Verde islands 385 miles off the west coast of Senegal. The Canary Current favoured them, as did the trade winds off the bulge of Africa. Rolling in the swells, the topgallants and stunsails set a billow of white canvas against a cerulean sky. Keeping each other in sight, the three ships ran down the coast before the breeze in harmony with sea and wind.[14]

On 28 March the ships caught up with an English transport and kept company with her until the following day. Soon after the *Agamemnon* took the *Pitt* in tow, for no other apparent reason than to catch up with the *Foudroyant*, which they had lost from sight. Twenty-four hours later they cast off the tow, still without sign of the *Foudroyant*.[15]

It is difficult to discern the islands of the Cape Verde archipelago from the sea. Accounts quite often mention ships approaching the islands finding the sun blocked by a dense cloud of fine sand carried aloft by the trade winds from the Sahara, sand that hampered vision making work aloft extremely hazardous. The *Agamemnon*'s log relates that one early morning after the wind subsided, the tall peak of Tope da Coroa came into view. She steered a passage through choppy seas between the Windward Islands, guided by the flame and smoke of the active volcano Fogo. The ships sailed through the narrows with sheer cliffs on either side. The *Agamemnon* and the little *Pitt* came to anchor in Praia Bay, at Sâo Tiago island, during the morning of 9 April. They were surprised at not finding the flag-ship there before them, but at 3pm she came into view around the headland, wallowing in the troughs.[16]

Placidly at anchor, Captain Rose boarded the *Foudroyant* to dine with the Admiral, his flag-captain, and Lt Perkins of the *Pitt*. Perhaps they talked about the aspects of the journey ahead, speculating on comments each had heard about Brazil. Fanciful legends of spiders big as crabs, iridescent butterflies and dripping rubbery vegetation. A country of brilliant plumed parrots, where monkeys bounded among the branches and dissolute planters smoked cheroots, drank brandy for breakfast and whipped their slaves, where no one condemned the habit of chaining a mad slave to the rooftop tossing him food to keep him alive as a sort of family pet or clown.[17] After such lively conversation, it is a reasonable assumption that the two captains, Hancock of the *Foudroyant* and Rose of the *Agamemnon*, with Lt Perkins of the *Pitt*, would have spread the chart of the South Atlantic upon the table between them and with pencils, rulers, and dividers, plotted their course southwest across the Atlantic ocean to Río de Janeiro.

Across the South Atlantic to Brazil

Since leaving Praia Bay, the *Agamemnon*, *Foudroyant*, and *Pitt* had steered a southerly course with the curve of the African continent receding to the east. The ships' commanders, Rose, Hancock and Perkins, had agreed to keep to it, with a tendency towards the west, until they had passed the Equator. Their concern was to steer clear of the Doldrums, that quiet span of hot sultry air between the trade-wind belts that spawns squalls and cyclones, while being windless within itself.

At Gibraltar the *Agamemnon* had taken on board two of the *Pitt*'s guns (6-pounders), complete with their carriages, harness, and ammunition. Without that extra weight, the *Pitt* sailed along much better keeping up with the two larger ships.[18]

Lanterns were lit at night to enable the ships to keep in sight of one another, but the *Foudroyant* tended to out-distance the *Agamemnon* and quite frequently had to shorten sail. The logs relate how the ships lost each other several times due to bad weather conditions but they managed to come together again.

During the daytime, the crews strung awnings above the quarter decks and partly across the well of the uppers to fend off the fierce heat of the sun. They opened gunports and hatches to catch the breeze and cool the stifling atmosphere below as the ships ran towards the Equator. The favourable hot dry winds, heated over desert sands, died to a siren's breath as they approached the invisible Equatorial Line. They crossed the Equator at last and the traditional tributes to Neptune, King of the Sea, were enacted.

The men caught rain in sails and funnelled it into empty casks. Drinking water, always a guarded commodity, was especially valuable in the tropics when the staple diet was beef or pork preserved in brine. Keeping the water consumption below the stipulated 4 pints (2 litres) per man, per day, was difficult, and grog took its terrible toll, as evidenced by the punishments meted out for drunkenness recorded in the logs. Due to the *Agamemnon*'s forlorn condition, as well as the continual heavy rains that penetrated the decks to the hold, much of her biscuit was spoiled, but it was eaten just the same.

When south by 4° latitude from the 'girdle of the world', the weather turned fine and clear. With the South Equatorial Current[19] in their favour, the ship caught the first vestiges of the southeast trade winds.[20] Schools of flying fish met the ships, taking off and soaring into the air around them, while porpoises and dolphins swam beside, diving under the hull and blowing and snorting to the amusement of the sailors.[21] By trolling a line with a fish-hook wrapped in dead bait or even chicken feathers, the men, off-duty, could catch bonitos and albacores, abundant at that latitude. Fish made a welcome addition to the usual dreary menu.

Sharks would feed off the waste from the galley, moving with their pilot fish to the bows at night, not to lose their source of food in the dark. During fair weather with a calm sea, green turtles were commonly sighted. They

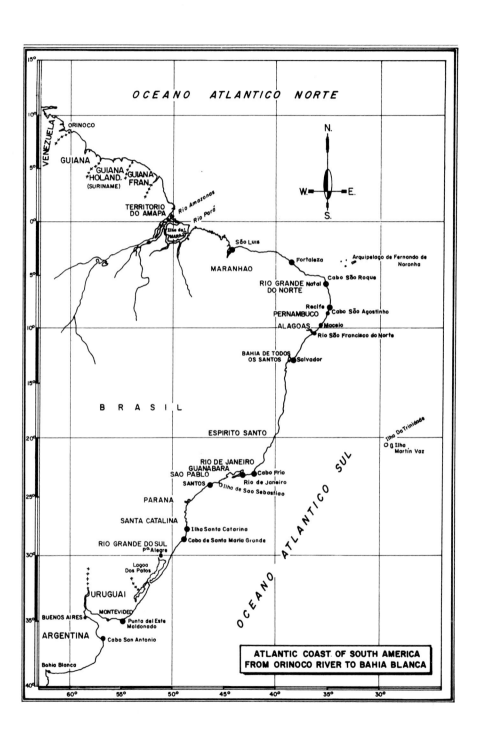

ATLANTIC COAST OF SOUTH AMERICA
FROM ORINOCO RIVER TO BAHIA BLANCA

would deceive the unsuspecting lookouts into thinking they were small up-turned boats, only to sink from the surface as the ship approached. These turtles migrated 1,215 miles from Ascension Island to the beaches of Brazil every year to lay their eggs before returning home. On their way they would surface from below to warm their shells in the sun until they could no longer stand the heat, then flip over and warm their bellies instead. A novelty, they entertained the crews with their languid behaviour. Whales were sighted several times during the trip, sometimes rather too close for comfort. One rose up near the ships revealing its frightening rock-like back amongst the waves. Awe-struck, the men watched with terror until it plunged beneath the surface, showing its flukes as it went.

Leaving Ascension Island some 200 miles to port the ships set a course past Martin Vaz and Trindade Islands, sighted on the morning of 7 May. A more uninviting apparition could not have met the eye, 27 days at sea notwithstanding. What confronted them was an arid mass of volcanic rocks thrown up from the ocean by some furious geological upheaval. The closest and more easterly of them were the smaller islets of Martin Vaz, steep and inaccessible. Twenty-six miles westward was the imposing rugged mass of Ilha da Trindade almost entirely surrounded by reefs and ledges of rock, on which the sea breaks in white fury. On its northern extremity rises Ponta Crista do Gallo like a cock's comb, and towards its centre, standing like a silent sentinel, stands Pico Desejado, nearly 2,000 feet (600 metres) high.

The *Agamemnon, Foudroyant* and *Pitt* sailed past the islands at a distance of 5 miles, leaving them to starboard. On being signalled by the *Foudroyant*, Captain Rose ordered the helmsman to steer a new course west by south ¼ west. They were now on the last leg of the voyage heading towards Cabo Frío on the Brazilian mainland.[22]

On 4 May a sail was sighted. The *Agamemnon* hove to and sent a boarding party to inspect the vessel. She proved to be the *Juliana* of Flamborough, sailing from the Rio de la Plata to Tonningen laden with a malodorous cargo of hides. They bid her 'God speed' and sent her on her way.[22]

Last leg to Río

Spurred on by the Brazil Current and the northeasterly trades, the ships picked up speed to cover the 765 miles from the island of Trindade to Cabo Frío in 6 days. Finally, through the rain of a northeasterly squall, the saddle-shaped heights of the Cabo loomed into view, growing in size as the ships approached until the vegetation on the hills could be clearly seen. Sailing close to shore they followed the coast westward towards Río de Janeiro. The ships dropped anchor at the entrance to the Bay of Guanabara, off Ponta de Santa Cruz and opposite the Sugar Loaf, on 14 May 1808. Riding to single anchor in the calm waters beneath the fort, they patiently waited. A day went by, and on the second, pilots came on board to guide the vessels into the Bay of Guanabara.[24]

It must have been a wondrous sight for the officers and crew as they sailed through the entrance into one of the most beautiful and sheltered harbours of the world. Bordered by lofty green mountains fading into the background in paler hues they slope gently down to shores of sandy beaches separated occasionally by short projections of rocks.

The *Agamemnon* and *Foudroyant* saluted the fort on Ilha das Cobras (Island of Snakes) with a salvo of twenty-one guns each. The salute that reverberated around the bay was returned in similar fashion from the fort. Rounding the headland, the vessels of the Brazil's squadron, moored off Ilha Fiscal, came into view. The three newcomers sailed slowly towards them under shortened canvas and coming up to them anchored close by.

Majestically floating at their moorings were: the brand new 74-gun *Marlborough*; the Slade-designed 90-gun *London*; the 74-gun *Bedford*; the 74-gun *Monarch*, also by Slade; and the 36-gun *Surveillante*, captured from the French. Closer inshore were anchored the sloop of war *Mistletoe* and the famous little 16-gun brig *Mutine*. Thomas Masterman Hardy, while still a lieutenant, had captured her from the French during the action at Santa Cruz, Tenerife, where Nelson lost his arm. Being in charge of the boats, Hardy had cut her out from the enemy ships under heavy fire. Most deservedly she became his first command and with her he fought at the Battle of the Nile in 1798.

After her arrival in Río, the *Agamemnon* stayed in port for a month, generally provisioning, repairing, caring for her sick, and attending to all the many dockside activities that arise after an Atlantic crossing. The sick were taken to the naval hospital to be given medical or surgical care, though many of the men were beyond recovery. The ship had also felt the rigours of the long sea voyage. Her seams had opened and she showed a general weakness, particularly when the wind blew fresh. Many old bolts of her hull were either broken or worn thin and though carpenters and riggers did their best her plight was irreversible.

NOTES

1. Admiralty: Captains' Logs (ADM 51): ADM 51/1855, HMS *Agamemnon*. Admiralty: Masters' Logs (ADM 52): ADM 52/3723, HMS *Agamemnon*.
2. The *Foudroyant*, the second of that name in the Navy List, was built in 1798. She became a training ship in 1862 and was eventually wrecked off Blackpool in her 99th year, in 1897.
3. Winston S Churchill, Vol. III, p 255.
4. Charles IV of Spain was the brother of Ferdinand IV of Naples.
5. 'El amado Fernando'.
6. J H Parry, *The Spanish Seaborne Empire* (University of California Press, Berkeley, 1990), p 348.
7. Sir Arthur Wellesley's army had been assembled in India for the purpose of invading the Spanish colonies in America. The expedition was cancelled when Napoleon invaded Spain making the Spanish *junta* Britain's ally.
8. Winston S Churchill, Vol. III, p 258. Dupont negotiated the capitulation with the understanding he and his troops would be sent back to France. The Spaniards did not keep their word and Dupont with his men were sent to work the galleys in Cadiz. Napoleon ill-treated Dupont for surrendering, but Dupont eventually got his own back as it was he who signed the Emperor's deportation to Elba.

9. Republished: Levi Scavarda, D. Joao VI, *Separata da Revista Marítima Brasileira* (Rio de Janeiro) 1967, pp 1–11.

10. Maria I suffered from fits of melancholia after the loss not only of her consort in 1786, but of her eldest son. In 1792, her mental state was further disturbed by the news of the French Revolution, and she ceased to reign. Her son, who on her death in 1816 was to ascend the throne as Joâo VI, became prince regent.

11. The Tsar had declared war on Great Britain on 31 October, 1807 and a short time later reprisals had been ordered in London against all Russian ships and goods. The Russian squadron under Vice Admiral Seniavin, comprising nine sail-of-the-line and a frigate, broke out into the Atlantic. They became intimidated by the large force of British ships that they saw on the horizon in every direction. Frightened, they ran down the coast of Portugal and put into the Tagus unseen, while both Portuguese and British squadrons were at sea on course for Brazil.

12. Levi Scavarda.

13. The fleet which carried the royal family to Brazil was made up of twenty Portuguese armed merchantmen and the following fifteen ships of the Portuguese navy: the 84-gun *Principe Reale*, 74-gun *Rainha de Portugal,* 74-gun *Conde Dom Henrique*, 74-gun *Medusa*, 74-gun *Principe de Brazil, 64-gun Alfonso de Albuquerque*, 64-gun *Dom Joâo de Castro*, 64-gun *Martin de Freitas*, 44-gun *Minerva*, 36-gun *Golfinho*, 32-gun *Urania,* a frigate name unknown, 22-gun *Voador*, 22-gun *Libre*, 20-gun *Vinganza* and the 12-gun *Curioza*. These constituted the whole of the serviceable ships of the Portuguese navy, excluding the 74-gun *Vasco da Gama*, which was being repaired. The British squadron was made up of the 98-gun *London* and the 74-gun ships *Marlborough*, *Monarch*, and *Bedford*. Laird Clowes, Vol. 5, p 233.

14. Admiralty: Captains' Logs (ADM 51): ADM 51/1855, HMS *Agamemnon*.

15. Ibid.

16. Ibid.

17. The exaggerated conceptions of Europeans about Brazil were still prevalent 57 years later. In 1865 Sir Richard Burton had been named consul to the port city of Santos, 230 miles south of Río de Janeiro, by the British foreign office. He and his wife Isabel sailed from England in July. On arrival in Brazil 'there were spiders as big as crabs. In the matter of tropical diseases it seems to have ranked with darkest Africa; there were slaves, too, often maintained in conditions of utmost savagery. It was the South America of which we get a glimpse in Gauguin's memoirs of his childhood: a steamy, brilliant landscape, where gaudy parakeets flashed through the rubbery vegetation, a dissolute society smoked huge cheroots, and drank brandy for breakfast, and no one condemned the habit of chaining a mad slave to the rooftop as a sort of domestic pet or clown.' Lesley Blanch, *The Wilder Shores of Love* (Carroll and Graf publishers, New York, 1985), p 51.

18. Admiralty: Captains' Logs (ADM 51): ADM 51/4078, HM Armed Brig *Pitt*.

19. The South Equatorial Current carries 6 million tons of water each second in a north-westward direction across the Equator. It is replaced by deep unseen flows of cold North Atlantic Water. National Geographic Society, *Atlas of the World* (Washington DC, 1966), p 163.

20. The trade winds drive surface water obliquely toward the Equator from both the North and South Atlantic, creating the great Equatorial Currents. In middle latitudes the westerlies take over as the driving force of the currents. As wind and currents approach the continents, they are deflected by the earth's rotation, clockwise in the North Atlantic, counter-clockwise in the South Atlantic.

21. The porpoise (*Phocoena phocoena*) has a rounded nose. The dolphin (*Delphinus delphis*) has a beak-like snout. Because of their blow and snort, they have been compared to ordinary land pigs. Hence the name that stems from the colloquial Latin, *porcus piscis*, 'hog fish'. De Lery-Whatley, pp 17, 233.

22. Admiralty: Captains' Logs (ADM 51): ADM 51/1855, HMS *Agamemnon*.

23. Ibid.

24. Ibid.

CHAPTER 13

Agamemnon in South America
1808–1809

Plots, true or false, are necessary things,
to raise up commonwealths and ruin kings.

Absalom and Achitophel, 1.83
JOHN DRYDEN (1631–1700)

Nelson's victory at Trafalgar ended the last Spanish attempt to reassert her sea power in the Atlantic. The defeat had further weakened Spain's control over her colonies, but other than the capture of Trinidad, Britain had not moved to take advantage of Spain's weakness. It was not for lack of desire, however, since the British government had long contemplated the conquest of some part of South America, but immediately after the battle, Britain was too hard pressed to get involved in such an undertaking. Furthermore, it had been Tory policy under William Pitt to secure the right to trade in preference to annexing territory. If not, Great Britain would encourage independence of the Indies, with trade as the ultimate objective. William Pitt died, however, on 23 January 1806, and with a Whig government in power, the first invasion of the Rio de la Plata was launched in May by Commodore Sir Home Riggs Popham.[1]

His squadron, consisting of eight men-of-war and a fleet of transports carrying some 5,000 troops under the command of Major General Sir David Baird, had sailed for the Cape of Good Hope, where first they reduced the Dutch colony. While anchored in the outer bay of the Cape, Popham received intelligence of the weak state of defence of Buenos Aires and Montevideo. Allured by dreams of conquest and booty, Popham persuaded Sir David Baird to embark the 71st Regiment of Highlanders under the command of Brigadier-General William Carr Beresford[2] and head for the Rio de la Plata. The expedition took on more troops and artillery at St Helena, arriving at their destination in the middle of June 1806. General Beresford landed 1,635 troops and moved on Buenos Aires. Finding little resistance, he marched through the city, took over the fort, and hoisted the British flag among much firing of cannon by the fleet and the artillery on shore. Shortly after, however, Beresford faced a popular uprising led by a French born nobleman, Jacques Antoine Liniers y Bremond (known as Santiago Liniers in Spanish circles). From then on things went from bad to worse for the British until eventually the situation became unsustainable.

On 12 August 1806, after hoisting the Spanish flag, Beresford came out of the fort at the head of his troops and surrendered to Liniers. British losses

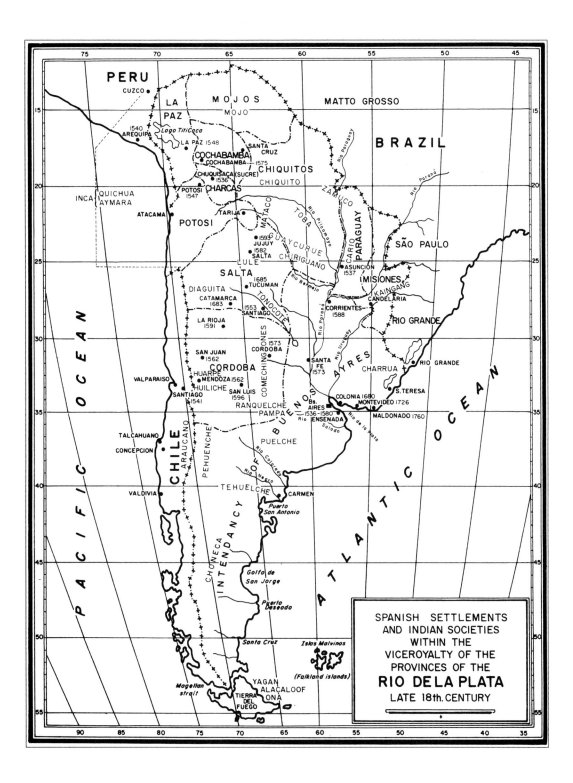

SPANISH SETTLEMENTS
AND INDIAN SOCIETIES
WITHIN THE
VICEROYALTY OF THE
PROVINCES OF THE
RIO DE LA PLATA
LATE 18th. CENTURY

Brigadier-General William Carr Beresford surrendering to Santiago
Liniers in Buenos Aires on 12 August 1806. Following his victory, Liniers
was appointed Viceroy of the Rio de la Plata by the Spanish Crown.
From a painting by Charles Fouqueray (1909). (Museo Histórico
Nacional, Buenos Aires)

amounted to 300 killed and wounded. Twelve hundred British soldiers laid
down their arms to become prisoners of war.

A second attempt to conquer the Spanish colony took place the following
year. By the end of May 1807, the British had assembled 12,000 men, a fleet
of eighteen warships, and over eighty transports. The command of the land
forces was conferred on Lieutenant-General John Whitelocke.[3]

To begin with, the British forces captured Maldonado, Montevideo, and
Colonia del Sacramento. On 28 June they landed on the south bank of the
Rio de la Plata and marched on Buenos Aires. Told to hold their fire until
they reached the Plaza Mayor, the patriots picked off the British troops from
the rooftops like fish in a barrel. Such was the carnage that by the end of the
day, 1,130 men lay dead or wounded, including 70 officers. Another 120
officers and 1,500 soldiers were taken prisoner.

Whitelocke capitulated to Liniers,[4] and on 16 July, after twelve days spent
embarking troops and war material, he sailed from Buenos Aires with the
remnants of his army. On 9 September he surrendered Montevideo and
returned to England. Shortly after his arrival he was tried by court-martial on

four different charges.[5] Found guilty on all but one of them he was 'cashiered and declaired totally unfit to serve His Majesty in any capacity whatsoever.' For many years after, a common toast in the officer's mess went: 'success to grey hairs, but bad luck to white locks.'

One year later, when the *Agamemnon* arrived at Rio de Janeiro, the world scene had changed. Due to the French invasion of Spain and Portugal, Britain became allied to the colonial power she had so recently attempted to displace.

Of greed and dreams of conquest

When the *Agamemnon, Foudroyant* and *Pitt* arrived, Rio de Janiero was still in a turmoil. The Portuguese royal family and court had landed only two months earlier, and 15,000 newcomers were still fighting for lodgings in the town. The city had 45,000 inhabitants but no facilities for sheltering such an influx of immigrants. Hasty preparations had been made to house the royal family, but all those having anything to do with the government, be they ministers or civil servants, also expected lodgings to be provided for them. To solve this problem, the regent had resorted to the simple procedure of confiscation.

Dom João dreamed of annexing the Banda Oriental, today Uruguay, then a part of the Spanish Viceroyalty of the Río de la Plata. By expanding his empire south he hoped to control the trade lanes of the great river and supply Buenos Aires, Montevideo, Asunción and eventually Perú, as well. He had appointed minister of internal affairs one who had been his last viceroy in Brazil, Marcos de Noronha e Brito, Conde dos Arcos. Noronha e Brito had considerable knowledge of the Río de la Plata, having fostered every effort, when viceroy, to protect and maintain the citadel of Colonia del Sacramento opposite Buenos Aires. A strategic outpost within Spanish territory, Colonia was a veritable bastion from where the Portuguese pursued their lucrative business of contraband with the Spanish colonies.

Noronha e Brito reasoned that the time was ripe to invade the Banda Oriental and the Río de la Plata, since Spain was at its lowest ebb having been overrun by Napoleon's armies and her king imprisoned in France. He therefore urged Dom João to act in the utmost haste. Further pressure was exerted on the regent by the minister for war, Rodrigo de Souza Coutinho. Both ministers knew, however, that the decision to invade might draw animosity, as Britain would be likely to suppress any act of aggression against the Spanish colonies while her alliance with the Spanish *juntas* lasted.

Further doubts bothered the Portuguese regent. There were, for instance, rumours that Britain herself planned a third invasion of the Provinces of the Río de la Plata to be commanded by Arthur Wellesley, the future Duke of Wellington. If the Provinces of the Río de la Plata were captured by the British it would annul any possibility of Portugal obtaining a part of them. Furthermore, there was talk about the Spanish viceroyalty declaring its independence which some linked to the purpose of the planned British invasion.

A view of Montevideo in 1807. The city was held by the British from
February to September of that year. (National Maritime Museum,
London)

This rumour made Dom Joâo and his ministers extremely anxious as the seeds
of liberty might eventually take root in Brazil, an event which would be
catastrophic for the House of Braganza. To add to his worries, the Spanish
viceroy in Buenos Aires was a French-born nobleman, Jacques Antoine
Liniers y Bremond (known as Santiago Liniers in Spanish circles, the same
Liniers who had accepted Beresford's surrender in 1806), who due to his
heritage was thought might seek Napoleon's support if threatened by Brazil.
In the final analysis, however, the insecurities of Dom Joâo and his two
favourite ministers induced them to favour invading the Banda Oriental immediately, reasoning that if the Viceroyalty of the Río de la Plata became
British, Brazil would have to give up her designs on the area; if the Spanish
colonies became independent, the infection might spread north to Brazil and,
finally, if they declared in favour of France, the French, with a foothold in
Buenos Aires, would later march on Brazil annexing, at least, their southernmost state of Rio Grande do Sul.

In Buenos Aires, Viceroy Liniers pledged he would remain loyal to Fernando,
'the well-beloved', opposing the very thought of any foreign intervention,
be it British, Portuguese, or French. He was equally adamant against the Provinces declaring their independence.[7]

Early in July 1808, Lord Percy Strangford arrived at Rio de Janeiro to take
up his duties as British minister plenipotentiary to the Portuguese court. On
the 25th of that month he informed George Canning by letter to the Foreign

Office that the Portuguese government in Rio de Janeiro had decided to occupy both banks of the Río de la Plata. The excuse given, he said, was that having conquered Spain and Portugal, Napoleon was almost certain to send an expedition to take over the Spanish viceroyalty. Far better, said Noronha e Brito to Lord Percy, that they occupy the territory themselves and defend it against the possibility of a French invasion. Foreseeing that the cities of Buenos Aires and Montevideo would put up a fight, the minister had explained that the Portuguese would have to resort to the use of arms. Their first objectives would be the towns of Asunción and Corrientes in the north and later in November, Buenos Aires, Montevideo and Maldonado in the south. The regent, he said, took for granted that Sir William Sidney Smith would assist their cause by blockading the Río de la Plata with the British squadron.

The proposed campaign conflicted with Britain's own plans for a third invasion of the Spanish viceroyalty to take place in October. All came to naught, however, on 2 September when Canning wrote to Lord Strangford emphatically opposing the Portuguese plan and asking him to inform the Portuguese minister of Britain's decision. In short order, the minister wrote to Canning stating that, due to Britain's request, Dom João would postpone, though not give up, his ambitions for seizing the United Provinces of the Río de la Plata.[8]

Sir William and Lord Percy

There were no friendly feelings between Lord Strangford and Sir William Sidney Smith. The two men had taken a dislike to one another when they had

Lord Percy Strangford, appointed British ambassador to the Portuguese court in Rio de Janeiro in July 1808. (Author)

met in Naples several years before. Sir William was a quarrelsome, vain character, always eloquent about his own exploits, a volatile mixture of conceit, insubordination, unpredictability, daring, resourcefulness and imagination. Those who knew him well said he was as French in spirit as he was English at heart, which explains his friendship with some notable Frenchmen, including the Comte de Liniers, brother of the Spanish viceroy at Buenos Aires. Sir William had lived in Paris between 1785 and 1787. He was later captured by the French and imprisoned for two years. When his active service was over, he would turn up as a spectator at the Battle of Waterloo and finally retire to live his last years in Paris.[9]

Lord Percy, on the other hand, was not a man of forceful character. He was handsome and had a soft persuasive manner which befitted his diplomatic rank, though according to Lord Byron he was only a mediocre poet.[10] Canning, however, thought much of this young Irish Viscount who shared his own farsighted views and had named him to the important diplomatic post in Portugal, over other more experienced candidates. His personal charm and sensible attitude would enable him to eventually become the most influential ambassador in South America.

Lord Percy had proven the loyalty of Britain towards her old ally Portugal and royal gratitude was not deaf to his petitions. During his stop in Bahía, on 28 January 1808, Dom Joâo had signed an exclusive treaty of free trade with Britain that provided for the importation of British manufactured goods to Brazil in return for the exportation of Brazilian agricultural produce to England. Later, in Rio de Janeiro, Strangford was granted by Dom Joâo an even more privileged treaty, which permitted British naval vessels the use of Brazilian ports to repair, water, and provision. It awarded the British navy the right to more than 3,000 miles of South Atlantic sea-board with the use of safe harbours. In addition, the treaty granted British Protestants religious freedom, and the privilege that legal cases involving British subjects in Brazil were to be tried only before judges appointed by the British crown.

Left pretty much to his own devices, Lord Strangford showed exceptional diplomatic skills for a man of twenty-eight. Shortly before his arrival in Rio, during 1806 and 1807, the British had mounted two successive attacks on Buenos Aires. Not only had they failed to hold the city but they had been repulsed in one of the most ill-managed military campaigns in British history. It fell to Strangford to heal the scars and bring about a reconciliation for the all important reason of securing the right to trade with the Spanish colonies.[11]

The intrigues of Carlota Joaquina and Sir William Sidney Smith

Carlota Joaquina, Infanta de España, was the eldest daughter of Spain's Carlos IV, sister to Fernando VII, 'the well-beloved' and niece of Fernando IV of Naples, Carlos IV's brother. She lived separately from her husband Dom Joâo.

Each had their own palace with a different group of courtiers, advisors, secretaries, and set of friends. Their's was simply a marriage of convenience, not one made in heaven.

Dona Carlota, as she was known in Portuguese circles, did her best to neutralise her husband's plans to annex her family's South American possessions, proposing that the Spanish colonies recognise her as the representative of the legitimate Spanish crown. She brazenly repeated that if asked she would remove herself to Buenos Aires to govern as regent of the Río de la Plata.

Sir William Sidney Smith had befriended Carlota since his arrival on station in May. He introduced to her court a British spy, Colonel Florence Burke. Burke, an Irishman, handsome, cultivated and sly, spoke French, Spanish, and German fluently, as well as English. He answered directly to Lord Castlereagh, the Secretary of State for War, who was also the Admiral's friend.

Using the ships of his fleet, Sir William kept Dona Carlota in contact with Liniers and the influential people in Buenos Aires and Montevideo, forewarning them of her husband's and his ministers' schemes.

The strange Paroissien Affair

Drawn by her ambitions of power and fuelled by the British Admiral's fawning flatteries, Carlota entered into a plot hatched by a patriot in Buenos Aires, Saturnino Rodríguez Peña. If it were successful, her aspirations of being appointed regent of the Provinces of the Río de la Plata representing her imprisoned brother Fernando would be satisfied. Since it would be seen as an affront for her to nominate herself, Peña and his friends decided to make it appear as if the citizens of Buenos Aires had requested that she take over the reins of government. If they could bring this about they predicted that Viceroy Liniers would have to resign and Carlota would succeed as their puppet with absolute power.

At Rodriguez Peña's suggestion, Carlota and Sidney Smith decided to send an emissary from Rio to Buenos Aires to promote the idea amongst the more influential members of creole society. Their choice for this undercover mission fell on a young British surgeon, Doctor James Paroissien.

Paroissien was instructed by Burke and the Admiral how to proceed and was given a memorandum explaining the project in detail as well as many letters of introduction to influential Buenos Aires citizens, including Saturnino Rodríguez Peña's brother Nicolás. Paroissien embarked aboard the British merchantman *Maria*, which would be escorted by the *Agamemnon* and the *Monarch* as far as Maldonado Bay.[12]

Before the ships set sail, however, Carlota's private secretary, Señor Presas, convinced her that among the letters given to the young British doctor were some that would prove that Rodríguez Peña was using Carlota as a means for turning the colony into a republic.[13] Convinced by Presa's lies, Carlota sent a secret agent of her own aboard the *Maria* with a letter to Viceroy Liniers

The Infanta Carlota Joaquina, daughter of Carlos IV of Spain, who despite being married to the Portuguese regent conspired against his plans to annex the Rio de la Plata to Brazil. (Author)

denouncing the unfortunate Paroissien as the bearer of seditious letters and asking that he be arrested and tried for treason upon arrival.[14]

The three ships sailed south down the coast and had an uneventful journey. On 11 October 1808, about 4 miles offshore from the entrance to Maldonado Bay, the *Maria* parted company and headed into the Río de la Plata towards Montevideo, while the *Agamemnon* and the *Monarch* with their large ships' companies made for the Bay to provision and water.

Sailing inside Lobos Island, famous for its many seals and giving Punta del Este a wide berth, they changed tack to round the northwestern point of Gorriti Island. Their destination was the usual anchorage within the bay, situated between the northern tip of the island and the shore. Cutting the distance too short the 74-gun *Monarch,* with its draught of over 24 feet aft (8 metres) took the shoal that runs from the northwestern extremity of Gorriti Island. She grounded on a rock 16 feet (5 metres) beneath the surface thereby baptizing the shoal forever with her name. It is known to this day as '*Bajo del Monarca*'.

The *Agamemnon* answered the *Monarch's* signal for assistance by sending boats to her aid. Having lightened ship, the *Monarch* slid off by the stern. Brought to safety by the efforts of oarsmen in the ship's boats she made for deeper water having sustained no major injury. Both ships of the line came to anchor later in the evening to leeward of the island.[15]

The *Maria* reached Montevideo the next morning and Paroissien was summarily arrested. It was discovered upon opening the letters he was carrying that there was not the slightest suggestion of treason in any of them. What did become plain to the authorities in Montevideo, however, was that Carlota was scheming to be named regent in place of Liniers.[16]

Yet another plot in the making

Naturally, the affair was embarrassing for those to whom the letters were addressed. Nicolás Rodríguez Peña, brother to Saturnino, was thrown in jail and his assets confiscated. The remaining recipients signed written affidavits declaring their total ignorance of the charges. For Carlota and Sydney Smith, however, it was only a momentary distress. They went back to their plots and conspiracies in short order.

While Rodríguez Peña was striving to extricate himself from the arms of the law, a number of prominent citizens in Buenos Aires, headed by Manuel Belgrano and the fiery fanatical Jacobin Juan José Castelli, signed a petition asking the Portuguese government in Rio to approve the nomination of the infante Don Pedro, a cousin of Carlota's, to be regent of the Viceroyalty of the Río de la Plata.

The Portuguese minister Souza Coutinho showed the request to Lord Strangford and Sydney Smith. Lord Percy opposed the plan as ludicrous while Sir William thought it a reasonable idea, though he slyly stated that in his opinion Carlota should be the candidate, not her cousin Pedro. When Carlota heard of the plan she decided to travel in person to Buenos Aires but Dom João forbade her. Nevertheless, she was not to be stopped. Discovering that the Spanish frigate *Prueba* was in port and bound for Buenos Aires she decided to disobey her husband and secretly take passage aboard her. She contacted Brigadier Ruiz Huidobro aboard the *Prueba* who in turn consulted Strangford. In consequence, Huidobro quietly weighed anchor early next morning and the *Prueba* slipped out of port unseen and unknown to Carlota.[17]

Lightning strikes at sea

The *Agamemnon* and the *Monarch* remained in Maldonado Bay until 29 November when they sailed up river to Montevideo. There they stayed for two weeks anchored in the shadow of the fort while taking on provisions.

Paroissien, who had been spared the firing squad, was in prison. The Governor of Montevideo, in a dispute with Viceroy Liniers, had refused to send him on to Buenos Aires, and though Captain Rose carried letters to Governor Elío, it proved impossible to persuade him to release the unfortunate offender.[18]

The two ships weighed anchor and sailed down the Río de la Plata from Montevideo to Maldonado. From there they headed north into the Atlantic on patrol. In sultry weather, on 28 November, a black threatening storm came upon them from the southwest. It engulfed them in rain, as lightning and thunder rent the sky. While men scampered up the ratlines onto the yards to furl the sails, the *Agamemnon* was struck by a bolt of lightning which shattered the main royal mast. The mast collapsed carrying shrouds and spars with it in a tangled heap upon the deck. Miraculously there were no casualties on board and both ships were able to head back to the relative safety of the Bay.[19]

Swimming, a rarity among seamen

While repairs were being carried out aloft on board the *Agamemnon*, on 11 December 1808, Captain Rose passed the order for a party to go ashore to replenish the ship's water. It was early morning, the sea was calm, and the two ships rode placidly to their single anchors a bare half mile off the northern tip of Gorriti Island.

One of the ship's cutters, carrying a large number of empty casks, set sail and tacking to and fro she headed for the shore. At the same time the ship's launch with ten men at the oars and a man at the tiller struck out on a straight course with the remaining empty casks towards the point where the rivulet La Aguada, fed by a fresh water spring, meets the sea. It took them nearly an hour to reach the appointed place and, while some held the boats, the rest brought the butts ashore and rolled them up the beach to submerge them in the waters of the rivulet. It was an easy task, the only effort needed was to heave the full casks back again into the waiting boats. The casks were stacked as neatly as before, though their weight was considerably more thus reducing their freeboard to a dangerous level. The cutter set sail for the ship with the wind abaft her beam. Rowing the launch, however, became more laborious task on the return journey. She moved steadily along, under oars, until she reached the approximate half-way point, when a long lazy wave rolled over the shoal where the *Monarch* had grounded and caught the overloaded launch broadside on. It sank with the full casks taking the men with it. The crew struggled in the water to get a grip on an oar, a bench, or anything floating but, nevertheless, five seamen were drowned before the eyes of their desperate companions aboard the ships. The tragedy has its explanation in the forgotten fact that few officers or seamen in this period knew how to swim.[20]

To perform the burial ritual the *Agamemnon* weighed anchor and sailed into the deeper waters of the Atlantic. Somewhere between Lobos Island and the shore the five bodies, sewn into their hammocks and weighted with shot, were committed to the deep. With the unpleasant formalities taken care of, the ship sailed back to the same place she had left in the bay, anchoring a cable's length away from HMS *Monarch*.

Of pestilence and heat

With the prospect of Rio's pestilent summer climate awaiting them, the ships lingered in Maldonado Bay over Christmas, savouring the comfort of its mild environment while preparing for sea. They left 4 days before the New Year, arriving in Rio de Janeiro on 16 January 1809.[21]

As a first duty Rose sent the *Agamemnon's* sick to the naval hospital on shore. A list of the infirm and injured was recorded and sent to the Commander-in-Chief who, having collected similar information from Captains of the other vessels of the squadron, forwarded the information by letter to the Admiralty:

> HM *Foudroyant* Rio de Janeiro 24th January 1809
>
> Sir,
> Enclosed I transmit for the information of my Lords Commissioners of the Admiralty 8 reports of surveys held by my order on the health of the officers and men as therein mentioned belonging to His Majesty's Squadron under my command.
> I have the honour to be, Sir,
> Your most obedient humble servant
>
> W Sidney Smith

Enclosed in this letter was the following which relates to the condition of men from HMS *Agamemnon*:

> We whose names are hereunto suscribed have been at the Naval Hospital at Rio de Janeiro and with the assistance of her respective surgeons have there taken a strict and careful Survey of the following Men sent there from the Ships of the Squadron for survey, and find them unfit for His Majesty's service owing to the diseases mentioned after their names.

Men's names	Quality	No. on Ships Books	Disease or Hurt
John Henwood	AB	264	Blind
James McAdams	Carpenter's mate	85	Lame
Mathew Scott	AB	208	Debility & Rheumatism
(?)Dunn	Ordinary	52	Debility, Piles & Prolapsus Ani
Robert Cooper	Do	230	Spitting of blood
George Mason	LM	602	Ophthalmia
Lawrence Hagan	LM	232	Asthmatic
John Wing	LM	605	Deranged
John Maxwell	PM	36.22	Fits
Charles Bradley	Do	26.4	Do
Wm.Cook	AB	452	Fistula

[The list continues with men from other ships, and is then signed underneath by
John Davey of the *Foudroyant*, Montagu Fabian of the *Mutine* and Doyle of the
Lightning][22]
AB: Able seaman; Ordinary: Ordinary seaman; LM: Landman.

Mentioned in the list were only the extreme cases. It is likely there were many
more that were not considered impaired enough to exempt them from work.
Human muscle was needed for practically every activity aboard ship. It was
the reason for so many men being confined in such a small space. Their work
was dangerous, food and conditions miserable, drinking water filthy, medical
knowledge primitive and all was magnified by the destructive, infectious
nature of the tropics that swiftly spread disease.

An invaluable record of Agamemnon's deplorable condition

The ship stayed in port for nearly two months, between 17 January and 6
March, the worst part of the year that anyone can choose to be in Rio, a time
when the heat of the upper deck becomes unbearable underfoot, when the
pitch in the deck-seams liquifies and the breeze dies to naught. At night the
surrounding mountains belch the heat that they have accumulated throughout
the day, and even the freshest food tends to rot before it can be eaten.
Mosquitoes and flies, roaches and bugs, all thrive in this habitat and behave as
if humans are an intrusion. It is difficult to work under these conditions but
Captain Rose went over his ship from stem to stern. Assisted by the ship's
carpenter, George Robbins, he compiled the following report of its deplorable
condition for the attention of Admiral Sir William Sidney Smith. It read:

Defects of His Majesty's Ship *Agamemnon* Jonas Rose Captain. Rio Janeiro.
March 28th, 1809.

1st.   Some of the Standard Knees and Hooks move considerably which re-
       quires additional fastening.
2nd.   The riders in general work much, some of them (from the labouring of
       the Ship) worked themselves ¼ of an inch in the Ceiling.
3rd.   The Ship shews her weakness in general, and particularly in the Wings
       when blowing fresh.
4th.   Several of the old Bolts are apparently broke and the beams work much
       in the Clamps, and the Scarfs of some of them work much which adds to
       the general weakness of the Ship.
5th.   Each Deck swags much and worn very thin; the Nail Heads (when
       labouring in the Sea) leak much, occasioned from the decay between
       wood and wood.
6th.   The Pawl Rim of the Capstan is broke and wants replacing.
7th.   The Water Cocks and Pipes want replacing.
8th.   The second Pintle from the Head of the stern Post works much up Hill
       upon the Brace and makes the Rudder work heavy.
9th.   Taylor and Nobles hand Pumps are much shook which occasions them
       to blow and deliver but little water.

10th. The Copper Pumps are worn very thin at the lower parts and want repairs.

11th. The decks of the Fore and After Cock Pits are worn very thin and want replacing.

12th. The facing piece of the Bitts is much worn.

13th. The after Hoods on the Stern frame of the Jack are much decayed, and one Chain Plate in the Larboard fore Channels wants replacing.

14th. Several of the Lower deck Ports are very much decayed and leak considerably when blowing fresh at Sea.

15th. Carried away and wants replacing the Cross Jack Yard.

Signed:
Jonas Rose   Captain
Geo.Robbins   Carpenter

Little was done, because there was little that could be done in Rio, to improve the desperate condition of the ship. Nevertheless, this document was later to become the most important piece of evidence for the defence at the later court martial of Captain Jonas Rose for the loss of HMS *Agamemnon*.

The final accounting

While scheming behind Lord Percy's back and not revealing to him their actions, deeds or plans, Sidney Smith and Burke kept the Secretary of State for War, Lord Castlereagh, fully informed, who in turn imparted his instructions to them behind Canning's back. Subterfuge appeared to be catching.

Castlereagh and Canning were enemies principally due to the long-standing divisions and intrigues in the cabinet provoked by both men and the groups that backed them. Castlereagh from his position in the War Department attempted at every turn to obstruct Canning in the Foreign Office, whatever be his purpose, and Canning simply could not stand Castlereagh because of his meddlesome behaviour in matters of foreign policy.

At Castlereagh's orders Rear Admiral Sidney Smith sent Burke from Rio with a letter to Liniers in Buenos Aires, composed of thirteen tightly-written pages, mainly trying to curry favour with the Viceroy. Liniers answered Sir William that he must know little enough about Burke's reputation to send him as his personal envoy since he was well-known in Buenos Aires as a British spy ('an agent of revolution', were his words) and that there was an order out for his arrest. This, he said, he would overlook since Burke was the admiral's messenger. He closed by saying that he had ordered Burke be banished from the Río de la Plata immediately aboard the British transport *Steady*.[23]

Word of this got to Canning at the Foreign Office who brought the matter up at a cabinet meeting. He charged that Sir William Sidney Smith with the aid of Colonel Burke had, on Castlereagh's orders, attempted to manipulate the delicate political situation of the Río de la Plata behind the backs of the

British ambassador and himself the head of the Foreign Office. Castlereagh made a lame excuse and the two men had a heated argument. Due to this and much to the relief of Lord Strangford, Sir William was recalled, being replaced as commander of the Brazils Squadron by Rear Admiral Michael de Courcy, who arrived in Rio to take up his post aboard HMS *Diana* on 2 May 1809.[24]

The affair, however, had an unpleasant aftermath. Later that year Canning held Castlereagh responsible for the disasters that overtook British arms at La Coruña in Spain and at Flushing (today Vlissingen) in the Netherlands. Canning insisted on Castlereagh's dismissal. He had already secured a secret agreement to replace him with the Marquis Wellesley. When Castlereagh heard about this they quarrelled and fought a duel on 21 September, Canning being wounded in the thigh. Both had already resigned. Canning did not return to public office for 13 years. Castlereagh, on the other hand, held office again in 1812 as secretary for foreign affairs and became leader in the House of Commons until in 1822 he suffered a mental breakdown. It developed into outright paranoia. Convinced he was being blackmailed on charges of homosexual acts, he finally committed suicide on 12 August 1822 by slitting his throat with a penknife.

Burke leaves Rio in disgrace

When Rear Admiral Sir William Sidney Smith sailed for England he offered Burke passage aboard his ship but Burke declined. Having rid himself of the admiral, Strangford set about getting rid of Burke. Burke was ordered by the police to leave Rio on the charge that he was suspected of spying. He was told that only a written document signed by his ambassador stating that he would be responsible for his behaviour could save him from banishment. Burke strived to attain it from Strangford, of course to no avail. Added to this, the Conde Linhares, minister of foreign affairs, made public that Burke was a 'perturbing element in the relations between Britain, Portugal and the Río de la Plata'. Burke sailed for England on 16 August 1809 aboard the *Confiance* never to return.[25]

During the year that Sir William Sidney Smith commanded the Brazils squadron rarely were there more than three or four British ships in the port of Rio. The admiral's crafty machinations and power plays kept his vessels busy beyond the usual naval tasks of patrolling the coast, keeping a watchful eye out for any French sails, and intercepting and boarding foreign ships. He made constant use of the British fleet during his sojourn in Rio for sending and bringing envoys and messengers and making a show of force before Montevideo and Buenos Aires, though for the most part he personally remained on shore. Perhaps all, except Carlota, were pleased to see him leave.

Notes

1. Sir Home Riggs Popham (1762–1820) was born in Tetuan, Morocco, where his father was British consul. He was his parents' twenty-first child, although his mother died giving birth

to him. (Through subsequent marriage his father is said to have sired forty-four children.) Educated at Westminster School and Cambridge University, he had an adventurous career but his greatest accomplishment was to provide the Navy with a new signal code. It was this code that was used by Nelson to send his 'England expects . . .' signal at Trafalgar. Carlos Roberts, p 311 and Grant Uden and Ricard Cooper, p 385.

2. Beresford (1768–1854) was later to become the general looked on by the Duke of Wellington as the man best-qualified to replace him should he be killed. The illegitimate son of the Marquis of Waterford, he entered the army at the age of sixteen and saw service at Toulon, Bastia, Egypt, the West Indies and the Cape of Good Hope. After his escape from Buenos Aires he later went on to command the Portuguese army in the Peninsular War.

3. Officially the illegitimate son of John Bulstrode Whitelocke, contemporary rumour held Whitelocke to be the son of a member of the British royal family. His appointment to command the South American expedition and to also serve as Governor-General, over the heads of men recommended by government ministers, and the fact that he was spared the firing-squad following the debacle of his command, only added to the currency of these rumours.

4. The conditions of Whitelocke's capitulation were stated in the following terms:

   I. There shall be from this time a cessation of hostilities on both sides of the River Plata.

   II. The troops of His Britannic Majesty shall retain for the period of two months the fortress and place of Montevideo, and as a neutral country there shall be considered a line drawn from San Carlos on the west to Parido on the east, and there shall not be on any part of that line hostilities committed on any side, the neutrality being understood, only that individuals of both nations may live freely under the respective laws, the Spanish subjects being judged by theirs, as the English by those of their nation.

   III. There shall be on both sides a mutual restitution of prisoners, including not only those which have been taken since the arrival of the troops under Lieutenant-General Whitelocke, but also all those of His Britannic Majesty's subjects captured in South America since the commencement of the war.

   IV. That for the prompt dispatch of the vessels and troops of His Britannic Majesty, there shall be no impediment thrown in the way of the supplies of provisions which may be requested for Montevideo.

   V. A period of ten days from this time is given for the re-embarkation of His Britannic Majesty's troops to pass to the north side of the River La Plata, with the arms which may be actually in their power, stores, equipage at the most convenient points which may be selected, and during this time provisions may be sold to them.

   VI. That at the time of the delivery of the place and fortress of Montevideo, which shall take place at the end of the two months fixed in the second article, the delivery will be made in the terms it was found, and with the artillery it had when it was taken.

   VII. Three officers of rank shall be delivered for and until the fulfilment of the above articles by both parties, being well understood that His Britannic Majesty's officers who have been on their parole cannot serve against South America until their arrival in Europe.

5. The essential points of these charges were as follows:

   1. That Whitelocke had sent a message to the Spanish commander demanding, among other things, 'the surrender of all persons holding civil offices in the government of Buenos Aires as prisoners of war.'

   2. That during the march from Ensenada to Buenos Aires he 'did not make the military arrangements best calculated to ensure the success of his operations against the town', and ordered his forces to enter the city with arms unloaded, and on no account to fire, thus unnecessarily exposing the troops to destruction, without the possibility of making effectual opposition.

   3. That he 'did not make, although it was in his power, any effectual attempt, by his own personal exertion or otherwise, to co-operate with or support the different divisions of the army under his command, when engaged with the enemy in the streets of Buenos Aires on the 5th of July.'

   4. That he, subseqently to the attack on the town of Buenos Aires, and at a time when the troops under his command were in possession of posts on each flank of the town, and of the principal arsenal, with a communication open to the fleet, and having an effective force of about 5,000 men, did enter into, and finally conclude a treaty with the enemy, whereby he acknowledged in the public dispatch of 10 July 1807, that he resolved to forego the advantages which the bravery of his troops had obtained, and which advantages had cost him about 2,500 men in killed, wounded and prisoner, and by such treaty he unnecessarily and shamefully surrendered all such advantages, totally evacuated the town of Buenos Aires and

consented to deliver, and did shamefully abandon and deliver up to the enemy, the strong fortress of Montevideo, which had been committed to his charge, and which, at the period of the treaty and abandonment, was well and sufficiently garrisoned and provided against attack, and which was not, at such period, in a state of blockade or siege. *Trial of Lieut.-Gen. Whitelocke*, Appendix, Vol. I, pp I–IV.

6. Ibid, Vol 1, pp I–IV.
7. Carlos Roberts, *Las Invasiones Inglesas Del Río de la Plata* (Buenos Aires, Jacobo Peuser Ltda, 1938), p 331.
8. Ibid, p 333. After William Pitt's death in 1806, the Duke of Portland became prime minister. He named George Canning as his foreign secretary, a remarkably intelligent man with a biting wit. He became a great orator in Parliament and had the uncanny gift for seeing in simple perspective the complicated political scene of world affairs. His views differed entirely from those conservative empire builders of his time, who were anxious to suppress the merest sign of colonial emancipation anywhere. Canning, on the contrary, strived to prevent any further European intervention in South America and was all for helping the rebellious Spanish colonies gain their independence. Chiefly remembered as foreign secretary, he taught the members of the Tory Party to take a more liberal view of many aspects of domestic, colonial and foreign policy. He was prime minister for a brief period in 1827.
9. Grant Uden and Richard Cooper, p 482. William Sidney Smith entered the British Navy at the age of thirteen. When war with France commenced in 1793, he arrived off Toulon in a small ship of his own and in short order was given an official command. Made prisoner by the French during an attack on Le Havre he escaped by an exploit comparable to the best Hollywood tradition. He brought the French army to a standstill before the fortifications of Acre, held by a Turkish garrison and a handful of his British seamen. In an unsuccessful introduction before the House of Lords of a bill to dissolve George IV's marriage to Queen Caroline due to her infidelity, Sir Sidney was cited as co-respondent. A committee of ministers found that he indeed had been her lover. (It was rumoured that Canning succeeded him in her favours.) Carlos Roberts, p 347.
10. Carlos Roberts, p 358.
11. Not only did he achieve the reconciliation with the authorities and general public at Buenos Aires, but he was later to help and encourage the patriots of the viceroyalty to gain their independence from Spain. Lord Strangford was granted the first honorary citizenship of the city of Buenos Aires ever awarded, though he personally never visited the city. The following is a translation from the letter sent to him on that occasion: 'It is our sacred duty, never to be forgotten, to officially express that Buenos Aires and her provincial dependencies are in your debt due to your good offices. This requires of us, in all justice, to state to you our public and constant gratitude.'
12. There were also letters to other prominent citizens such as: Castelli, Alzaga, Vieytes, Casamayor (General Beresford's friend), Maestre (*aide de camp* to Liniers), Miguel Irigoyen, Mattos and Esquerrena. (In the letter to Castelli, Sidney Smith mentions Colonel Florence Burke as their mutual friend.) Carlos Roberts, p 350.
13. By coincidence this was, more or less, the truth.
14. Carlos Roberts, pp 351–352.
15. Admiralty: Captains' Logs (ADM 51). ADM 51/1934, HMS *Agamemnon*.
16. Carlos Roberts, p 350.
17. Carlos Roberts, pp 349–353.
18. Dr James Paroissien was imprisoned for eighteen months in Montevideo accused of treasonous intent. He was released in May 1810. Paroissien later became chief Surgeon General to José de San Martin's Army of the Andes. After the expedition that liberated Peru from spain (1820–1821) he was promoted to Brigadier General, Councillor of State and Envoy to Europe. Carlos Roberts, p 352.
19. Admiralty: Captains' Logs (ADM 51): ADM 51/1934, HMS *Agamemnon*.
20. Ibid. Many seamen regarded it as tempting fate to learn to swim.
21. Ibid.
22. ADM 1/19 Admiralty. Secretary's Department in-letters Admiral's Despatches; Brazils 1807–1809.
23. Carlos Roberts, p 357.
24. Ibid, p 359.
25. Ibid, p 360.

CHAPTER 14

The Last Voyage: Maldonado Bay 1809

> We rounded Pt. Este, and sailing inside Lobos
> Island, famous for its many seals, entered
> Maldonado Bay. This little harbour seemed but
> little protected, should the wind choose to blow
> hard from seaward. It is but a shallow bay
> surrounded by mud-banks, with one little island
> called Goriti, overgrown with wild asparagus, and
> inhabited by rabbits alone, in the centre of it. It
> was here that HMS *Agamemnon*, Nelson's old
> vessel, was lost.
>
> The Cruise of the Falcon
> E F KNIGHT (1887)

The ritual of daily life aboard the *Agamemnon* was shaken on 17 March 1809 by seaman Luke Knighton striking his senior officer Lieutenant William Edwards. Knighton was confined to the bilboes[1] and one month later, on 20 April, was tried by court-martial. Though the episode evoked general condemnation throughout the ship, it was mixed with feelings of distress and pity for the prisoner, whose child-like simplicity had turned aggressive under the influence of alcohol and the airlessness of the lower deck. This mingling of pity and righteous indignation was reflected later in the sentence handed down by the court. The all-powerful tribunal, made up of five captains of the squadron, assembled in the stern cabin of the *Agamemnon*. Captain McKenzie of the *Bedford* presided, as the unfortunate Knighton was brought in to face trial. Four days later they forwarded the minutes of the proceedings to the Commander-in-Chief Sir William Sidney Smith:

HMS *Agamemnon*
Rio de Janeiro
24th April 1809

Sir,
We the undersigned members of the Court Martial assembled on board His Majesty's Ship *Agamemnon* in pursuance of your order of the 20th instant to try Luke Knighton, seaman, belonging to the said ship on charges exhibited against him by a Lieut. William Edwards for having on or about the 17th day of March last behaved in a mutinous manner and having struck him, the said Lieut. William Edwards his superior officer when in the execution of his office which court martial having found the prisoner guilty, and agreeable to the 22nd article

sentenced him to be hung by the neck until he is dead, do in consequence of its having appeared in evidence of his defence, that he is subject to occasional fits of insanity when intoxicated, caused by his skull having been fractured some years since, which deprives him at the time of all power of reason and direction, do therefore recommend him to mercy.

We have the honour to be, Sir, your most obedient and humble servants,

A McKenzie
Jonas Rose
John Hartley
C M Schomberg
John Davies[2]

Sir William, in his turn, showing the clemency recommended by the court, informed his superiors at the Admiralty:

Aboard HMS *Foudroyant*
Rio de Janeiro
12th May 1809

Sir,
I have the honour to transmit for the information of the Lords Commissioners of the Admiralty the minutes of the proceedings with the original sentence of a court martial held by my orders as Commander in Chief for the trial of Luke Knighton, seaman, belonging to HMS *Agamemnon* for striking Lieut. William Edwards. I send likewise a letter which I have received from the members composing the court, recommending him for reasons herein stated as an object for mercy. In consequence of which I did not order him for execution observing that from the circumstances of his general outrageous conduct in striking others and indeed all who came near him at the time, that the act could not be considered as one of premeditated mutiny or intentional resistance of authority, but rather an act of temporary insanity produced by intoxication. I did not however take on me to promulgate a free pardon of him but have ordered him to be discharged into HMS *Diana* for a passage to England, there to await the King's pleasure. I venture at the same time most humbly to recommend him as an object for mercy. His Captain and Officers having giving him a general good character when I admonished the ship's company of the *Agamemnon* on the occasion, and have myself observed that every purpose of example was operated on their minds by the sentence and the admonition with a humble confidence in the known mercy of their Sovereign whom they have long served loyally and faithfully.

I have the honour to be, Sir, your most obedient and humble servant,
W Sidney Smith

PS The prisoner is under charge of James Channon Master at Arms of this ship, who officiated as Provost Marshal on the occasion.[3]

Anticipation of danger

Ever since Napoleon had invaded Spain and placed his brother Joseph on the Bourbon throne, it was reasonable to expect that he would also move to take over the Spanish territories of the Viceroyalty of the Río de la Plata. The British were on guard, attempting to keep the French in their sights, while viewing the future of the area with considerable anxiety.

The day after his arrival in Rio de Janeiro to relieve Sir William Sidney Smith as Commander of the Brazils, Rear Admiral Michael de Courcy addressed the subject in a letter to the Admiralty:

> As it has been understood, previously to my departure from Plymouth, that a French Squadron had escaped from L'Orient it appeared important to me to endeavour to trace their route. Accordingly I called at the Madeira, Canary and Cape Verd[e] Islands, but without obtaining the desired information. From Madeira where the *Diana* arrived on the 20th March, a course was shaped for Teneriffe, but the winds and currents having set the ship far to the eastward it became expedient [to call] on the 23rd March at Gran Canaria where her water was in a few hours completed.[4]

The rumour that a French squadron had evaded the British blockade and escaped into the Atlantic from the Mediterranean naval base of L'Orient had gained momentum. Embellished by the latest sensational but inaccurate information, it was recorded and sent by letter on 12 March to de Courcy. It caught up with him at Rio de Janeiro two months later. He responded to it in the following terms:

> Aboard HMS *Diana*
> Rio de Janeiro
> 14th May 1809
>
> Sir,
> I have the honour to acknowledge an order from the Lords Commissioners of the Admiralty, which has been brought hither by the *Elizabeth*, bearing date the 12th March and addressed to me on board the *Diana* in Cawsand Bay[5], directing that I should proceed to sea with all possible despatch, make the best of my way to my station, and on my arrival at Rio de Janeiro, to proceed with the whole of the force under my command to the mouth of the Río de la Plata for the purpose of taking such a station as might intercept an enemy's squadron from L'Orient, or in the event of their arrival to endeavour to destroy them requiring also that I should communicate their Lordships' instructions to His Majesty's Minister at this place, to the end that such measures might be taken as might be deemed most effectual for apprising the Government of Buenos Aires and Montevideo of the approach of the force under my command for their protection.
>
> And in answer I have to request you will acquaint their Lordships that I shall lose no time in carrying their orders into execution, after Rear Admiral Sir Sidney Smith, to whom I have communicated their Lordship's instructions, with Sir George Collier's letter of information, shall transfer to me the command of his Majesty's Squadron. I have further to acknowledge your letter of the same date referring to their Lordships' order and acquainting me by their Lordships' desire, of a Rumor which had reached them, that Charles IV, late king of Spain, had been embarked on board a French Squadron destined to

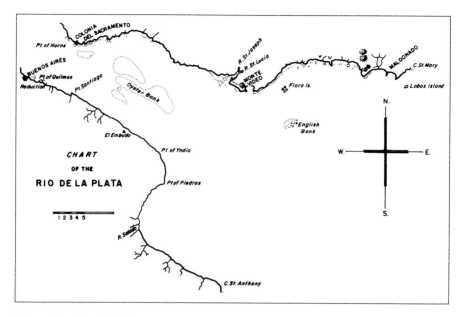

Chart of the Rio de la Plata

Buenos Aires with a view of distracting the attention of the Spaniards in South America and shaking their allegiance to Ferdinand VII and further pointing out to me that His Majesty's Minister at Rio de Janeiro would best judge of the use to be made of this information, to whom I was to communicate the same.

I have the honour to be, Sir, your most obedient humble servant.

M de Courcy, Rear Admiral.[6]

While the ships of the squadron were provisioning and getting ready for sea, de Courcy sought information from all incoming vessels hailing from Buenos Aires or Montevideo. His inquiries, however, revealed no evidence of any French presence in the vicinity of the Río de la Plata. He informed the Admiralty to this effect:

Aboard HMS *Diana*
Rio de Janeiro
20th May 1809

Sir,
The command of HM Squadron on this coast having been made over to me on 18th instant by Rear Admiral Sir Sidney Smith KG, I beg leave to state for the information of the Lords Commissioners of the Admiralty, that with the ships named in the margin I shall pursue the service as pointed out in their Lordships' instructions of the 12th March, as soon as the different ships' stores and provisions shall be complete and a court martial which has been appointed by my predecessor in command shall terminate its proceedings.

At the same time I have reason to suppose that the French Squadron, whose operations I am to endeavour to counteract, has not come into this sea, vessels having arrived at Rio de Janeiro from various parts of the coast, and letters being received (sea-ways) from Montevideo under date the 24th April, without any information on the subject.

I have the honour to be, Sir, your most obedient and humble servant

M. de Courcy, Rear Admiral
[The ships named in the margin are: *Foudroyant, Elizabeth, Bedford, Agamemnon, Mutine* and *Mistletoe*][7]

The day before the squadron sailed there was great activity at the naval base of Fiscal Island where the British were moored. Boats plied to and fro among the ships of the squadron and the shore. Victuals, kegs of water, barnyard animals, powder and shot came aboard while sails were bent to the yards and hoist after hoist of signals flew aboard the flagship.

In the early morning on 26 May with a light breeze hazy with rain the ships got slowly under way to the wafting sounds of fifes and fiddles as the capstans hauled aboard their anchor hawsers. *Foudroyant*, in the lead, was followed out of harbour by the *Elizabeth*, the *Bedford*, the *Agamemnon*, the *Brilliant*, the *Mutine* and the *Mistletoe*, four ships of the line, a frigate, a brig and a schooner. Clawing out from the lee of the mountains their masts and yards broke into pyramids of white as they set course for the fort of Santa Cruz rising majestically at the entrance to the bay.[8]

At noon the wind died to a whisper and the ships wallowed helplessly until their boats were lowered and sent ahead in tow. The *Agamemnon*, sailing abreast of *Mutine*, swung her bows to starboard as she drifted in the swell. Falling foul of the brig, she carried away her jib-boom. The ships' bows were separated by the towing boats and held on course until the breeze picked up once again and *Mutine* was able to pass under the stern of *Agamemnon* and move into open water.[9]

For the first few days the winds were fickle and the ships progressed slowly southward until they had crossed the Tropic of Capricorn. Out of the tropics the difference in latitude made itself apparent. The wind blew fresh and bracing from the south, after its passage across Antarctic seas. It was a great change from sultry Rio and heavier clothes became necessary. Most of the men reached for their waistcoats to wear under their jackets while the officers changed cottons for woollens and buttoned up against the wind.[10]

Rear Admiral Michael de Courcy, his pennant flying aboard *Foudroyant*, was the opposite to his flamboyant predecessor Sir William Sidney Smith. When in Rio de Courcy lived aboard his flagship, keeping out of from court affairs and devoting his time to his squadron. His second-in-command was captain of the *Elizabeth*, the Honourable Henry Curzon. It was the first voyage to the Río de la Plata for the admiral, whose knowledge of the Spanish colony would have been scarce indeed, except perhaps for accounts he might have heard from naval officers who had been present at the British invasions two years before. Lord Strangford would, however, have briefed de Courcy before his departure about politics and the nature of the viceroyalty's population, their frustrations and their wrath at Spain's administrative policy based on a system of privilege and discrimination. It would have given de Courcy much to ponder as the ships sailed steadily southward over a thousand miles of sea.

The howling storm

On 3 June, before the Brazils squadron had reached the halfway point on their voyage from Rio de Janeiro to Maldonado Bay, a furious storm with a *Pampero* wind from the southwest beset the ships. 'Hard gales and squally, furled the courses and set the main staysail' is recorded in the *Agamemnon*'s log during the morning watch. Again in the evening a similar entry: 'Struck topgallant masts and lowered down the gaffs. Handed the fore and main topsails and set the fore and main staysails. Admiral in company. At 9 pm hard gales with lightning and rain at times, at 12 [midnight] set the mizzen storm staysail.'[11]

The following day the weather worsened, the main topsail being split and a new one bent onto the yard to replace it. That night the ships hove to and rode out the gale hoping not lose sight of one another. The manoeuvre in such heavy weather was demanding and dangerous. The topgallant sails, courses, jibs and staysails were clewed up. Trimmed down to the mizzen and three topsails only, with weather braces hauled in tight, the helm was put down to leeward and secured. This caused the vessel's bows to come to and then fall off the wind but always head up out of the trough. The ships drifted slowly on the quarter using oil-bags to calm the breaking waves. Under extreme conditions such as these a guiding rule prevailed: the less the onward motion the safer the vessel, which simply meant that it was preferable to ride out the gale than try to make progress on the voyage. (For a day-by-day notation of the wind's direction during the voyage from Rio to Maldonado, see Note 12.)

The weather continued foul and very cold for two more days reaching the critical point where, aboard the *Agamemnon,* the standing rigging slackened and Captain Rose wore ship to tighten the shrouds on both sides.[13] During the storm the pumps were constantly manned and the ship's hull had to be frapped with hawsers to hold her planks together, a precaution that Rose had thought of applying anyway if the *Agamemnon* were ordered to return to England.

The weather started to gradually improve on 6 June as illustrated by the entries in the ship's log: 'AM. Strong gales and squally, at 7 moderate and clear, [wind from the south-southwest] Broached a cask of rum No. 22 = 35 gallons. Out second and third reef of the topsails. Loosed the small sails to dry. Unbent the storm staysails. Flag and squadron in company.' From fresh and blustery the weather slowly quietened becoming mild and clear until at last, on 13 June it is recorded 'light airs inclinable to calm'.

The 'Banda Oriental'

The sun's first rays brought the loom of land off the starboard bow, the northeastern reaches of the Viceroyalty of the Río de la Plata known as the 'Banda Oriental'. The climate, the colour of the sky, and the lack of vegetation that grows so luxuriantly in Brazil, showed they had indeed left the torrid zone. On sailing closer to land it proved to be a low shore of beaches backed by sandy dunes and hills of no great altitude, a desert-looking country where thistles and aloes seemed specially to thrive.

Since very early days, this wild coast was a terror to mariners with its few landmarks and powerful and unpredictable ocean currents. Shipwrecks were so frequent here that on the shore among the surf still can be found the skeletons of many an ill-fated vessel caught in the struggle of sea and wind. Due to their deep draught the ships of the squadron stood warily out to sea as they coasted along the dreary sandbanks.

The morning of 15 June found the squadron approaching the Rio de la Plata in foggy weather with the little *Mistletoe* ahead and to landward of the main force. Cautiously sounding every half hour the larger ships made little headway tacking against light winds and a strong adverse current.

At noon, the *Mistletoe*, with a lively spread of canvas, passed the granite sentinel of Lobos Island that guards the northern approaches to the great river and the entrance to Maldonado Bay. Sighting a Spanish vessel she hauled her wind and came about. Closing with the stranger she backed her foretopsail to speak to it and then hove to off Punta del Este to wait the arrival of the rest of the squadron.[14]

Fast approaching the winter solstice, the sun was setting when the flagship ahead of the rest passed the *Mistletoe*, bore up, and at 5:45pm came to with her bower anchor in 15 fathoms off Maldonado roads. Wisely, de Courcy had decided to defer entering the bay with its many hidden hazards until dawn the following morning.[15]

Maldonado Bay

Maldonado Bay is a crescent of beaches that stretches some 6 miles from its eastern to its western tip, backed in its entirety by tall sand dunes. Off centre to the southeast it encloses Gorriti Island with its southernmost point a bare mile and a quarter distant from the mainland.

The bay is not a truly reliable harbour. Like the rest of the estuary of the Rio de la Plata it lies in a region of storms and extraordinary electric disturbances.[16] Only a very small portion of the bay known from ancient times as 'The Shepherd's Anchorage' (Puerto de la Pastora) situated midway between

The lookout tower overlooking Maldonado Bay, built in 1801, to give warning of the approach of hostile ships. It was from here that the alarm was raised on 29 October 1806 when a British squadron landed 400 troops and took the town. (Author)

the northern tip of Gorriti Island and the mainland, offers protection from the infamous southwesterly *pamperos* winds. Acting like electrical fuses in sultry weather they bring down the temperature of the atmosphere dramatically as the winds thunder across the Pampa from the Andes. Rolling clouds and sometimes flattening trees and dwellings before them they can become veritable hurricanes in their fury. In the past, their dramatic reputation accounted for seasoned Cape-Horners (a title accorded to only those that sailed past the Horn from east to west) bending on their best sails before reaching the estuary of the Río de la Plata as a precautionary measure.

Taking its name from its whale-like appearance, Punta Ballena is the western extremity of the bay, the termination of Sierra de la Ballena. The eastern extremity, on the other hand, is a low spur of volcanic rock projecting southwestward for a mile and a half from the general line of the coast. A prosperous and developed resort today, Punta del Este, as this peninsula is called, marks the geographical boundary of the Rio de la Plata and the Atlantic Ocean. The extensive estuary of the river, the widest in the world, is entered by crossing an invisible line drawn between this point and Cabo San Antonio, on the Argentine mainland, some 120 miles to the southwest.

Four and a half miles off Punta del Este, into the Atlantic, lies the famous seal sanctuary Lobos Island. Rugged and barren, the craggy reefs surrounding it have claimed many a ship taken unaware as it sailed in or out of the estuary in bad weather or in the dead of night.

Within the bay, the little island of Gorriti affords shelter to vessels of shallow draught that can anchor in its lee. Nowadays covered by pine trees, in early times palm trees and wild asparagus grew over it which for a time gave it the name of Palm Island (Isla de las Palmas), until the British chose to call it the Green Island (Isla Verde), instead.

In 1794 the Spaniards built four batteries on it and gave each a name, or rather two.[17] On the mainland there were also two primitive fortifications: Batería del Medio beneath the town towards the centre of the crescent and the other protecting the bay's most valuable asset, a natural stream of clear spring water, known simply since time immemorial as La Aguada ('The Watering Place'). There were some alternative sources of water along the coast but none were as close to a protected anchorage, had as excellent spring water, or were as readily accessible from the sea as this one. It was a treasured gift of nature that became as widely known by the early navigators and explorers as it has been forgotten today.[18] In fact, there was no other convenient place to water for 700 north until on the Brazilian coast the Arroyo San Miguel runs into the sea opposite Santa Catalina Island. The same can be said for almost a similar distance south to the Rio Negro or further still to Puerto San Matías, today called Golfo Nuevo, on the southern side of Patagonia's Peninsula Valdez, unless the alternative was chosen of sailing up the Rio de la Plata, an off-course excursion of some 100 miles.

The town above the bay

In the centre of the crescent, two miles from the shore and built on a rise 250 feet above sea level, stands the little town of San Fernando de Maldonado. It takes its name from Francisco Maldonado who had a primitive hide industry there in 1730, a successor to the one established by the French buccaneer Esteban Moreau in 1717. Moreau constructed the first buildings and fortified the place with four cannon. The Spaniards dislodged him, Francisco Maldonado took over the premises and the town grew up around the site, retaining his name.[19]

In the early days, there was genuine nervousness amongst the towns-folk that they might be attacked from the sea. As a precautionary measure Antonio Salguero, who held the post of Regidor of Maldonado, instructed his people that in the event of danger he would order the firing of two cannons. This would be the signal for those that owned carts to move their women and children inland as well for those with cattle and horses to do likewise.

The alert system was improved in 1801 by the construction of a look-out tower placed on a bluff at the edge of the town. It provided a sweeping view east and west of the coastline as far as the eye could see. The Regidor wisely thought that keeping a man on duty in the turret would enable him to be informed of any approaching sails long before the ships could anchor and resort to mischief on shore. What he and the inhabitants envisioned were pirates, marauders, or, at worst, the Portuguese. A full military encroachment was inconceivable until, to their astonishment and utter dismay, it came upon them from the most unlikely quarter.

On 29 October 1806, a squadron of British ships of the line, with several transports in company, came into view across the horizon. Anchoring at short distances from one another, they spread out across the width of the bay. Sails were furled and clewed signals broke from mastheads, commands were shouted. Hundreds of soldiers teemed about the upper decks as boats were lowered into which they climbed. Muskets and ammunition were passed down to them from above.

One can imagine the terrified faces of the townspeople grouped around the look-out tower, the warning boom of the town's two cannons, the authoritive figure of the Regidor perched in the tower spying the scene through his telescope while calling out orders to the militia below. Why was this happening? Whatever the reason, they were now at the mercy of the British. Fear was added to consternation, uncertainty to confusion.

It was a sight such as this that greeted the lookouts above Maldonado on 29 October 1806, when a British squadron landed 400 soldiers and captured the town. (National Maritime Museum, London)

Those who owned horses or oxen either saddled up or yoked them to the shaft of their wagons and with their womenfolk astride, or up on the transverse seat clutching their possessions, they made haste for San Carlos, the nearest town. Others of less means and those whose duties did not permit them to leave — officials, the clergy, members of the military units together with the simple folk — waited in fear of the oncoming legions.

The British disembarked 400 men of the 38th Regiment, with an additional force of seamen and marines. They advanced on Maldonado from Punta Ballena in three columns, bayoneted muskets at their shoulders. The Spaniards attempted to defend the village but they were overwhelmed losing fifty men while many were made prisoners. The following day the batteries on the coast were taken. It was an easy task as the guns faced seaward and the British fell upon them from the rear. In the meantime, Sir Home Popham, the British naval commander, directed an assault on Gorriti Island. The Spanish garrison, battered by the guns of the squadron, hastily surrendered having spiked some of their own guns. They were rounded up and then taken and stranded on Lobos Island. Thirty-seven of them managed to escape in boats ingeniously made from seal-pelts, to the annoyance of the British. The remaining half-starved prisoners were eventually removed and confined aboard HMS *Lancaster* to work her pumps as she was leaking badly.

After Maldonado fell, three horrifying days and nights followed as the troops ransacked the little town as stated in the following eye-witness account:

> . . . not only did they destroy many effigies of saints that they found in the homes but without the slightest shame they revised the women-folk for money or anything of value. Some they partially undressed, ravishing others irrespective of tears, supplications, age or virginity. Added to the number of more than three thousand soldiers were sailors from the seventy ships anchored in the bay. They prowled the streets at night by the light of candles they had stolen from the church. The only dwellings spared were those in which distinguished officers had taken residence. Horses, bullocks and sheep were stolen and, who will deny, it being recognised worldwide, that under these circumstances public archives and hospitals are always spared desecration. Not so here by the British. All the papers and documents of the Ministry, of the Real Hacienda and the Superintendency of these new settlements, those pertaining to the Military Command and of your illustrious *Cabildos* [the account was written to inform the members of the *Cabildo*, or City Council, of Montevideo], all of them were either torn up, strewn on the streets, or destined for other uses such as making cartridges. Our hospital was sacked the first night and all we were given in prison were three ears of corn per person and stagnant water to drink from an old disused well. Our sadness grew when we saw our parish priest and his acolyte flung into our jail cell the next morning regardless of the assurances we had been given by the British general that they would be respected. Both men [the priest and the acolyte] had been arrested while burying the dead of both sides. They shared our cell for a short time while the general was advised. Learning what had happened he ordered them released giving word that they would not be further molested.

Those were three days of tribulation. On the fourth a proclamation was posted, signed by General Blackhouse [he was actually a Lieutenant-Colonel in charge of operations] and his secretary declaring that all inhabitants that had fled should return home to their respective tasks as [from now on] they and their property would be protected. Later that day Colonel Vassal of the British 38th regiment was named governor of this township. He seemed to take compassion of us and as he showed a desire to correct the excesses that had been committed, we believed we saw the dawning of serenity.

As a first measure, while our priest was still detained in custody, Colonel Vassal ordered that the vestments stolen be returned to the church and that our religious services be respected and celebrated freely in accordance with instructions given by his government. Our parish priest had determined to suspend any church services until everything stolen from the church had been returned. Not only did this occur but Colonel Vassal went personally to our priest's house taking two boxes containing some of the church's stolen paraphernalia, though incomplete, that had been found in one of the king's storerooms. Furthermore, he posted a sentry at the door of the church which he kept throughout their stay so that no one would disturb our pious celebrations. But there is no doubt that these and other measures had no other object than to save him and his countrymen from the reckoning they deserve due to the atrocious treatment to which they submitted the people of this poor and innocent town.

The chronicle of these events, sad products of the murk and messiness of war, continues at length. It was addressed to the King of Spain, from his subjects in Maldonado, and dated 24 July 1807.[20]

When the news reached Montevideo that Maldonado had fallen to the British, 400 men under Lieutenant Abreu were sent to surround the town and fight the enemy with partisan tactics. Disobeying orders Abreu instead fought an open battle near San Carlos. He was defeated, slain, and his men dispersed. After this misfortune, Colonel José Moreno carried out the guerrilla tactics neglected by his predecessor. He deprived the British of horses for their cavalry, as well as cattle and provisions, to the extent that Popham had to bring in stores by sea from Rio de Janeiro.

The British stayed in Maldonado for ten weeks until General Auchmuty ordered that they be embarked to join in Whitelocke's disastrous invasion of Buenos Aires. These happenings took place two years and eight months before Rear Admiral de Courcy and his squadron entered Maldonado Bay on the fateful morning of 16 June 1809.

NOTES

1. 'Confined to the bilboes' means placed in irons. The manacles were known as the bilboes, a word probably derived from the town of Bilbao in Spain, famous for its iron foundries. Grant Uden and Richard Cooper, p 223.
2. Letter included in Qa 4: William Sidney Smith, aboard HMS *Foudroyant*, Rio de Janeiro, 12 May 1809.
3. Letter Qa 4: William Sidney Smith, aboard HMS *Foudroyant*, Rio de Janeiro, 12 May 1809.
4. Letter Qa 1: Rear Admiral M de Courcy on board HMS *Diana* at Rio de Janeiro, 3 May 1809. Para. 2.

5. Cawsand Bay in England is close to Plymouth although further west, in Cornwall, while Plymouth is in Devon.
6. Letter Qa 124: Rear Admiral M de Courcy, aboard HMS *Diana* at Rio de Janeiro, 14 May 1809.
7. Letter Qa 3 [Volume 2]: Rear Admiral de Courcy aboard HMS *Diana* at Rio de Janeiro, 20 May 1809.
8. Admiralty: Captains' Logs (ADM 51): ADM 51/1934, HMS *Agamemnon*.
9. Ibid.
10. Admiralty: Captains' Logs (ADM 51): ADM 51/1921, HMS *Brilliant*. The *Brilliant*, the 28-gun frigate that had set out from Río in company with the squadron, put back because the convoy she was escorting to England was unable to keep up due to their heavy burden and 'calms and thick weather with rain'. She got under way again but did not remain near the squadron for long. She arrived with her convoy in The Downs on 25 August 1809.
11. Admiralty: Captains' Logs (ADM 51): ADM 51/1934, HMS *Agamemnon*.
12. Ibid. The following is a day by day notation of the wind's direction during the voyage from Río de Janeiro to the Río de la Plata, as taken from the columns of the *Agamemnon*'s log book. Note that there are several different entries for the same day, since the master was obliged to note changes in wind direction when they occurred (not at fixed times). I have only noted the actual hours the wind changes occurred on the last day, the day of the loss.

May 26th WSW SW Vble SW Calm
     27th Calm SWbW Vble SWbW Calm
     28th Calm SbW WSW Vble
     29th NE
     30th NE NNE
     31st NNE North
June 1st SWbS from SSW to ESE [actual log entry]
     2nd Calm North NNW Calm Vble
     3rd WSW West NNW
     4th WSW SW
     5th WbN West WbS
     6th SSW SSW SWbW
     7th SWbW SWbS Vble
     8th SWbW NE
     9th NbE NW
     10th NW WSW Vble
     11th SbW Vble
     12th South SbE SEbS
     13th NNE NW
     14th WSW WbS
     15th WSW Vble SW Vble South
     16th [1 am] ENE [5 am] ENE [7 am] NNE [9 am] ENE
          [1 pm] East

13. Ibid.
14. Admiralty: Captains' Logs (ADM 51): ADM 51/2581, HMS *Mistletoe*.
15. Ibid.
16. In his book, *A Naturalist's Voyage Around The World*, relating his famous circumnavigation in HMS *Beagle*, Darwin mentions the extraordinary electric disturbance in the area of the Rio de la Plata: 'The neighbourhood of the Rio Plata seems peculiarly subject to electric phenomena. In the year 1793 [Felix de Azara's *Voyage*, Vol. 1, p 36] one of the most destructive thunderstorms perhaps on record happened at Buenos Aires: thirty-seven places within the city were struck by lightning and nineteen people killed. From facts stated in several books of travels, I am inclined to suspect that thunderstorms are very common near the mouths of great rivers.'
17. Batería de la Boca Grande on the island's western side was named San Pedro. Batería del Cañón on its northern shore was San Santiago. Batería de la Boca Chica to the east was San Carlos and, finally, Batería del Puerto, looking south was named San José.
18. Following are the names of some of the most famous of the early visitors that called in to water their ships at Maldonado Bay, (in chronological order):

1501–2 Amerigo Vespucci
1514   Joao Lopes de Carvalho with João de Lisboa.

1516	Juan Díaz de Solís.

1516   Juan Díaz de Solís.

1520   Fernâo de Magalhaes (Ferdinand Magellan) with Juan Sebastián Elcano.

1525   Juan Sebastián Elcano, second in command of an expedition to Loaisa in which he lost his life.

1527   Sebastian Cabot, born in Bristol, and son of John Cabot, (Giovanni Caboto, born in Genoa, discoverer of Newfoundland.)

1527   Diego García.

1530   Martín Alfonso de Souza and his brother Pedro Lopes de Souza.

1535   Pedro de Mendoza.

1542   Alvar Núñez Cabeza de Vaca. Hernando Arias de Saavedra.

1573   Ortíz de Zárate accompanied by Martín del Barco Centenera.

1578   Sir Francis Drake.

1582   Edward Fenton accompanied by Francis' brother, John Drake.

19. Carlos Seijo, *Maldonado y su Región* (Montevideo, 1945), pp 5–6.

20. Francisco Bauzá, *Exposición de los vecinos de Maldonado al Cabildo de Montevideo sobre la conducta de los ingleses. Documento probatorio No. 4.*

CHAPTER 15

The Wreck 16 June 1809

Thus while he spoke, around from man to man
At either pump a hollow murmur ran:
'For, while the vessel through unnumbered
   chinks,
Above, below, th'invading water drinks,
Sounding her depth they eyed the wetted scale,
And lo! the leaks o'er all their powers prevail:
Yet at their post, by terrors unsubdued,
They with redoubling force their task pursued.

The Shipwreck (1762)
WILLIAM FALCONER

Jonas Rose was a mere sea-officer with little to commend him except perhaps what he had learned during a lifetime aboard ships of the fleet. He had joined the navy in 1771 as a youngster of ten or eleven, was given a berth aboard HMS *Arethusa* and entered on the ship's books as Captain's Servant. He was lucky in this as his captain was a first-rate seaman who took the boy under his wing. After four years young Rose was rated a midshipman aboard HMS *Levant*. Recommended for examination in October 1779 he was commissioned lieutenant aboard the *Santa Margarita*. The ships he later served on, the *Defence, Duke, Glory* and *Resolution*, were assigned to stations as diverse as the Mediterranean, the North Sea, the coast of North America, the West Indies and the English Channel. He held the rank of commander for five years before being appointed captain of the *Jamaica* in 1801. Later he transferred to the *Circe* and in June 1806 was given command of Nelson's favourite, HMS *Agamemnon*. In recognition of his appointment to the illustrious old ship, in January 1807, Lady Hamilton sent Rose a lock of Nelson's 'Dear Hair', cut off after his death in accordance with his isnstructions, and set in oval frame. The accompanying note was signed 'your affectionate and grateful *but unhappy* Emma Hamilton'.[1]

A reconstruction of the events of 16 June 1809

Three years after his appointment to the *Agamemnon*, almost to the day, Captain Rose stepped out onto the quarter-deck from the warmth of his cabin wrapped in his blue woollen jacket. It was two bells[2] in the early morning watch, dark and cold with a slight breeze from the east-northeast. He turned to the marine sentry at the door and with a nod of his head bid him good morning. His greeting was answered in a similar manner as the man sprang to

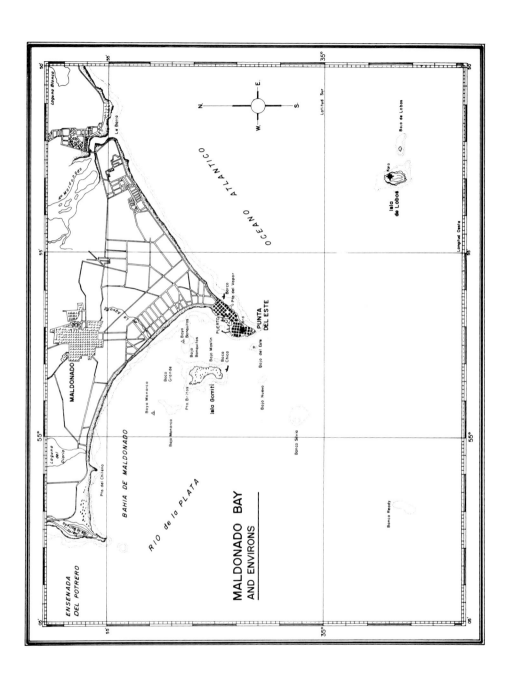

MALDONADO BAY
AND ENVIRONS

attention. The sky was dark grey and it was difficult to discern whether it was clear or had a covering of cloud. He glanced at the binnacle and then through narrowed eyes at the pendant on the head of the main mast checking the wind's direction. The first lieutenant walked across the deck, touching his hat he said 'Good morning sir.'[3]

'Good morning Mr Parr' answered Rose. He paused by the larboard rail and glanced around him at the surrounding sea. Not far off he could make out the silhouette of the flagship riding at anchor and further away the lights of the other ships blinking in the darkness.

At three bells the *Foudroyant* fired a gun followed by a blue flare that soared up into the sky and burst casting a ghostly fluorescence in the early dawn, the prearranged signal for the squadron to weigh anchor and prepare to get under way.[4] There were many people on the quarterdeck now, the master, the quartermaster at the wheel with his assistant, the signal midshipman and the captain's clerk, the marine sergeant with his small armed detachment as well as the ship's surgeon and a cluster of others.

Captain Rose and his first lieutenant, hands clasped behind their backs, paced up and down alert but aloof to the sudden activity. From the hatchways of the upper deck bare feet came racing up from below as the creaking capstan announced the bower anchor being hauled aboard to the squealing sounds of fife and fiddle encouraging the hands at the capstan bars.

Five bells. The ship's corporal in a subdued voice reported 'All's well', repeated by the sentinels in turn at their various stations. Aboard *Foudroyant* two hoists of signals broke out, high above her topsail yard. The first hoist ordered the *Bedford* to lead the squadron to the proper anchorage and the second commanded the *Agamemnon* to proceed and place a buoy upon the shoal where the *Monarch* had once grounded.[5]

The day was dawning fast with a light breeze from the east-northeast. The *Agamemnon*'s men seethed about her upper deck and aloft along the yards loosing the sails. A few minutes later, with the anchors catted and her topsails sheeted home, the ship got under way close-hauled. She sailed past Lobos Island and Punta del Este on a broad reach, then, nearing the northern entrance to Maldonado Bay, Rose gave the order to head up and lower the cutter and the launch. The master, Thomas Webb, was given the task of placing a flag-buoy off the shoal where the *Monarch* had grounded the year before.[6] As the launch pulled away from the ship the coxswain, young Samuel Winspear, remarked to Webb about an open plank he had detected between the first and second sheets of copper on the starboard side of the old ship's hull, slightly forward of the fore and main channels.[7] Leaving Webb and his men to their task, Rose signalled the flagship for permission to proceed to the anchorage within the bay.

(*left*) A map of Maldonado Bay, showing the 'Bajo Monarca' (Monarch shoal), named for HMS *Monarch* which grounded there in 1808.

The crew stood at their assigned posts in silence as the *Agamemnon* worked her way down the channel between Gorriti Island and the shore. Only the voice of the leadsmen in the chains were heard calling out the soundings as they heaved the lead. Ahead was the *Bedford* while astern, rounding the buoy off the Monarch shoal and on the larboard tack, was the flagship followed closely by the *Elizabeth*, the *Mutine* and the *Mistletoe*. All headed to their chosen places in the anchorage under easy sail, having clewed up and furled their topgallants and courses. At one time or another each of the ships had been in the bay, the *Agamemnon* on three occasions, and though it was the Vice Admiral's first visit, the captains knew the place sufficiently well to trust the spot they had chosen to anchor.

As the *Agamemnon* glided smoothly down the channel the only sound aboard was that of creaking blocks and gently straining ropes and sailcloth. Rose stood beside the quartermaster at the binnacle with the Spanish chart of the bay in one hand.[8] He also held another with the soundings of Captain Ross Donnelly's survey taken during the British occupation two years before. Navigating by dead reckoning he neared the place where he remembered anchoring eight months before. The quartermaster at the wheel watched the captain with painful anxiety. 'Bear up, port your helm', said Rose. The ship began its turn to windward.

The cables were flaked neatly on the deck, the anchors clear on the cats with a buoy attached to the bower anchor's fluke. All remaining sails had now been furled.

'Luff up, handsomely now!' said Rose as the ship slowly continued the turn bringing her bows to the wind. With no jib to swing her, she barely moved.

There was a splash of the lead and the cry 'By the mark five . . . yo ho, yo ho . . . and a quarter four', chanted the man heaving the lead in the chains. The bottom was shelving fast. 'Hoist the jib, look lively. Helm a-port,' said Rose in a loud, nervous voice while muttering under his breath, 'My God, we've got to wear her bows around before she takes the ground.'

The order had a curiously powerful effect as the sense of urgency reached the deck. 'Let go and haul,' said Rose as men on the forecastle payed out one jib sheet to haul on the weather one in hope of gaining enough steerage way to veer the ship into the channel again. Her head had fallen off, however, and she faced the wind with a shivering sail.

'Stream the buoy,' called out Rose. The anchor buoy was thrown overboard by the bows and floated off ahead.

'Let go anchor!' There was not a moment to be lost. The splash of her best bower anchor shattered the silence, pulling coils of heavy rope with it through the hawse hole as the jib was hastily lowered.[9] A stopper of thin, pliable rope was made fast to the hawser and thrown over the bitt head. The ship reacted smartly to this as the anchor checked and held her bows to the wind. For an instant she seemed secure but then the anchor lost its grip on the sea-bed 4½ fathoms below and the hull drifted to starboard. For two anxious minutes she floated free until, with a gentle shudder, she took the ground by the stern and then swung around until she lay with her starboard side to the shoal. Down came her ensign, to be immediately rehoisted upside down, the signal of distress.

Rose ordered the boats out. The pinnace carried the kedge anchor towards the northeast, in the direction the ship had drifted, while the launch carried the stream anchor in the same direction. Both were lead to the stern of the ship. From the stern the kedge hawser was taken to the capstan on the lower deck. Heaving upon it the men managed to move the ship some 3 or 4 feet. The strain upon the hawser, however, was more than the rope could bear and it stranded. Then the stream cable was brought to the capstan instead but some strong gusts of wind came off the land at that moment and the anchor came home.

The inrush of water into the hull was not instantly apparent but by the time the *Mistletoe* had moved in close enough to carry the small bower anchor out to windward a half hour had passed and the sad truth became clear. Water was rushing into her hull below deck at a rate the pumps could not handle. The flow gained steadily until it became evident that all further effort was useless.[10]

The *Agamemnon* had signalled she was aground and needed assistance. The admiral, in turn, asked from *Foudroyant* if she needed boats with anchors and ordered the other ships of the squadron to send help. He also ordered the *Mistletoe* to go to *Agamemnon*'s assistance and the *Mutine* to anchor near by.

At about this time Thomas Webb returned from placing the buoy on the shoal to find 4½ feet of water in the *Agamemnon*'s bilges. He reported to the captain on the quarter-deck and then, fearing the ship might capsize, he got the spanker boom and two of the lower spars overboard to support her on the starboard side.

The *Mutine* had anchored 1½ cables to windward of the foundered ship.[11] Sending one of his boats to sound around the *Agamemnon* Captain Fabian found that she had run aground on a knoll no more than 3¾ fathoms beneath the surface.[12] He also ascertained that the fluke of her starboard anchor had caught on her keel and broken through her bottom, abreast of the fore chains, when she listed over on her starboard side.[13]

The *Mistletoe* manoeuvered close to *Agamemnon*. Assisted by the ship's launch she hung one of the *Agamemnon*'s smaller anchors to her own stern and carried it out to windward, anchoring it with considerable difficulty. She then came along side the stricken ship to lend assistance. Despite the substantial purchase on the anchor by means of a cable to the mainmast and the spars placed to keep her upright they could not stop the list. Rose then put the crew to unload stores, sails and cordage, attempting to lighten the ship. He then proceeded to take bearings on the surrounding geographical points to fix his position. These he recorded on a slate using a personal interpretation of the Spanish names. Later that night he laboriously entered them into his log thus:

Point of Gaula [Gorriti] SW by W 1/2 W

Guard Point [Main] SSE 1/2 E
Belone [Ballena] Point W 1/2 N
PM. Fresh Breezes & cloudy all the Pumps working Empd unriving the running
rigging & unShipping the Topmasts loading the boats with various Stores
at 3 left off Pumping water gaining fast & the Ship setting down at 5 got the
Fore & Main Yard over for Shores Struck Topmasts at 8 Moderate & Hazy
Water above the Lower Deck Ports on the Starbd Side & the Orlop Deck
within at Midnight Modte & hazy Weath.[14]

By sunset the *Agamemnon* had settled down, with the water above the lower-
deck ports and the orlop deck flooded. Rose had a frugal meal with his officers
in the stern cabin, then taking off his jacket and shoes he climbed into his
swinging cot. Covering himself with a blanket and closing his eyes he attempted to block out the cold and the tragedy that had befallen him.

Saturday 17 June dawned with a light haze that soon cleared with the help of
the pale winter's sun and a light northeastern breeze. Daylight found the ship settled in the water with her maindeck ports barely 2 feet from the surface of the sea.

Gorriti Island in Maldonado Bay, in a recent photograph. The cross in
the upper right of the picture shows the location of the wreck. (Barbara
Brown)

De Courcy had instructed the captains of the *Elizabeth, Bedford, Foudroyant* and *Mutine* to take their masters and carpenters aboard the stricken ship and adopt any feasible measures for saving the *Agamemnon* from shipwreck. If this proved impossible, they were to send their boats to unload *Agamemnon*'s stores mindful that their warrant officers were to inventory every item removed. At midday they gathered on *Agamemnon*'s tilted upper deck to evaluate the situation. After a brief inspection each group in turn pronounced the old ship doomed. The reports of the masters and the carpenters, penned before leaving the ship, were handed to the captains, who in turn forwarded them with their own report to de Courcy aboard *Foudroyant* as follows:

In pursuance of an Order of the Honourable Michael de Courcy Rear-Admiral of the White and Commander in Chief of His Majesty's Ships & Vessels in the Brazils and South America.

We, the undersigned, the Captains of His Majesty's Ships the *Elizabeth, Bedford, Foudroyant* and *Mutine* Brig, have been with our Masters and Carpenters on board His Majesty's Ship *Agamemnon*, to examine into her present state, and it appears to us that the ship is settled in the mud, bilged and full of water, and heeling over to starboard with her Main Deck Scuppers in the Sea, and we are of opinion from her present state and the reports of our Masters and Carpenters, and that of the Master and Carpenter of the *Agamemnon*, as annexed, that any attempt to heel her the contrary way so as to stopp [sic] the leak is not likely to be attended with success, and if effected would not answer the purpose of saving the ship, and therefore recommend that every exertions should be used for the saving of her Furniture and Stores.

Given under our hands in Maldonado Bay this 17th day of June 1809
[signed]
H Curzon, Captain of the *Elizabeth*
A Mackenzie, Captain of the *Bedford*
R T Hancock, Captain of *Foudroyant*
C Montagu Fabian, Captain of the *Mutine*

This was followed by the masters' report, as follows:

We, the undersigned Masters of His Majesty's Ships *Foudroyant, Elizabeth, Bedford, Agamemnon* and *Mutine* Brig, having in pursuance of directions from the Honourable Michael de Courcy, Commander in Chief, etc etc, examined into the state and situation of His Majesty's Ship *Agamemnon* are of opinion that it would be an useless effort and tended with much loss of time to attempt to save the ship in her present situation, shee [sic] being bilged and her Main Deck Scuppers under water, and likewise a great heel to starboard, but are of opinion that a great part of her Stores above water may be saved and we are fully convinced in our present opinion for the very advanced season of the year.

Given under our hands on board the said ship, Maldonado Road, 17th June
[signed]
James Sutherland, Master of *Foudroyant*
John King, Master, *Elizabeth*
John Engeldice, Master, *Bedford*

Thomas Webb, Master, *Agamemnon*
Thomas Humphreys, Master, *Mutine*

Then the carpenters reported as follows:

> We the undersigned Carpenters of His Majesty's Ships *Foudroyant, Elizabeth, Bedford, Agamemnon, & Mutine* Brig do unanimously think, and it is our opinion, that in case the *Agamemnon* can be righted and brought on even keel, that it is possible to stopp the leak and clear the ship of water by pumps & buckets bailing, but we are further of opinion that with any superficial repairs we could make on her here, she never could be seaworthy.

> Given under our hands on board His Majesty's Ship *Agamemnon* in Maldonado Bay, this 17th of June 1809
> [signed]
> G Monilaws, Carpenter, *Foudroyant*
> W Berry, Carpenter, *Elizabeth*
> James Boddin, Carpenter, *Bedford*
> George Robbins, Carpenter, *Agamemnon*[15]

While the townsfolk of Maldonado gathered around the look-out tower watching the activities in the bay below with much apprehension, men in launches and boats of the squadron clustered around the *Agamemnon* and set about picking the ship clean of every movable oject. They started by taking off the boatswains', gunners' and carpenters' stores, then sails, cordage, yards and spars. From storerooms on the orlop deck and from the hold they recovered casks of salt beef and pork, pease, rice and sugar, rum and wine. 'Everything that appeared useful', went over the side to be distributed among the remaining ships of the fleet.[16] By evening the *Agamemnon* had settled further into the seabed, the scuppers of her upper deck were under water and she had listed further on her starboard side.

Sunday 18 June dawned with barely a breeze from the northeast and a midwinter sky of grey that threatened rain. Parties of men from the ships of the squadron continued dismantling the wreck and removing stores while carpenters scuttled the decks of the ship to gain easier access to the storerooms. Four carronades were dismounted and swung over the side while men from the *Bedford* set out to salvage the best bower by reeving a hawser to the stranded one. The sheet anchor was recovered and the fore topmast was hoisted overboard.[18]

The afternoon turned cold and hazy with light showers of rain when officers and men gathered on the sloping upper deck of the *Agamemnon*. Rose bid the ship farewell as the men, clutching their hats in their hands bowed their heads. An old boatswain's mate, one of the many whom had served under Nelson's command made a stab at a cheer but faltered, drawing back among his shipmates with a mournful shaking of the head. According to one of her gunners, some of the men cried like children when Rose gave the order to abandon the old ship.

Over the side they went into the waiting boats. The last man off the ship was Captain Rose. He climbed down and settled into the bows of his waiting gig larger than life in his foul-weather clothes. Pulling the collar of his jacket up around his neck he voiced 'Away!' with a constricted throat as he signalled the coxswain to cast off.

All that could be heard in the surrounding silence was the rhythmic plop of the oars as the boat pulled away from the wreck ahead of the others. It was almost dark. The wind had increased slightly, sweeping away the haze and replacing it with weeping grey clouds from the west. Halfway to the *Bedford*, Rose raised his hand for the men to pause. Resting on their oars they looked back at the stricken *Agamemnon* now tilted on her side with the water reaching up to the ports of her gun deck. The men gazed with half closed eyes, tears mixed with rain on their rugged faces.

That night in the cabin assigned to him aboard the *Bedford*, Rose removed the log book from its oilskin wrapping. He lit a candle and seating himself at the ledge that served as a table, he opened the book to complete the last entry. Dipping his quill in the inkwell he shook his head and paused in thought. Names harkened from the past: Caldwell, Nelson, Smith, Fancourt, Harvey, Berry, Searle. He heaved a sigh, and putting quill to paper, simply wrote:

at 6 I left the Ship with the rest of the Officers —

I Rose Captain

NOTES

1. This lock of hair was sold, with the letter, on 18 February 1988 by Laurence Fine Art in Crewkern, Somerset, for the sum of £ 5,500.

2. Ship's Bells

No. of Bells	Hour	(A.M. or P.M.)	
1	12:30	4:30	8:30
2	1:00	5:00	9:00
3	1:30	5:30	9:30
4	2:00	6:00	10:00
5	2:30	6:30	10:30
6	3:00	7:00	11:00
7	3:30	7:30	11:30
8	4:00	8:00	12:00

3. Lieutenant A F Parr, one of four brothers in the Royal Navy, was born in Portsmouth in 1786 and entered the service in 1796. He served as midshipman in the *Swiftsure* in the battle

of the Nile in 1798, and took part in operations on the coast of Egypt in 1801. He served as midshipman in the *Agamemnon* in the battles of Trafalgar, 1805, and Santo Domingo, 1806. After this he was promoted Lieutenant. He was also present at the capture of the *Lutine* and the expedition to Copenhagen in 1807. He died in 1856. Colonel Robert Holden Mackenzie, *The Trafalgar Roll* (George Allen, London, 1913), pp 269, 270.

4. Admiralty: Captains' Logs (ADM 51): ADM 51/2581, HMS *Mistletoe*.
5. Admiralty: Captains' Logs (ADM 51): ADM 51/1934, HMS *Agamemnon*.
6. Thomas Webb was appointed Master, RN, in 1799. He served as master of the *Agamemnon* during the battles of Trafalgar in 1805, and Santo Domingo in 1806. He died in 1823. *The Trafalgar Roll*, p 268.
7. Admiralty: Court-Martial of Captain Jonas Rose, ADM 1/5399.
8. The 1789 Spanish chart by Felipe Bauzá, cartographer to the Malaspina scientific expedition sent from Spain in 1788 to survey its colonies.
9. Anchors: Best Bower — bow anchor carried on port side. Sheet anchor — the biggest anchor on the ship, 25 per cent bigger than best bower. Stream anchor: a smaller anchor for short term use in light weather. Kedge anchor: even smaller and could be used in boats. Kedging: taking the anchor out in a boat then dropping it and hauling up on a cable to move ship.
10. When George Robbins, carpenter of the *Agamemnon*, later testified at the court-martial he was asked, 'From the body of water that rushed into the ship, could the pumps and bailing in your opinion have left her clean?' He responded, 'No, nor all the pumps in the squadron!'
11. Admiralty: Captains' Logs (ADM 51): ADM 51/2565, HMS *Mutine*.
12. A cable or 'a cable's length' was 100 fathoms or approximately 600 feet (607.56 feet, according to the *Oxford English Dictionary*).
13. Ibid.
14. Admiralty: Captains' Logs (ADM 51): ADM 51/2581, HMS *Mistletoe*. *Mistletoe*, when she was 2 cables to windward of *Agamemnon*, gave the following bearings, although unfortunately no distances:

    West end of Goritti   SW by 1/2 W
    East point of Maldonado   SSE
    Point Raya   W by N

    [Point Raya is known today as Punta del Chileno]
    Admiralty: Captain's Logs (ADM 51): ADM 51/2581, HMS *Mistletoe*.
15. Admiralty: Captain's Logs (ADM 51): ADM 51/1934, HMS *Agamemnon*.
16. Admiralty: Captain's Logs (ADM 51): ADM 51/2019, HMS *Bedford*.
17. *The Trafalgar Roll*, p 266.
18. The ship's company was distributed between the *Foudroyant, Elizabeth* and *Bedford*. Captain Rose, three lieutenants, the master, surgeon, purser, a marine officer and six petty officers were taken aboard the *Bedford*. Admiralty: Captain's Logs (ADM 51): ADM 51/2019, HMS *Bedford*. Admiralty: Captain's Logs (ADM 51): ADM 51/1934, HMS *Agamemnon*.

CHAPTER 16

The Aftermath

> And meet it is, that over these pastures, wide
> rolling watery prairies and Potters' Fields of all
> four continents, the waves should rise and fall, and
> ebb and flow unceasingly; for here, millions of
> mixed shades and shadows, drowned dreams,
> somnambulisms, reveries; all that we call lives and
> souls, lie dreaming, dreaming, stll; tossing like
> slumberers in their beds; the ever-rolling waves
> but made so by their restlessness.
>
> *Moby Dick*, ch.111.
> HERMAN MELVILLE, (1851)

Four days after the *Agamemnon* foundered, the Admiral weighed anchor with the *Elizabeth*, the *Bedford* and *Mistletoe* and proceeded to sea. The first port of call on their return to Rio would be Santa Catalina off the Brazilian coast, to water and provision.

Shortly after leaving Maldonado the *Mistletoe* chased a Spanish ship but was recalled from further action. In the evening the Admiral passed the word for his secretary and seating himself at the table in the aft cabin he dictated the following report:

Latitude 33° 55' S
Longitude 52° 11' W

Foudroyant at Sea, 23rd June 1809

Sir,
I beg of you to acquaint the Lords Commissioners of the Admiralty that in obedience to their Lordships' commands of the 12th of March, I lost no time in proceeding with the Squadron, as stated in the margin [*Foudroyant, Elizabeth, Bedford, Agamemnon, Mutine, Mistletoe*] from Rio de Janeiro towards the Rio de la Plata, having sailed on the 26th of May and arrived at Maldonado on 16th June. The winds during the greater part of the passage were unfavorable and the weather boisterous. No vessel was met with from which information could be obtained relative to the object in pursuit. On the 16th instant, having passed the Isle of Lobos, the *Bedford*'s signal was made to lead to the proper anchorage, while the *Agamemnon* (each ship having been previously at this rendezvous) was directed to place a flag upon a shoal whereon the *Monarch* had once grounded. Those services being performed with precision, the *Agamemnon* asked permission to enter the harbour, but very sorry am I to add, that after so ably denoting its principal difficulty, she appeared to have too implicitly trusted to Stofino's survey, whereby in seeking a well sheltered berth, she ran upon a muddy bank

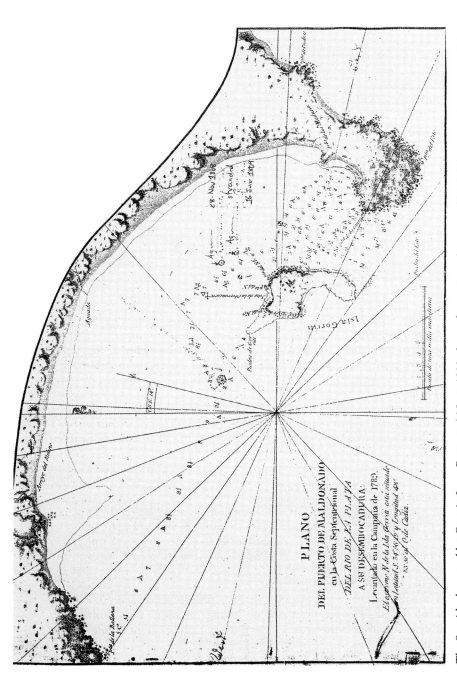

The Spanish chart used by Captain Jonas Rose on 16 June 1809, drawn from a Spanish survey of 1789. The annotations, presumably made at the time of Rose's court-martial show where *Agamemnon* was hit by lightning on 28 November 1808 and (lower) the approximate position where she was wrecked. (Public Records Office)

to the North Eastward of Gorriti. No effort was omitted by the Squadron to heave her into security. The *Mutine* and *Mistletoe* were anchored within a cable's length of her stern, and the boats of every ship were occupied with hawsers, stream anchors &c. But although the water was quite smooth, and the ground soft, the unfortunate *Agamemnon*, by resting (as it is supposed) on an anchor which she had let go on approximating shoal water, bilged, heeled and so became hopelessly lost.

Although I have great concern in stating this disaster, some consolation is to be derived from a knowledge of previous circumstances. Our officers and company had long been of the opinion that her decayed state rendered her unfit for at least a wintry passage to Europe, and it appears that during the storms which she met from Rio de Janeiro her leaks were very great and it became expedient to frap her with hawsers so as to bind her frame together.

After the misfortune as above recited, the Squadron as per margin [*Foudroyant, Elizabeth, Bedford, Mutine, Mistletoe*] remained in the occupation of saving as far as possible the *Agamemnon*'s stores. But finding on that day, that it was no longer practicable to obtain any articles of importance, and considering the anchorage during the Winter solstice to be improper for large ships, I have proceeded with them to sea, and have left the *Mutine* with orders to collect and transport to the uninhabited Isle of Gorriti, whatever might be still be obtained, and to protect them till transports should be sent for their reception from Rio de Janeiro. Having received no intelligence of the French Squadron of which I had come in pursuit, I am led to conclude its destination cannot have been La Plata, and therefore, if circumstances shall justify it I mean on my return towards Janeiro, to look into St. Catherine's, in order to ascertain whether the enemy may have made that port their rendezvous, and in any event to show to any French Spies or Agents, that the English Squadron may be expected on every part of the Coast.

While at Maldonado, I transmitted to Liniers, the Viceroy of Buenos Aires, and to Elio the Captain-General of Montevideo, despatches with which I have been entrusted by His Majesty's Minister at Brazil, accompanying them with a statement of the motive which drew the English Squadron to La Plata, and adding an assurance of the Zeal with which the English were always disposed to adopt any measure for the prosperity of Spain and the discomfort of its enemies.

As soon as a sufficient number of Captains can be assembled for constituting a court martial, an enquiry shall be instituted into the cause and circumstance of the *Agamemnon*'s loss &c and I will take the first opportunity of transmitting to your office, the inventories of such of her stores as are in charge of the respective warrant officers of this Squadron, 22 of them having been left to assist the operations of the *Mutine*.

I take this opportunity of mentioning that I last night communicated with the Spanish Frigate *Prosepina* from Cádiz, having on board the Admiral Don Hidalgo Ciscenisos (whose name I could not comprehend) for Montevideo in lieu of Elio.

I have the honour to be, Sir, your most obedient humble servant

M de Courcy[1]

Salvage operations in the Bay

The day that the Admiral weighed anchor and left with the other ships of the squadron, Captain Fabian, commander of the brig *Mutine*, sole vessel left in the bay, punished seaman James Blair with twenty-four lashes for drunkenness. The penalty exacted, he then sent a sergeant and six marines to guard the stores on the island.

The stores were neatly piled on high ground. Boatswains', carpenters' and gunners' stores filled a fair-sized ledger and, as property of the King, every item had to be meticulously accounted for. The inventories survive today and it is fascinating to read the many components that were necessary aboard a fighting ship of the line.

On 24 June after a violent *pampero* gale from the southwest, Captain Fabian sent a boat to the wreck and found that the storm had shattered her masts and broken her hull in two, between the main channels and the after hatchway.[2] He later reported to de Courcy by letter that the violence of the storm had

A gun barrel found recently in the surf on Gorriti Island in Maldonado Bay, at low tide after a storm. Although great efforts were made to salvage *Agamemnon*'s armament, study of the contemporary sources suggest that eighteen guns were not recovered. (Author)

also blown up her decks and nearly overwhelmed her with sand, leaving little hope of more than nine of her lower deck guns being saved.[3]

A lot of attention was given to salvaging the guns. It must have been an arduous task. Firstly, the crew had to manoeuvre each cannon into position on deck, then hoist it over the side in a sling, using blocks and tackle. There were then two options: either to lower the cannon gently into an open boat or submerge it in the water. In this latter case, the waiting boat would be rowed into the sling so that the cannon hung beneath it. This system, however, was more commonly used for moving a gun from ship to ship as it needed a depth of water beneath. We can therefore assume that the *Agamemnon*'s guns were taken to the island lying on the bottom of a boat and then hoisted out with tackle attached to a triangle of spars. It was no simple task on a rocky shore.

The *Mutine*'s log makes reference to thirty-eight salvaged guns in total and of these twenty-three were reported to have been landed on Gorriti Island. It is difficult to be precise, since the log does not always distinguish between the raising of a gun, an operation in itself and the landing of the same gun on Gorriti, except where it occasionally says 'got a gun and landed it on shore'. It is, however, fairly obvious that none of the guns were loaded straight away onto the other ships of the squadron, as if we look at the date that the *Mutine* started work on the salvage of them, the first mention is on 22 June, by which time the other ships had departed. An additional eight upper deck guns were possibly salvaged during August and September by the transports *Neptune* and *Kingston*. Added to the thirty-eight saved from the wreck by the *Mutine* it would leave eighteen guns still unaccounted for but being on the lower deck it is possible they could not be retrieved.

We know from the inventories that twelve carronades were put aboard the other ships of the squadron. *Foudroyant*, *Elizabeth* and *Bedford* acknowledged receiving four each. Carronades, however, were not included as part of her official amount of sixty-four guns.

The *Mutine* continued her solitary vigil, slowly removing every possible item from the wreck to the island. On 17 July her log reports another gale. This time the *Agamemnon*'s cutter was lost with fourteen oars, her mast, sails and rudder. By the end of the month the hull had sunk low into the sea-bed and the water had reached the upper deck ports. A boat sent from *Mutine* to inspect the wreck, after the storm, found that due to the rising water the casks in the hold, had jammed everything solid inside.

HMS Nancy *escorts the transports* Neptune *and* Kingston *to Maldonado Bay*

Rear Admiral de Courcy wrote to the Admiralty from Rio de Janeiro. Following is an extract from the letter:

Aboard *Foudroyant*, at Rio de Janeiro, 22nd July 1809

I lost no time in sending hence, under protection of the *Nancy* armed brig, two transports to Maldonado, for the purpose of bringing back all such stores belonging to the *Agamemnon* as may have been collected by the *Mutine*, and am in hopes that one of His Majesty's ships of war may soon reach this port, whereby an opportunity would occur for instituting an enquiry into the cause and circumstances of that Ship's loss &c. The *Agamemnon*'s Captain & Officers, with many invalids, are placed on board the *Dawn* transport for the purpose of profiting (after the meditated Court Martial) of the first convoy bound to England. I regret to mention that the remainder of her Complement will scarcely suffice to complete the companies of His Majesty's Ships on this station. All the ships were deficient and so ill-manned was the *Foudroyant* in particular, that on blowing hard during her late wintry cruise, the Topmen were afraid of venturing on the Yards. The climate is very weakening. One effect of it is to produce numerous ulcers on the legs. Much relief was nevertheless obtained by lately leaving this burning port. I enclose lists of such stores belonging to the *Agamemnon* as have been brought away by this Squadron.[4]

The direct involvement of HM Brig *Nancy*, Commander S A Killwick, with the salvage of the *Agamemnon* was fairly minimal. It was very useful, however, as the *Nancy* recorded information about the two transport ships, *Neptune* and *Kingston*, which were used to take away the salvaged equipment and stores. Their own logs unfortunately do not survive. For selected items of interest taken from the entries in *Nancy's* log see Appendix 7.

The *Nancy* proceeded to sea in company initially with the transport *Kingston*. She spent the next day working out of the bay and rounding the island of Lobos. There she parted company with the *Kingston*. On Friday 15 December she entered the harbour of Rio de Janeiro. She found the *Foudroyant, Bedford, Elizabeth, Mutine* and *President* already there.

Rear Admiral de Courcy had written to the Admiralty on 20 August. The following is an extract from the third paragraph of his letter:

Aboard *Foudroyant* at Rio de Janeiro, 20th August 1809

From different causes and infirmities many seamen of the Squadron have also been invalided (for it is a climate very pernicious on the strength of Europeans). To lighten government [illegible word] as far as practicable of the expense of providing for them a conveyance to England, I have permitted such of them as possessed sufficient strength to work their passages homewards in merchant vessels, the Masters whereof having stipulated to deliver them to the first vessel of His Majesty which they should meet in English ports. Others go by the *Dawn* transport, which I had previously appointed for the conveyance of the Captain, Officers and part of the Crew of His Majesty's late Ship *Agamemnon*. Such Guns of that ship as had been brought from Maldonado go by the same conveyance and here I take opportunity of mentioning that from the last letter I have received from Captain Fabian of the *Mutine*, I have reason to believe he has been assiduous in endeavouring to save the *Agamemnon*'s remaining Stores. Yet, he says that a violent gale of wind from the South West, had on the [looks like] 25th of June shattered her Masts, blown up her Decks, and nearly overwhelmed her with sand, and left but little hopes of more than nine of her Lower Deck Guns being saved.[5]

The court-martial at Rio de Janeiro for the loss of HMS Agamemnon *as reconstructed from the official records*[6]

A court-martial was automatic when any naval ship was lost. It was convened by the commander-in-chief, so he could not serve on it himself. His second-in-command usually presided over a court of senior officers. It was always a painful ordeal for the captain of the lost ship. The officers were invariably asked if they had any complaints to make against their captain and captain if he had any against the officers. An advisor to the court on legal matters, the judge advocate to the fleet, or one of his deputies, attended the trial to assure it was conducted correctly.[7]

The flag was hoisted above the *Bedford* and a gun echoed across the bay as the captains solemnly assembled for the court-martial. Haze was coming off the water magnifying the surrounding mountains, bathing them in hues blue and green. The bay of Guanabara is spectacularly beautiful in the forenoon but despite its shimmering brilliance each captain stepped through the entry port of the *Bedford* solemn as an owl. Greeted with due respect they were escorted by the first lieutenant into the great stern cabin.

The formality of the occasion was matched by their attire. All wore their full-dress jackets, with gold braid, epaulettes and white breeches. Two rows of gold lace round their cuffs denoted their rank as captains of at least three years' seniority. Cocked hats edged with more gold lace and polished silver buckles on their shoes added much dignity to the occasion.

A second gun boomed and the master-at-arms stood to attention. The door opened and Captain Rose entered the great cabin with his officers behind him. Hat under his left arm, figure erect, he bowed to the president of the court, the Honourable Henry Curzon, Captain of HMS *Elizabeth* and second-in-command of His Majesty's ships and vessels on the Brazil station. Unbuckling his sword he placed it on the table before him. He then turned slightly and bowed to the captains on the right, Adam Mackenzie, and Richard Turner Hancock, and again to Charles Marsh Schomberg, and James Lucas Yeo, on the left. With a nod of his head the president bid Captain Rose and his officers to sit.

The judge advocate proceeded to read the document before him requiring the court to assemble 'by order of the Honourable Michael de Courcy, Rear Admiral of the White and Commander-in-Chief of His Majesty's ships and vessels on the coast of Brazil and South America, dated the 4th instant, directs the Honourable Henry Curzon, captain of HMS *Elizabeth* and second officer in the command of His Majesty's ships and vessels on the Brazil Station, to enquire into the cause and circumstances of the loss of His Majesty's late ship *Agamemnon*, and to try Captain Jonas Rose, late commander of that ship, her officers and company, for their conduct on that occasion.'

Following the reading, the members of the court and judge advocate took the oaths 'directed by Act of Parliament, made and passed in the twenty second year of the reign of his late Majesty King George II . . .' The atmosphere in the great stern cabin was grave.

Captain Rose's letter to Admiral de Courcy, with the account of the incident that caused the loss of his ship, was read aloud by the judge advocate as were the reports of the captains, masters and carpenters sent to review the wreck. Immediately afterwards Henry Curzon, senior captain and president of the court-martial looked sternly at the prisoner. Thus commenced the inquiry: 'Captain Rose, have you any complaint to proffer against any of the Officers or Crew of His Majesty's late Ship *Agamemnon* for not using their utmost endeavour to preserve or get off the said Ship, or since her loss for not having been obedient to orders, or for not having used their utmost endeavours to save the Ships Stores?'

Captain Rose stood up and answered firmly: 'None.'

All the witnesses were ordered to withdraw from the court except Lieutenant Blissett of the *Agamemnon* who was sworn in.

Question by the Court: Was the Signal made by the Admiral giving permission for the *Agamemnon* to anchor in Maldonada Roads?
Answer: I cannot say, being unwell at the time.

Lieutenant Blissett withdrew. Lieutenant Parr was sworn in.

Court: Was the Signal made by the Admiral giving permission for the *Agamemnon* to anchor in Maldonada Roads?
Answer: I believe it was.
Court: Were you on the Quarter Deck of the *Agamemnon* at the time she struck, and were the leadsmen in the Chains?
Answer: Yes.
Court: Was the *Agamemnon* by the Wind or sailing large when she first came into shoal water?
Answer: Clean full.
Court: Under what sail?
Answer: The Jib, the other sails having been taken in and furled for anchoring.
Court: Was it supposed the Ship being in shoal water was owing to her not being sufficiently amid channel?[8]
Answer: I believe it was.
Court: Was the Ship kept away for the purpose of getting amid channel?
Answer: Yes.
Court: Upon running more amid channel and finding the water still shoal what was done to prevent the Ship taking the ground?
Answer: The anchor was let go.
Court: Did the Ship bring up to her anchor?
Answer: Yes.
Court: Had the Ship any way?
Answer: About half a knot.
Court: How happened it that the anchor checked her?
Answer: Capt. Rose ordered it to be stoppered.
Court: And the Ship took the ground immediately afterwards?

Answer: Yes.

Court: After the Ship took the ground what was done to get her off?

Answer: The boats were hoisted out, the Kedge and Stream Anchors carried out on the larboard quarter and brought to the Capstan on the lower deck, and hove a great strain, till the Hawser that was bent to the Kedge stranded, which obliged us to stand fast till the Hawser was bent afresh; then hove again, found the anchors came home. At 10 the Carpenter reported the Ship had sprung a leak that four feet six was in the Hold, the Pumps were set to work. At 1/2 past 10 found the water increasing, I believe to nine feet.

Court: Was any signal made to the Admiral of the situation of the Ship?

Answer: Some, I don't know what they were, but understood they related to the situation of the Ship.

Captain Rose now questioned the witness.

Rose: Do you know if the Ship drew off the ground at the time the Hawser stranded and stopped the Capstan?

Answer: I cannot say, for I was on the lower Deck at the time.

Rose: If the Hawser which was made the Messenger to the stream Cable had not stranded and occasioned the Capstan to stop is it your opinion that the Ship would have hove off?[9]

Answer: I think she might.

Rose: Was the Anchor let go the moment the Ship began to shoal her water?

Answer: Yes.

Rose: How long was the Ship aground before she made water?

Answer: To the best of my knowledge not more than twenty minutes.

Rose: Did the Ship lay so quiet on the ground that standing on the fore part of the Quarter Deck it would not have been known?

Answer: Yes she did.

Rose: Is it your opinion that the pumps could have kept the Ship clear?

Answer: No.

Rose: Was all the pump gear in good order, then, and all the time you had been in the Ship?

Answer: I think it was.

Rose: Were the Cables ranged, the Anchors clear and everything ready for coming to an Anchor on the Morning of the 16th June when going into Maldonada Roads?

Answer: Everything.

Rose: Had the *Agamemnon* been in any tolerable state of strength, could she have got afloat without much injury?

Answer: I think she might.

Rose: How were we at the time the Jib was run up; were we nearer the Main or the Island?

Answer: Nearer the Main.

Rose: From your observations when at Maldonada Roads three times before, did it appear to you that the *Agamemnon* was running into danger?

Answer: No.

Rose: Have you ever trawled[10] with one of the Boats in Maldonada Roads? If you have, did you apprehend that there was any bank in the position where the *Agamemnon* grounded that would have brought her up?

Answer: Yes I trawled there once, and close over to the Main but I could not tell without a lead, and I had none in the Boat.

Rose: After the Ship struck the ground, was every possible exertion made use of on my part to get the Ship off, with the assistance of the Squadron?

Answer: Yes, every exertion was used.

Rose: Were there any men sent from the Squadron and how many, to work at the Pumps?

Answer: There were some but I can't say the number.

Rose: In what state were the Hawsers of the *Agamemnon*, and if defective from what cause?

Answer: All good except two, which were eaten by the rats and rendered useless.

Rose: Did you, as doing the duty of 1st. Lieut. or Officer of the Watch visit the Cockpits and Wings every Morning, and what was the state of the Ship?[11]

Answer: Every morning when I had the morning watch. I found her in a very bad state due to the gales of the 3rd, 4th and 5th of June. In going the rounds I used to find the riders, which were in the Wings work from side to side half an Inch some of them, and one or two of the Bolts drew in and out. We kept the hand pumps going during the Gale.[12]

Rose: Could you have put in your hand or a small book between the riders when the Ship rolled over to leeward?

Answer: I think I could to some of them at times when she took heavy lurches.

Rose: During the gale abovementioned and clearing her of a good deal of water that she had unexpectedly made, was the hand Pumps kept constantly going and relieved every half hour during your watch?

Answer: Yes.

Captain Rose turned to the president of the Court and nodded his head. Lieutenant Parr was asked to withdraw. Lieutenant L'Estrange was sworn in and questioned by the court.

Court: Where were you stationed?

Answer: On the forecastle.

Court: State to the court the circumstances which occurred relative to the *Agamemnon*'s getting aground, and what was done to get her off.

Answer: We tacked about half past eight to stand in for the anchorage. After we got into the bay we bore up from the weather shore, clued up and furled the sails. We received orders to have the best bower Anchor clear about ten minutes before it was let go. We had hoisted the Jib to wear the Ship round finding we had got into shoal water but it was scarcely up before I was ordered to haul it down again. About two minutes after the Anchor was gone I felt the Ship touch the ground. All the boats were got out: the Pinnace carried the Kedge out to the NE, the launch carried the stream Anchor out in the same direction. We brought the Kedge Hawser to the Capstan first and after we began to heave upon it I think we moved the Ship about three or four feet when we stranded the Kedge Hawser. We then brought the stream Cable to the Capstan. By this time we found the Ship had made a great deal of water, we got all hands to the Pumps, but found the Water gained upon us and we stopped pumping. About two o'clock in the afternoon two rough Spars and the spanker-boom were got

An anonymous watercolour from *circa* 1819 of the stern great cabin of a ship
of the line. The court-martial of Captain Jonas Rose, following the loss of the
Agamemnon, was held in the great cabin of HMS *Bedford* (74) in the bay of
Guanabara near Rio de Janeiro. (National Maritime Museum, London)

over on the starboard side, finding the Ship began to settle down. The Lower
Yards were got over in the afternoon to shore the Ship. At Sunset she had
settled down with the Water above the Lower deck Ports and above the Orlop
Deck within. The Sails were all unbent and every dispatch was made in order to
save the Stores by the Squadron. On the morning of the 17th purchase was got
from the Main mast head on the small bower Cable to prevent the Ship settling
down any further.

Court: Have you ever been at Maldonado before?
Answer: Three times.
Court: Have you any reason to suppose from what you know of the place that
when the sails were taken in for anchoring the Ship was in an unsafe berth?
Answer: I had not.

The court then authorised Captain Rose to question the witness.

Rose: Did you apprehend that to be the best berth which the Ship was in, to
protect her from the prevailing winds?
Answer: I did.

Rose: If the Hawser had not stranded, which occasioned the Capstan to stop, was it your opinion that the Ship could have been hove off?

Answer: If we had not been delayed by the Hawser stranding and the Ship making water, it is probable she might have been hove off.

Rose: Had the Ship any motion until we began to move her off the ground?

Answer: No.

Rose: In what state were the Hawsers of the *Agamemnon*?

Answer: In general very bad, mostly eaten by the Rats.

Rose: Had the *Agamemnon* been in any tolerable state of strength could she have been got afloat without much injury?

Answer: She might, but I cannot answer.

Rose: Were the Cables clear and everything ready for coming to Anchor on the morning of the 16th of June, you having the forenoon watch?

Answer: Everything was ready.

Rose: How much from the centre of the Channel was the *Agamemnon* when we hoisted the Jib, to run her more to leeward, and was she nearer the Main or the Island?

Answer: I think she was nearer the Main.

Rose: Did you when Officer of the Morning Watch in general visit the Cockpits and Wings and report them to me agreeable to the regulations of the Ship?

Answer: Yes.

Rose: What was the general state of the Ship during her last cruise, particularly during the gale of the 3rd, 4th and 5th of June when you visited the Wings?

Answer: The Ship was extremely leaky in the Wings, not a dry part to be found fore and aft. In the Larboard Wing I observed one of the sleepers where the bolts played half an inch in and out when the Ship worked, and in both Wings the leaks appeared to have come through the side.[13]

Rose: During your watch in the gale of the 3rd, 4th and 5th of June was the hand pump kept going at intervals and relieved every half-hour?

Answer: It was.

Rose: How long was the Ship aground before she made water?

Answer: To the best of my recollection about an hour and a half.

Rose: Could the Pumps have kept her clear of the body of water which rushed into her?

Answer: The water gained upon the Pumps.

Rose: From your own knowledge were all the Pumps and Gear in the best condition?

Answer: I do not think they were.

Rose: After the Ship was on shore was every possible exertion used to get her afloat?

Answer: To the best of my knowledge there was.

Rose: Have you always seen me particularly anxious in conducting the Ship?

Answer: Yes.

Rose: What do you judge from?

Answer: From seeing you always on deck when Anchoring or weighing and always at sea when there was any danger.

Rose: Have you heard me express my opinion of the Ship latterly, and what I proposed doing to secure her?

Answer: You have mentioned your intention of frapping her in case of being ordered home.[14]

Lieutenant L'Estrange withdrew. Lieutenant Rudall took the oath and was questioned by the court.

Court: Were you attending the Signals the day the *Agamemnon* got on shore?
Answer: Part of the time.
Court: Did you see the Signal made by the Admiral giving permission for the *Agamemnon* to Anchor in Maldonada Road?
Answer: Yes.
Court: When the *Agamemnon* got on shore were any Signals made to the Admiral of her situation and circumstances?
Answer: There were.
Court: Were any Signals made from the Admiral in consequence and what were they?
Answer: He asked by telegraph if we wanted Launches with Anchors, or without. He made the Signal for the Boats of the Squadron and the *Mistletoe* to come to our assistance and the *Mutine* to Anchor near us.

The witness was then questioned by Captain Rose.

Rose: How long had the Ship grounded before she made water?
Answer: I believe about half an hour.
Rose: Were all the sails furled before we hoisted the Jib to run the Ship more to leeward, and which shore were we nearest at the time?
Answer: All furled except the mizzen-topsail which they were then furling, and the Ship was nearer the Main.
Rose: Was the anchor let go the moment you heard the leadsman give notice of our shoaling the water?
Answer: It was let go as we were shoaling water, but I cannot answer for the exact moment.
Rose: When the Ship lay aground did she lay quiet?
Answer: After she began to make water.
Rose: Had she much motion before or any?
Answer: Some, but not much.
Rose: Do you know if the Ship drew off the ground after we hove?
Answer: She did.
Rose: Do you suppose that to be about the time she began to make water?
Answer: Yes.
Rose: Describe the state of the Ship during the gale of the 3rd, 4th and 5th of June last when going through the wings and cockpits in your morning watch.
Answer: I observed the riders work a great deal several of the bolts loose, and the Ship made water.
Rose: If the Ship was in any tolerable state of strength would she have got off without much injury?
Answer: I should suppose a strong Ship might from hearing the report of the officers.
Rose: After the Ship was on shore was every possible exertion used to get her off?
Answer: Yes.

Lieutenant Rudall withdrew. Mr Webb the master took the oath.

Court: Where were you at the time the *Agamemnon* got on shore?
Answer: I was in one of the boats laying a buoy on a shoal by Capt. Rose's order, in consequence of the Admiral's having made a signal for that purpose.
Court: At what time did you return on board the *Agamemnon* and what was the state of the Ship at that time?
Answer: I returned at forty minutes past nine, and the Ship was then aground. She had a kedge anchor out astern and hove taut, and the launch was carrying the stream anchor out.
Court: Was every exertion used in your opinion to get the Ship off?
Answer: Yes it was.
Court: How often have you been in Maldonada?
Answer: Three times before that.
Court: From what you know of the anchorage should you have supposed the *Agamemnon* was standing into danger in the place she then was, had you been on board?
Answer: No.
Court: Was every exertion used to save her stores after the idea of getting her off was given up?
Answer: Yes, every exertion was used.

The witness was questioned by Captain Rose.

Rose: Did you suppose when you left the buoy to join the Ship, that she was aground or in an unsafe berth?
Answer: I did not.
Rose: Have you ever anchored the *Agamemnon* near that spot before, and what distance do you suppose by the bearing?
Answer: About a cable and a half to the westward of that bearing.
Rose: Have you ever seen a man-of-war at anchor nearer to the Island than where the *Agamemnon* lay aground?
Answer: Yes I have.
Rose: What ships were they if more than one?
Answer: Two Spanish frigates.
Rose: With the Spanish as well as the English Charts and Capt. Ross Donnelly's survey should you have hesitated to run the ship into Maldonada Roads as I had done?
Answer: No I should not by either of the surveys.
Rose: Have you any reason to suppose from the situation of the Roads that sand banks are liable to be formed there?
Answer: Yes I have.
Rose: Do you remember when the *Monarch* was moored that she brought home her anchors and that Captain Lee said it was in consequence of having broke a wreck loose from the bottom, which must have drifted up the roads with the gale?
Answer: Yes I saw the *Monarch* drive, and heard Captain Lee tell Captain Rose so.
Rose: Are the soundings in the Chart correctly laid down?
Answer: No.

Rose: When the boat joined you on the shoal, did the coxswain make any observations on the state of the Ship, and what were they?

Answer: Yes he did. There was a plank started about a streak above the copper.[15]

Rose: Did you hear me point out to Sir Sidney Smith before we went to Sea, how much the Ship had sunk abaft?

Answer: Yes I did.

Rose: Have you always seen me particularly anxious about the safe conducting of the Ship?

Answer: Yes always.

Mr Webb withdrew. Mr Robbins the carpenter was then sworn in.

Court: Relate to the Court the circumstances and state of the *Agamemnon* after she got on shore.

Answer: From about a quarter of an hour after the Ship struck she made no water, there was no more than 15 inches which remained from the night before. At seven o'clock Capt. Rose sent for me on the Quarter Deck to know whether the Ship had made any water, I told him not. He desired me then to rig the hand pumps and pump that water out. The hand pumps were rigged and set to work. I then went down and ordered all the spare pump gear both for the lower and main deck to be brought up immediately, which was done and rigged. I called to the man in the well, Wilson, Carpenter's Mate whom I had placed there on the Ship's fore.

Court: Was every exertion used to save the Ship, and the Pumps worked as long as they could be of any use?

Answer: In my opinion there was.

Court: Was everything done possible for saving the Ship's stores?

Answer: Every exertion possible was used.

Captain Rose examined the witness.

Rose: From the body of water that rushed into the Ship could the pumps and bailing in your opinion have left her clear?

Answer: No, nor all the pumps in the squadron.

Rose: Was all the Pump gear in very good condition?

Answer: They were, and Capt. Rose had proved them three days before with the assistance of Lt. Parr. They delivered a great body of water, as much as they would when first put into the Ship.

Mr Robbins withdrew and the prosecution closed. Mr Sutherland, Master of *Foudroyant*, was then called by Captain Rose as evidence in his defence.

Rose: With the Spanish Chart, [the chart was produced as evidence], as well as the one by R Smith, and sanctioned by Capt. Ross Donnelly, would you have hesitated to run the Ship you are master of into Maldonada Roads on the same bearings that the *Agamemnon* now lays?

Answer: From the Charts, I should not have hesitated a moment in running the Ship in.

Mr Sutherland withdrew. Mr King, Master of *Elizabeth* took the oath.

Rose: Have you the bearings of the *Agamemnon* on the shoal in Maldonada Road?
Answer: Yes.
Rose: Is its bearings shown with the Chart correct to the best of your recollection?
Answer: Yes.
Rose: With the Spanish Chart as well as the one by R. Smith and sanctioned by Capt. Ross Donnelly would you have hesitated to run the Ship you are Master of into Maldonada Roads on the same bearings that the *Agamemnon* now lays?
Answer: Certainly not.

Mr King withdrew. Mr Engledue, Master of *Bedford* was then sworn in.

Rose: Have you been in Maldonada Roads and how often?
Answer: Twice.
Rose: Have you the bearing of the shoal where the *Agamemnon* now lays, and is the bearing now with the Chart correct to the best of your knowledge?
Answer: Yes.
Rose: With the Spanish Chart as well as the one by R. Smith and sanctioned by Capt. Ross Donnelly, would you have hesitated to run the Ship you are master of into Maldonada Roads on the same bearing that the *Agamemnon* now lays?
Answer: Not at all.
Rose: Were you aware of any shoal running out so far from the island as that which brought up the *Agamemnon*?
Answer: No I was not, as the bearings of the *Agamemnon* almost agrees with that of the *Bedford* the first time she anchored there.
Rose: Had the *Monarch* stirred up any wreck during the time you were first in Maldonada Roads?
Answer: Not to my knowledge.

Mr Engledue was asked to withdraw.

Rose: I wish the president and other members of the court who were present at Maldonada on the 16th June, whether with the confidence of the Charts before them, they would have had any apprehension in running their Ships where the *Agamemnon* grounded?
Answer: As the Charts are laid down certainly not.

Mr Samuel Winspear, coxswain, was called and sworn.

Rose: What remarks did you make on the state of the Ship when you were sent with Mr Webb the Master who was laying down the buoy?
Answer: I observed a plank being open between the first and second sheet of copper on the starboard side in the wake of the main channels and as far forward as betwixt the fore and main channels.
Rose: Did you report it to the Master?
Answer: I did.

The last of Nelson's 'Agamemnons'. In June 1840
Frederick Cruickshank painted this portrait of John
Adams ('alias Wilkinson'), who had been boatswain
of HMS *Agamemnon* during Nelson's command of her
from 1793–1796. (National Maritime Museum,
London)

With nothing further to offer in Captain Rose's defence, the court was
cleared and the members of the panel proceeded to deliberate the evidence.
Within 30 minutes, they reached a verdict. The Corporal of Marines opened
the door to re-admit Rose and his officers, who filed in and stood facing their
judges. Peering intently at the disconsolate Rose, Captain Curzon, president
of the court, instructed William Brenton, the judge advocate, to read the
verdict. He did so in a firm but expressionless voice:

> The court having carefully and deliberately weighed and considered the evi-
> dence on the part of the Crown as well as the defence of the Prisoner, were of
> opinion that His Majesty's late Ship *Agamemnon* was run upon the shoal owing
> to the incorrectness of the Chart or a Bank recently strewn up, and that no
> blame attaches to Captain Jonas Rose; that he, the Officers and Ships Company
> appear to have done their utmost to get the Ship off, and afterwards save her
> Stores. In consequence thereof the Court has acquitted Captain Jonas Rose, the
> Officers and company for the loss of the said Ship.

The strain of the day lifted almost visibly from the shoulders of the assembled men. Respectful murmurs of congratulations were heard all around; there was a humbled shaking of hands. Captain Curzon got to his feet and smiled. He picked up Rose's battered sword from the table, and holding it by the scabbard, held the hilt towards the shaken man. Rose reached for the sword with bowed head, no doubt overwhelmed in his moment of absolution. His naval career, which had reached its height as captain of HMS *Agamemnon*, had also nearly shared her depths. He was a relieved man, cleared of all wrongdoing. But he would no more grace the quarterdeck of a ship so famous. Unfair or no, his naval reputation would suffer the strain of implication until his death on 20 July 1820.[16]

Notes

1. Letter Qa 6: M de Courcy, *Foudroyant* at Sea, 23rd June 1809.
2. Admiralty: Captains' Logs (ADM 51): ADM 51/2565, HMS *Mutine*.
3. Letter Qa 10: Rear Admiral de Courcy aboard *Foudroyant* at Rio de Janeiro, 20 August 1809.
4. Letter Qa 7: Rear Admiral de Courcy aboard HMS *Foudroyant*, Rio de Janeiro, 22 July 1809.
5. Letter Qa 10: Rear Admiral de Courcy aboard *Foudroyant* at Rio de Janeiro, 20 August 1809.
6. Admiralty: ADM1/5399 Court Martial Proceedings on Captain Jonas Rose and crew for the loss of HMS *Agamemnon*. Text and spelling true to the original document.
7. Brian Lavery, *Nelson's Navy* (Conway Maritime Press, London, 1989), p 217.
8. Shoal, a term synonymous with shallow. W A Falconer, p 467.
9. Messenger: in a ship is a large rope used to unmoor or heave up anchors by transmitting the efforts of the capstan to the cable. This operation is performed by fastening one end of the messenger to the cable in several places, by a particular kind of rope called nippers, and by winding the other end onto the capstan. W A Falconer, p 275.
10. To trawl means to tow a large bag-like net behind a boat or fishing vessel to catch fish living on the bottom or lower layers of the sea. Grant Uden and Richard Cooper, p 531.
11. Cockpit: in the old sailing ships there were two cockpits, fore and aft. The after cockpit was on the lowest deck. Dark and stuffy, it housed the 'young gentlemen', or midshipmen who shared their unattractive quarters with the Master's Mates and other lesser folk. In battle it was used as an emergency sick-bay for the wounded, and was the scene of many an amputation by the surgeon. The fore cockpit in the bows was the quarters of the boatswain and the carpenter. Grant Uden and Richard Cooper, p 90.

    Wings: A name given to those parts of the hold and orlop deck which are nearest to the sides. This term is particularly used in the stowage of the various materials used in the hold; as in 'Stow the large casks amidships, and the smaller barrels in the wings'. W A Falconer, p 634.
12. Riders are a sort of interior ribs fixed opposite the timbers to which they are bolted. They reach from the keelson to the beams of the lower deck in order to strengthen the frame.
13. Sleepers: the knees which connect the transoms to the fore and after-timbers on a ship's quarter. They are fitted within the side to strengthen the bows and stern-frame. W A Falconer, p 484.
14. To frap a ship means to pass four or five turns of a large cable-laid rope round the hull or frame of the vessel, in the middle, to support her. A method used sometimes in a storm when it is felt that she is not strong enough to resist the violent efforts of the sea. W A Falconer, p 158.
15. In naval terms, to start, when applied to liquid means to empty, but when applied to solids, e.g. an anchor, a plank, etc., it means to move or moved. W A Falconer, p 499.
16. After the court-martial for the loss of the *Agamemnon*, Jonas Rose does not appear to have been given another ship. He was on half pay, as a ten-shilling-a-day captain, for most of the time between July 1809 and his death in 1820. It is just possible, though unlikely, that he got a command in between. There is a note on the Half-Pay Register, ADM 25/191 which says, 'Dead-20 July [1820]' after which is written, 'His money was paid on 17 October to Claude & Co. for H B Molework, sole executors', and then an illegible notation.

APPENDIX 1

'Agamemnon': a short history of the name

In the sixteenth century BC powerful dynasties established their authority over the great citadels of mainland Greece. The most important of these was Homer's Mycenae 'rich in gold', which acquired, in the ancient world, even more glory than Athens itself.

Agamemnon, the most famous descendant of those kings, was the son of Atreus and brother of Menelaus. After the murder of their father by Thyestes' son Aegisthus, Agamemnon and Menelaus took refuge with Tyndareus, King of Sparta, whose daughters Clytemnestra and Helen respectively they married. With Clytemnestra, Agamemnon had a son, Orestes, and three daughters, Iphigenia, Electra and Chrysothemis. Menelaus suceeded Tyndareus while Agamemnon recovered his father's kingdom.

After Paris, son of King Priam of Troy, had carried off Helen, Agamemnon called on the princes of the country to unite in a war against the Trojans. He himself furnished 100 ships and was chosen as commander-in-chief of the combined forces. The fleet assembled at the port of Aulis but was prevented from sailing by calms and adverse winds sent by the goddess Artemis because Agamemnon had offended her. To appease the wrath of the goddess, Agamemnon was forced to sacrifice his own daughter, Iphigenia.

After the capture of Troy, Cassandra, the daughter of Priam, fell to Agamemnon's lot in the distribution of the prizes of war and he took her as his concubine.

Soon after stepping ashore in his homeland, after a stormy voyage, Agamemnon and his comrades were invited to Aegisthus' palace. Aegisthus, who had seduced Clytemnestra, Agamemnon's wife, during his absence, treacherously murdered Agamemnon and his comrades. Cassandra was murdered by Clytemnestra. The Greek poet Aeschylus, however, attributed the crimes to Clytemnestra alone.

Eight years later, Agamemnon's son Orestes returned and, incited by his sister Electra, avenged his father's death by slaying both his mother and her lover Aegisthus.

APPENDIX 2

HMS *Agamemnon* 1781–1809

Particulars

Length of Gun Deck .... 160' 2"

Length of Keel .... 131' 10¼"

Extreme Breadth .... 44' 5"

Depth in Hold .... 18' 11"

Displacement (approx.) .... 2,578 tons

Burthen .... 1,384 tons

Iron Ballast .... 70 tons

Shingle Ballast .... 277 tons

Draught Forward .... 12' 1"

Draught Aft .... 17' 3"

Draught Forward When Victualled .... 20' 11"

Draught Aft When Victualled .... 22' 7"

Foremost Port to Surface of Water .... 4' 10"

Midship Port to Surface of Water .... 4' 4"

After Port to Surface of Water .... 4' 9"

Armament

Gun Deck 26 24-pounders

Upper Deck 26 18-pounders

Quarter Deck 10 9-pounders

Forecastle 2 9-pounders

Total Number of Guns .... 64 guns

Total Number of Carronades 12 24-pounders

Total Weight of Armament   . . . . 141½ tons

Admiralty Records 95/36: Sailing Qualities of Ships 1791–96: HMS Agamemnon

[Sailing Quality Reports were forms required to be filled in and returned to the Navy Board at the end of commission or periods at sea. The captain's answers are reproduced below *in italics.*]

Her best Sailing Draft of Water, when victualled and stored for Channel Service, *given this 25th Day of September 1796.*
  Afore *20 ft. 4 in.*
  Abaft *21 ft. 4 in.*
Her lowest Gundeck Port will then be above the Surface of the Water
  Afore *8 ft. 1 in.*
  Abaft *4 ft. 8 in. or more.*
How she behaves close haul'd, and how many knots she runs
  in a Top-gallant Gale: *6 knots*
  in a Top-sail Gale: *5½ knots*
How she Steers, & how she Wears & Stays
  steers easy
  stays indifferent
  wears tolerably well
  Under her Reef Topsails
  5½: pitches much in a head Sea
  Under her Courses
  not try'd
In each Circumstance above mentioned (in Sailing with other Ships) in what Proportion she gathers to Windward, and in what Proportion she fore Reaches, and in general her Proportion of Lee-way
  a good Company keeper, about ½ + ½ point Leeway.
How she proves in sailing thro' all the Variations of the Wind, from its being a point or two abaft the Beam, to its veering forward upon the Bow-line in every strength of Gale, especially in a stiff Gale, and a head Sea; and how many Knots she runs in each Circumstance, and how she carries her Helm:
  in general as well as most Ships of her Class
  carries her Helm but indifferent
The most Knots she runs before the wind, and how she rolls in the Trough of the Sea:
  9 knots — rolls easy
How she behaves in lying Too or a Try, under a Main-Sail, and also under a Mizon ballanc'd:
  never try'd

What for a Roader she is, and how she careens:

indifferent Roader, never Careen'd

The Trim of the Ship:

Rigging slacks with Safety. Foremast upright, Main & Mizzen Masts a small inclination Aft.

Topmasts in line with the Lower Masts.

[signed] *S Smith*

[This is probably Captain John Samuel Smith who was in command of *Agamemnon* from 11 June–19 September 1796.]

APPENDIX 3

Demands of the Nore Mutineers
20 May 1797

On 20 May 1797, Richard Parker and the delegates of the mutiny sent Vice-Admiral Charles Buckner, commander-in-chief at the Nore, the following statement of demands:

1. That every indulgence granted to the fleet at Portsmouth be granted to his Majesty's subjects serving in the fleet at the Nore and places adjacent.
2. That every man, upon a ship's coming into harbour, shall have liberty (a certain number at a time, so as not to injure the ship's duty) to go and see their friends and families, a convenient time to be allowed to each man.
3. That all ships, before they go to sea, shall be paid all arrears of wages, down to six months, according to the old rules.
4. That no officer that has been turned out of any of his Majesty's ships shall be employed in the same ship again without consent of the ship's company.
5. That when any of his Majesty's ships shall be paid that may have been some time in commission, if there are any pressed men on board that may not be in the regular course of payment, they shall receive two months' advance to furnish them with necessaries.
6. That an indemnification be made to any man who ran, and may now be in his Majesty's service, and they shall not be able to be taken up as deserters.
7. That a more equal distribution be made of prize-money to the crews of his Majesty's ships and vessels of war.
8. That the Articles of War, as now enforced, require various alterations, several of which ought to be expunged therefrom; and, if more moderate ones were held forth to the seamen in general, it would be the means of taking off that terror and prejudice against his Majesty's service, on that account too frequently imbibed by seamen, from entering voluntarily into the service.

This statement was forwarded to the Admiralty, which on 22 May replied refusing some of the demands but promising forgiveness to the men if they would return to duty.

Sir Hyde Parker's Signal No 39 'Discontinue the Action'

The following is a letter written by Ole Feldbaek and published in *Mariner's Mirror*, Vol 73, No 3, August 1987. It refers to Mr Feldbaek's book *Slaget pa Reden (The Battle of Copenhagen)*, which was published in Copenhagen as the first of a series called *Highpoints, Dramatic Events and Upheavals in Danish History*.

Referring for more detailed references to my book on the Battle of Copenhagen (reviewed in *Mariner's Mirror*, 72 (1986), p 226) I would like to comment upon the query about Sir Hyde Parker's signal No 39 'Discontinue the action'. The relevant contemporary evidence consists of the following: Lieutenant-Colonel William Stewart's diary for 2 April and his letter 6 April to Sir William Clinton: Rear Admiral Graves' letter 3 April to his brother; the Earl of St Vincent's conversation with George Rose on 22 April; and the logs of the vessels in Nelson's and Parker's division. Stewart's Narrative from 1809 should in my opinion be treated with caution.

The signal No 39 is neither referred to in Nelson's report of the battle nor in Parker's covering letter to the Admiralty. Nevertheless, it is a fact that the signal was made, that it was made 'General' (that is: directed to every individual captain in Nelson's division), and that its urgency was marked by a gun from the flagship. It is likewise a fact that the signal was read by every British ship in the King's Channel, even by the southernmost such as the frigate *Désirée* and the bomb vessel *Volcano*. And there is no evidence that this was a pre-arranged discretionary signal.

We know enough about Nelson's reaction to the signal from Parker to say that he confined himself to hoisting the answering pendant, not repeating the signal, and that he kept his original signal No 16 from the commencement of the battle flying 'Engage the enemy more closely'.

We also know that some confusion arose on board the ships in Nelson's division as a result of Parker's signal. Some ships — among them the *Agamemnon*, the *Désirée* and the *Cruiser* — did in fact repeat signal No 39, thereby obeying it. But seeing Nelson confining himself to just answering the signal, and keeping the original No 16 flying, they acted as Rear Admiral Graves on board the *Defiance* who asked if Parker's signal was repeated by Nelson, and being told that it was not, said: 'Then we have nothing to do with it.' The only ships to obey Parker's signal and to leave the battle were the frigates of Captain Riou's squadron. And their logs — written after the battle — testify to their discomfort at having been the only ships to obey the order of the Commander-in-Chief.

By not allowing the *Elephant* to repeat signal No 39 (but only answering it) and by not cancelling his original signal 'Engage the enemy more closely', Nelson deliberately left it to each of the captains in his division to make his own decision on his own responsibility. Trusting Nelson more than Parker, each of his captains took upon himself the grave responsibility of disobeying the direct, explicit and unmistakable order of his Commander-in-Chief. In the words of the master of the *Bellona*: 'the Commander-in-Chief made the signal to discontinue the action, which was not obeyed by our squadron'. And by doing so they saved the Baltic fleet from a military disaster.

Ole Feldbaek is a professor of History at the University of Copenhagen. He is a specialist in Danish history from 1730 to 1814 and in particular in the Anglo-Danish conflicts of 1800–1801 and 1807–1814, about which he has already published a number of articles.

APPENDIX 5

Excerpt from *The Times*, London Thursday 7 November 1805

ADMIRALTY OFFICE, Wednesday, Nov. 6. Dispatches, of which the following are Copies, were received at the Admiralty this day, at one o'clock, A.M., from Vice-Admiral Collingwood, Commander in Chief of his Majesty's ships and vessels off Cadiz.

Euryalus, off Cape Trafalgar, Oct. 22, 1805.

Sir:

The ever-to-be-lamented death of Vice Admiral, Lord Viscount Nelson, who in the late conflict with the enemy fell in the hour of victory, leaves to me the duty of informing my Lords Commissioners of the Admiralty that on the 19th instant it was communicated to the Commander in Chief, from the ships watching the motions of the enemy in Cadiz, that the combined fleet had put to sea; as they sailed with light winds Westerly, his Lordship concluded their destination was the Mediterranean, and immediately made sail for the Streights entrance with the British Squadron, consisting of twenty-seven ships, three of them 64s, where his Lordship was informed by Captain Blackwood (whose vigilance in watching and giving notice of the enemy's movements has been highly meritorious) that they had not yet passed the Streights.

On Monday, the 21st instant at daylight, when Cape Trafalgar bore E. by S. about seven leagues, the enemy was discovered six or seven miles Eastward, the wind about West, and very light. The Commander in Chief immediately made the signal for the fleet to bear up in two columns as they are formed in order of sailing; a mode of attack his Lordship had previously directed to avoid the inconveniences and delay in forming a line of battle in the usual manner. The enemy's line consisted of thirty-three ships (of which eighteen were French and fifteen Spanish), commanded in chief by Admiral Villeneuve: the Spaniards under the direction of Gravina, were with their heads Northward, and formed their line of battle with great closeness and correctness; but as the mode of attack was unusual, so the structure of their line was new; it formed a crescent, convexing to leeward, so that in leading down to the centre I had both their van and rear abaft the beam, before the fire opened, every alternate ship was about a cable's length to windward of her second ahead and astern, forming a kind of double line and appeared when on their beam to leave a very little interval between them; and this without crowding their ships. Admiral Villeneuve was in the *Bucentaure* in the centre, and the *Prince of Asturias* bore Gravina's flag in the rear; but the French and Spanish Ships were mixed without any apparent regard to order or national squadron.

As the mode of our attack had been previously determined and communicated to the Flag Officers and Captains, few signals were necessary, and none were made except to direct close order as the lines bore down.

The Commander in Chief, in the *Victory*, led the weather column, and the *Royal Sovereign*, which bore my flag, the lee.

The action began at twelve o'clock by the leading ships of the column breaking through the enemy's line, the Commander in Chief about the tenth ship afore the van, the Second in Command about the twelfth from the rear, leaving the van of the enemy unoccupied: the succeeding ships breaking through in all parts, astern of their leaders, and engaging the enemy at the muzzles of their guns. The conflict was severe: the enemy's ships were fought with a gallantry highly honourable to their Officers, but the attack on them was irresistible, and it pleased the Almighty Disposer of all events to grant his Majesty's arms a complete and glorious victory. About three P.M., many of the enemy's ships having struck their colours, their line gave way: Admiral Gravina with ten ships joining their frigates to leeward, stood towards Cadiz. The five headmost ships in their van tacked, and standing to the Southward, to windward of the British line, were engaged, and the sternmost of them taken; the others went off, leaving to his Majesty's squadron nineteen ships-of-the-line (of which two are first-rates — the *Santissima Trinidad* and the *Santa Anna*), with three Flag Officers, viz., Admiral Villineuve, the Commander in Chief; Don Ignacio, Maria D'Aliva, Vice Admiral and the Spanish Rear Admiral, Don Baltazar Hidalgo Cisneros.

After such a victory it may appear unnecessary to enter into encomiums on the particular parts taken by the several Commanders, the conclusion says more on the subject than I have language to express; the spirit which animated all was the same; when all exert themselves zealously in their country's service, all deserve that their high merits should stand recorded; and never was high merit more conspicuous than in the battle I have described.

The *Achille* (a French 74), after having surrendered, by some mismanagement of the Frenchman took fire and blew up; two hundred of her men were saved by the Tenders.

A circumstance occurred during the action which so strongly marks the invincible spirit of British seamen, when engaging the enemies of their country, that I cannot resist the pleasure I have in making it known to their Lordships. The *Téméraire* was boarded by accident or design by a French ship on one side and a Spaniard on the other; the contest was vigorous, but in the end the Combined Ensigns were torn from the poop and the British hoisted in their places. Such a battle could not be fought without sustaining a great loss of men. I have not only to lament in common with the British Navy and the British Nation in the fall of the Commander in Chief, the loss of a hero whose name will be immortal and his memory ever dear to his country; but my heart is rent with the most poignant grief for the death of a friend to whom by many years intimacy and a perfect knowledge of the virtues of his mind, which inspired ideas superior to the common race of men, I was bound by the strongest ties of affection; a grief to which the glorious occasion in which he fell does not bring the consolation which perhaps it ought. His Lordship received a musket ball in his left breast about the middle of the action, and sent an Officer to me immediately with his last farewell, and soon after expired.

I have also to lament the loss of those excellent Officers Captains Duff, of the *Mars* and Cooke of the *Bellerophon*; I have yet heard of no others. I fear the numbers that have fallen will be found very great, when the returns come to me; but it having blown a gale of wind ever since the action, I have not yet had it in my power to collect any reports from the ships.

The *Royal Sovereign* having lost her masts, except the tottering foremast, I called the *Euryalus* to me while the action continued, which ship lying within hail, made my signals — a service Captain Blackwood performed with great attention; after the action I shifted my flag to her, that I might more easily communicate any orders to, and collect the ships, and towed the *Royal Sovereign* out to seaward. The whole fleet were now in a very perilous position, many dismasted, all shattered, in thirteen fathoms of water off the shoals of Trafalgar; and when I made the signal to prepare to anchor few of the ships had an anchor to let go their cables being shot; but the same good Providence which aided us through the day preserved us through the night, by the wind shifting a few points, and drifting the ships off the land, except four of the captured dismasted ships, which are now at anchor off Trafalgar, and I hope will ride safe until those gales are over.

Having thus detailed the proceedings of the fleet on this occasion, I beg to congratulate their Lordships on a victory which I hope will add a ray to the glory of his Majesty's crown, and be attended with public benefit to our country, I am, & c.,

C. COLLINGWOOD

William Marsden, Esq.

The order in which the ships of the British Squadron attacked the combined Fleets on the 21st of October, 1805:

VAN.	REAR.
Victory	*Royal Sovereign*
Téméraire	*Mars*

Neptune   Belleisle
Conqueror   Tonnant
Leviathan   Bellerophon
Ajax   Colossus
Orion   Achille
Agamemnon   Polyphemus
Minotaur   Revenge
Spartiate   Swiftsure
Britannia   Defence
Africa   Thunderer
Euryalus   Defiance
Sirius   Prince
Phoebe   Dreadnought
Naiad
Pickle Schooner
Entreprenante Cutter

C. COLLINGWOOD

General Order

Euryalus, October 22

The ever-to-be-lamented death of Lord Viscount Nelson, Duke of Bronte, the Commander in Chief, who fell in the action of the twenty-first in the arms of victory, covered with glory, whose memory will ever be dear to the British Navy and the British Nation, whose zeal for the honour of his King and for the interests of his country will ever be held up as a shining example for British Seamen, leaves to me a duty to return my thanks to the Right Honorable Rear Admiral, and Captains, Officers, Seamen, and detachment of Royal Marines serving on board his Majesty's Squadron now under my command for their conduct on that day; but where can I find language to express my sentiments of the valour and skill which were displayed by the Officers, Seamen, and Marines in the battle with the enemy, where every individual appeared an hero on whom the glory of his country depended? The attack was irresistable and the issue of it adds to the page of Naval Annals, a brilliant instance of what Britons can do when their King and their Country need their service.

To the Right Honorable Rear Admiral the Earl of Northesk: to the Captains, Officers, Seamen, and to the Officers, Non-commissioned Officers, and Privates of the Royal Marines, I beg to give my sincere and hearty thanks for their highly meritorious conduct both in action and in their zeal and activity in bringing the captured ships out from the perilous situation in which they were after their surrender among the shoals of Trafalgar in boisterous weather.

And I desire that the respective Captains will be pleased to communicate to the Officers, Seamen, and Royal Marines this public testimony of my high approbation of their conduct and my thanks for it.

C. COLLINGWOOD

General Order

The Almighty God, whose arm is strength, having of his great mercy been pleased to crown the exertion of his Majesty's fleet with success in giving them a complete victory over their enemies on the 21st of this month; and that all praise and thanksgiving may be offered up to the Throne of Grace for the great benefits to our country and to mankind.

I have thought proper that a day should be appointed of general humiliation before God, and thanksgiving for his merciful goodness, imploring forgiveness of our sins, a continuation of his divine mercy and his constant aid to us in the defence of our country's liberties and laws, without which the efforts of man are naught. I direct, therefore, that a proper day be appointed for this holy purpose.

Given on board the *Euryalus* off Cape Trafalgar, 22 Oct. 1805.

C. COLLINGWOOD

To the respective Captains and Commanders: The fleet having been dispersed by a gale of wind, no day has yet been able to be appointed for the above purpose.

Euryalus, off Cadiz, Oct. 24, 1805

Sir:

In my letter of the 22nd, I detailed to you for the information of my Lords Commissioners of the Admiralty, the proceedings of his Majesty's Squadron on the day of the action and that preceding it, since which I have had a continued series of misfortunes, but they are of a kind that human prudence could not possibly provide against or my skill prevent.

On the 22nd, in the morning, a strong Southerly wind blew, with squally weather, which, however, did not prevent the activity of the Officers and

Seamen of such ships as were manageable from getting hold of many of the prizes (thirteen or fourteen) and towing them off to the Westward, when I ordered them to rendezvous round the *Royal Sovereign* in tow by the *Neptune*; but on the 23rd, the gale increased and the sea ran so high that many of them broke the tow rope and drifted far to leeward before they were got hold of again; and some of them, taking advantage in the dark and boisterous night, got before the wind, and have perhaps drifted upon the shore and sunk; on the afternoon of that day the remnant of the Combined Fleet, ten sail of ships who had not been much engaged, stood up to leeward of my shattered and strag-gled charge, as if meaning to attack them, which obliged me to collect a force out of the least injured ships and form to leeward for their defence; all this retarded the progress of the hulks and the bad weather continuing determined me to destroy all the leewardmost that could be cleared of the men, consider-ing that keeping possession of the ships was a matter of little consequence compared with the chance of their falling again into the hands of the enemy; but even this was an arduous task in the high sea which was running. I hope, however, it was accomplished to a considerable extent; I entrusted it to skillful Officers who would spare no pains to execute what was possible. The Cap-tains of the *Prince* and *Neptune* cleared the *Trinidad* and sank her. Captains Hope, Bayntun, and Malcolm, who joined the fleet this moment from Gibral-ter, had the charge of destroying four others. The *Redoubtable* sunk astern of the *Swiftsure* while in tow. The *Santa Anna*, I have no doubt, is sunk, as her side was almost entirely beat in; and such is the shattered condition of the whole of them, that unless the weather moderates, I doubt whether I should be able to carry a ship of them into port. I hope their Lordships will approve of what I (having only in consideration the destruction of the enemy's fleet) have thought a measure of absolute necessity.

I have taken Admiral Villeneuve into this ship; Vice Admiral Don Aliva [sic] is dead. Whenever the temper of the weather will permit and I can spare a frigate (for there were only four in the action with the fleet, *Euryalus*, *Sirius*, *Phoebe*, and *Naiad*; the *Melpomene* joined the 22nd and the *Eurydice* and *Scout* the 23rd) I shall collect the other Flag Officers and send them to England with their flags (if they do not all go to the bottom) to be laid at his Majesty's feet.

There were four thousand troops embarked under the command of General Contamin, who was taken with Admiral Villeneuve in the *Bucentaure*. I am,

C. COLLINGWOOD

Excerpts from HMS *Agamemnon* Log
2–24 March 1806

The log is given in the original wording, except for the notes in square brackets, where the author has paraphrased and added extra comments.

Sunday 2nd March 1806
Employd unreaving the running rigging for survey Struck main Yard and TopGallant Mast &c [crew employed working on the rigging and the sails for much of the time]

Monday 3rd
[A couple of seamen punished for theft; the Main Mast was sprung; a gang of hands employed at the Dockyard with the boats & carpenter.]

Tuesday 4th
Arrived HM Brig *Eperion*

Wednesday 5th
[Carpenters and sailmakers at the dockyard. Still employed about the rigging.]

Friday 7th
[HM Brig *Nimble* arrived; carpenters and sailmakers still at the dockyard; ship's company about the rigging; HMS *Carysfort* arrived.]

Saturday 8th
AM At 8 made the Signal for a Pilot with a Gun Hoisted in the Launch Sent William Reed First Officer & Alexander McIntosh to the Hospital

PM At 2 weighed and warped At 2.30 made Sail At 3 dischargd the Pilot Joined company HMS *Carysfort*

Sunday 9th
AM *Carysfort* in company At 5 exchanged numbers with HM Sloop *Hippopotamus* Saw a Strange Sail north At 8 Do Wr Carysfort & *Hippopotamus* in company At 11.30 joined company HMS *Galatea* Several Strange sail in sight At noon *Carysfort Galatea* & *Hippopotamus* in company
   Bearing & Distance at Noon Body of Descada W S W 1/2 W 3 Leagues
   At 1 a strange Schooner in sight

Monday 10th
[no change: *Carysfort* & *Hippopotamus* in sight or in company]

Tuesday 11th
Bearing & Distance at Noon Bridgetown Barbados E N E 5 miles
   PM Working into Carlysle Bay At 1.45 came too with the Best Bower in 17 fathoms Bridgetown N 1 mile Found lying here HM Ships *Northumberland, Dolphin, Ethalion, Carysfort, Unicorn* & several sloops Sailed HMS *Ethalion* and *Dart* sloop
[From this date until Saturday 15th inclusive *Agamemnon* remained at Carlysle Bay, Barbados]

Wednesday 12th
[*Wolverine* arrived with a prize]

Thursday 13th
[*Unicorn* & *Carysfort* departed]

Friday 14th
[*Heureux* departed]

Saturday 15th
[*Hippopotamus* departed, and in the afternoon the *Wolverine*]

Sunday 16th
PM Made sail at 3 South Point of Barbados N W 6 or 9 miles

Monday 17th
[nothing eventful]

Tuesday 18th
AM At 8 saw a sail NNW Bore up & made sail in chace At 10 shortened sail & hove too & boarded her She proved to be an English ship from Liverpool to Barbados Pressed 3 men from her
   PM At half past 3, 3 Sail in sight, one of them in chace of a Schooner supposed to be a Ship of War Made all sail in chace of the Schooner At 4 Do Wr in chace all sail set Fired at the Chace as convenient HM Ship *Heureux* did the same At 7.40 brought to & boarded the Chace She proved to be *La Dame Ernouf* French Privateer Schooner mounting 19 Guns and 81 Men from Guadaloupe [she] Had made no captures Left her in charge of the *Heureux* Wore & made sail Fresh Gales & cloudy Made & Shortened Sail & Tackd occasionally Modte & Cloudy
   [The notorious French privateer *La Dame Ernouf* that had ravaged British shipping in the West Indies had been seized by HMS *Curieux* in February 1805 only to be recaptured by the French shortly after. It was a brilliant coup for Captain Berry to capture her, finally putting and end to her piratical career.]

Wednesday 19th
AM At 7 saw a Sail NNE At half past tackd in chace At 8 in chace of a Brig Empd occasionally Carpenters repairing the Launch Sailmakers repairing Sails

At 11 Fired a shot at the Chace Hove too & Boarded her Found her to be an
American Brig from Newhaven to Barbados
   Bearing & Distance at Noon Bridgetown S 73 miles

Thursday 20th
AM At 6 saw a sail SW by W Bore up Made Sail in chace Killed an Ox 494 lbs
At 8 fresh Gales & Squally with constant Rain In chace Made & Shortend sail
occasionally Fresh Breezes & Cloudy Split the ForetopGallant Sail & Starboard
Main TopGallant Steering Sail Bearing & Distance at Noon North Point Barbados S 64 W 46 miles
   PM Fresh Breezes & cloudy Firing at the Chace occasionally At Quarter Past
1 brought her too and boarded her She proved to be an English Schooner with
the Mail from Demerara to Barbados In 2nd reef Topsails Sailmakers preparing
the Main Topsail in the Top Unbent the split ForetopGallant Sail and bent
another at 3 filled and Made Sail At 4 Tackd At 6 Squally with Samll Rain at
times At Quarter past seven the North point of Barbados S S W 1/2 W 6 or 7
Leagues At 7.30 furld TopGallant Sail ·

Friday 21st
AM Killed an ox 384 lbs at Daylight saw a Sail SSW bore up & Made Sail in
chace at 6.40 hauld the wind on the Larboard Tack the Chace proved to be an
American Brig at 8 Fresh Breezes & Cloudy 3 Sail in sight to the westward
Punished James Stapleton with 36 lashes for striking his Officer

Saturday 22nd
At 5 killed an ox 444 lbs at 4 saw a Sail N by E at quarter past brought her too
with a Gun and spoke her an American Brig from Norfolk to St Vincents at 5 a
Schooner in sight to Starboard at Noon a Brig in sight bearing east hoisted
American colours
   Bearing & Distance at Noon Body of the island of Barbados W 1/2 S 11 or
12 Leagues
   PM 11.40 saw 2 Sail N 1/2 E Observed 1 to burn a Blue Light

Sunday 23rd
AM at 4 killed an Ox 475 lbs

Monday 24th
AM Fresh Breezes & Squally at 4 Do Wr at 5 carried away the Jib Stay Hauld it
down and spliced it at 6 saw 2 Sail NE sailing Large a Ship & a Brig at 6.30 the
Ship fired 2 Guns & hoisted English colours at 6.40 wore in chace of the Brig
the Ship showed her Pendant to the *Carysfort* at 7 the chace hoisted French
colours and fired Several guns at 7.30 the chace Struck after our firing 39 shott
at her she proved to be *La Lutine* National Brig of 16 guns from L'Orient bound
to Martinico [Martinique] out 33 days and made no Capture Employd taking
out Prisoners
   Bearing & distance at Noon Point Caracal Martinico S 80 W 141 miles
   PM Fresh Gales & Cloudy Boats employd taking the Prisoners from the Prize to
the *Carysfort* at half past 2 hoisted the Boats up Wore & made Sail parted company
with the *Carysfort* & Prize at 3 split the Main Topgallant Sail unbent it and bent
Another at 6 Modte unbent the Spanker to alter it Sailmakers empd about it

[For comparison it is interesting to read the entry in the log of HMS *Carysfort* concerned with this action. Although the Captain's log does not survive, the Master's does. (Admiralty: Masters' Logs (ADM 52): ADM 52/3591 HMS *Carysfort*.) Her entry is reproduced as follows:]

Sunday 23rd March 1806
Bearing & Distance at Noon Barbados S 45 W 203 miles
    PM at 5 saw a Strange Sail on the Wd Beam bore up on the Larboard Tack at 6 the chace WSW 3 Miles at 11 lost sight of the Strange Sail

Monday 24th March
AM Strong Breezes at 1.30 carried away the Main Top Gt Mast got the Yard and Stump of the Mast down and made Sail as needful at Daylight the Chace SW by S 2 miles fired several 6ps shotted at the Chace at 7 shewed our Privte [private signal] to HM Ship *Agamemnon* and made Signal of an Enemy in Sight at 8 they shewed French Colours fired a Broadside and hauld them down Shortened Sail and hove to and Exchanged the Prisoners she proved to be the French National Brig *Lutine* mounting 16 long pieces [in the margin is the entry: 'Sent an Officer & 10 Men to take possession']
    PM at 3 made Sail *Agamemnon* parted Company Recd 9 Men from the Prize [The log goes on to record that the *Carysfort* took charge of the Prize. On Wednesday 26th March she put into Carlysle Bay, Barbados, and discharged the prisoners into the Prison Ship *Sally*.

Excerpts from HM Brig *Nancy's* log 4 August – 28 November 1809

Tuesday 4th August 1809
AM Light Breezes and hazy Wr At 8 made the Island of Lobos distance 2 Leagues Employed working into the Bay at Maldonado At 11 came too within 7 Fathoms Veerd out half a cable found lying here HM sloop *Mutine*, and the remains of HM late Ship *Agamemnon*. The convoy at anchor.

Wednesday 9th August
PM Modte Breezes

[Note: this particular log-keeper still seems to be using the old log notation of PM first then AM, even though the Admiralty convention had changed by this date.]

AM Received from HM Sloop *Mutine* 20 supernumeraries belonging to HM late Ship *Agamemnon* and 8 belonging to HM *Mutine*

Thursday 10th August
PM Modte Breezes and Clear Wr Transports Empd getting off the stores of HM late Ship *Agamemnon*

AM The Armourer and Carpenter on shore making Gun Carriages

Friday 11th
The Transports boats Empd as yesterday

Saturday 12th the transports Empd as before

Monday 14th
Transports boats Empd bringing off Stores belonging to the late Ship *Agamemnon*

Tuesday 15th
The Transports Empd cutting away the *Agamemnon's* masts Sailed HMS *Mutine* and proceeded up the River Plate Remained here HM late Ship *Agamemnon*, *Kingston* and *Neptune* transports

Wednesday 16th
The Transports Empd stripping the *Agamemnon*'s Main Mast

Thursday 17th
The Transports Empd getting the *Agamemnon*'s Fore Mast on shore onto the Island of Gorriti

Friday 18th
The Transports Empd off the *Agamemnon*'s Main Mast the Rigging &c

Saturday 19th
Transports Empd as Yesterday

Monday 21st
Transports stripping the *Agamemnon*'s Main Mast

Tuesday 22nd
The Transport Boats as Yesterday

[Note: during all this activity by the transports, the *Nancy* herself appeared to be making considerable repairs to her own rigging and yards etc. There are notes about fitting new fore lifts etc. It is not clear whether items are being used from the wreck of the *Agamemnon*, or whether they were already carried as spares by *Nancy*.]

Thursday 24th
Transports as yesterday At 4 saw a strange Sail standing into the Harbour Proved to be HMS *Mistletoe* came too outside the Island of Gorriti 15 days from Rio de Janeiro.

Wednesday 30th
The transports towing on Shore the Main Mast of the late *Agamemnon*

Thursday 31st
PM Pleasant Breezes and Clear Wr The Transports towing on Shore a spare Yard and Top Mast lent from HM Brig *Nancy* for a Triangle to get off the Guns of HM late Ship *Agamemnon*

Friday 1st September
The Transports rigging a Triangle on Shore for getting off the Guns of the late *Agamemnon*

Saturday 2nd
Empd getting the *Kingston* Transport alongside the late *Agamemnon* to endeavour to get out Guns that remain on the upper Deck.

[Note: There was a heavy gale on the 3 and 4 September. It appeared that no work was done on the *Agamemnon* during this time.]

Tuesday 5th September
The *Kingston* Transport getting out the Guns of the late *Agamemnon*

Wednesday 6th
The *Kingston* Transport as yesterday Sailed the *Saint Jose* Brig and proceeded up the River. Remains the *Kingston*, *Neptune* Transport and the remains of HM late Ship *Agamemnon*

Thursday 7th
Transport as yesterday

Friday 8th
Transports getting out the Gun Carriages of the *Agamemnon*

Saturday 9th
The Transports as most required

Saturday 11th
The *Kingston* raising a purchase for getting the Guns off the Island belonging to the late *Agamemnon*

Wednesday 20th
At 5pm Arrived HMS *Hyacinth* and the *Brother* merchantman from Rio de Janeiro Remained here the HMS *Hyacinth*, the *Kingston* and *Neptune* Transports the *Brother* merchantman and the remains of the HM late Ship *Agamemnon*

Thursday 21st
Lent the Kingston a 4 inch hawser to get the *Agamemnon*'s Guns off the Island

Friday 22nd
At 5 am sailed the *Neptune* Transport for Buenos Aires Remained HMS *Hyacinth*, *Kingston* Transport, *Brother* and the remains of the late HMS *Agamemnon*

Sunday 24th
Sailed HMS *Hyacinth* for Montevideo

Monday 25th
The *Kingston* getting Guns from the Island

Tuesday 26th
The *Kingston* as yesterday
[Note: this is the actual log entry, not my interpretation]

Wednesday 27th
The *Kingston* as yesterday

Thursday 28th
The *Kingston* as yesterday

Friday 29th
The *Kingston* as yesterday

Saturday 30th
The *Kingston* as yesterday

Tuesday 3rd October
Strong gales [Note: these gales kept up for 2 days]

Thursday 5th October
AM Strong Breezes and Cloudy Wr 1.30 heavy Gales with thunder and lightning and heavy Squalls of Hail and Rain The Sheers for getting off the Guns of
the late *Agamemnon* washed away by the surf Perceived a great many casks and
other articles drifting about but impossible for Boats to go and save them

Saturday 7th October
The *Kingston* raising the Triangle that washed down during the Gale

Sunday 8th
Sailed the *Brother* merchantman for Buenos Aires

[On Wednesday 11th the *Nancy* shifted her position to 'get a better berth'.]

Thursday 12th October
Sent the Sergeant and 2 Marines to look out for things that might float from the
Agamemnon

Saturday 14th
PM Fired a Royal Salute of Guns, it being the King of Spain's birthday

[On Monday 16th the *Nancy* shifted position once again.]

Wednesday 18th
The *Kingston* getting off Guns

Thursday 19th
One cask of Wine on board the *Kingston* to be taken on charge being a cask that
came out of the *Agamemnon*

Friday 20th
The *Kingston* as before

Saturday 21st
The *Kingston* as yesterday

Sunday 22nd
Sent a cask of Rum on board the *Kingston* Transport to be taken on charge
being a cask that came out of the *Agamemnon*

Wednesday 25th
Fired a Royal Salute and dressed ship in honour of His Majesty's Ascension to
the Throne

Thursday 26th
The *Kingston* as yesterday

Friday 27th
The *Kingston* as yesterday

Saturday 28th
The *Kingston* getting off the [illegible word] and iron ballast belonging to the late *Agamemnon*

Monday 30th
The *Kingston* as yesterday

Tuesday 31st
The *Kingston* employed purchasing the *Agamemnon*'s Anchor

Wednesday 1st November
Kingston as yesterday

Friday 5th
Launch Empd getting out a cask of Wine from late *Agamemnon*

Monday 6th
Sent a cask of Wine got out of the *Agamemnon* on board the *Kingston* transport

Friday 10th November
Lent the *Kingston* two Carpenters to prepare her for sea

Thursday 16th
AM Strong Breezes and Cloudy with Rain At 10 am down TopGallant Masts at 11 strong Gales struck lower Yards and Top Masts Heavy gales with squalls of rain At 2 pm passd by HMS *Mutine* at 10 observed the *Agamemnon* to have parted in two

Friday 17th
At daylight found the Brig had drove during the night about a cables length to the East No part of the wreck of HM the late Ship *Agamemnon* to be seen

PM More Modte Sent the Launch on shore Found the Wreck to be all in pieces along the Beach

Saturday 18th
Modte Breezes and Clear The launch Empd along the beach to preserve what necessary things might be found

Sunday 19th
Arrived at 10.30 HMS *Bedford*

Wednesday 22nd
At 12 sailed HMS *Bedford*

Saturday 25th
Empd as required Watering the Brig and getting ready for Sea

Tuesday 28th
At 9.30 weighed and ran into the fairway

Glossary

backstays: long ropes extending from all upper masts to both sides of the ship. Part of the standing rigging (*q.v.*)

beakhead: the foremost part of the ship, forward of the forecastle

binnacle: a wooden case or cabinet on the deck of a ship holding a ship's compass, and a lamp so that the compass could be read at night

Boatswain: warrant officer (*q.v.*) responsible for the sails and rigging of a ship

catspaws: name given to a light and intermittent gust of wind, so-called for the impression it makes on the surface of the sea

cat-head: stout timber protruding from the bows, used to raise anchors

catted (of anchors): to raise the anchor up to the cat-head (*q.v.*)

chain-shot: a type of shot made up of two balls joined by a chain or bar, used to damage the enemy's rigging

clew (verb): to haul sails up to their yards by lines attached to their clews (lower corners); used to shorten sail temporarily

come home (of anchors): an anchor was described as 'coming home' when it came free of the sea-bed and was dragged along by the ship

Commodore: a temporary rank given to a captain in command of a particular squadron

compass timber: any curved, crooked or arched timber used in shipbuilding

Comptroller of the Navy: the Chief Commissioner of the Navy Board (*q.v.*). The Comptroller was always an experienced naval captain

cutter: a small clinker-built rowing and sailing boat. A ship of the line officially carried two 25ft cutters, employed for carrying light stores and passengers

Flag captain: commander of an admiral's flagship

frapp, frapping (a ship): to bind a ship's hull with heavy ropes to hold it together

futtocks: the separate pieces of timber that compose the lower parts of the frame of a ship

grape-shot: a charge of grape-shot consisted of a cluster of ½-pound balls. Used principally for anti-personnel fire.

hawse-holes: cylindrical holes cut through the bows of the ship on either side, through which the anchor cables pass

jib: a large triangular sail, on *Agamemnon* the sails on the bowsprit

junta: local Spanish provincial governments formed after the French takeover in 1808

knees: generally, a right-angled piece of timber used as a bracket to secure surfaces together, e.g. the deck beams to the ship's sides

launch: the largest boat carried aboard a ship of the line, approximately 30ft long, better under oars than under sail and capable of carrying heavy loads

leeward: the side opposite to that from which the wind is blowing

lugger: a small sailing vessel with four-cornered sails set fore and aft on two or three masts. Usually a fishing vessel

Master (of a ship): the senior warrant officer (q.v.) aboard a ship, responsible for the navigation of the ship

Navy Board: the body responsible for the technical and financial aspects of naval administration, e.g. shipbuilding and repairs, dockyard administration, supply and appointment of warrant officers

orlop deck: the lowest deck of a ship, often no more than a series of platforms forward and aft of the hold

petty officer: the lowest class of non-commissioned officer

pinnace: a 28ft carvel rowing and sailing boat, one of which was carried by a ship of the line primarily as the officers' or captain's transport

Post-Captain: denotes an officer with the full rank of Captain, qualified to command all ships of 20 guns and above.

Purser: the warrant officer (q.v.) in charge of the ship's provisions and clothing

quartermaster: a petty officer (q.v.), assistant to the master

ratlines: ropes running horizontally across the shrouds (q.v.)

Rear Admiral: the most junior rank of admiral. The term originally referred to the commander of the third division of the fleet, dating from the 17th century when the fleet fought in three divisions, with the Vice Admiral in the rear and the Admiral in the centre

running rigging: the 'moving' rigging used for trimming and setting the sails

shrouds: the lower and upper standing rigging (q.v.), running from the mast head to the sides of the ship

sounding: measuring the depth of water by the use of a lead-weighted line

standing rigging: the permanent rigging that supports the masts. *See* stays and shrouds

'starter': a short length of rope or a cane carried by petty officers (q.v.) aboard ship for informal corporal punishment of the men

stays: standing rigging (q.v.) running from the masthead forward

'thick stuff': strokes above and below the wales (q.v.) that were thicker than the normal planking though not as thick as the wales themselves

Vice Admiral: The second most senior rank of Admiral, originally commanding the second division of the fleet (*see* Rear Admiral *above*).

wales: extra thick strokes of planking to give the hull additional longitudinal strength; usually positioned beneath each tier of gunports

warrant officer: a non-commissioned officer appointed by the Navy Board (q.v.)

warp (verb): to move a ship by attaching a light rope or hawser ('a warp') to a fixed object (usually the ship's anchor) and then using the capstan to move the ship

Bibliography

Primary sources

Admiralty papers in the Public Record Office
ADM 1/5399: Court-Martial of Captain Jonas Rose
Captains' Logs ADM 51/1855, HMS *Agamemnon*
      ADM 51/1104, HMS *Agamemnon*
      ADM 51/1361, HMS *Agamemnon*
      ADM 51/1576, HMS *Agamemnon*
      ADM 51/1921, HMS *Brilliant*
      ADM 51/1934, HMS *Agamemnon*
      ADM 51/2019, HMS *Bedford*
      ADM 51/2565, HMS *Mutine*
      ADM 51/2581, HMS *Mistletoe*
      ADM 51/4078, HM Armed Brig *Pitt*
Masters' Logs ADM 52/2113, HMS *Agamemnon*
      ADM 52/3723, HMS *Agamemnon*
Ship's Musters ADM 7/437, HMS *Agamemnon*
Half-pay Register: ADM 25/191

Published sources

Blackburn, Graham, *The Overlook Dictionary of Nautical Terms*, Woodstock, NY 1981
Blanch, Lesley, *The Wilder Shores of Love*, New York 1984
Bradford, Ernle, *Nelson: The Essential Hero*, London 1977
Bradford, Gershom, *The Mariner's Dictionary*, Massachussetts 1972
Bryant, Sir Arthur, *Nelson*, London 1970
Chatwin, Bruce, *In Patagonia*, 1977
Churchill, Winston, *A History of the English Speaking Peoples*, London 1957
Conrad, Joseph, *The Mirror of the Sea*, 1906
Deane, Mary, *The Book of Dene, Deane, Adeane: A Genealogical History*, London 1899
De Grasse, Alexandre, *Notice bibliographique sur l'Amiral Compte de Grasse d'apres les documents inedits*, 1840

De Lery, Jean (trans. J Whately), *History of a Voyage to the Land of Brazil, otherwise called America*, Berkeley 1990

Driver, Christopher & Berriedale-Johnson, Michelle, *Pepys at Table*, Berkeley 1984

Elvin, J, *Handbook of Smooth Bore Cannon*, 1805

Falconer, W A, *A New Universal Dictionary of the Marine*, London 1815, repr. 1970

Fraser, Flora, *Emma, Lady Hamilton*, New York 1987

Gilbert, Arthur N, 'Buggery and the British Navy', *Journal of Social History* (1976), Vol 10

HMS Victory: *Official Guide*, 26th impression 1984

Heaps, Leo, *Log of the* Centurion, New York 1973

Holland, A J, *Buckler's Hard, A Rural Shipbuilding Centre*, Emsworth, Hampshire 1985

James, William, *The Naval History of Great Britain*, 1822

Knight, E F, *The Cruise of the Falcon, a Voyage to South America in a 30-ton Yacht*, London 1887

Laird Clowes, William, *The Royal Navy: A History from Earliest Time to the Present*, London 1898

Lavery, Brian, *The Ship of the Line*, London 1983

Lobo & Riudavets (compilers), *Manual de la Navegación del Rio de la Plata*, Madrid 1868

Mackenzie, Robert Holden, *The Trafalgar Roll*, London 1913

Mossiker, Frances, *Napoleon and Josephine: The Biography of a Marriage*, London 1965

National Geographic Society, *Atlas of the World*, Washington 1966

Oman, Carola, *Nelson*, London 1947

Parry, J H, *The Spanish Seaborne Empire*, Berkeley 1990

Pocock, Tom, *Nelson and His World*, London 1974

Preston, Antony, *History of the Royal Navy*, Greenwich 1980

Roberts, Carlos, *Las Invasiones Inglesas Del Rio de la Plata*, Buenos Aires 1938

Rodger, N A M, *Naval Records for Genealogists*, London 1984

——   *The Wooden World*, London 1988

Seijo, Carlos, *Maldonado y su Región*, Montevideo 1945

Swaine, Thomas, *The Universal Directory for Taking Alive, or Destroying, Rats and Mice*, 1788

Tucker, Jedediah Stevens, *Memoirs of Admiral The Right Honourable the Earl of Vincent*, London 1844

Uden, Grant & Cooper, Richard, *A Dictionary of British Ships and Seamen*, London 1980

Warner, Oliver, *A Portrait of Lord Nelson*, London 1987

Index